Audiovisual Translation and Media Accessibility at the Crossroads

APPROACHES TO TRANSLATION STUDIES
Founded by James S. Holmes

Edited by   Henri Bloemen
                    Cees Koster
                    Ton Naaijkens

Volume 36

Audiovisual Translation and Media Accessibility at the Crossroads

Media for All 3

Edited by

Aline Remael, Pilar Orero and Mary Carroll

Amsterdam - New York, NY 2012

Cover image: www.idea.pt

Cover design: Studio Pollmann

The paper on which this book is printed meets the requirements of "ISO 9706:1994, Information and documentation - Paper for documents - Requirements for permanence".

ISBN: 978-90-420-3505-8
E-Book ISBN: 978-94-012-0781-2
© Editions Rodopi B.V., Amsterdam – New York, NY 2012
Printed in The Netherlands

To Juan, Michael A. and Raymond

Table of contents

Acknowledgements 11

Audiovisual Translation and Media Accessibility at the Crossroads
Aline Remael, Pilar Orero, Mary Carroll 13

Section 1 – Extending the Borders of AVT 23

From Fan Translation to Crowdsourcing: Consequences of
Web 2.0 User Empowerment in Audiovisual Translation
Minako O'Hagan 25

Exploring New Paths towards Game Accessibility
Carmen Mangiron 43

Graphic Emoticons as a Future Universal Symbolic Language
Junichi Azuma 61

Mapping Digital Publishing for All in Translation
Lucile Desblache 85

Section 2 – Interpreting Sight and Sound 109

Quality in Live Subtitling: The Reception of Respoken Subtitles
in the UK
Pablo Romero-Fresco 111

Applying a Punctuation-based Segmentation to a New Add-on Display
Mode of Respoken Subtitles
Juan Martínez Pérez 133

Experimenting with Characters: An Empirical Approach to the
Audio Description of Fictional Characters
Nazaret Fresno 147

Audio Description Made to Measure: Reflections on
Interpretation in AD based on the Pear Tree Project Data
Iwona Mazur & Agnieszka Chmiel 173

The In-vision Sign Language Interpreter in British Television Drama
Alex McDonald 189

Section 3 – The Discourses of Audiovisual Translation 207

AVT Classics Revisited
Voice-over or Voice-in-between? Some Considerations about Voice-Over Translation of Feature Films on Polish Television
Monika Woźniak 209

Surtitling for the Stage and Directors' Attitudes: Room for Change
Anika Vervecken 229

Bilingualism, Multilingualism and Its Consequences
Old Films, New Subtitles, More Anglicisms?
Henrik Gottlieb 249

Audiovisual Information Processing by Monolinguals and Bilinguals: Effects of Intralingual and Interlingual Subtitles
Dominique Bairstow & Jean-Marc Lavaur 273

Heterolingualism in Audiovisual Translation: *De Zaak Alzheimer/ La Memoria del Asesino*
Anna Vermeulen 295

'You Fancying Your *Gora* Coach Is Okay with Me': Translating Multilingual Films for an Italian Audience
Vincenza Minutella 313

AVT, Film Language and Corpora
The Enriching Functions of Address Shifts in Film Translation
Maria Pavesi 335

Exploring Greetings and Leave-takings in Original and Dubbed Language
Veronica Bonsignori, Silvia Bruti & Silvia Masi 357

What AVT Can Make of Corpora: Some Findings from the *Pavia Corpus of Film Dialogue*
Maria Freddi 381

Multisemiotic and Multimodal Corpus Analysis in
Audio Description: TRACCE
Catalina Jiménez & Claudia Seibel..409

Notes on contributors..427

Index 433

Acknowledgements

It seems that our *Media for All* series of conferences and publications has become a landmark in Audiovisual Translation (AVT) and Media Accessibility studies. The 2009 *Media for All* 3 conference, organised by Aline Remael and her support committee from Artesis University College Antwerp was the catalyst of this publication, *AVT and Media Accessibility at the Crossroads*. This third *Media for All* volume with its diverse collection of contributions is not only living proof of the growing scope of the field but also an insightful survey of the valuable and varied research fields of many of our colleagues.

First and foremost, we would like to acknowledge and thank the contributors for sharing their work with us. Second, we owe thanks to our TransMedia colleagues, Jorge Díaz Cintas, Anna Matamala, Josélia Neves and Diana Sánchez, for their friendship, enthusiasm and support in compiling this edition. The contribution of the scientific committee of the *Media for All* conference was invaluable in both selecting the abstracts for the conference and subsequently assisting with the reading of the some 70 contributions submitted for publication. For the blind peer reviewing, we are also indebted to the numerous specialists from the AVT field who graciously offered their active support. Their rigour in the selection and their timely collaboration have been greatly appreciated.

The publication of this book has also been made possible thanks to a grant from the Catalan Government Fund 2009SGR700 as well as research funds made available by the Spanish Ministry of Science and Innovation FFI2009-08027, Subtitling for the Deaf and Hard of Hearing and Audio Description: Objective tests and future plans.

Special mention must be made of Jimmy Ureel's significant contribution. He was in charge of revising and formatting the text and his care and diligence deserve the highest praise. Our gratitude is also extended to our Rodopi editor Esther Roth for her advice and encouragement, and to the series editors of Approaches to Translation Studies, Henri Bloemen, Cees Coster and Ton Naaijkens, for their continued interest and support.

Last but not least, our thanks and recognition go to our partners for their generosity and understanding when so much of our time needs to be devoted to ostensibly invisible activities, such as the editing of the present volume.

Aline Remael
Pilar Orero
Mary Carroll

Audiovisual Translation and Media Accessibility at the Crossroads

Aline Remael
Artesis University College (Belgium)

Pilar Orero
Universitat Autònoma de Barcelona (Spain)

Mary Carroll
Titelbild (Germany)

Translation Studies (TS) appears to be developing in cycles, and audiovisual translation studies (AVTS) is no different. Far from being an ugly duckling at the periphery of TS, AVTS has evolved into a discipline in its own right. Its fledgling concerns with a focus on the specificity of AVT and its constraints first led to much fragmentary research conducted by practitioners. Now, a decade into the 21st century, AVTS is a mature field of studies in its own right, with AVT researchers adopting detached, comprehensive, descriptive and scientific approaches. Today, much research into AVT is taking the discipline back into the sphere of TS. At the same time, closer collaboration with AVT practitioners is evident and it is reaching further afield into new (sub)disciplines. Additionally, the link between AVT and accessibility in the broader sense – a novel stance in *Media for All 1* (Díaz Cintas, Orero & Remael 2007) – is now a generally accepted notion. In many ways, the new trends in AVTS reflect overall developments in TS, as translation continues to diversify, and TS too forges links with an increasingly broader spectrum of related disciplines.

From the practitioners' viewpoint, rapid advances in technology and the myriad of innovations in speech, text, software and translation applications impact on work processes, and increasingly blur the contours of AVT. On the research side, these same developments are leading to new methodologies and their application across TS subdisciplines (e.g. multimodal corpus analysis) and far beyond. This is resulting in increased collaboration between AVTS and linguistics, psychology, sociology and other human sciences, more often than not in combination with approaches from engineering, information technology and statistics.

However, such diversification also has its downside. Some areas remain underdeveloped because (1) they require expertise from (too) many different disciplines, (2) they do not fit neatly into any specific category for academic funding or (3) they are of no interest to the industry. Viewed from a more theoretical perspective, diversity and diversification also mean that it is becoming increasingly difficult to identify future directions of AVT and what constitutes 'state-of-the-art' research. Although TS in general faces this dilemma, AVT may well be more radically affected as a result of its dependency on technology, the development of which is fast and unpredictable.

Given the pervasiveness and significance of technologies and the interfaces between such technologies and people in daily life and work processes, designers, developers and implementers have an important – and unprecedented – responsibility to incorporate user concerns, reception and behavioural patterns into their respective fields of expertise, taking full account of how people perceive information, interact socially and use and interact with technologies. We believe that AVT is already playing an important role in this research and development. Undoubtedly, it entails collaboration with experts from other fields. Translation specialists are now often part of or may have to become part of human-centred computing (HCC), which has emerged from the convergence of multiple disciplines and research areas that deal with understanding human behaviour, human communication, and the design of computational devices and interfaces. AVTS will increasingly embrace the study of 'content' and the form of content to be supplied to technologists. The concept of content, too, is changing. It is extending beyond the study of written and spoken languages into the study of emotions, facial gestures and behaviour, the effect of texts in new formats on individual viewers, and the role and types of metadata in an increasingly non-linear, globalized, hybrid and multi-device audiovisual world.

Take, for instance, the relaunch of 3D, now digitally mastered. This has interesting repercussions for AVT practice and research alike. How should subtitles be projected? How should such apparently unstable texts be studied? Which standards will eventually be applied? Or will new developments appear on the horizon even before final decisions are taken? It would be foolish to assume that decisions will be based on translation requirements rather than on commercial interests and politics. Yet, in this context, too, AVTS has an important role to play to ensure accessibility for all. Another example is the renewed interest in translation, speech and speech-to-text technologies in AVT. Google subtitle and Google translate may not produce professional translations at this stage, but as AV text types to be translated become more varied, the use of machine translation and translation memories

– only rarely considered for the translation of fiction films in the past – becomes a more feasible solution. The range of AVT has expanded, not least as a result of new technologies. Corporate videos (a genre on the rise), technical texts and e-learning have become commonplace, adding to the demand for specialised AVT. Respeaking software, used to produce live subtitling for the deaf and hard of hearing in some countries, is still far from perfect, but improving quickly in certain languages. Such improvements come from the development of the software but also from research into respeaking techniques and error analysis as well as audience needs.

Three other relatively new developments deserve some attention at this point: (1) the use of eye-tracking, (2) the development of multimodal corpora and (3) Web 2.0 and its newer variants. Both the use of eye-tracking and the development of mulimodal corpora have paved the way for new research methodologies in AVTS, enabling the discipline to progress from the original case studies mentioned above. The development of multimodal corpora enables researchers to trawl much larger AVT corpora and to draw on the different semiotic channels of AVT products. The third development – Web 2.0 and its newer variants – is causing a veritable upheaval in translation. More information about these developments will be provided in our introduction to the contributions below.

AVTS is not only about keeping up with new technologies. Not all existing translation modes are becoming obsolete today. Since AVTS must examine content for technology, the presentation of content through technology and how it influences or modifies existing translation formats, we should not dispose of the old in embracing the new. Established themes must continue to be studied, from new angles, or in newly arising contexts. Glances into our heritage, into AVT history, may be equally enlightening. Indeed, some classic forms of AVT – such as subtitling – are taking on new forms, adapting themselves to new contexts and encountering new challenges, such as increased multilingualism, greater linguistic variety, more demanding and diversifying audiences and, last but not least, accessibility on new devices.

To conclude, we feel a word of warning is in order too. We are currently engaged in a paradigm shift, one that extends beyond the boundaries of TS: the dominance of the information society appears to be under threat from a new dominance, the index society. Economists and market forces use indices such as the Financial Times 100, the Dow Jones or Nikkei 225 to study performance. Today, education and many other social spheres are managed by economists, and they have imported their methodologies and ethos to evaluate success by means of indices. In translation practice and research this can lead to a focus on quantity rather than quality, a trend that is supported by technology as well. The need to draw attention to this threat and to counter the trend of giving priority to quantifiability and quantity over quality in AVT practice and research were underlying themes at the third international *Media for All* conference, which was held in Antwerp (Belgium) in October 2009: *Audiovisual Translation: Quality Made to Measure*. The present book is loosely based on the conference. We are aware that a degree of quantifiability in research is required, but our concern with quality and the need to give smaller, new research the time to grow remains. Nevertheless, the recent developments in AVT described above and the contributions that we received prompted us to choose another title for this *Media for All 3* volume: *Audiovisual Translation and Media Accessibility at the Crossroads*.

The number of manuscripts that were submitted testifies to the fact that AVTS is very much alive today. We received 70-odd contributions. After a stringent blind peer-review process, we retained 19 contributions. Our choice was based on research quality and methodology, as well as the current relevance of the topic. We also wanted to give a voice to young researchers and include contributions which presented different AVT modalities, functions and topics, including small-scale research. As a result, the book contains contributions on new directions in AVT as well as studies focusing on more established modalities, be it with a new twist or angle, reflecting the interdisciplinary nature of much research. This is also the reason why AVT and accessibility have not been subsumed under two different headings. Some methodologies are now applied to both subdisciplines. In addition, the differences between both subdisciplines seem less relevant than the similarities in the research methodologies applied to the 'raw' material. In short, AVTS is at the crossroads in many ways and this accounts for the diversity in the topics included in most collections of articles on AVT today.

Media for All: Audiovisual Translation and Media Accessibility at the Crossroads is divided into three sections, with a selection of contributions in each section: (1) Extending the borders of AVT (four contributions), (2) Interpreting sight and sound (five contributions) and (3) The discourses of audiovisual translation (ten contributions).

Section 1, *Extending the Borders of AVT*, comprises contributions that look into new research areas, relatively marginal to AVT up to now, but reflecting today's social reality. This section starts with a contribution from **Minako O'Hagan**, who analyses the effects of the collaborative principle of Web 2.0 from a translation perspective. *From Fan Translation to Crowdsourcing: Consequences of Web 2.0 User Empowerment in Audiovisual Translation* looks at the actors in the organisation of crowdsourced translation within AVT and the shift in basic concepts such as quality, which should be at the heart of any translation. Volunteer translation, collaborative efforts and crowd wisdom give rise to a new product which may in turn lead to new market models, working practices and a renewed need for research.

Carmen Mangiron considers issues of accessibility within the popular field of video games localization. In *Exploring New Paths towards Game Accessibility*, video game developers are held responsible for including the many features that can be provided for accessible gaming from the early design stages, going beyond their translation and localization into different languages. In a society where technological development is user-centric, video user groups with special needs should be no exception. Moreover, accessible games provide more than entertainment alone: they can contribute to improving the lives of people with visual, auditory, cognitive and physical disabilities.

In *Graphic Emoticons as a Future Universal Symbolic Language*, **Junichi Azuma** proposes the use of a computer-mediated universal symbolic language which goes beyond specific language differences. Emoticon usage is on the increase, providing not only a synthetic and fast form of communication, but also an international code which supersedes translation. Azuma's contribution focuses on extreme examples of the hieroglyphic use of graphic emoticons, which may lead to the emergence of a universal symbolic language in the future. It also looks at the role that insights from the psychology of vision may play in this endeavour.

In the last contribution in the first section, **Lucile Desblache** offers some insights into new online publishing trends and their contribution to different types of accessibility in *Mapping Digital Publishing for All in Translation*. Desblache traces the ways in which the growth of open-access online publications in (AV)TS is contributing to changes in attitudes towards translation and related research. Desblache's contribution focuses on five themes which are at the heart of online publication today: (1) access versus finance, (2) quality versus speed, (3) digital versus print, (4) multiculturalism versus globalisation and (5) open access versus accessibility.

The second section of the book, *Interpreting Sight and Sound*, is devoted to specific issues within already established disciplines that are faced with new challenges, both in practice and research, as a result of recent developments in technology, legislation or user needs. The section starts with two contributions on live subtitling.

In the first contribution, *Quality in Live Subtitling: The Reception of Respoken Subtitles in the UK*, **Pablo Romero-Fresco** looks at comprehension, perception and viewer preferences in live subtitles in the UK, making use of a detailed questionnaire disseminated to users in collaboration with the Royal National Institute for Deaf People. The results show how the existing settings and assumptions shared by various TV stations offering live subtitling may need to be reconsidered or modified. In the second contribution entitled *Applying a Punctuation-based Segmentation to an Add-on Display Mode of Respoken Subtitles*, **Juan Martínez Pérez** focuses on ways to improve live subtitling transmission speed while achieving an optimum display mode for respoken live subtitles. Two different formats are tested and compared. Both Romero Fresco's and Martínez Pérez's contribution on live subtitling with respeaking pave the way for a change in the production of live subtitles, demonstrating how theory and academic studies may have a direct impact on the industry and established practices.

Working within a different area of accessibility, that of audio description, **Nazaret Fresno** also looks at existing conventions in her contribution *Experimenting with Characters: An Empirical Approach to the Audio Description of Fictional Characters*. The ultimate aim of Fresno's research is to develop alternative narrative modes that will produce more user-friendly descriptions.

Also within the field of audio description, **Iwona Mazur** and **Agnieszka Chmiel** discuss the results of the pan-European audio description project entitled *The Pear Tree Project*, which looks at – among other things – the reception of visual input in different cultures and languages. Mazur and Chmiel's contribution *Audio Description Made to Measure: Reflections on Interpretation in AD Based on the Pear Tree Project Data* demonstrates that while cultures vary, film director techniques and film language cross national barriers, permitting the creation of an AD narrative that can be enjoyed regardless of national background. This, in turn, makes the translation of existing audio descriptions for new audiences feasible.

The last contribution in the second section is from **Alex McDonald**, who discusses the quality of sign language in *The In-vision Sign Language Interpreter in British Television Drama* and develops a concept for sign language interpretation for this popular TV genre. McDonald first explores the interpreter's role in assisting the audience in negotiating the interaction of the competing visual images. Sunsequently, McDonald identifies the challenges and demonstrates how in-vision interpreters can become an additional element in the semiotic web of the drama itself.

The third section of the book, *The Discourses of Audiovisual Translation*, is divided into three subsections and looks at challenges which local traditions and global trends present to traditional and newer forms of AVT and AVT research. The first subsection, *AVT Classics Revisited*, illustrates, on the one hand, the diversity of AVT traditions beyond the mainstream and the desire to uphold and develop regional practices. On the other hand, it shows new and growing demands created by increasing cross-border cultural exchange.

In *Voice-over or Voice-in-between? Some Considerations about Voice-Over Translation of Feature Films in Polish Television*, **Monika Woźniak** casts a new light on a translation mode that has been neglected in recent academic research: voice-over translation for fiction films. Focusing on the interaction between the three key factors in successful voice-over, Woźniak reaches the conclusion that the voice-over of feature films not only deserves much more attention than it has been receiving, she also points out how the practice of voice-over could be improved by transforming it into a 'voice-in-between' technique.

Turning to translation for the stage, in *Surtitling for the Stage and Directors' Attitudes: Room for Change*, **Anika Vervecken** challenges the established views of many theatre directors who consider surtitles a disruptive influence on their productions. After providing the reader with a detailed analysis of the surtitling process, Vervecken offers a step-by-step outline of how the process can be optimised and what role a theatre director could ideally play in achieving optimisation.

The second subsection, *Bilingualism, Multilingualism and Its Consequences*, groups contributions that demonstrate how today's increased interaction between local and global cultures leads to new linguistic challenges for AVT, but also how AVT itself can offer support to language acquisition. In *Old Films, New Subtitles, More Anglicisms?*, **Henrik Gottlieb** revisits subtitling history, calling for more systematic diachronic studies of screen translation and looking into the degree to which subtitles do or do not act as motors in the Anglicization process of Danish.

Dominique Bairstow and **Jean-Marc Lavaur**, in their contribution *Audiovisual Information Processing by Monolinguals and Bilinguals: Effects of Intralingual and Interlingual Subtitles*, look at the didactic possibilities offered by various forms of subtitling. Bairstow and Lavaur investigate the effects of language fluency and the use of both intralingual and interlingual subtitles on film comprehension and, ultimately, foreign language acquisition, on the basis of two controlled experiments with language learners.

In the following two contributions, the challenges that different types of multilingualism pose for audiovisual translation are investigated. In *Heterolingualism in Audiovisual Translation: De Zaak Alzheimer / La Memoria del Asesin*, **Anna Vermeulen** investigates the demands of subtitling or dubbing into Spanish of a film marked by Dutch linguistic variations. Vermeulen highlights a new direction for research in this region, recognising Belgium's linguistic diversity and heterolingualism as a prominent and characteristic feature of many of the country's film productions.

In *'You fancying your gora coach is okay with me': Translating Multilingual Films for an Italian Audience*, **Vincenza Minutella** investigates how multilingual films are translated for an Italian audience, focusing on three films by South Asian diasporic directors. For her research, Minutella makes use of a small bilingual parallel corpus with transcriptions of the original, dubbed and subtitled film dialogues, tagged for some of the main aspects of multilingual films: instances of cultural references, code-mixing, code-switching and ethnolects, which Minutella proceeds to analyse in detail. Both of the above contributions offer translational insights into challenges faced by many audiovisual translators today.

Minutella's contribution also provides a bridge to the third and last subsection in the third section of this book, *AVT, Film Language and Corpora*. The contributions in this last subsection also embrace the use of (multimodal) corpora for AVT research, which brings them in line with methodological trends in other areas of TS. Three contributions offer detailed linguistic analyses of specific translation choices; one is also of special methodological interest in that the very possibilities of multimodal corpus analysis constitute its topic.

In *The Enriching Functions of Address Shifts in Film Translation*, **Maria Pavesi** examines address modes such as vocatives and second-person pronouns, which express social roles and interpersonal relationships in translated film dialogue. Their shift tends to indicate mutations in the interactants' attitudes or status. Zoning in on a selection of contemporary American and British films dubbed into Italian, Pavesi's contribution focuses on the specific issue of transitions from formal to informal address in the target texts. This focus reveals that there are different contextual and paralinguistic causes that can function as triggers for such shifts.

Veronica Bonsignori, **Silvia Bruti** and **Silvia Masi**, look at another, equally complex and interactionally motivated linguistic phenomenon, in their contribution *Exploring Greetings and Leave-takings in Original and Dubbed Language*. Using a pilot Italian film corpus, Bonsigniori, Bruti and Masi identify and describe translation trends in this area, paying special attention to such features as the coherence of register across turns and between characters, as well as translator choices when dealing with idiolects and connoted slang varieties.

Focusing on methodology, **Maria Freddi** looks at *What AVT Can Make of Corpora: Some Findings from the Pavia Corpus of Film Dialogue* in her contribution. More specifically, Freddi presents findings based on the *Pavia Corpus of Film Dialogue*, a parallel corpus of original British and American film dialogues and their dubbed Italian versions. Freddi demonstrates how corpus methods can be of use to AVT.

Whereas the Pavia corpus was designed for research into traditional forms of AVT, in particular dubbing, the TRACCE corpus was intended for research in accessibility in a broader sense. In *Multisemiotic and Multimodal Corpus Analysis in Audio Description: TRACCE*, **Catalina Jiménez** and

Claudia Seibel present the results of this project, the objective of which has been to design the structure of an accessible audiovisual product database,

We hope that *Media for All: Audiovisual Translation and Media Accessibility at the Crossroads* will provide you with new insights for further research in our ever-expanding discipline and will provide stimulus to its readers on which turn to take. The preparation of this volume has been a pleasure for its editors, and we wish to thank all the contributors once againfor their hard work and inspiring contributions.We hope that all our colleagues and all others who have an interest in audiovisual translation and media accessibility will also find the book a pleasure to read.

References

Díaz Cintas, Jorge, Anna Matamala and Josélia Neves (eds) 2010. *New Insights into Audiovisual Translation and Media Accessibility* (Approaches to Translation Studies 30). Amsterdam: Rodopi.

Díaz Cintas, Jorge, Pilar Orero and Aline Remael (eds) 2007. *Media for All: Subtitling for the Deaf, Audio Description and Sign Language* (Approaches to Translation Studies 33). Amsterdam: Rodopi.

Section 1

Extending the Borders of AVT

From Fan Translation to Crowdsourcing: Consequences of Web 2.0 User Empowerment in Audiovisual Translation

Minako O'Hagan
Dublin City University (Ireland)

Abstract

Addressing the overarching question of 'quality made to measure' in the context of audiovisual translation (AVT), this contribution turns the attention to the emerging model of crowdsourcing (Howe 2006, 2008) applied to translation where the members of the undefined 'crowd' act as volunteer translators. Advancing Internet technology has ushered in the second generation Internet age of Web 2.0, promoting user participation through large-scale online collaboration and social networking. Ranging from the fan translation of popular culture domains to the user translation of *Facebook*, translation has become an illustrative example of participatory culture (Jenkins 2006). Taking the case of TED.com's Open Translation Project, where video clips of high-profile speakers are subtitled by volunteers, this contribution explores implications for AVT of this newly emerging model, with a focus on the issue of quality. The findings indicate that organisers of crowdsourced translation indeed implement quality control measures. However, these are not motivated by the same set of principles that apply to traditional translation-quality measures, but privilege online collaboration and the wisdom of the crowd. Framing the general trend of user empowerment and user-based translation in the concept of abusive subtitling (Nornes 1999), this contribution points to the evidence of subtitles as "vulnerable translation" (Díaz Cintas & Remael 2007). The contribution highlights the increasing need for adaptability of the AVT community of practitioners and researchers facing dynamically changing digital environments, while calling for more dialogue between the AVT community and crowdsourcing organisers.

Keywords
abusive subtitling, crowdsourcing, fans, TED.com, translation quality, user-generated content, users

1. What is crowdsourcing?

In his 2006 article in *Wired* the journalist Jeff Howe coined the term 'crowdsourcing'. Clearly associated with the business concept of outsourcing, this new term was defined as "the act of taking a job traditionally performed by employees and outsourcing it to an undefined, generally large group of people in the form of an open call" (Howe 2006). It exploits the Internet's global connectivity to tap into users' collective intelligence and self-motivation to solve problems and create new values. The year 2006 – the year in which the term 'crowdsourcing' was coined –

was also the year in which *Time* (13 December 2006) chose the annual "Person of the Year" to be "you" in recognition of the increasing visibility of user-generated content (UGC) on the Internet. Focusing on users and their tangible contributions, the authors of *Wikinomics* (Tapscott & Williams 2006) described a new kind of economy arising from mass collaboration through "peering technology" afforded by the second-generation Internet and collectively referred to as Web 2.0. Having emerged as a slogan from the 2004 O'Reilly[1] conference (Berry 2008: 13), Web 2.0 environments facilitate active user participation and are conducive to the now widespread development of both social networking as well as UGC.

Other technological advancements also played a critical role in such developments. For example, affordable yet sophisticated digital cameras have had a significant impact on photography, with amateur photographers now being able to produce pictures which have become as visible as the pictures by professionals in certain contexts and for certain purposes, as is evident on websites such as *Flickr* and *iStockphoto* (Howe 2008). Similarly, in the area of audiovisual translation (AVT), tools that were once specialised and intended for professional subtitling are now available – in some cases as freeware, pared-down versions without sophisticated professional features – making subtitling technically accessible to lay volunteers. Citing examples from a wide range of professional domains, Howe (2008) highlights how volunteer contributions from general Internet users are eroding some professional territories, in no small part owing to the availability of relevant tools. Indeed, such developments are seen by some as worrisome (Keen 2007) because of the fact that they place certain professions and professionalism at risk. However, others (Howe 2008, Tapscott & Williams 2006) hold the view that crowdsourcing is a natural consequence of technological advancements and can be seen as opening up new opportunities. As demonstrated by *Wikipedia*, collaboration by the Internet crowd can lead to meaningful contributions, in this case affording the creation of the biggest multilingual encyclopedia in the world within a relatively short time-frame. Both its domain and language coverage would not have been feasible without the mass scale of contributions. The volunteers' varying competence is subjected to the watchful eyes of the general crowd among whom are those with more knowledge of and expertise in a given domain, willing to mend other contributors' deficiencies almost instantly or with little delay. Such a mechanism is afforded by the appropriate technological platform – in this case *Wiki* – to enable collaborative authoring, and cannot be matched by a more rigid and closed conventional editorial structure drawing on a pre-determined relatively small group of experts.

Unique to the concept of crowdsourcing is a reliance on unspecified self-selected Internet users who respond to an open call to take on specific tasks.

In turn, this raises concerns over the impact on quality found in such user contributions. Yet, the findings of a 2005 comparative study by *Nature* (Giles 2005) which – in terms of accuracy – showed minor differences between *Wikipedia* and *Encyclopedia Britannica* are often cited to demonstrate the effectiveness of the concept of the "wisdom of crowds" used in the title of his book by (Surowiecki 2005). In addition, the findings also add that – unlike the inaccuracies found in *Encyclopedia Britannica* – the inaccuracies in *Wikipedia* were reportedly fixed by the time *Nature* published the report. This suggests that while the openness of *Wikipedia* may make it vulnerable to substandard contributions or – worse still – to forms of vandalism, it gives an unprecedented opportunity for a far wider coverage of topics, up-to-date information and a rapid rate of contributions (Tapscott & Williams 2006: 75). This is analogous to running massive, parallel, 24/7 operations on a global basis. Above all, the *Wikipedia* case suggests that a self-regulating quality-control mechanism could indeed kick in, effectively culling weaker contributions in a timely fashion. Focusing on the issue of quality, Brunette and Désilets (2008:55-56) call this a "self-repairing community approach" as opposed to the conventional "watchdog approach", where a small closed group of experts are responsible for checking quality.

Currently (first quarter of 2010) crowdsourcing is gradually creeping into translation discourse. To date, the single most significant event to highlight the link between crowdsourcing and the field of translation was the application of this crowdsourcing approach/model by *Facebook*. In December 2007 it launched the purpose-built crowdsourcing translation platform *Facebook Translations*[2] in an attempt to involve its more than 30,000 users to help translate the *Facebook* website into its 16 launched languages, with 60 additional languages under translation (Losse 2008). The first Spanish version was ready in one week. Likewise for the German version, which was followed by the French version, which took only 24 hours. This, in a context in which "most LSPs (Language Service Providers) would struggle to produce a 300,000-word project in a week, let alone within a day" (DePalma & Kelly 2008: 12). Within translation circles it was the localisation sector which first recognised this trend as something significant. Interest is evident at localisation conferences such as *Localisation World* in October 2007, the *Localisation Research Centre (LRC)* conference in October 2008 and *LISA (Localisation Industry Standards Association) Forum* in November 2008, where the topic was features as a key theme. According to the *LISA* report (Ray 2009: 2-3), "crowdsourcing is now on most people's radar" in the business sector with many high-tech companies implementing or seriously investigating this new translation model to facilitate their globalisation goals. A literature survey points to a high level of interest in this model from the commercial sector, resulting in a number of industry reports.

Chief among them are those by *CommonSense Advisory* (DePalma & Kelly 2008), *Translation Automation Users Group* (TAUS 2008, 2009) and *LISA* (Ray 2009). In the academic literature, the topic of crowdsourcing is beginning to appear, largely in relation to localisation and translation technology as is the case in the entry for localisation in the *Routledge Encyclopedia of Translation Studies*. Here, Schäler (2009: 161) introduces the concept as a new localisation framework which serves wider globalisation interest beyond purely commercial concerns. Schäler also mentions *Wikifization* in reference to *Wiki* applications enabling large-scale collaboration in translation and localisation. In relation to the latter, lines of research have been established to develop a computer-aided translation (CAT) platform to facilitate translator collaboration (Bey et al. 2006, Désilets 2007). Crowdsourcing is also discussed by Garcia (2009) and O'Hagan (2009) as a major potential factor to influence the future working environments of professional translators and localisers.

Having covered the background context of crowdsourcing, I would like to examine – particularly from the point of view of AVT – this new phenomenon in the remainder of this contribution. Given the relative newness of the concept and the paucity of prior work – especially in the field of AVT – the nature of this contribution is exploratory. Taking the case of *TED.com*'s *Open Translation Project* as a main example directly relevant to AVT, this contribution attempts to shed light on how quality issues are approached by an organiser of crowdsourcing. It also seeks to consider wider implications of crowdsourcing for the AVT profession. Nornes's concept of abusive subtitling (Nornes 1999) is used as a broad framework in an attempt to understand this new phenomenon, which is profoundly affecting the AVT profession and potentially challenging AVT norms. We begin our journey with the subtitling of anime by fans as a forerunner of volunteer AVT practices on a broader scale.

2. Fansubs as a forerunner of crowdsourced translation

Among the earliest and most conspicuous forms of 'user-generated' AVT of any significant quantity are 'fansubs', a term used to refer to subtitles created by fans of foreign films. The term, in its narrower sense, refers to subtitles created by fans to facilitate the free circulation of Japanese animation (hereafter referred to as anime) (Leonard 2005). Fansub practices were initiated in an attempt to bridge the subtitling gaps in official translations, which were the result of three possible factors: (1) the complete absence of subtitles, (2) considerable delays in subtitling production and (3) a reaction to over-editing, which was commonly – particularly in the early days of anime import – exercised by American television networks. Typically applied in dubbed form, such editorial changes affected anime both visually and in terms of narratives, where "Japanese names may be Americanized, and elements of Japanese culture may be edited out of the story" (Cubbison 2005: 52). Fansub practices have been in existence since the 1980s despite the formidable technical challenges of the pre-digital era before DVDs, AV authoring/editing tools and any ready access to the Internet. However, despite technical difficulties and also their shaky legal status appropriating copyrighted materials, fansubs have continued to develop and flourish in the digital age (Cubbison 2005). More recently, the fansub phenomenon has captured the attention of a few AVT scholars, who have shed some light on the following three fansub features: (1) fansub processes and their quality (e.g., Díaz Cintas & Muños Sánchez 2006), (2) the interventionist goals of fansubs in contributing to the globalisation of anime (Pérez González 2006) and (3) the potential merits of fansubs for translator training (O'Hagan 2008). These prior studies all recognised that these are highly organised, albeit organically formed, group-based collaborations with clear workflow put in place. There is a strong feeling of resistance to the dominance of Western popular culture among fans (Cubbison 2005: 45), which characterises fan participation in translation, in turn fuelling strong motivation and devotion. Fan translators also seem to treat translation as an opportunity to demonstrate their expert-like domain knowledge and the resulting respect earned within the fan groups as a reward. Indeed, the fan translators' domain-knowledge of anime is something which works to their advantage when translating – even if they lack formal translator training and skills (O'Hagan 2008). Furthermore, genuine fansub groups clearly distinguish themselves from bootlegging operations intended to make a profit by trying to sell their translations (Leonard 2005).

The most problematic and controversial aspect of fan translation is the issue of legality. Although fansub groups declare that they withdraw their work as soon as the official translation is released, their ethical arguments are based on their own internal logic and are contestable in a strictly legal sense. Such a tendency of being a law unto themselves and their activist spirit can also be seen in the fan translators' translation approaches. For most of these groups, the main intended audience comprises fellow fans (Díaz Cintas & Muños Sánchez 2006). Their work is therefore based on the assumption that the viewers' values are similar to those of fan-activist-cum-translators in that they are all in quest of authenticity, wishing to experience the "original form as seen by Japanese audiences" (Cubbison 2005: 47). Such an approach may at times manifest itself in a drastic procedure, which possibly includes leaving certain words untranslated on purpose, inserting gloss or translators' notes in the middle of the on-screen image and using colours and fonts to match the mood of the predominant theme, regardless of legibility. These approaches are experimental and clearly do not conform to AVT norms. At the same time, they can be regarded as serving the intended purpose for the assumed viewers. Given these contexts, it can be argued that conventional translation quality measures are neither relevant nor productive in assessing fansubs. The concept of abusive subtitling presented by Nornes (1999) provides a framework to focus on how fan translators project their voices against the prevailing revisionist approach[3], which was evident in this particular genre especially in the early days of anime circulation. Nornes's concept draws on abusive translation as advocated by Venuti (1995). Venuti's concept of abusive translation was based on poststructuralist ideas such as those of Lewis (1985: 42), who encourages experimental translation as a way to "rearticulate analogically the abuse that occurs in the original text". The whole resistive translation framework goes hand in hand with the fundamental reasoning of fans to take on these laborious tasks of their own accord in the first place. From a film-studies perspective Nornes (1999: 18) insists that some professionally produced subtitles are simply "corrupt" and conspire to hide the work of translation, succumbing to "the violent reduction demanded by the apparatus" without attempting to resist them in order to present the original with its abuse. Nornes (1999: 18) advocates inventive ways in which some fansubbers try to convey the potent force or "the unfamiliar" present in the original and he observes the following:

> Working outside the mainstream translation industry, lacking any formal training, these fans have produced abusive subtitles *quite by instinct*. In scenes with overlapping dialogue, they use different-coloured subtitles. Confronted with untranslatable words, they introduce the foreign word into the English language with a definition that sometimes fills the screen. (Nornes 1999: 31-32)

From a different perspective, fansubs which break AVT norms and the conventions of the target language can be considered simply as instances of poor translation, stemming from an obvious lack of translator training as well as necessary linguistic knowledge. And yet, the concept of abusive subtitling raises a question about the relevance of conventional translation-quality criteria used to assess fan-produced subtitles, given the underlying motivations and intended goals. In the meantime, culture-specific references depicted in anime may be becoming less foreign to an increasing number of viewers, who are now more familiar with Japanese culture in general and some of the anime-specific conventions in particular. It is also likely that as anime increasingly occupy the position of a "canon" within film genres on the global stage, less revisionist approaches may be taken in their translations. In fact, today's fansub practices seem to be more motivated by the time factor, that is, the wish to make new Japanese anime recently aired on Japanese television quickly available to overseas fans. Nevertheless, they may have succeeded in planting seeds of resistance not only to over-editing but also to accepted AVT norms. As Nornes (2007: 187) maintains, "'abuse' [in abusive subtitles] is directed at convention, even at spectators and their expectations" and "there is nothing holding us back from subjecting the most nonviolent films to abuse". By extension, we can hypothesise that AVT may see further disturbances to established norms and conventions (in the case of crowdsourced AVT legitimising indiscriminate user participation), for better or worse and for all the right or wrong reasons.

Some of the characteristics of fan translation can be seen as shared with crowdsourced translation. For example, self-motivation and drive are always considered hallmarks of crowdsourcing (Howe 2008). Another similarity is a community spirit, with volunteer translators sharing a common goal and purpose, which unite the participants who work together. Such a trait may be most evident with volunteers working for minority languages, which are usually not considered commercially viable and therefore often excluded from officially supported languages. Despite these similarities, one of the key and crucial differences between fan translation and crowdsourced translation lies in that crowdsourced translation legitimises the concept of free translation. As discussed above, fansub translations have been largely treated as underground activities. Although tolerated, they are practices which have never been officially endorsed as wholly legitimate. This is why fan translation remains primarily 'unsolicited' work whereas crowdsourced translation is 'solicited' by its organisers even though no remuneration is offered and no specific individuals are sought for help. Crowdsourcing is therefore fundamentally different from fan translation in the sense that it has been taken up by businesses and initiated from the start by a top-down mechanism. By contrast, fansubbing is the result of a genuinely bottom-up formation of fans' grassroot efforts. Despite their increasing visibility on the Internet, fansubs remain resolutely esoteric, niche activities focused on specific (sub)culture genres which nevertheless enjoy a strong following of fans. By comparison, the volunteer translation phenomenon through crowdsourcing looks set to become a legitimate translation model applicable to broad areas of translation, a model which responds to the needs of both non-profit and for-profit organisations. In the next section, I will provide a closer look at the case of *TED.com* with its use of a crowdsourcing model in making AV material accessible to those who do not speak English.

3. Translation as user-generated content: TED.com

Different aspects of AVT have seen changes in the digital age and further changes are set to emerge as a result of the proliferation of AV content made available at the fingertips of worldwide audiences. Such materials range from purpose-designed streamed video clips on corporate websites to a large array of UGC – including fansubbed anime. UGC became most visible on platforms such as *YouTube*, which – in turn – are linked to or embedded in various websites, mutually contributing to the further distribution of such content. In this way, different types of AV content – including copyrighted sources such as commercial films, television programmes and personal creations by individuals – are now potentially distributed to global audiences. This general climate of shared AV materials circulated as free UGC has created a new demand for AVT and seems to have contributed somewhat to the expectation that translations are to be provided free to accompany the otherwise free content. With the notable exception of fansubs, subtitling was not considered until recently something which non-professionals could readily attempt to undertake because of the need for specialised tools to create, synchronise and insert subtitles in the given audiovisual material, not to mention the specialised translation techniques required. With the advance of technology, together with the trend of freely distributed open source products, free or affordable tools have now become available. Organisations applying crowdsourcing to AVT are well aware of such trends and are further developing purpose-built applications designed both to avoid steep learning and to better facilitate the task for volunteer translators. *Facebook*'s translation platform, for example, simplified the job for the volunteers and "eliminated the need for manual processing beyond translation" (DePalma & Kelly 2008: 13). While a closer study into translation tools is beyond the scope of this contribution, any apparent impact on translation quality arising from the technical platform will be commented on below. We will now examine a recent crowdsourcing project set up with a view to subtitling motivated by the need to reach a global audience.

TED (Technology, Entertainment, Design) is a non-profit, US-based organisation established in 1984 with the mission to disseminate novel and inspirational ideas by inviting high-profile experts in a given field to give 18-minute talks at TED conferences, which were initially focused on the three professional fields of technology, entertainment and design. The current setup has now been expanded to cover other fields. TED launched its crowdsourcing platform *Open Translation Project* in May 2009 to subtitle video clips of TED Talks available in English on its website as explained in its press release as follows: "A year in the making, the project offers video subtitles, time-coded transcripts and the ability for volunteers worldwide to translate any talk into any language" (TED Open Translation Project 2009). According to the statistics provided by the TED.com home page (www.ted.com), as of April 2010 it has published almost 6,000 talks in over 70 languages with the help of 2,300 volunteer translators. The website indicates Spanish as the most translated target language, followed by

Bulgarian, Brazilian Portuguese, Chinese (simplified) and Arabic. Each language group is shown to have covered in excess of 300 talks. Looking at the range of languages in this list, it becomes obvious that the list is missing some of the languages which are usually considered commercially significant languages. This aligns with prior experiences by organisations using crowdsourcing (such as *Facebook*) which discovered that less commercially oriented or minority languages seem to be even more well served by a crowdsourcing approach as they tend to attract volunteers who have a particularly strong sense of mission about the preservation of such languages (Losse 2008). A desire to reach many languages is detectable in the statement by TED Media's Executive Producer June Cohen, who declares the following:

> Volunteer translation will be increasingly important for anyone trying to reach a global audience ... It's the only feasible way to reach all the world's languages. Crowd-sourced translation creates communities of volunteers who are passionate about producing great work, accountable for the accuracy of their translations, and invested in evolving the system itself. It turns users into true participants, helping to spread ideas. (TED Open Translation Project 2008)

The reasoning behind the crowdsourcing translation paradigm presented above reflects a number of key issues regarding this new model. Firstly, the language coverage problem comes down to economics, where demand and sales have to justify the level of investment in commissioning professional translations. A second point relates to the question of quality, where it seems to be argued that volunteer translators' innate enthusiasm and their self-organising dynamics will make them accountable, which, in turn, will ensure accuracy. While this justification partly matches the general 'wisdom of the crowd' logic discussed earlier, it also highlights the fundamentally different approach to translation quality from that in the conventional model familiar to professional and academic contexts of translation studies. It is this shift in thinking about how to organise translation and how to ensure quality which is significant and of interest. Garcia (2009: 210) highlights how the traditional localisation framework was already being questioned in relation to the effectiveness of the conventional translation quality control model of "translate-edit-proofread (TEP)" (Beninatto & DePalma 2008, cited in Garcia 2009). A new collaborative translation model proposes to replace TEP with a parallel approach by mass collaboration between translators and subject specialists, designed, unlike the TEP model, to eliminate mistakes from the outset rather than at the end. While the collaboration between professionals discussed by Beninatto and DePalma (2008) is not the same as crowdsourcing, the general shift towards collaboration and the move away from the closed-liner approach is clearly shared with the concept of crowdsourcing. Similarly Brunette and Désilets (2008) advocate the efficient quality control achieved by *Wikipedia*, leading them to conclude that the conventional approaches are not suitable for massive online collaboration and that "they must be replaced by more organic, open, self-repairing models" (Brunette & Désilets 2008: 56). *Facebook* also implemented two steps of "immediate feedback and correction" to ensure quality in addition to conventional translation steps such as "style specification, glossary development, and linguistic quality assurance" (DePalma & Kelly 2008: 13).

With these insights in mind, we examined the approach to quality by TED.com's Open Translation Project on the basis of translation guidelines prepared by TED. The specific quality measures used are laid out under "Becoming a TED Translator" (TED Becoming a TED Translator n.d.) guidelines on the TED.com website which are divided into the following headings: (1) working with other translators, (2) style guidelines for translators and (3) terms and conditions. In section (1), TED.com's principles on translation approaches are clearly formulated based on collaboration although translators can also choose to work alone initially to produce their translations. Registered volunteer translators are put in touch with other translators who have translated TED clips from the same language group in order to facilitate collaboration in any way that they feel is appropriate. With the initial freedom on how translation may be done individually, in pairs or in groups, a key quality measure is introduced in the form of a separate reviewer (also a volunteer), with whom the translator must work by means of interaction through the TED e-mail system. The reviewer's task is to spot any translation errors and assist the translator with interpretation and style issues. The guidelines also refer to a specific instruction directing reviewers to give priority to "most universally understood among all dialects of your language" when resolving differences of opinion between the translator and the reviewer. A fairly detailed list of guidelines intended for the reviewer is provided for "a successful collaboration". It is beyond the scope of this contribution to delve into the work ethics of online collaboration which the guidelines detail. However, it is relevant to point out that the list prompts the reviewer to report translators' lack of competence in addition to any instances of disruptive behaviour. On the basis of these guidelines, we can suggest that one of TED's key approaches to ensuring quality is to assign a separate independent reviewer irrespective of whether the initial translation was conducted individually or in collaboration.

Some guidelines provided to the reviewers are repeated in the style guide for the translators under (2). The overall emphasis is on being "extremely accurate" and on reflecting "the spirit and flow of the speaker's style" (TED Style guidelines for translators n.d.). In order to address these two key points, the guideline is then subdivided into 4 sections: (1) assess your own fluency,

(2) TED style, (3) technical style and (4) specific guidelines. Under (1), while translators are not required to have any formal translator training, they are expected to be "fluently bilingual" (TED Style guidelines for translators n.d.) and "take seriously the role of translating another person's idea" (TED Style guidelines for translators n.d.). While a specific emphasis is placed on quality, the recruitment of translators is – true to the spirit of crowdsourcing – primarily left as self-selection. As for specific translation styles, the guidelines in TED Style (2) suggests informal over formal, modern over traditional, personal over generic and global over regional on the basis that "TED speakers are all at the edge of their fields, and therefore the edge of language. So being current, as well as fluent, is key" (TED Style guidelines for translators n.d.). There are also specific instructions for not translating idioms literally as well as titles of works mentioned in talks ideally being translated by using the same words if translations already exist in the target language. Proper nouns are meant to be transliterated and the units of measurements are to be converted into the most familiar units of measurement for the target audience. TED punctuation guidelines do not include any subtitle-specific rules and make references only to readability, the flow of the original speech and target language punctuation rules. While intended to ensure translation quality, the guidelines are laid out as if they are intended for translating documents. Finally, the terms and conditions (item 3 in the list above) stipulate the nature of the translation work as voluntary and indicate an incentive different from the incentive for paid commissioned work. The terms and conditions section states this as follows: "We don't pay translators for their work ... But we place a great emphasis on crediting you for your work" (TED Terms and Conditions n.d.). In addition to using the leader-board concept commonly found in other organisations which use crowdsourced translation to recognise contributions made by particularly prolific volunteer translators, TED also credits the translators' and reviewers' names in the translated clips. In turn, this must be designed to make the volunteer translators feel accountable for their efforts as well as to provide them with a moral reward. In other words, the crediting of names can be considered as a means of quality control. Additionally, any viewer can send feedback to the translators by simply clicking on their names, which are shown with the video clip.

The analysis outlines the direction of translation quality control principles adopted by TED. These principles also serve as a translation brief to the translators, spelling out the intended purpose of use of the translation as well as providing broad criteria for the quality sought of their translations. The most conspicuous absence is that of subtitle-specific guidelines such as text-reduction requirements in consideration of viewer reading speed or image/text synchronisation while accuracy in translation and reflecting speaker style are stressed. This in turn can be seen as relating to the particular way in which the subtitling procedure and the technical platform is set up in TED. Firstly, the transcripts in English are generated in-house professionally and approved by speakers, in effect providing volunteer translators with the source text (dialogue list) to work with. This is considered by TED as one of their quality measures which ensures that "all translations are based on the same source document" (TED Open Translation Project 2009). In terms of technical subtitling tools, TED volunteer translators work on a web-based subtitling platform provided by dotSUB[4] which largely removes the freedom of segmentation and cueing of speech for purposes of subtitle-speech synchronisation, speaker style and the viewer reading speed. And yet these are integral parts of key considerations in professional subtitling. The transcript in the source language is broken into lines, each of which is cued and presented to the volunteer translator, who is merely required to translate line by line without the burden of cueing or segmentation. This is reminiscent of the recent template-based approach used in the AV industry with master titles made available – usually in English – already shortened and cued and provided in so-called 'genesis files'. From these files DVD subtitles in multiple languages may be generated (Díaz Cintas & Remael 2007: 35). Some TED subtitles also seem to follow a verbatim approach. However, there is ambiguity with respect to whether or not these subtitles are truly intended to serve deaf and hard-of-hearing viewers as is the case for subtitling for the deaf and hard-of-hearing (SDH) proper. The ambiguity about the purpose of the subtitles is clear given that TED clearly recognises the advantage of subtitles over dubbing by acknowledging the additional benefits (of subtitles) of "making our talks available to audience members who are hearing-impaired", stated under TED Help for translators (TED Becoming a TED Translator n.d.).

As a final part of our analysis of the approach to quality adopted by TED, some end-user comments were sought. For practical reasons, only an informal survey was feasible. This survey was designed to gain impressionistic feedback and consisted of 36 responses provided by 13 undergraduate and 23 postgraduate translation students. The group of translation students consisted of native and non-native speakers of English, most of whom had no formal knowledge of AVT. The voluntary survey[5] consisting of six questions was made available in October 2009 on the virtual learning environment Moodle, which was used for the module taught by the author. For the purpose of the survey, the students were free to choose any TED video clips taking into account their language combinations and their interests in particular topics or speakers. In the group of undergraduate translation students, the most commonly selected target language was Spanish (6 students). In the group of postgraduate translation students, the most commonly selected target language was French (10 students). In both groups, German was the second most popular language. The majority of the 13 undergraduate translation students was positive about the subtitles in terms of informativeness, although three students (23%) commented that (1) some translations were too literal, (2) the length of subtitles was too long and (3) subtitles contained minor linguistic errors. Similarly, the group of 23 postgraduate students was generally positive about the informativeness of the subtitles, although 16 respondents (70%) had suggestions for improvements with respect to, for example, the speed with which the subtitles were presented. In addition, some subtitles were considered too fast and some translations too literal. Furthermore, some subtitles also contained some spelling errors, questionable word choice, poor cohesion and problems with synchronisation. When asked if they were prepared to offer their comments to the translator, 9 students from the undergraduate group (69%) and 14 students from the postgraduate group (61%) said that they were prepared to do so. A few students specifically commended the accessibility provided by the extra information appropriate for hearing-impaired viewers included in the subtitles, making references to SDH features in the particular clips that they had chosen.

4. Conclusions

The recent development of crowdsourcing is putting AVT at a crossroads: it draws special attention to the need for AVT as a result of an increasing volume and range of AV content now available on the Internet while at the same time possibly opening a floodgate to a potentially massive number of volunteers who would gladly take on subtitling assignments free of charge. This contribution set out to investigate the emerging translation model of crowdsourced subtitles as illustrated in the relatively recent case of the TED Open Translation Project at the time of writing. On the face of it, a non-profit organisation seeking to spread inspirational messages from leading professionals, themselves donating their time, seems just. An analysis of the organisers' approach to quality control also indicates that some well-considered measures are in place to maximise and manage the unknown quality of volunteer translators' contributions. TED assign separate reviewers and also credit both the translators' and the reviewers' names on the clip visible to the public, who, in turn, can send translators post-viewing feedback in the action of a single click. In addition, TED encourages and facilitates collaboration between the registered volunteers within the same language group, which would also function to reduce errors. A small-scale informal survey conducted among translation students suggests that the subtitles of the clips that they randomly reviewed were mostly informative and without major errors. These findings appear to prove only that there is room for volunteer translators in AVT and indeed that crowdsourcing might well be the only way to have all kinds of AV material – especially materials intended for a non-profit good cause – circulated on the Internet and made available to a worldwide audience in a timely fashion.

And yet a question remains. The students in training still noticed spelling errors, literal translations not in keeping with the style of the speakers, subtitles that appeared too fast and some synchronisation problems, which one would be less likely to see repeated in commercial cinema today. Subtitled TED video clips probably get the most important messages across to viewers but perhaps only with some compromises in the form of awkward literal translations, less than optimal segmentation. The consequence appears to be that the translations often miss out on the speakers' great styles and flair in delivering the messages. Unlike commercial movies in cinema or DVDs, these AV materials – including subtitles – are free so these shortcomings are probably accepted as minor glitches. Many viewers perhaps do not even notice them. However, one student expressed the thought that while the crowdsourced subtitles met TED's goal of "spreading ideas", they perhaps did not meet their other goal of "inspiring", which would have required the subtitles to be of a higher quality.

Subtitles are a long suffering mode of translation, having long been regarded as something short of translation proper because they are a reduced form of what is actually being said. Most of all, the original speech is always there to remind the viewers of the subordinate status of subtitles. In the digital age, fan-translated subtitles are becoming more visible and establishing themselves as somewhat edgy, while professional subtitles may be seen as a somewhat staid and even "corrupt" (Nornes 1999), not always trying hard enough to convey the force which is present in the source text. Indeed, on many levels subtitles are vulnerable translations as acutely observed by Díaz Cintas and Remael (2007). The digital era seems to do nothing but further highlight such vulnerability by inviting what Nornes (2007) calls "the abusive turn" (176-187). In the advent of crowdsourced subtitles, what is a poor subtitle and what is a truly innovative attempt can be further blurred and increasingly difficult to distinguish by all but a few discerning viewers. That said, as most students commented, the subtitles probably do the job of conveying the key ideas, and crowdsourcing has the advantage of quickly covering a large number of language groups. Furthermore, the time-coded transcripts in all languages in which TED talks are available allow viewers to perform keyword searches using search engines and also to access the exact point of the speech in the clip where the words appear. Having launched the TED Open Translation Project, Michael

Smolens – the CEO of the project's technology partner dotSUB – is clear about the next step with crowdsourcing subtitles:

> The real challenge will then be to take this learning and convince traditional owners of video content of any type, in any industry, that crowd sourcing can work, can help them spread their message, engage their audience, lower their costs, while at the same time embracing openness instead of feeling threatened by *new standards of quality*. (quoted in the TAUS report 2009, my emphasis)

This statement directly addresses the question of quality made to measure. Now more than ever is the time to rethink the meaning of quality in AVT in the context of the digital era and – more fundamentally – to ask ourselves how AVT as a profession and an academic discipline can flourish in the dynamic new environments that are unfolding. If we fail to do so, users will lead the way, be it abusive or not. This calls for more dialogue between the AVT community, crowdsourcing organisers and platform providers.

---

[1] O'Reilly and Associates publishes open-source software technical manuals, and is concerned with software developments and the future direction of the Internet, which they were discussing at the conference in question (Berry 2008: 203).

[2] Facebook filed for patent appliation to the US Patent and Trademark Office in December 2008 for its concept of community translation processes and it is currently pending. Full application is available at: http://appft.uspto.gov/netacgi/nph-Parser?Sect1=PTO2&Sect2=HITOFF&p=1&u=/netahtml/PTO/search-ool.html&r=1&f=G&l=50&col=AND&d=PG01&s1=facebook.AS.&s2=translation.AB.&OS=AN/facebook+AND+ABST/translation&RS=AN/facebook+AND+ABST/translation

[3] The revisionist approach refers to radical editing strategies which used to be freely applied to anime, typically by American television networks, in an attempt to remove any Japanese flavour to Americanize the content as detailed by Cubbison (2005).

[4] See the demo link to the dotSUB platform: http://dotsub.com/demo.jsp

[5] Because the survey was conducted as an anonymous, voluntary online questionnaire administered on the virtual learning environment (LVE) which the students were using for the course taught by the author, no specific ethical approval was sought. However, the students were informed that the results were to be used for research purposes. The number of students taking the course consisted of 24 undergraduate and 45 postgraduate students. Therefore, the response rates were 54% and 51% respectively.

References

Berry, David. 2008. Copy, *Rip, Burn: The Politics of Copy Left and Open Source*. London: Pluto.

Bey, Youcef, Christian Boitet & Kyo Kageura. 2006. 'The TRANSBey Prototype: An Online Collaborative Wiki-based CAT Environment for Volunteer Translators' in Yuste, Elia (ed.) *Proceedings of the Third International Workshop on Language Resources for Translation Work, Research & Training (LR4Trans-III)*. 49-54.

Brunette, Louise & Alain Désilets. 2008. 'Quality in Collaborative Translation and Terminology' in *Multilingual* (September): 55-58.

Cubbison, Laurie. 2005. 'Anime, Fans, DVDs, and the Authentic Text' in *The Velvet Light Trap* 56(1): 45-57.

DePalma, Don & Nataly Kelly. 2008. *Translation of, for, and by the People*. Lowell, MA: Common Sense Advisory.

Désilets, Alain. 2007. Translation Wikified: How will Massive Online Collaboration Impact the World of Translation? *ASLIB Translating and the Computer 29 Conference Proceedings*, London: ASLIB.

Díaz Cintas, Jorge & Pablo Muños Sánchez. 2006. 'Fansubs: Audiovisual Translation in an Amateur Environment' in *The Journal of Specialised Translation* 6: 37-52. On line at: http://www.jostrans.org/issue06/art_diaz_munoz.php (consulted 15.03.2010).

Díaz Cintas, Jorge & Aline Remael. 2007. *Audiovisual Translation: Subtitling*. Manchester: St. Jerome.

Garcia, Ignacio. 2009. 'Beyond Translation Memory: Computers and the Professional Translator' in *The Journal of Specialised Translation* 12: 199-214.

Giles, Jim. 2005. 'Internet Encyclopedias Go Head to Head' in *Nature* 438(531). On line at: www.nature.com/news/2005/051212/full/438900a.html (consulted 15.032010).

Howe, Jeff. 2006. 'The Rise of Crowdsourcing' in *Wired* 14(6). On line at: http://www.wired.com/wired/archive/14.06/crowds.html (consulted 15.03.2010).

Howe, Jeff. 2008. *Crowd Sourcing: Why the Power of Crowd Driving the Future of Business*. London: Random house.

Jenkins, Henry. 2006. *Fans, Bloggers and Gamers: Exploring Participatory Culture*. New York: New York University Press.

Keen, Andrew. 2007. *The Cult of the Amateur*. New York: Doubleday.

Leonard, Sean. 2005. 'Progress against the Law: Anime and Fandom, with the Key to the Globalization of Culture' in *International Journal of Cultural Studies* 8(3): 281-305.

Lewis, Philip. 1985. 'The Measure of Translation Effects' in Graham, Joseph (ed.) *Difference in Translation*. Ithaca, NY: Cornell University Press. 31-62.

Losse, Kate. 2008. Achieving Quality in a Crowd-source Translation Environment. A keynote paper given at the Annual Conference of Localisation Research Centre XIII, 2-3 October 2008, Merino Institute of Education, Dublin, Ireland.

Nornes, Abè Mark. 1999. 'For an Abusive Subtitling' in *Film Quarterly* 52(3): 17-34.

Nornes, Abé Mark. 2007. *Cinema Babel: Translating Global Cinema*. Minneapolis, MN: University of Minnesota Press.

O'Hagan, Minako. 2008. Fan Translation Networks: An Accidental Translator Training Environment? In Kearns, John. (ed.) *Translator and Interpreter Training: Issues, Methods and Debates*. London: Continuum. 158-183.

O'Hagan, Minako. 2009. Evolution of User-generated Translation: Fansubs, Translation Hacking and Crowdsourcing in *The Journal of Internationalization and Localisation* 1(1): 94-121. On line at: http://www.lessius.eu/jial/ (consulted. 17.04.2010).

Pérez González, Lewis. 2006. 'Fansubbing Anime: Insights into the "Butterfly Effect" of Globalisation on Audiovisual Translation' in *Perspectives* 14 (4): 260-277.

Ray, Rebecca. 2009. *Crowdsourcing: The Crowd Wants to Help You Reach New Markets*. Romainmôtier: Localisation Industry Standards Association (LISA).

Schäler, Reinhard. 2009. 'Localisation' in Baker, Mona & Gabriala Saldanha (eds.) *Routledge Encyclopedia of Translation Studies*. London: Routledge. 157-161.

Surowiecki, James. 2005. *The Wisdom of Crowds: Why the Many are Smarter than the Few*. London: Abacus.
Tapscott, Don & Anthony Williams. 2006. *Wikinomics: How Mass Collaboration Changes Everything*. New York: Portfolio.
TAUS. 2008. 'Community Localisation inside SecondLife'. On line at: http://www.translationautomation.com/best-practices/community-localisation-inside-second-life.html (consulted 17.04.2010).
TAUS. 2009 'Community Translation for TED.com'. On line at: http://www.translationautomation.com/user-cases/community-translation-for-tedcom.html (consulted 17.04.2010).
TED n.d. 'Becoming a TED Translator'. On line at: http://www.ted.com/pages/view/id/293 (consulted 17.04.2010).
TED 2009. 'Open Translation Project'. On line at: http://ted.streamguys.net/TED_announces_OTP_release.pdf (consulted 17.04.2010).
TED n.d. 'Style guidelines for translators'. On line at: http://www.ted.com/pages/view/id/295 (consulted 18.04.2010).
TED n.d. 'Terms and Conditions'. On line at: http://www.ted.com/pages/view/id/297 (consulted 18.04.2010).
Venuti, Laurence. 1995. *The Translator's Invisibility*. London: Routledge.

Exploring New Paths towards Game Accessibility[1, 2]

Carmen Mangiron
Universitat Autònoma de Barcelona (Spain)
Dublin City University (Ireland)

Abstract

Over the course of the last four decades video games have become a world-wide entertainment phenomenon. One of the keys to the success of this multibillion-dollar industry lies in video game developers' drive to reach as many gamers as possible by designing games of universal appeal and localising them into different languages. However, in their race to make games as universal as possible, developers are leaving behind an important segment of the market: people with disabilities. Naturally, people with visual, auditory, cognitive and physical disabilities also enjoy playing games because of the fun and entertainment that such games provide. In addition, games can contribute to improving the quality of life of people with disabilties and to increasing their sense of inclusion. This contribution explores the current issues associated with games accessibility and explores new paths towards a design for all that strive to include rather than exclude gamers with disabilities, truly providing fun for all.

Keywords

accessibility, design for all, gamers with disabilities, universally accessible video games, video games

1. Introduction

The entertainment software industry, also known as the video game industry, is a relatively young industry that – in less than four decades – has grown to become a world-wide phenomenon, generating billion-dollar sales across the globe. It represents a powerful source of competition to other entertainment industries – such as the music and the movie industry – to the extent that it has surpassed the movie industry in revenue in countries such as the UK (Radd 2010). Games graphics and sound quality are constantly improving to the point that games are starting to resemble movies extremely closely, mainly due to their use of cinematic scenes, which are also known as *cutscenes*. Development costs are soaring and are expected to continue to do so, with the average cost of multiplatform games of the next generation estimated between 18 and 28 million dollars (Crossley 2010). In order to maximise their returns on investments, developers and publishers need to increase their potential target markets by aiming their products at the widest possible audience and by designing games that appeal to both genders, to different age groups and to international audiences.

That said, developers seem to be leaving behind an important segment of the population: people with disabilities, who – according to the UN – account for 10 to 12 per cent of the word population (The World Bank 2009). People with sensorial (visual, auditory), cognitive and physical disabilities also enjoy playing video games since such games are fun and provide hours of entertainment. In addition, games can have an educational value, as they can help players (1) improve hand-eye coordination and motor skills, (2) develop problem-solving skills and (3) improve reading skills. For example, there are games specifically designed to educate children by teaching them how to read and write, by developing their mathematical skills, or by raising awareness about issues such as health, the environment or human rights, to mention but a few. These kinds of games are known as edutaintment, a portmanteau of the terms *education* and *entertainment*. Furthermore, games can have a therapeutic value, and some mainstream games, such as *Wii Fit*, are used in hospitals and rehabilitation centres to help patients improve their balance, endurance and strength (WKYC 2008).

Games can undoubtedly contribute to improving the quality of life of people with disabilitites, increasing their sense of social inclusion. Unfortunately, most mainstream titles are designed without taking into account accessibility issues, which means that most games are not suitable for disabled players. It is ironic that as game technology becomes more advanced, games are becoming less accessible for players with special needs. For example, the transition from fifth-generation consoles, such as the PlayStation 1, which used CD-ROM as a storage medium, to sixth-generation consoles, such as the PlayStation 2 and Microsoft Xbox, which use DVD as a storage medium, allowed, for the first time, the introduction of recorded human voices and fully fledged cinematic scenes. While 'old-fashioned' games that used speech balloons to present the dialogue between characters had been fully accessible for deaf and hard-of-hearing (DHH) players to that point, the introduction of voiced-over dialogues meant that unless these were subtitled, parts of the game were in fact inaccessible for DHH players.

Accessibility barriers can be the source of great frustration and emphasise the marginalisation and the exclusion that people with disabilities often endure. This contribution explores the current issues associated with video-games accessibility. It provides a definition of game accessibility, states the benefits of promoting game accessibility, presents an overview of the current situation, focuses on the main accessibility challenges facing different groups of players and explores different paths for improving game accessibility.

2. What is game accessibility?

The Merriam-Webster's online dictionary defines *accessibility* as the noun corresponding to the adjective *accessible*, which – in turn – is defined as follows:

1: providing access
2: (a) capable of being reached <accessible by rail>; also: being within reach <fashions at accessible prices> (b) easy to communicate or deal with <accessible people>
3: capable of being influenced: open <accessible to new ideas>
4: capable of being used or seen: available <the collection is not current ly accessible>
5: capable of being understood or appreciated <the author's most access ible stories> <an accessible film>

The concepts of *access, within reach, easy to communicate or deal with, capable of being used or seen, being understood or appreciated* describe the many meanings that the adjective accessible can have, and are applicable to physical spaces, media and new technologies. Accessibility to new information technology and the media has attracted considerable attention over the past few years. In particular, accessibility to TV has been given a great deal of attention by scholars. It has become the subject of several studies triggered by the switch from analogue to digital TV in Europe by 2012,[3] which provides new opportunities for improved access to TV programmes for users with sensorial disabilities. There are also specialised conferences focusing on media accessibility, such as the biennial Media for All conference series, which started in 2005, bringing together academics and scholars from different countries to discuss accessibility issues such as subtitling for the deaf and hard-of-hearing (SDH) and audio description for the blind.

However, game accessibility remains a largely unexplored field of study, as a result of several factors, such as the relatively young age of the video-game industry and the fact that for many years video games have been considered a pastime for children and teenagers. In addition, video games have only recently become the subject of academic study, with the year 2001 considered year 1 in game studies (Aarseth 2001). Most of the research conducted on game accessibility to date has been carried out by academics from engineering- and computer-studies backgrounds, such as the Universally Accessible (UA) Games research group at the Human-Computer Interaction Laboratory of ICS-FORTH in Greece, and a handful of industry professionals interested in the topic, such as the Game Accessibility Special

Interest Group (SIG) at the International Game Developer Association (IGDA).

A key difference between traditional media accessibility, such as movies, and game accessibility lies in the interactive nature of video games. A movie spectator receives the movie passively, while video-game players are agents and must perform certain actions to be able to progress in the game. As a result, game accessibility poses a higher challenge than accessibility to other traditional media because the physical and cognitive efforts demanded from players is much higher. Players are not only required to process and understand information, they must also take actions and control their own progress in the game by carrying out certain tasks.

Thus, the interactive nature of games brings their accessibility issues closer to those associated with accessibility to other new digital media, such as software applications and websites. Microsoft (2010) states that "accessibility makes the computer easier to see, hear, and use", and adds that this definition "includes both accessibility settings built into programs and specialty assistive technology products". This definition highlights the two key solutions to improved accessibility to electronic media: (1) an accessible design and (2) the application of assistive technology to existing products. IBM (s.d.), on the other hand, summarises software and web accessibility in the following fashion:

> Understanding accessibility requires an awareness of the special needs of multiple user groups, including people with disabilities and mature users with age-related disabilities. A person with a disability may encounter one or more barriers that can be eliminated or minimized by the software or Web developer, the assistive technology, or the underlying operating system software and hardware platform.

The view expressed in the quote above highlights the importance of designing software that meets the needs of users with disabilities by eliminating barriers through an inclusive design or by using adaptive technologies. This can also be applied to video games, which are also a form of interactive software. However, the main difference between video games and other types of software lies in the entertaining nature of video games, as opposed to the more functional nature of business software applications.

From a game-accessibility perspective, this contribution adopts a wide definition of the term *accessibility*, which not only refers to accessibility for those players with disabilities, but also to players of different ages and levels of ability and experience.[4] Accessibility is therefore understood as a combination of usability and adaptability in an attempt to make games available to the widest possible set of users. The concepts of usability and adaptability are explored in more detail in the following subsections.

2.1. Usability

Usability is defined by the ISO 9241-11 norm as "the extent to which a product can be used by specified users to achieve specified goals with effectiveness, efficiency and satisfaction in a specified context of use" (UsabilityNet, 2006). Despite the fact that this definition originally referred to the use of software applications, it can be extended to any other instance of human-computer interaction, such as the use of websites or video games. In order to play a game successfully, the user interface must be effective and efficient so that it facilitates progress and provides a satisfactory gameplay experience to the players by engaging them and immersing them in the game world.

Some authors have captured the importance of the "satisfaction" and entertainment factor in game usability by providing more specific definitions of usability in the game-industry context. For example, usability has been defined as "delivering a better and deeper experience with less unnecessary interruptions or challenges that have not been designed by the developers" (Laitinen 2005). Glinert (2009) focuses on four dimensions of usability: (1) learnability, (2) simplicity, (3) efficiency and (4) aesthetics. Learnability emphasises the fact that a novice player should be able to learn easily how to play a game. Simplicity refers to the fact that controls should be as easy and intuitive as possible, while still keeping the gameplay engaging. Efficiency, on the other hand, guarantees that tasks which are to be performed can be carried out quickly and efficiently. The aesthetic dimension is the dimension that developers often focus on, as a game should have a pleasant aesthetic, making it enjoyable to use (Glinert 2009). The aesthetic and ludologic dimensions are crucial in games since their primary function is to entertain, which is reflected in the terms *player* and *gamer* in contraposition to the more general term *user*.

2.2. Adaptability

Adaptability is defined here as a game-design characteristic aimed at fostering compatibility of game software and hardware with existing assistive technological solutions in an attempt to meet the specific needs of different groups of users. Adaptability through the application of assistive technologies is particularly relevant to players with physical disabilities who are not able to play a game with the standard controllers or keyboard. For example, games that are compatible with adapted digital controllers are more accessible because they allow gamers with reduced mobility to play games by pressing fewer buttons or simply one single switch. Unfortunately, many recent games do not support non-standard and non-analogue controllers (Ellis 2006).

3. Reasons for advocating game accessibility

There are several reasons to champion game accessibility and these may be of an economic, social, educational, therapeutic and moral nature. While the financial benefits of localisation are generally accepted by the game industry, the benefits of accessibility for players with disabilities have been largely disregarded. However, there are also economic arguments in favour of improving accessibility for players with disabilities since game companies could theoretically gain from a potential sales increase of up to 12 per cent, considering that there are approximately ten to twelve per cent people in the world with disabilities. Despite the fact that many of them already play games regularly, as proved by numerous websites and blogs catering for disabled gamers,[5] the more accessible games become, the more likely players with disabilities will buy them.

In addition, enhanced accessibility features aimed at young, elderly and novice players are generally popular among players, as shown by the remarkable success of Nintendo's *Touch! Generations* series of games for their Wii and DS consoles, designed for people of all ages and levels of gaming experience.

Accessibility can also foster the sense of social inclusion of gamers with disabilities as well as improve their quality of life by providing them with increased entertainment options. Games can also be infused with educational and therapeutic value. However, if they are not accessible, disabled players cannot benefit from this.

Furthermore, accessibility can be considered a moral issue. According to the UN Universal Human Rights Declaration, we are all equal, have the same rights and should not suffer discrimination of any kind. Because of this statement, providing accessibility to games and virtual platforms could in time become a legal issue (Bierre 2005). In the USA, the use of accessible technology in governmental agencies is a legal requirement according to section 508 of the Rehabilitation Act of 1973. There is also existing legislation providing equal access in many areas (Americans with Disabilities Act), which may be extended to video games and virtual environments over the coming years (Bierre, 2005). In Spain, video games have been considered 'cultural products' by the Spanish government since 2009. As accessibility gains prominence in Spanish society, the possibility that the government will eventually create legislation in favour of equal access to culture – including video games – will become more likely.

4. A state of affairs of accessibility in games

Many mainstream games are not accessible for players with disabilities. Some games do offer certain accessibility features but these features are often not specifically designed for accessibility purposes, but rather as a means of innovating game design to facilitate and enhance all players' gaming experience. For example, the demo mode recently included in the *New Super Mario Bross* (2009)[6] for the Wii console allows players who cannot progress past a difficult part of the game to switch to automatic mode so that the game will do it for them and they can resume playing when they are ready. This accessibility feature is useful for young and elderly players, novice players, and casual players, as well as players with cognitive and physical disabilities. While hardcore gamers may object to this feature, arguing that having this kind of built-in 'cheat' feature defeats the purpose of gaming, it can also be argued that this is an optional feature that does not necessarily have to be used. The idea behind universal accessibility is to allow for a high degree of customisation of games, so that different players can choose the features that best suit their specific needs.

There are also a number of mainstream games which currently provide subtitles. For example, French developer and publisher Ubisoft has included subtitles in all of its in-house developed games since 2008. A few games also provide subtitles that include descriptions of sound effects – known in the industry as *closed captions* (CC) – such as *Zork: Grand Inquisitor* (1997), *Half-Life 2* (2004) and *Dragon Age Origins* (2009). Some commercial games have been made accessible for DHH players by means of modifications called *mods*, made by gamers or independent developers to an existing game, such as the first-person shooters *Doom 3* (2004) or *Quake 4* (2005). Both games were modified to include close captions, including not only subtitles for audio, but also for sound effects. The modified versions are known as the '*Doom 3* [CC] mod' and the '*Quake 4* [CC]' mod.

In addition, there are a number of accessible games specifically designed for players with a certain types of disability, such as audio games – games based only on sound – for blind players and one-switch games for players with reduced mobility. However, these are considered too specialised and therefore not attractive for many mainstream developers.

There are also games designed for players with cognitive disabilities, such as games designed for autistic children. The game *Terraformers* (2003), developed with partial financial support from the Swedish Handicap Institute, deserves attention in this respect since it is a 3D adventure game that can be played both in a visual and an audio mode. Consequently, it is fully accessible to blind players by means of an audio-based user interface and the provision of sonars to identify and locate objects.

However, focusing on creating special games for players with specific disabilities does not address the issue of segregation between these gamers and other gamers. By extension, such special games do not assist in the social inclusion of gamers with specific disabilities (Grammenos & Savidis 2006). For this reason, a universal game design which focuses on usability and adaptability and provides a high degree of customisation to players seems to be the best path to improved accessibility.

5. Challenges in game accessibility

The main challenge in game accessibility lies in the whole gamut of users with different types of disability combined with the interactive nature of games. It is extremely challenging – and some may even say impossible – to develop games that are universally accessible and can be played by any gamer with any type of disability. For example, it is particularly difficult to provide blind players with accessibility to mainstream games. While the use of assistive technologies is essential and extremely beneficial for gamers with disabilities, usability and adaptability issues should be taken into account from the development stages of a game – rather than as an afterthought – to pave the way for a Design for All.[7]

Different players face different accessibility barriers, as shown in the table below, which lists a number of examples of the accessibility issues faced by groups of players with disabilities in mainstream games.

Table 1. Accessibility barriers in video games (adapted from Bierre 2005)

Type of player	Accessibility issue
Players with cognitive disabilities including: special learning needs, dyslexia, attention deficit disorder, autism, memory loss, Asperger syndrome, etc.	• level of difficulty of games, leading to comprehension and usability problems • reading ability (small font, enough time to read a message, etc.) • lack of tutorial mode • high difficulty levels • lengthy tutorials and manuals • use of complex language

Exploring new paths towards game accessibility

Table 1 (contd.). Accessibility barriers in video games (adapted from Bierre 2005)

Type of player	Accessibility issue
Players with auditory impairments (deaf players and hard-of-hearing players)	• extracting information from non-subtitled audio-based elements in cinematic scenes due to lack of subtitles • missing information and clues provided by sound effects • solving tasks or play minigames based on sound
Players with visual impairments	
blind players	• Extracting information from visually based elements in a game
players with low vision	• Reading small font, icon, recognising and using small icons, objects, etc.
colour-blind players	• Solving colour-based tasks and minigames
Players with physical impairments (reduced mobility and dexterity)	• Hand-eye coordination issues • Use of controllers, keyboards • High speed of some games

6. Towards improving game accessibility

The accessibility issues described in the previous section pose different barriers to diverse groups of players. As already mentioned, the solution to overcoming those barriers lies in the creation of games that are as universal as possible, that apply Design for All principles, and that enable the use of assistive technology.

6.1. Universal game design

A universal game design is related to the implementation of enhanced, highly customisable usability features that facilitate access to video games to a wider spectrum of the population. While universally accessible, mainstream, commercial games may seem a distant fantasy to many, change is possible. If accessibility awareness is raised and developers start applying the principles of Design for All to their games, the accessibility landscape will gradually start to change. The UA Games research group (2007) has outlined some guidelines for the developers of universally accessible game design,[8] some of which are quoted here. The guidelines have been grouped according to the type of accessibility issue that they address:

Accessibility for players with physical disabilities
- Avoid simultaneous button pressing.
- Allow the controls to be redefined, that is, allow players to assign new buttons or keys to perform certain actions in the game.
- Allow the game to be played with a smaller number of controls, even with a single switch (button).
- Support alternative input techniques.
- Provide control over game speed.

Accessibility for young, elderly and novice players and players with cognitive disabilities
- Provide a tutorial mode.
- Allow adjustment of difficulty level.
- Use simple language and provide easy to understand instructions.

Accessibility for players with visual impairments
- Do not rely on colour alone.
- Allow magnifying of the text and graphics.

Accessibility for players with auditory impairments
- Provide 3D audio cues.
- Provide separate volume controls for music, speech and sound effects.
- Provide closed captions for dialogue and sound effects.

These guidelines can be applied to any game at the conceptual development stage, and they can facilitate accessibility for gamers with different needs. For example, players with reduced mobility will be able to play games that do not require the player to press several buttons at the same time and that can be played with one single button. Players with cognitive disabilities and young, elderly and inexperienced players will benefit from a tutorial mode, simple instructions and adjustable levels of difficulty. Players with low vision will particularly benefit from magnifying texts and graphics, while colour-blind players will be able to play games that do not rely on colour. DHH players will have an enhanced gameplay experience if closed

Exploring new paths towards game accessibility

captions are avaible. Many of these accessibility guidelines can also be beneficial to both expert players and players without disabilities since they can facilitate engagement and immersion in the games by making the games more accessible and usable. As a result, games can become more enjoyable and less frustrating when the set goals can be achieved more simply and efficiently.

Apart from the inclusion of closed captions, there are other solutions that could be applied to universal game design to improve game accessibility, particularly for DHH players. For example, the use of haptic feedback with the controller to replace sound cues.[9] The PlayStation DualShock controller provides this kind of vibration feedback, which could be used more often as an alternative to sound or visual stimuli. In addition, in the article *The Sound Alternative*, game designer and accessibility researcher Richard Van Tol (2006) makes interesting proposals to complement the use of closed captions, providing examples of games currently using these options. The proposals incude the following features:

- **Speaker portraits** to identify the character who is speaking, as in the game *Freedom Force vs the Third Reich* (2005);
- **Action captions** similar to those used in comics to replace more traditional captions, as in the game *XIII* (2003);
- **Speech balloons** to indicate which character is speaking, as in the game *Mario and Luigi, Partners in Crime* (2005);
- **Sound visualisations** accompanied by an animation to indicate that an object, such as a phone, is moving, as in the game *The Sims 2* (2004);
- **Video clips** displayed in a small part of the screen or a split screen to indicate an action that is happening elsewhere and that players would normally identify by sound, such as the sound of a helicopter firing a rocket, as in the game *Indigo Prophecy* (2005);
- **Danger meters** to replace the function music to indicate that danger is approaching, in the game *Lupin the 3rd: Treasure of the Sorcerer King* (2002);
- **Visual sound radars** to indicate where a sound is coming from, as in the game *Doom 3* [CC] mod;
- **Use of sign language**, either by means of an avatar in a small corner of the screen or the option to watch the game with sound language as opposed to written language There are currently no games using this, but it is an option that should be further explored in order to improve accessibility for deaf and hard of hearing players.

In addition to Van Tol's suggestions, there are other possibilities to depict sound in games, such as the following:

53

- **Use of icons** to describe sound effects, for example, a phone to indicate a phone is ringing;
- **Use of emoticons** to describe the emotion of a character speaking;
- **Use of small character portraits** displaying the emotion of the character speaking.

Despite the fact that there are different possibilities for making maintream video games more accessible to DHH players, the biggest challenge to creating universally accessible game design lies in designing mainstream games that are accessible to blind players. This is the result of the highly visual nature of the medium. Issues such as the potential application of audio description to mainstream games to audio describe non-verbal elements in cut-scenes, as well as the possibility of playing games with an audio-based interface should be further explored.

6.2. Use of adaptive technology solutions

There are several existing technological solutions that can be applied to games to facilitate accessibility to players with reduced mobility as well as to blind and low-vision players. For example, players with reduced mobility can benefit from using simplified controllers (including the one-switch controllers), head mice, sip-and-puff devices, which allow the users to control the game with their mouths, and speech recognition software to give instructions to the game and to execute commands. With respect to blind players and those with low vision, screen-reading software can facilitate these players' access by providing them with text-based information that would otherwise remain inaccessible to them. More research on effective, easy-to-use and compatible assistive technology solutions is required to improve accessibility.

6.3. Implementation of an accessibility information system

Another measure that would contribute to improving accessibility consists of introducing an information system, using a label similar to that used by the game ratings boards, such as PEGI, to classify the content of games (Ellis 2006). This kind of label would inform consumers of the degree of accessibility of a game, so that potential buyers could judge whether the game would be suitable for them or not. Japanese developer Namco designed a label with the logo 'Barrier free entertainment' for their accessible products, while in the 1980s Atari also indicated on the boxes of their products whether games could be played by young children (Ellis 2006).

Developer 2K, creator of games aimed at young audiences, such as those based on the popular cartoon character Dora the Explorer, includes a 'Kid tested' label on their games to inform parents that a game can be played by young children, including those who cannot read.

6.4. Fostering research in game accessibility

Research projects on game accessibility are few and far between. An interdisciplinary approach, bringing together academics from different disciplines, such as engineering, computer studies, psychology, media studies, translation studies and the humanities, as well as industry professionals, is required to champion research in this field. In addition, collaboration between industry and academia is crucial to explore the best solutions for improved accessibility, as well as test suggested solutions by means of conducting reception studies, in which interviews and eye-tracking technology can be used. The results of these studies could help the industry design more accessible and immersive games for all.

In particular, subtitling in games, and more specifically SDH and the potential application of audio description to games are areas worthy of attention. Because of the relative young age of the game industry there is still no standard in place for subtitling in games. Subtitles currently vary in length from one to three or more lines in some games, often with a very small font and without taking into account the semantic unit when dividing the subtitles. Studies in this area will help establish what kind of subtitles are more appropriate for different genres of games, considering factors such as font type and size, position, length of time that subtitles appear on screen, the most effective way to indicate that a character is speaking (use of name tags, use of different colours, use of speech balloons as in comics). This type of research would follow on from the work of similar studies focusing on the reception of subtitles for movies, such as the European Commission-sponsored DTV4ALL project, and would try to validate if the results of such projects are applicable to video games or if there are any significant differences resulting from the interactive nature of games.

Empirical reception studies with subjects using eye-tracking technology will provide objective data regarding the most effective subtitles for games, similar to the kind of research currently conducted with movie subtitles. For example, the Spanish research project *La subtitulación para sordos y la audiodescripción: Pruebas objetivas y planes de futuro* (Subtitling for the deaf and audio description: Objective tests and future plans) was set up to analyse the reception of movie subtitles with eye-tracking technology. The next step of the author's research in accessibility will consist of empirical research on the reception of game subtitles and alternative ways to describe sound effects in video games for DHH players using interviews and tests with eye-tracking technology.

6.5. Raising awareness

The lack of accessibility to games is – to a great extent – the result of the lack of awareness shared by developers, publishers and the gaming community in general about the accessibility barriers present in games. As research in this field progresses and is disseminated in books, journals, specialised gaming sites, blogs and reports, different parties will gradually become more aware of this issue. There are already some initiatives in place, such as the UA Games project, which have been set up with a view to raising awareness among developers. Another interesting project, led by the Universidad Francisco de Vitoria in Spain, is *Iredia*, which is a video game designed to raise awareness among young children about deafness and the implications of being deaf.

Governments in different countries have dedicated agencies and bodies dealing with accessibility issues, such as the IMSERSO (*Instituto de Mayores y Servicios Sociales*, Institute for the Elderly and Social Services) in Spain or the Enabling Accessibility Fund in Canada, which provide grants and subsidies for the development and implementation of accessibility-related projects. If representatives of the different groups involved (gaming industry, associations of people with disabilities, academics) initiate a dialogue with such government agencies about the provision of funding to encourage the industry to implement accessible design guidelines, developers who may be reluctant to do so(because of possible cost implications) will be more likely to apply such guidelines.

7. Concluding remarks

To date game accessibility has received little attention from the industry and academia, despite the fact that further research in this area and the application of research results to game design can be beneficial for all parties. For developers and publishers, accessibility can help increase their potential market size. Accessibility can also foster the sense of social inclusion of disabled players and improve their quality of life by providing them with alternative entertainment, educational and therapeutic options. The gamers community in general, and more particularly casual, novice, young and elder players can also benefit from more customisable, usable and accessible games whose difficulty settings and controls can be personalised to suit gaming needs. Cooperation between academics from various disciplines and the industry can foster research in game accessibility and contribute to raising awareness about the far-reaching benefits of accessibility, paving the way for a universally accessible game design that truly provides fun for all.

---

[1] This research, partially presented at the Media for All Conference 3 in Antwerp in 2009, is supported by a postdoctoral fellowship funded by the Agència de Gestió d'Ajuts Universitaris i de Recerca (AGAUR), Generalitat de Catalunya, Spain.

[2] This research is also supported by the grant from the Spanish Ministry of Science and Innovation FFI2009-08027, Subtitling for the Deaf and Hard of Hearing and Audio Description: objective tests and future plans, and also by the Catalan Government funds 2009SGR700.

[3] For example, the DVT4ALL project, which brings together academics from different universities as well as broadcasters from several countries accross Europe.

[4] Accessibility is also used to refer to the provision of equal access rights to media and new technologies, regardless of users' socioeconomic backgrounds and resources. Accessibility can also refer to being able to access content in a different language by means of translation. However, due to the limited scope of this contribution, accessibility will primarily focus on accessibility to games for people with disabilities, be they casual, young, elderly or novice players.

[5] Some of the better known sites for gamers with disabilities are www.ablegamers.com, www.deafgamers.com, www.audiogames.net and http://www.oneswitch.org.uk/

[6] When games are cited, their names and the years of original release are indicated in the body of the text. In the gameography, which may be found at the end of the contribution, the names of the developers, followed by the name(s) of the publisher(s), if different, are also stated.

[7] Design for All is defined by Stephanidis et al. as "the conscious and systematic effort to proactively apply principles, methods and tools, in order to develop IT&T products and services which are accessible and usable by all citizens, thus avoiding the need for a posteriori adaptations, or specialised design" (1998: 3).

[8] For the complete list, see http://www.ics.forth.gr/hci/ua-games/game-over/game_levels.html

[9] Haptic feedback is a design element for human-computer interaction. It uses the sense of touch to provide information to users by means of vibration, motion, etc. Most game controllers are designed so that they can provide this kind of feedback to users, enhancing the game-playing experiences of players. For example, racing games often incorporate this technology for increasead realism when the players' cars collide with other vehicles.

References

Aarseth, Espen J. 2001. 'Computer Game Studies, Year One' in *Game Studies* 1(1). On line at: http://www.gamestudies.org/0101/editorial.html (consulted 07.04.2010).
Bierre, Kevin. 2005. 'Improving Game Accessibility' in *Gamasutra*. On line at: http://www.gamasutra.com/features/20050706/bierre_01.shtml (consulted 07.04.2010).

Caili, Eric. 2008. 'Ubisoft Backs Hearing-disabled Gamers with Subtitles Initiative'. On line at: http://www.gamasutra.com/php-bin/news_index.php?story=20175 (consulted 07.04.2010).

Chandler, Heather M. 2005. *The Game Localization Handbook*. Hingham, MA: Charles River Media.

Chandler, Heather M. 2006. 'Taking Video Games Global: An Interview with Heather Chandler, Author of The Game Localization Handbook' in *Byte Level/Research*. On line at: http://bytelevel.com/global/game_globalization.html (consulted 06.04.2010).

Crossley, Rob. 2010. 'Study: Average Dev Costs as High as $28m' in *Develop*. On line at: http://www.develop-online.net/news/33625/Study-Average-dev-cost-as-high-as-28m (consulted 06.04.2010).

Ellis, Barry. 2006. 'Physical Barriers in Video Games' in *OneSwitch.org.uk*. On line at: http://www.oneswitch.org.uk/2/ARTICLES/physical-barriers.htm (consulted 06.04.2010).

Glinert, Eitan. 2009. 'Upping Your Game's Usability' in *Gamasutra*. On line at: http://www.gamasutra.com/view/feature/4110/upping_your_games_usability.php (consulted 06.04.2010).

Grammenos, Dimitri & Anthony Savidis. 2006. 'Unified Design of Universally Accessible Games (Say What?)' in *Gamasutra*. On line at: http://www.gamasutra.com/features/20061207/grammenos_01.shtml (consulted 12.04.2010).

IBM. n.d. 'Understanding Accessibility' in *Human Ability and Accessibility Center*. On line at: http://www-03.ibm.com/able/access_ibm/disability.html (consulted 06.04. 2010).

Lommel, Arle & Rebecca Ray. 2007. 'The Globalization Industry Primer'. On line at: http://www.lisa.org/Globalizatio.468.0.html (consulted 06.04.2010).

The World Bank. 2009. 'How Many Disabled People Are There World-Wide?' in *Disability and Development*. On line at: http://web.worldbank.org/WBSITE/EXTERNAL/TOPICS/EXTSOCIALPROTECTION/EXTDISABILITY/0,,contentMDK:21150847~menuPK:420476~pagePK:210058~piPK:210062~theSitePK:282699,00.html#HowMany (consulted 06.04.2010).

Laitinen, Sauli. 2005. 'Better Games through Usability Evaluation and Testing' in *Gamasutra*. On line at: http://www.gamasutra.com/features/20050623/laitinen_01.shtml (consulted 07.04.2010).

Merriam Webster's Online Dictionary. n.d. Online at: http://www.merriam-webster.com/ (consulted 07.04.2010).

Microsoft. 2010. 'Accessibility'. On line at: http://www.microsoft.com/enable/ (consulted 07.04.2010).

Radd, David. 2010. 'Game Revenue Surpasses Movies in UK' in *Industry Gamers*. On line at: http://www.industrygamers.com/news/game-revenue-surpasses-movies-in-uk/ (consulted 07.04.2010).

Stephanidis, Constantine et al. 1998. 'Toward an Information Society for All: An International R&D Agenda' in *International Journal of Human-Computer Interaction* 10(2): 107-134. On line at: http://www.ics.forth.gr/proj/at-hci/files/white_paper_1998.pdf (consulted 10.04.2010).

UA-Games. 2007. 'What are UA Games?' in *Human-Computer Interaction Laboratory FORTH-ICS*. On line at: http://www.ics.forth.gr/hci/ua-games/ (consulted 07.04.2010).

UsabilityNet. 2006. 'International Standards for HCI and Usability'. On line at: http://www.usabilitynet.org/tools/r_international.htm#9241-1x (consulted 10.04.2010).

Van Tol, Richard. 2006. 'The Sound Alternative' in *Game Accessibility*. On line at: http://www.accessibility.nl/games/index.php?pagefile=soundalternative (consulted 10.04.2010).

WKYC. 2008. 'Road to Recovery with Nintendo Wii' in *WKYC.Com*. On line at: http://www.wkyc.com/news/local/news_article.aspx?storyid=90212&catid=3 (consulted 10.04.2010).

Gameography

Doom 3 (id Software/Activision 2004)
Dragon Age Origins (Bioware/EA Games 2009)
Freedom Force vs. The Third Reich (Irrational Games/VU Games-Jester Games 2005)
Half-Life 2 (Valve Corporation/Sierra Entertainment – Valve Corporation 2004)
Indigo Prophecy (Quantic Dream/Atari 2005)
Lupin the 3rd: Treasure of the Sorcerer King (Banpresto/Bandai 2002)
Mario and Luigi, partners in crime (Nintendo 2005)
New Super Mario Bross (Nintendo 2009)
Quake 4 (Raven Software-id Software/Activision Blizzard 2005)
Terraformers (Pin Interactive 2003)
The Sims 2 (Maxis/EA Games 2004)
XIII (Ubisoft 2003)
Zork: Grand Inquisitor (Activision 1997)

Graphic Emoticons as a Future Universal Symbolic Language

Junichi Azuma
Ryutsu-kagaku University (Japan)

Abstract

This contribution discusses the possibility of implementing a universal, computer-mediated symbolic language that will overcome the barrier of language differences. The current state of emoticon usage in cyberspace will first be described, with special emphasis on the recent popularity of graphic emoticons especially favoured by young Japanese people. Extreme examples of the hieroglyphic use of graphic emoticons will also be discussed. It is argued that these new types of graphic emoticons will lead to the emergence of a universal symbolic language in the future, making translation tasks much easier. To support this vision of a computer-mediated universal symbolic language, a brief sketch of the psychology of vision will be provided, as well as comic book dynamics, that is, how we extract important components from a complicated story line just by seeing a single picture or a few panels of a comics segment. Some tentative syntactic and semantic rules of the universal symbolic language will be also proposed. Actual icon-like visual signs meant for disaster-related warnings will be also proposed.

Keywords

cartoon, comics, emoticons, graphic emoticons, psychology of vision, universal symbolic language

1. Introduction

We are increasingly relying on cyberspace. It is not too much to say that at no other time in history have we witnessed such a strong reliance on technology and such a keen attachment to cyberspace. But what is cyberspace made of? It is of course filled with various types of files and huge amounts of information. However, in principle, it is written language that makes up cyberspace and it is impossible to bring cyberspace into existence without language. We communicate with language when we use emails or blogs. We search for necessary information and desired files by means of language. And we engage in *social-bookmarking* using language.

1.1. Nature of cyberspace communication

Communication in cyberspace by means of written language has some unique features. Features such as gestures, posture and facial expressions are not yet part of cyberspace communication. Unless we use messaging services or other types of audiovisual modes of communication on the Internet, we cannot convey non-verbal information and prosodic features such as intonation, rhythm or stress in cyberspace. This situation naturally leads to the difficulty of engaging in comfortable and smooth communication in cyberspace as a result of the fact that purely linguistic elements are said to convey only about 5 per cent of the content of face-to-face communication, while non-verbal information can account for about 65 per cent and prosodic features can comprise 30 per cent of the content of face-to-face communication as Nakatsu (2010: 64) describes, based on the results of past research on communication.

In fact, it is rather difficult to have conventional language-only communication online, especially if both parties have just encountered each other for the first time and share little information about each another. In real life, the first encounter will of course put some pressure on both parties but probably with the help of paralinguistic and prosodic information accompanying the language, they will understand each other quickly and communication between them will become relatively smooth in a short time. Importance of paralinguistic and prosodic features in our daily communication was already pointed out in as early as 1966 by Crystal (1966: 93-108).

In cyberspace we often encounter extremely violent arguments or in a sense, furious verbal fights. Such fights might not erupt if the parties encountered each other in real life and initiate discussions face-to-face. In such severe verbal fights in a Bulletin Board System (BBS) or in a social network service, we often see postings such as *I did not mean that in my previous posting*. In such situations the clarifications or meta-clarifications of past postings add more oil to the flames and the situations will often become uncontrollable.

2. Emoticons as paralinguistic and prosodic features in cyberspace

Emoticons or smiley/s have gradually entered cyberspace to provide language-only and seemingly logic-only cyberspace communication with an emotional and human touch. In a sense, emoticons are considered to function as prosodic or paralinguistic features in cyberspace. As is the case in the sentence *This paper looks quite strange ;-)*, they are often added at the end of a sentence or a phrase to show the emotional state of the writer. Thus,

Graphic emoticons as a future universal symbolic language

emoticons are typographic versions of paralinguistic features. In East Asia, especially in Japan, people have developed their own style of emoticons, or in the Japanese language, *kaomoji* (face words or face characters). Normally these East Asian emoticons are to be read vertically like a sentence *Well, this paper is not so bad as you might think (^_^)*. Although their style is different

Icon	Meaning	Icon	Meaning	Icon	Meaning
(^_^)	smile	(^o^)	laughing out loud	d(^_^)b	headphones or listening to music; thumbs up
(;_;) or (T_T) or (T^T)	sad (crying face)	(-_-)Zzz	sleeping	(z_z)	sleepy person
\(^_^)/	cheers, "Hurrah!"	(*^.^*)	shyness	(>_<) or (;_;) or (T_T)	sweating (as in exasperated)
(*_*)	"Surprise !"	(?_?)	Nonsense, I don't know	(^_~) or (^_-)	wink
(o.O) or (o_O)	shocked, disturbed, stunned, raised eyebrow	(<.<)	shifty, suspicious; could also be sarcasm or irritation	(>'.')> or (>'.')> # or (>'.')>~~~	"Have a cookie/waffle/drink from a cup with a spiral straw"

from the Western style, they are also relatively intelligible to people all over the world. Figure 1 below shows some examples of East Asian emoticons.

Figure 1. Examples of East Asian emoticons - from http://en.wikipedia.org/wiki/Emoticons (consulted 07.09.2010)

Many East Asian languages have double-byte character code systems. These allow for more variety in the number of emoticons in East Asian languages used in cyberspace. The examples in Figure 2 show some Japanese double-byte code emoticons expressing the emotion of *fear*. Note that emoticons showing an acute emotional state are normally accompanied by actual linguistic expressions or interjections. The Japanese characters shown in Figure 2 are the interjections representing the feelings of *fear*. Various Japanese writings in kana (phonographic writing) all represent some aspect of the feelings of fear.

```
('-'*)コワイヨコワイヨ
(((p(>o<)q))) ギャアァア！！！
／(・．＼   コワイヨー
~m( --)m(/;° ロ° )/ アレー
ギャアァァァ（＞＜;)//
(*ノ・)ノギャーーー！！
バタバタ、、(≧▽≦)// キャー
("  ロ")ヤメテー
＼(><)シ ぎょぇぇぇっ
．・ヾ(。><)シ ぎょぇぇぇ
＼(><)／ギャー！
＼(>o<)／ギャーッ！
(((p(>v<)q)))！！
(((p(>o<)q)))いやぁぁぁ
ウギャーー((((/＊o＊;)/
＼(O_o)／コワイヨー
```

Figure 2. Examples of Japanese double-byte code emoticons showing the emotion of *fear* - taken from http://www.kaomoji.com/kao/text/kowagaru.htm (consulted 07.09.2010)

3. Graphic emoticons as linguistic units

When we access the web-based free email services of famous portal sites, we notice that graphic emoticons are also becoming popular in today's cyberspace. Even when we input typographic emoticons, some software programs such as Microsoft Word or email client programs display the result in graphic emoticons. In Japan, mobile phones also need special kinds of Japanese input systems similar to the computer-based systems and they

Graphic emoticons as a future universal symbolic language

normally support the input of graphic emoticons. All the major Japanese providers are moving towards the standardisation of the codes for graphic emoticons and the use of graphic emoticons is now quite common in mobile-phone communication among young Japanese people.

Computer-based network communication of course is no exception. Many Japanese blog services as well as social networking services now support HTML-based postings with graphic emoticons (see Figure 3). Although the input system is still primitive and the repertoire of graphic emoticons is still limited, the use of graphic emoticons is expanding.

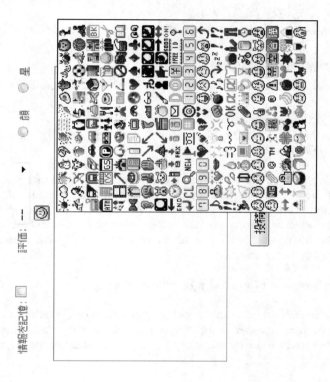

Figure 3. Input menu for graphic emoticons (all in colour on the original page) - Livedoor Blog in Japan (http:// blog.livedoor.jp/ (consulted 07.09.2010)

3.1. New wave of graphic emoticon usage among Japanese young people

Today, young people (especially girls) in Japan have a tendency to use graphic emoticons together with relevant words in sentences. This often results in the duplication of vocabulary, that is, words and graphic emoticons often represent the same meanings of words and are placed side by side. Here are some examples taken from the actual blog postings of female university students:

Meaning in English: ' (▽ ﾉ)🍴 dinner 🍴(▽ ﾉ)φ(c·ω·) eating…'

Meaning in English: ' Found a letter 📧 and felt glad. 💗 '

Meaning in English: 'Got up at 5 💤 and went to Sannomiya by subway. 🚇 '

As is clear from these examples, young people in Japan use emoticons not only at the end of sentences or phrases, but also tend to use them within sentences for emphasis or simply for the purpose of decorating words or phrases. Let us call this type of emoticon use emphatic use and differentiate it from the traditional paralinguistic use of emoticons, which functions as a 'lubricant of communication'.

3.2. Replacement of words by graphic emoticons

The most recent trend in the use of graphic emoticons is extreme and some young people in Japan omit words in sentences and use only graphic emoticons to illustrate the meanings of the words. Some examples are shown below:

Meaning in English: '…then, suddenly 📱 broke down. (;＿;) '
(📱 = mobile phone)

Meaning in English: 'I was busy because of the part-time job and the 🚗 training. ≡3 '

(🚙=automobile)

わたし決してこの🎄をバックにしては📷撮らん☹🍂

Meaning in English: 'I will never take a 📷 with this 🎄 behind me! ☹🍂,

(📷=photo, 🎄=Christmas tree)

These examples are extreme and of course there are not so many people in Japan who always adopt this style of writing for blog postings or email communication. In addition, many conservative adults – especially educators – consider this type of writing to be quite childish and absurd. However, in some sense this tendency of using graphic emoticons as replacements for words leads to an innovative future style of communication, namely communication by means of universal symbolic language. Such use will be referred to as lexical use in this contribution.

4. Descriptive study of graphic emoticons

To investigate the extent to which the new styles of graphic emoticons, that is, emphatic use and lexical use, are popular, actual blog articles were analysed. All the emoticons that appeared in blog postings created by AS and AM (the initials of two female college seniors) between August and October 2007 on Rakuten Blog, one of the largest free blog hosting sites in Japan, were analysed and categorised into four types: (1) paralinguistic use (graphic emoticons), (2) paralinguistic use (traditional character-based), (3) emphatic use and (4) lexical use. The results of the analysis are shown in Figures 4a and 4b, which show the actual numbers of tokens and the percentages of each usage category. As the figures show, the paralinguistic use of emoticons is dominant even today. We can also see a substantial amount of character-based or ASCII-based emoticons of paralinguistic use (20% in AS's postings and 11% in AM's postings).

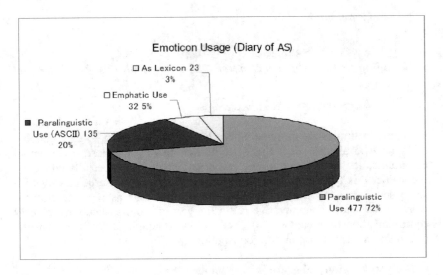

Figure 4a. Analysis of emoticon use (AS)

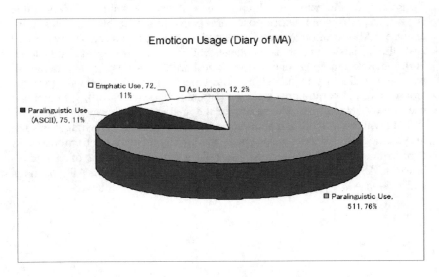

Figure 4b. Analysis of emoticon use (AM)

The proportion of the new usage of graphic emoticons (emphatic and lexical) was about 10% in both cases, though there were individual differences and preferences concerning the type of usage, whether emphatic or lexical. For example, AM strongly preferred the emphatic use of graphic emoticons to the lexical use (11% and 2% respectively). As was expected, no character-based emoticons were found that were used in emphatic or lexical contexts.

5. Power of graphic emoticons in international communication settings

If graphic emoticons work as lexical items, they are considered to function as ideographic words, like Chinese characters. And if the meanings of graphic emoticons are extremely easy to recognise intuitively among people who speak different languages, they are (in a sense) said to behave as lexical items of a primitive universal symbolic language. An international experiment was conducted to test this hypothesis, using a small number of Japanese university students at the University of Marketing and Distribution Sciences in Kobe (14 students in total) and Austrian university students and young researchers at Graz University of Technology (9 students in all).

As is also described in Azuma and Ebner (2008: 974-975), a special community blog site compatible with graphic emoticons was opened at TU Graz LearnLand (https://tugll.tugraz.at/emotions/) and everyone was instructed to use as many graphic emoticons as possible in the postings, where the common language to be used was set to English. In a sense, participants were told to use graphic emoticons and to write in English when they could not express their meaning in graphic emoticons properly. The assumptions of this project were as follows:

(1) Even in an international context where the native language of users is not English, simple communication will be feasible with the help of graphic emoticons.
(2) Participants in the experiment will have no difficulties in inventing ways to use graphic emoticons as lexical items. This will cause a dramatic increase in the lexical use of graphic emoticons in blogs.

Communication for the period from 11 October to 26 November 2007, that is, all postings including comments on main postings, was analysed. Communication seemed quite active, although the contents of the communication were not always serious and perhaps even shallow in nature, partly because the number of emoticons available was limited. It can be concluded that the first assumption of the project was verified. However, it should also be noted that communication problems sometimes occurred. A good example is " how is ♡ 🌳 in 🏠? in araz onlv 🌳." In this context the Austrian member thought it would be appropriate to use a graphic emoticon of a mountain (like Mount Fuji) to show the meaning of *Japan*, but Japanese participants did not understand the meaning.

Another example which created increased communication difficulty was " A weekend full of ⬚⬚⬚ ". Japanese participants did not at all understand the intended meaning of this posting, which originated from an Austrian member. However, since the writer in question was a young Austrian researcher who had to write a lot of academic papers and proposals, it was later understood to mean *A weekend full of paper writing, with the deadline drawing near and a lot of business telephone calls*.

The author also analysed all the writings in these community blog pages and categorised all the emoticons used here into four types once again: (1) paralinguistic use (graphic emoticons), (2) character-based paralinguistic use, (3) emphatic use and (4) lexical use. The results of the analysis (see Figure 5) show that the lexical use of graphic emoticons prevailed (477 cases, 56%) throughout all communication instances. Since participants were instructed only to use as many graphic emoticons as possible, and were not told how to use the graphic emoticons, it seems that they did indeed learn by themselves how to use graphic emoticons as ideographic lexical items. On this basis, we believe that the second assumption of the research project was also verified.

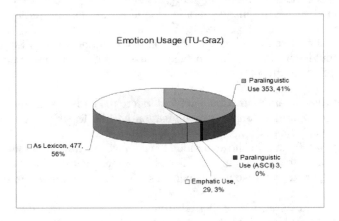

Figure 5. Emoticon use at TU Graz LearnLand community

6. Universal symbolic language as a future language

If the trend to replace linguistic units with graphic emoticons osberved in the communication behaviour of young Japanese people continues to develop, we will be able to devise universal symbolic signs that work as a special kind of auxiliary language used for communication using computers, mobile

Graphic emoticons as a future universal symbolic language

phones and other computer-based devices. As such, a symbolic language is expected to make use of simple and easy-to-understand pictures. It is expected to make international communication easy, overcoming the barrier of language differences.

It is true that we already have a long history of using pictures for communication visible in examples from Sumerian picture language, Egyptian hieroglyphs or Chinese inscriptions on bones and tortoise carapaces (see Horn (1998: 23-26) for a detailed description of the history of visual language). The last system developed into Chinese characters, but in the Western world, hieroglyphic culture disappeared during in the course of history. Sometimes artificial pictorial languages were devised for universal communication but they were not put to general practical use in real life as an auxiliary language. For one thing, they often needed a large amount of learning to use them properly. To take some modern examples, both Blissymbolics (BCI (2004), McNaughton (1985) or Hehner (1986)) and LoCos (Ota, 1993: 220-221) are really well designed and well organised visual languages but they require a certain amount of learning before one can use and understand the system (for example, see the LoCos message for *A postman brought me a happy letter from my hometown this morning* below).

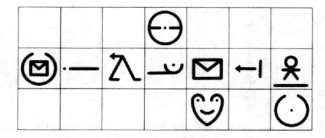

Figure 6. Example of LoCos message: from Ota (1993: 160)

Some Blissymbolics vocabulary elements shown below (Figure 7) illustrate the semantic and morphological structure of words. However, the rules still seem quite primitive since we cannot see which morpheme or constituent is the core part and which part modifies the core part. It seems that the rule implicitly assumes that the right or the rightmost part is the core symbol of the whole word or the phrase. Yet, even the production of an actual Chinese character is not so simple. Language is not just a simple juxtaposition of symbols anyway.

Junichi Azuma

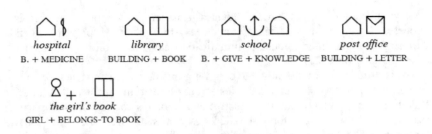

Figure 7. Basic rules for Blissymbolics word formation: from "The fundamental rules of Blissymbolics: creating new Blissymbolics characters and vocabulary" - http://www.blissymbolics.org/downloads/bliss-rules.pdf (consulted 07.09.2010)

Another problem with regard to Blissymbolics is its syntactic structure. As Figure 8 indicates, Blissymbolics seems to imitate the structure of English and appears to be a so-called Subject–Verb–Object (SVO) language. In addition, the writing goes from left to right. However, considering the variety of languages in the world, these ideas might cause problems for people whose native tongues are not English.

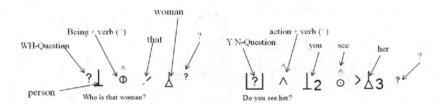

Figure 8. Word order of Blissymbolics: from Blissymbolics Communication International - http://www.blissymbolics.org/WebTraining/Lessons/ Lesson_9.doc (consulted 07.09.2010)

Another serious problem of existing modern pictorial languages is that they were invented before the emergence of the personal computer and the Internet. Since they depend on printed media or other types of fixed analogue media, they unfortunately lack the flexibility of communication and ease of authoring. Of course Blissymbolics, LoCos or other types of modern visual languages may have a brighter future in the new era of ICT, but if we look at the rapid development of real-life communication employing graphic emoticons, it seems more probable that the descendants of these graphic emoticons will evolve into the future symbolic language for global communication.

Graphic emoticons as a future universal symbolic language

6.1. Proposal of universal symbolic signs in the digital age

If we are to communicate in the future using universal symbolic language in computer-mediated environments, and if we render a definite visual rule to certain categories of vocabulary in the symbolic language, then the structures and the meanings of sentences will be much more easily perceivable. For example, using Flash technology or GIF animation, we can add a slight vibrating movement to action verbs (in this contribution action verbs will be highlighted using light grey backgrounds since it is impossible to show any movement in writing). Let us agree that if a verb governs an object, a simple line will be drawn from the verb to the icon of the object. If a noun is modified by an adjective or a different noun, the modifier will be enclosed by a light grey square-shaped line and the whole noun phrase will also be enclosed by a square-shaped line, but in this case the colour will be black. The line with two arrowheads will illustrate *from* or *to* depending on which end the arrowheads are attached to. Let us also agree to use a circle with a dot near the bottom border to denote the meaning of first person singular (i.e., *I*). We place the entire picture-like symbols within a square-shaped border to illustrate that the total set of pictures make one simple sentence. It should also be noted that since these visual rules exist, this system is completely free of any word-order constraints. With these rules, we can draw the picture shown in Figure 9 to convey the meaning of *I drive a car from my house to the library*.

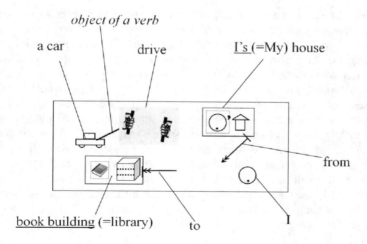

Figure 9. Proposed symbolic language for the simple sentence *I drive a car from my house to the library*

Junichi Azuma

If you would like to indicate the tense, it is possible to add a visual time-line to some place within the picture above. For example, if you want to add the meaning of *three days ago*, then you can draw a simple time-line picture as is the case in Figure 10. The centre of the time-line is *now* and the sun-like mark with the number '-3' denotes that the contents of the statement happened *three days ago*.

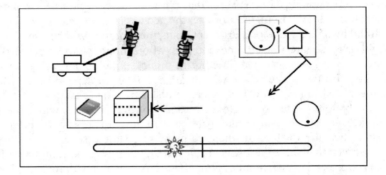

Figure 10. A simple sentence with time-line

We can easily recognise that the new linguistic system proposed here is much stronger in demonstrating the structure and the meaning of a sentence compared with conventional pictorial languages. The new innovative visual language is free of word-order constraints and rules with respect to the direction of writing (right to left, left to write, top to bottom) since the relationships between the iconic words are visually well defined. Consequently, people are free to arrange the pictorial words. When people need to compose a complex sentence, the subordinate clause modifying the main clause, also enclosed within the square-shaped line, can be embedded within the square of the main clause. The vocabulary of the new visual language will be rather small since combinations of two or several pictorial words will form one compound word and slight modifications in the *behaviours* of certain words can create different derivative words, just as a slightly vibrating movement of a *glass of beer* can create an expression of *drink a glass of beer*.

6.2. Implementation of universal symbolic language in a limited-application scenario

As has been argued, new symbolic signs in the digital age will create new frontiers for universal visual communication. However, it is thought that the actual implementation of such a universal symbolic language will take time. If we limit the application of this type of innovative visual language to certain areas of our lives, the idea will move away from a world of fantasy to a concrete realistic application.

In today's world, especially in crowded areas, the importance of disaster-prevention management has been well recognised and appropriate infrastructure and hardware systems have been developed and are well maintained. However, the organisation of the communication sector for disaster alert systems has advanced more slowly than the development of hardware systems. Today's metropolises attract people from all over the world, which makes a megalopolis a multiracial, multicultural and sometimes multilingual melting pot. In such a situation, disaster alerts or warnings cannot be disseminated in a single language. Multilingual alert messages may be effective but in today's metropolises, English and Chinese plus some major European languages are not enough. If there are a myriad of translations into different languages, it will be extremely difficult to single out appropriate languages for inhabitants. Considering such complicated situations, alert messages in universal symbolic languages ought to be considered.

For example, if you want to transmit a disaster alert such as *Severe rainfall will cause flooding in 30 minutes. Go up to the second floor or onto the roof,* you can use the pictures depicted in Figure 11. The triangular frame (actually in yellow) implies that the danger is imminent (in reality the GIF animation enables the pictures of the rainfall and the flood water to move slightly, showing the rainfall becoming heavier and the amount of flood water increasing). The square frame (actually in red) can imply that people are expected to behave in a certain way. In this case, because of the flood water, they are expected to move to the second floor or – if the house is just a one- storey building – onto the roof.

Junichi Azuma

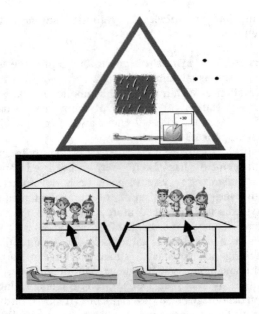

Figure 11. Example of disaster alerting using pictures

In addition, we can connect the two pictures (sentences) by means of a conjunction. To illustrate the meaning of *therefore*, a mathematical *therefore sign* may be used.

7. What optical illusion tells us about visual perception

Keeping in mind that pictorial languages have strong advantages in today's ICT age, let us reconsider the nature of pictures at this point. We tend to think that pictures, pictograms or other visual signs are still and motionless. However, from a psychological point of view this is not completely true. The fact is that it is our brain and not our eyes which sees the world.

For example, let us look at the famous figure-ground illusion (Figure 12). Although it is just a single picture, the figure and the vase become reversible depending on our capricious preference for seeing the picture.

Graphic emoticons as a future universal symbolic language

Figure 12. Example of figure-ground illusion - from
http://en.wikipedia.org/wiki/Optical_illusion (consulted 07.09.2010)

The case of the Kanizsa Triangle is more special (Figure 13). We can see a floating white triangle, which does not actually exist. Our brain also tells us that there is another lined triangle below the *white triangle*. Actually, no physical triangles are drawn in this picture, but our brain insists that there are two different triangles, with the one with black outline below the completely white one.

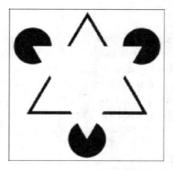

Figure 13. Example of the Kanizsa Triangle - from
http://en.wikipedia.org/wiki/Optical_illusion (consulted 07.09.2010)

Pictures or illustrations are of course two-dimensional but normally we get three-dimensional information from them. Figure 14 shows another famous illusion called the Ponzo Illusion, which illustrates how our perception is easily fooled by the seemingly three-dimensional situation. Our brain interprets that the image higher in the picture field is farther away, so our brain makes us believe that the light-coloured bar at the top is larger than the light-coloured bar at the bottom. Of course, the sizes of the two light-coloured bars are the same. Even today, more and more research is being done into optical illusion, and new types of optical illusion are often presented by researchers (see, for example, Kitaoka 2008 or Amer and Ravindran 2010).

Figure 14. Example of Ponzo Illusion - from
http://en.wikipedia.org/wiki/Optical_illusion (consulted 07.09.2010)

7.1. Showing various degrees of motion or feelings by modifying the same picture

We can add some decorative drawings to the same picture and modify the degree of motion or a person's feelings. This is one of the techniques used in comics but it can also be put to effective use when creating future symbolic signs. Figure 15 is an excerpt from a famous Japanese cartoon series called *Sazae-san* by Machiko Hasegawa (Hasegawa 2003: 27) with the leftmost picture being the original used for the actual episode. This shows the scene where the main character, Sazae-san, is running with a bucket full of horse manure.

Figure 15. Sazae-san running with a bucket full of horse manure (Leftmost picture is the original) – from Hasegawa (2003: 27)

Graphic emoticons as a future universal symbolic language

As the middle picture shows, if the drops of sweat and the lines behind her which appear to show the speed of the movement are deleted, it looks as though Sazae-san is carrying the bucket rather effortlessly. On the other hand, the rightmost picture with more drops of sweat, more lines, and some puffs tells you that for Sazae-san carrying the bucket is strenuous.

Figure 16. Cartoon panel showing a man jumping towards a building (McCloud 1994: 112)

Showing motion by using a special drawing technique is not limited to Japanese cartoons or comics. McCloud (1994: 112), for example, gives similar examples of comic panels showing motion. In Figure 16, the *path* of motion is drawn over the scene, and this gives us the impression that the man has jumped towards the building, though such a lengthy jump would be almost impossible in the real world. If the path of this motion had not been shown, the picture would be almost meaningless and would simply show a man floating, as it were, in the air.

Figure 17 is an example of a technique which is called "multiple images" (McCloud 1994: 112), which gives us the impression that the man is running extremely quickly. Figure 18 also gives us a similar impression using "photographic streaking effects" (McCloud 1994: 112). Note that these

79

special drawing techniques commonly found in comics do not actually produce any movement. Instead, our brain perceives and creates the movement because of the addition of lines, multiple figures and/or multiple shadow-like objects.

Figure 17. Cartoon panel showing a man running fast (multiple images)
(McCloud 1994: 112)

Figure 18. Panel showing a man running (photographic streaking effects)
(McCloud 1994: 112)

7.2. The power of multiple cartoon panels

A picture of course tells us something about what is happening at a certain point in time. But as we have seen, it also tells us what happened just before and what is going to happen after the scene is over. Even a single picture tells

Graphic emoticons as a future universal symbolic language

us more than many words. Thus, we can learn a lot from the way in which comics and their characters are drawn.

When multiple panels are juxtaposed – as is the case in Figure 19 (McCloud 1994: 66) – the space between the panels tells us more than simply that there is a space. The space combines two separate images and lets us form a concrete idea. Of course, nothing exists between these two panels but the reader nonetheless develops certain assumptions based on the space. As McCloud (1994: 68) argues when he writes that "[E]very act committed to paper by the comics artist is aided and abetted by a silent accomplice. An equal partner in crime known as the reader". In a sense, a series of discontinuous panels with space between them lets the readers participate in the plot of the comic, in the creative process. In this case, readers participated in the murder in a proactive manner, holding the axe themselves.

Figure 19. Two comics panels and the power of the space between them
(McCloud 1994: 66)

In fact, the author would like to emphasise that we should analyse the drawing techniques used in the visual arts, including comics and animated cartoons, and reconsider their communicative power. Comics and animated cartoons have long been considered simply as vulgar entertainment. However, they seem to include a potential to change our entire communication style in the age of ubiquitous computing. It should also be noted that even manually drawn cartoons or cartoon-like pictograms were used as signs for EXPO 2002 in Switzerland (see Abdullah and Hübner 2006: 184-191).

8. Conclusion

So far it has been argued that the development of emoticons – especially graphic emoticons – popular among Japanese young people using mobile phones and computers will lead to the next-generation universal symbolic language. Of course, conventional language will also feature in future communication using computers or other computer-based devices but we are likely to see more situations where universal symbolic signs are used. Such a universal symbolic language will be especially useful in multilingual situations.

Suppose that we have a set of core symbolic signs corresponding to the core vocabulary of a language. If several different languages have similar sets of core vocabulary, we can create a link between signs and corresponding words or phrases in each language. If this process is implemented electronically, it will be quite easy for us to create an electronic multilingual dictionary (see Figure 20).

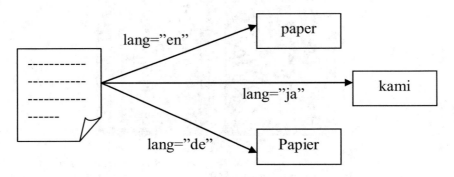

Figure 20. Sign of "paper" and multilingual lexical explanation as metadata

This looks just like a multilingual version of the famous *Duden Bildwörterbuch* (Duden 2005). Yet, the difference is that the sign and the lexical explanation in the language do not exist in the same object. The lexical explanation in each language exists as metadata outside the picture as shown in Figure 20. This means that the same picture object can be used as many times as required. If a phrase *cut the paper with a knife* is included in the electronic multilingual dictionary, we can use the same sign for the *paper* to illustrate the meaning of the phrase. Even composing a simple sentence combining symbolic signs will be possible. If this is implemented, communication during meeting with people from different countries speaking different languages will become much easier. Any participant can consult the electronic dictionary to identify the sign or the sequence of the signs and show it to other participants. All participants will understand the meaning instantly and – if necessary – another person can consult the same dictionary switching to their own language, with the result represented by means of symbolic signs.

In the near future, public signs, signs in tourist areas, disaster alerts, instructions for vending machines and other interactive machines could all be programmed to use such a universal symbolic language. Physically handicapped people will also enjoy the benefits of this new visual language. Even people who speak different languages may be able to communicate through email just by using the symbolic signs. Meetings in multilingual contexts may become much easier because of the new type of symbolic language. Even if n different languages are spoken in an international meeting, the translation will be a matter of n versus 1 (universal symbolic language) rather than n versus n-1. Dynamic and animated symbolic signs may also be integrated into this next-generation visual system. In fact, as Maurer et al. (2003: 312) argued, within a decade or so, we will be carrying a tiny but powerful computer capable of presenting high-resolution movie images and compatible with new types of symbolic signs. In addition, all kinds of signs on the streets and tourist sites will be in some way or other controlled by a computer. Dynamic and universal visual language will feature everywhere in the real world too. If this new system of universal symbolic language is implemented, and if the set of symbolic signs is truly universal, that is, without language- or country-specific variations, our world together with cyberspace will be a much more comfortable place to live in.

References

Abdullah, Rayan and Roger Hübner. 2006. *Pictograms, Icons & Signs*. London: Thames & Hudson.
Amer, Terek S. and Sury Ravindran. 2010. 'The Effect of Visual Illusions on the Graphical Display of Information' in *Journal of Information Systems* 24(1): 23-42.
Azuma, Junichi and Martin Ebner. 2008. 'A Stylistic Analysis of Graphic Emoticons: Can They Be Candidates for a Universal Visual Language of the Future?'. In Luca, Joseph and Edgar R. Weippl (eds.) *Proceedings of World Conference on Educational Multimedia, Hypermedia and Telecommunications 2008*. Vienna: AACE. 972-979
Blissymbolics Communication International (BCI). n.d. 'The Fundamental Rules of Blissymbolics: Creating New Blissymbolics Characters and Vocabulary'. On line at: http://www.blissymbolics.org/downloads/bliss-rules.pdf (consulted 13.09. 2010).
Blissymbolics Communication International (BCI). n.d. 'Lesson 9 Questions'. On line at : http://www.blissymbolics.org/WebTraining/Lessons/Lesson_9.doc (consulted 13.09.2010).
Crystal, David. 1966. 'The Linguistic Status of Prosodic and Paralinguistic Features' in *Proceedings of the University of Newcastle upon Tyne Philosophical Society* 1(8): 93-108.
Duden. 2005. *Bildwörterbuch: Deutsch als Fremdsprache*. Mannheim: Duden Verlag.

Hasegawa, Machiko 2003. *The Wonderful World of Sazae-san*. Tokyo: Kodansha International.
Hehner, Barbara (ed.) 1986. *Blissymbolics for Use*. Don Mills, ON: Blissymbolics Communication International.
Horn, Robert E. 1998. *Visual Language: Global Communication for the 21st Century*. Portland, OR: XPLANE Press.
Kitaoka, Akiyoshi 2008. 'A New Type of the Optimized Fraser-Wilcox Illusion in a 3D-like 2D Image with Highlight or Shade' in *Journal of Three Dimensional Images* 22(4): 31-32.
Maurer, Hermann, Robert Stubenrauch and Daniela G. Camhy. 2003. 'Foundations of MIRACLE: Multimedia Information Repository, A Computer-Supported Language Effort' in *Journal of Universal Computer Science* 9(4): 309-348.
McCloud, Scott. 1994. *Understanding Comics: The Invisible Art*. New York: Harper Perennial.
McNaughton, Shirley (ed.). 1985. *Communicating with Blissymbolics*. Toronto, ON: Blissymbolics Communication International.
Nakatsu, Ryohei. 2010. *Tekunoloji ga Kaeru Komyunikeshon no Mirai* (Future of Communication Changed by Technology). Tokyo: Ohmsha.
Ota, Yukio 1993. *Pikutoguramu "emoji" dezain (Pictogram design)*, Tokyo: Kashiwashobo.

Mapping Digital Publishing for All in Translation

Lucile Desblache
Roehampton University (United Kingdom)

Abstract
Expanding the concept of accessibility beyond its usual definition in media, this contribution examines accessibility in the context of publishing in translation studies. In particular, it maps ways in which the growth of open-access online publications in translation studies is contributing to changes in attitudes towards translation, sometimes perceptibly, sometimes imperceptibly. First, the notion of translation invisibility is considered and contextualised in the area of publishing in translation studies. In spite of its presence in contemporary intellectual debates, translation as a discipline is still often considered to be the poor relation of more established subjects in the humanities such as linguistics, sociology or literature. Similarly, translation-studies publications frequently evade the word *translation* in their titles, contributing to further invisibility. New developments in online publishing, combined with a surge of interest in translation and translation-related subjects, are key to dismantling barriers of invisibility. Online publishing reaches audiences in spectacularly wide, fast and efficient ways. Its development in translation studies can contribute to the full recognition of its importance as a discipline. Yet, there are challenges in these developments. They will be considered in relation to five binary themes: (1) access vs finance, (2) quality vs speed, (3) digital vs print, (4) multiculturalism vs globalisation and (5) open access vs accessibility.

Keywords
accessibility, invisibility, online publishing, open access, translation journals

1. Introduction

While translators and translation-studies scholars aspire to increase comprehension and improve communication, translation journals could be described as a reflection of the post-Babelian world that we live in. Only a handful of translation journals are internationally recognised as reputable scholarly publications. Moreover, translation resources are indexed in ways which often hinder the visibility of the discipline. I would like to discuss how this hindrance manifests itself and how e-publishing and, more specifically, open-access online journals can be helpful in combatting it. The notion of open access can have several meanings and as highlighted by Davis, who says that open access has a long historical record. Its general meaning of unrestricted admission or access is documented by the Oxford English Dictionary as far back as 1602. In library science, the phrase can be traced to 1894 with reference to patrons' unrestricted access to the publications kept on library shelves (Davis 2009).

However, in the context of contemporary journal publishing, open access is generally understood as follows:

[F]ree availability [of scholarly and scientific research texts] on the public internet, permitting any users to read, download, copy, distribute, print, search, or link to the full texts of these articles, crawl them for indexing, pass them as data to software, or use them for any other lawful purpose, without financial, legal, or technical barriers other than those inseparable from gaining access to the internet itself. The only constraint on reproduction and distribution, and the only role for copyright in this domain, should be to give authors control over the integrity of their work and the right to be properly acknowledged and cited" (BOAI 2010).

In the scientific world, a staggering number of journals have become available as open access. This phenomenon is highlighted by Suber, who writes the following about open access:

[M]ore than 30 subscription journals converted to open access in 2008, including six venerable ones over 25 years old. More than a dozen subscription journals converted just their backfiles to open access, including another six over 25 years old (Suber 2009).

In spite of these developments, open access does not always equate with an accessible approach. First, because smaller disciplines are not promoted as they could be. Second, because few online translation publications implement accessibility in relation to disability.

With regard to the promotion of small disciplines and by way of focus on the field of translation studies, no translation entry exists in the main journals directories. In Ulrich's periodical directory or in the Directory of Open Access Journals – the two main directories – translation is invisible and must be searched using other disciplines such as linguistics or literature. In addition, only a relatively small number of translation-related publications are included in the main directories available. Among the selected list of 878 titles listed on the Open Journal System site, for instance, one journal currently relates to translation (the recent *Translation and Interpreting*).

The drive towards more online and open-access development was initiated by universities in the late 1990s. Subsequently, it was encouraged by the European Research Council, who issued an official statement on the importance of open-access development in 2006 and who made it a requirement for ERC-funded research projects open access to be set up within six months of their publication (ERC 2006, 2007). The European Reference Index for the Humanities (ERIH) was created in 2007 as part of this intention to structure and to open up information, and to create a bibliometric system for the Social Sciences and Humanities (Hicks & Wang 2009). ERIH attempted to publish a league of scholarly journals (published in the humanities), in which translation journals were listed as part of linguistics, one of the sixteen areas considered. Of the 596 scholarly journals listed under linguistics, 24 focus primarily on translation and/or interpreting issues. However, this classification was highly criticised by scholars and academic journal editors as divisive and inadequate. After a wave of protest, the grade classification was dropped by the European Science Foundation in January 2009 with a view to replacing it with written descriptors by the end of 2010 (Corbin 2009; ERIH). A second ranking list was published in 2011. In the field of translation, the index was generally perceived by scholars and editors as a tool which further marginalised an area already struggling for visibility.

Only six journals were initially rated as A journals by ERIH:[1] (1) *Interpreting*, (2) *Machine Translation*, (3) *Meta*, (4) *TTR: Traduction Terminologie et Rédaction*, (5) *Target* and (6) *The Translator*. *Interpreting* and *The Translator* were founded in 1996 and 1995 respectively. The other journals are more than thirty years old (*Meta* 1955, *Machine Translation* 1986, *TTR* 1988, *Target* 1989). Other well-rated journals, such as *Terminology* (founded in 1994), belong to neighbouring fields. Paradoxically, as we shall see, only one of these A-graded publications currently has a policy of open-access archives. All the other journals remain accessible only by subscription. This is in spite of the fact that (and as a study conducted in 2008 shows)

> [i]n the humanities, e-only journals were the most commonly cited genre of content, followed by discussion forums. Resources facilitating informal exchange, like discussion forums and blogs, appeared more frequently in the humanities than in the other subject areas (Maron Smith 2009).

It may be argued that these figures are reasonable within the context of a small area. Yet, if we compare the field of translation studies with another small field such as gender studies, we find that in ERIH's initial list, for example, gender studies is identified as a discipline and comprises 33 journals, among which nine were graded A. Besides, the growth in the number of translation-studies journals in the last few years has been spectacular. A few recent titles include *New Voices in Translation Studies* (2005), *1611 A Journal of Translation History* (2007), *Translation Studies* (2008), *Translation and Interpreting* (2009) and *Monti* (2009).

Some journals are established among the specialist readers that they target (e.g., *InTRAlinea*) but many are not widely known among members of the translation community. To return to our comparative example above, the quantitative output between the fields of gender studies and translation studies is analogous but the infamous question of the invisibility of translation emerges once more.

2. Translation studies and invisibility

It seems that just as translational texts are doomed to a lapsarian status as they are judged less worthy than original ones, translation journals are also considered to be lacking in authenticity and associated with loss, with a lack of originality, discussing what is seen as – in Umberto Eco's words – *dire quasi la stessa cosa*, which states that almost the same thing is still perceived as lacking (Eco 2003). I would like to consider in this contribution how the expansion of open-access online publications in translation studies is contributing to changes in attitudes towards translation, sometimes perceptibly, sometimes more imperceptibly.

One may argue that translation has more visibility than it has ever had in the modern Western world. In the current globalised context, we are confronted not only with the need to transfer languages but with the evidence of cultural translation. Some thinkers (Bruno Latour, Homi Bhabha and Edouard Glissant among them) have broadened the notion of translation as the practice of mediation in relation to migration and transformation. They argue that this practice is necessary for crosscultural hybridisation. In the present era of constant change, the process of transcending borders and expressing cultural variation, which is inherent in our cultures, can be seen as translation.

Yet, this widening of the notion of translation has not necessarily made its agents more valued or more visible. Stripping translation of the inescapably dualistic nature of an instance of transfer from one language and culture to another, and turning it into a metaphor can also be reductive, and disinvest it of some of its importance. Translation may provide striking metaphors in the realm of transplanetary connections, respacialisations and deterritorialisations of our times but promoting it "as descriptive of social processes rather than merely language-based systems" (Bhabha 1995) has not substantially enhanced the profile of translators or the status of translation. In the professional world of translation, translators are more anonymous than ever, through an increased and often compulsory use of specialist software and ready-to-use text, which can transform them into post-editors, and through crowdsourcing, which forces them into cyber-collaborations which can challenge their roles as individual experts (see Garcia 2009).

Theorists can contribute to a depreciation of translation and its agents when they disseminate tropes of translation that equate transfer with the inauthentic. Thus 'translated' people are no more than displaced, suffering rather than enriched people.

In cultural mediation, people are more frequently represented as caught in the in-betweens of cultures rather than empowered by their gift for translation. This is the case in many recent films or works of fiction such as *Lost in Translation* (both in Eva Hoffman's 1989 novel and Sofia Coppola's film from 2003), or Jhumpa Lahiri's *The Interpreter of Maladies* (2000) to give just a couple of examples. In the latter work, Mr Kapasi, the main protagonist in the eponymous story *The Interpreter of Maladies*, remains unsuccessful in his attempt to mediate, incapable of communicating with the person in need of his gifts. Failing in his task, he is dismissed as "not even important enough to be properly insulted" (Lahiri 2000: 66). Lahiri's image echoes common contemporary beliefs that translation and translator have both reached an impasse. It evokes not only an insignificant and failed mediator but questions the possibility of translatability.

In the publishing world, the word *translation* is sometimes avoided, as if it needed to be transcended into a more worthy notion: *Meta*, *Target*, *Babel* are examples of this verbal escapism. In addition, the polysemous meanings of translation reinforce its invisibility. For instance, the widespread use of the medical sense of the word *translation* in some publication directories enhances this invisibility. A search for translation journals in the Ulrich's directory of periodicals in October 2009 reveals 43 references to electronic journals. However, only eight are translation journals as such.

3. Translation studies nurtured or neutered by other disciplines?

Faced with this marginalisation, many translation scholars – at least in the English-speaking world – seem to meander through various disciplines to publish their research. In the UK, young researchers are frequently advised to write their work under the guise of disciplines such as French/Italian/Hispanic Studies, with the promise that it will enhance their career opportunities and their chances of successfully ensuring grant applications. A great number of journals which host translation articles have titles which suggest more allegiance to linguistics than to translation studies. This is particularly the case for journals which have a reasonably long history of publication predating the era of translation studies as such. The example of *Linguistica Antverpiensia New Series*, a major journal in the field, is a potent illustration of this. In 2009, its title was changed to *Linguistica Antverpiensia New Series: Themes in Translation Studies*, in an attempt to remedy this lack of visibility.

As Michaela Wolf reminds us, translation studies is "by nature located in contact zones 'between cultures' [..] and calls for us to go beyond disciplinary boundaries" (Wolf 2010: 31). Although this leads translator scholars and practitioners to map their subjects in relation to different disciplines, this transdisciplinary essence is not always read as a sign of "recognition within the scientific community" (Wolf, Michaela, 2010: 29). The fact that the field of translation studies can be defined in parallel with the paradigm shifts that it engages with – be they linguistic, cultural or sociological – can also make it vulnerable as a discipline.

Thus, translation figures as the theme of a large number of philology, linguistics, communication and literature journals in special issues but does not figure as a mainstream topic. Recent examples include the *Journal of Romance Studies* 8(3), "Translation, adaptation, performance" winter 2008; *Quaderns de Fiolologia, Estudis Literaris XIII* "Traducció creativa", 2008; *Comparative Critical Studies* 6(1), 2009, which all focused on translation issues in an invisible way. While seasoned researchers may meander successfully and end up finding these issues, access to such journals requires some research expertise.

Finding niches for translation subfields has been even more challenging. Audiovisual translation (AVT) research in its increasingly diverse forms – from accessibility to video games localisation – has struggled to establish itself as a discipline. As Díaz Cintas wrote, audiovisual translation's "long journey to academic acknowledgement" (Díaz Cintas 2004: 50) is still in process. Association with overarching frameworks or fields (e.g., cognitive studies, sociology, film studies) has tended to relegate AVT to a theme discussed in major disciplines or frameworks, rather than a subject in its own right. The dedication of a small group of researchers who have woven strong relationships with the media industry has allowed AVT to emerge as a field of studies.

Whereas interdisciplinarity affects and enriches most fields of studies, there is a sense in the field of translation studies – particularly in AVT – that established subjects remain central and translation peripheral, often fragmented in its interests. The ideal picture of translation nurtured by other subjects is often substituted with that of translation pushed to the periphery of intellectual debates.

In the UK, most research councils and established institutions tend to spurn translation studies. The example of the Arts and Humanities Research Council, one of the main British sources of funding for humanities scholars, can be highlighted in this respect. Once more, in this case, translation is not a category as such but if we consider some of its bordering subjects, the following statistics are eloquent:

- Of 195 awards in 'Modern Languages-French Studies' (all schemes recorded between 1998 and 2009), 2 projects were translation-related

(but not by translations scholars: both professors specialised in the medieval period: Professor Penny Eley and the late Professor Peter Noble);
- Of 28 awards in 'Modern Languages-Comparative Studies' (all schemes recorded between 2000 and 2009), none relate to translation;
- Of 19 awards in 'Modern Languages-Area Studies' (all schemes recorded between 2004 and 2009), none relate to translation;
- Of 149 'French language and culture' awards (all schemes recorded between 2003 and 2009), no translation project is included;
- None of the nine successful entries in 'Language' (between 2006 and 2009) (all schemes between 2006 and 2009) included translation;
- None of the '1945-present' category 65 awards included translation (AHRC 2009).

Linguistic subjects are listed under extremely precise areas such as morphology and phonology, semantics, phonology, etc. but the 'Application of Linguistics' search, the search most likely to include translation projects, gave similar results to the ones above.

Of 34 successful submissions in these subjects (all schemes recorded since 1998), one award in translation was made: Professor Mona Baker's *Translation in Conflict* (2004). A few successful translation grants were awarded in fields not considered above, such as cultural studies. Nevertheless, in light of these figures, it is not surprising that translation studies scholars have sought alternative platforms for discussion and dissemination.

4. Translation studies and online publishing

Many of these platforms are provided through internet technology. As the European Society for Translation Studies website states,

> Our discipline suffers from poor coverage of TS literature in university libraries. In such a context, online resources are particularly valuable (EST no date).

This enthusiasm for online publications from the academic world is revealed in statistics.

Ulrich's periodicals online listed 18,563 academic and scholarly periodicals refereed and online in October 2009. In other words, such resources are clearly valuable across the disciplines. In fact, online academic publications constitute most of the online periodicals corpus, as Figure 1 shows.

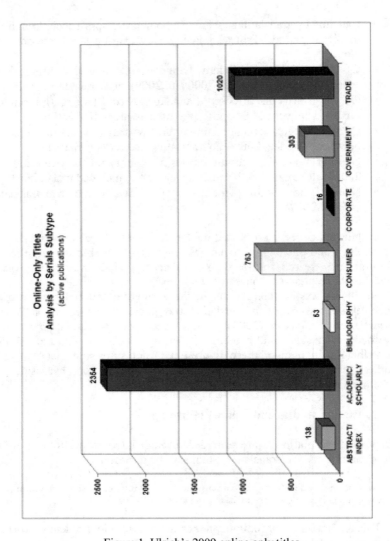

Figure 1. Ulrich's 2009 online only titles

Initially, scientific disciplines drove this online and open-access trend but a survey of the Directory of Open Access Journals shows that quantitatively, the humanities, law and social sciences are now on a par with respect to scientific output. A major publisher such as Cambridge University Press now offers more than 230 online journal titles, most of which are available by subscription although they state that "[a] significant number of Cambridge Journals now offer Open Access articles which are free to all readers" (Cambridge Journals).

Moreover, "at present, 95.7% of academic publishers make their journal back volumes available online" (Waltham 2009: 8). Björk et al. (2008) calculated that of the estimated 1,350,000 journal articles published in 2006, 19.4% were freely accessible (4.6% openly accessible immediately on publication, 3.5% freely accessible after an embargo, usually at least one year; and 11.3% through self-archiving).[2] These figures tend to increase towards more open access. Table 1 shows how rapid and continuous the expansion of access journals is.

Table 1. The expansion of access journals (Source: Directory of Open Journals)

Date	Number of journals included in the DOAJ (created in 2003)
January 2006	2000
10 October 2009	4365
16 October 2010	4372
08 March 2010	4844
27 April 2010	4991
30 June 2010	5140
08 November 2010	5633

Recent research (e.g., Taler 2008) shows that the increase has been steady and regular since 2000. Figures taken from the Directory of Open Access Journals at a few days interval indicate that increase is visible within days of monitoring.

In addition, peer-reviewed electronic journals are now recognised as being on an equal footing with print journals. As late as 2002, Boismenu and Beaudry wrote that "institutional recognition of digital publication is often perceived as a significant issue" (2004: 120). Quoting relevant studies, they emphasise that "[t]he reception and legitimacy of a digital journal [are largely conditional on...] the retention of print media in parallel" (Boismenu & Beaudry 2004: 133). This discriminative attitude has been quietly receding in the last few years, for two main reasons: (1) the adoption by the scientific publishing world of e-publishing, which suited the sort of computational contents of the articles and (2) the fact that most print journals started to offer e-versions of their issues. Because of their power of dissemination, online journals – and particularly open-access journals – are increasingly favoured by authors. A recent study on the open availability of journals in which 1104 scientific academics around the world participated, shows that although reasons for their motivations vary (according to whether or not they are tenured, for instance), they are in favour of adopting open-access publishing.

The main factors of influence are the unique visibility provided by open access and what is perceived as the technological advantage that it offers (Park 2009). The array of technological means provided by online publications is certainly attractive in the variety of ways information is disseminated. Videos in particular provide a useful contrast to peer-reviewed articles for interviews and other communication-based features. Curiously, although videos are widespread in online teaching, they are not common as a resource for online journals. A few scientific and well-established journals provide them. The journal *Nature*, first published in 1969, is one of them. But it is unusual in the online publication world.

The translation-studies community does offer some video materials, in particular in the UK through the Routes to Languages programme funded by the Higher Education Funding Council for England, which provides an array of videos on the translation profession (National Network for Translation). However, the translation-studies publishing network has been slow to open up to not only resources such as videos but also – more surprisingly – e-journals as most translation journals seem to remain conservative in their publication modes. For instance, *Meta*, one of the most established journals, does have an online version of the journal, archiving articles which are two-years old or older but it has not attempted to develop any other electronic features. *The Translator*, which came into existence at the dawn of e-publishing in 1995, follows the same pattern, although its archive is not open to free access. Although more recent journals tend to include electronic tools as part of their publication (e.g., *inTRAlinea*), translation e-journals tend to remain print media on line. *The Translation Journal*, the pioneer of electronic resources, is an exception but prioritises professional information, is not peer-reviewed and features advertising very heavily.

Developments on various e-platforms for information exist and provide useful information. Mona Baker's translation resources pages is a good example. However, such pages – the updates to which are generally reliant on the unstable staffing of doctoral students – are often not maintained or updated regularly.

In a wide range of disciplines, online publications can be innovative, can facilitate research functions and can display information in ways which are much more suitable than traditional print formats. The move towards e-publishing and online journals, –even more acutely in small fields such as translation studies than in mainstream fields – is primarily driven by considerations of finance and dissemination. Yet, online publishing is key to the propagation of translation studies and can be one of the prime factors furthering its visibility.

5. Challenges of online publishing

JoSTrans, The Journal of Specialised Translation, first published in January 2004, will be considered as an example to highlight trends, challenges and issues that are faced in online publishing in our discipline. Five key areas will be considered, among which some issues are relevant to all online journals while others are specific to translation. These areas have been grouped into binary oppositions:

(1) access vs finance
(2) quality vs speed
(3) digital vs print
(4) multiculturalism vs globalisation
(5) open access vs accessibility

Let us take a closer look at these binary oppositions

(1) Access vs finance

There is no doubt that open access online materials are the most efficient media for reaching readerships and web users. *JoSTrans*, a small player in the publishing world, has a much wider audience than a publication of its calibre in print media and it has grown exponentially in the last few years, both as regards number of readers/viewers and international participation. As an indication of this development, below are statistics on the number of *JoSTrans* pages viewed in the last four years. The increase since 2006 is two-hundred-fold:

Table 2. JoSTrans pages viewed in the last four years
(Source: Ghostgator Awstats statistics provider)

Date	*JoSTrans* pages viewed
April 2006	354
April 2007	648
April 2009	25,406
April 2010	35,164
October 2010	45,601
April 2011	68,177

However, everything has a price, and free access also has to be paid for. Using Salaün's eloquent words: electronic "information is expensive to produce but cheap to reproduce" Salaün (2001: 3).[3] The main options available to cut costs include running a sponsored commercial site (e.g., *The*

Translation Journal), asking authors to contribute financially for their publications (scientific model), being entirely subsidised by an academic institution (unless you are head of a department and control the budget, it is more and more unlikely), using fees paid for association membership (e.g., *New Voices in Translation Studies*), through contract with a commercial publisher (e.g., *Translation Studies*), or running an income-generating venture which subsidises the journal (e.g., *JoSTrans*).

The fallacy that e-publishing reduces costs to an absolute minimum is less prevalent than it used to be. Production costs are reduced, printing costs avoided and many tasks such as peer-reviews and other editorial work are carried out by volunteers. However, there are other services to be budgeted for in e-journal publishing: dissemination, maintenance, updates and archiving are all expensive and require a high degree of expertise. The fact that academics are increasingly expected not only to contribute to most aspects of the process but also find funding is a cause for concern. Whether in the creative or academic arena, "the Internet creates communities, but it doesn't pay them" (Gomez 2008: 190). Oxford Journals' announcement in June 2010 that more than two-thirds of its journals will be in open access if authors pay a publication charge can be quoted as an illustration of this practice:

> Today, six Oxford journals are fully open access and over 90 are hybrid open access, where authors of accepted papers are given the option of paying an open access publication charge to make their paper freely available online immediately (Oxford Journals 2010).

(2) Quality vs speed

Peer-reviewed journals go through a quality process, which is long and at times slow. As far as e-journals are concerned, the turnout expectations are higher than for print journals. Authors find it quite acceptable to wait a couple of years for the publication of a book but they expect an e-article to be online within a matter of weeks or months of its submission. The use of an editing platform used by some journals (e.g., *Perspectives*) mechanises the process and makes it more visible to authors. However, it does not shorten the process. The process can be summarised as shown in Figure 2.

Mapping digital publishing for all in translation

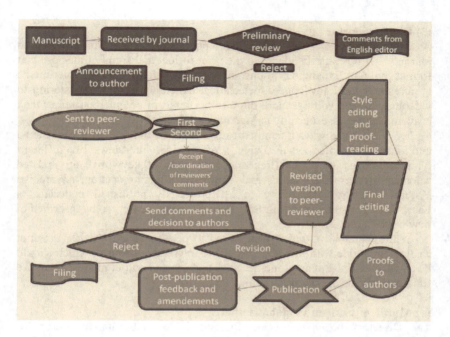

Figure 2. The peer-reviewing process

In an area where developments happen much faster than in most areas of the humanities, the print format is often inadequate since information may be irrelevant when it is made available. However, this puts pressure on online journals to have a fast turnover and in this respect, *JoSTrans* follows a scientific model more than a humanities one. Recent research shows that while in some cases – such as the open-access journal *Optic Express* – the publishing process takes "an average time of 56 days (7 to 8 weeks) from article submission to publication (online only and by the article), [… a group of Humanities and Social Science journals including the PMLA reports] "around 18 months"…and "… around 5 months before submission to vendor and then 3 months in production" (Waltham 2009: 7). Digital publishing also offers new forms of practice in peer-reviewing which can be explored, such as 'crowd-peer-reviewing, which offers the public opportunities to comment on articles and take part in their revision (Cassella 2010). However, these experiments also take time to set up and implement, in an area which is already short of experienced scholars.

(3) Digital vs print

As we have seen, most online academic publications – including translation journals – still primarily adhere to the print format and simply transpose that format online. Expanding publishing to the palette of available media requires a broad knowledge and technical expertise, from webmastering to videomaking and editing, more often to be found in commercial rather than academic contexts, especially in humanities subjects.

JoSTrans has always attempted to break out of the limits of print media and to use electronic tools available. It offers video interviews, two different types of search functions (free and by means of keyword), an updated calendar of events, a readers and viewers' comments section, an archive system ensuring accessibility to all previously published materials, a Facebook page and it offers an RSS feed, allowing readers to be informed of new issues.

While biannual output is well suited to peer-reviewed articles, it is not easily compatible with the development of interactive features, which should be added to the site at any time. Regular updates and output in these areas are time-consuming and require technical expertise.

(4) Multilculturalism vs globalisation

The Directory of Open Access Journals is the authoritative source for journals published in over 100 countries in more than 50 languages.[4] The World Wide Web offers the possibility of a presence to all languages including minority languages, and the non-English online presence has grown in the last decade.[5]

However, the current trend for academic publications is to publish them in English, with a general acceptance of Anglo-Saxon publishing models. In the world of peer-reviewed scholarly language, the dominance of English has steadily increased since the 1950s . In fact, it is "homogenizing knowledge worldwide. Not only is English the dominant language, but its relationship with the controlling trends in international science and scholarship is a powerful combination of forces contributing to decreasing diversity of themes and methodologies" (Altbach 2007). The English-speaking countries remain relatively inhospitable to translations into English from other languages. All in all, there were only 14,440 new translations in 2004, accounting for a little more than 3% of all books on sale. The 4,982 translations on sale in the US was the highest number in the English-speaking world, but was less than half of the 12,197 translations reported by Italy in 2002, and less than 400 more than the 4,602 reported by the Czech Republic in 2003. Almost three-quarters of all books translated into English from other languages last year were non-fiction. The Open Journal System provides multilingual support and automated translation but no comments are made on the quality and effectiveness of the translations (Bowker 2004).

Ulrich's periodicals online takes Spanish as a case study. It shows that while the number of publications in Spanish grew in the first years of development of the Internet, it has very much decreased since the turn of the century.

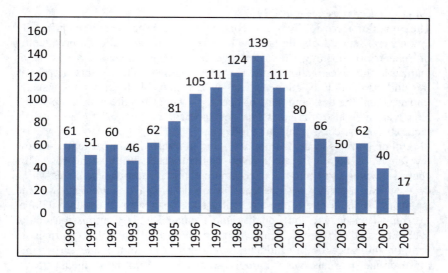

Figure 3. Ulrich's Spanish periodicals online

This reflects a trend towards more, rather than fewer publications in English. For instance, a high-ranking journal such as the PMLA, which publishes a wide range of articles on translation, has shown no signs recently of opening up to either multilingual output or non-Anglo-Saxon authors. In a study of 25 articles published in 2007, 21 authors were North American, two Australian, one South African and one Peruvian (Waltham 2009: 6).

This form of censorship does not come from the publishers only, but also from the authors, who are often under pressure to publish in English, for dissemination purposes, but also because their institution rates publications in English higher than in other languages. *JoSTrans* always stated its intention to be a multilingual journal but an extremely large proportion of submissions (95%) are in English. Articles in languages other than English are in major languages (French, German and Spanish). Sadly, minority-language authors feel more marginalised by not publishing in English than they do publishing in English.

In spite of the apparent trends towards more accessibility, which AVT scholars are well aware of, globalisation seems to have taken over from localisation, in ways which can and do consolidate the hegemony of Anglo-Saxon cultural and epistemological systems. Moreover, this drive towards more English is not without its problems as a large number of authors do not write comfortably in English.

(5) Open access vs accessibility

The notion of accessibility in this contribution has been considered primarily in a general sense, focusing on how internet technologies allow a broadening of readership, opening up knowledge to a larger audience in terms of numbers. The investigation of the slow development of accessible support as it is understood in translation studies – with various platforms for the visually impaired and the deaf and hard-of-hearing – would require a separate study. However, it is also vital that this development be mapped to have a true picture of open-access publishing today.

Online journals in the humanities – and in translation in particular – show few signs of complying with Web content accessibility standards. This contrasts with a large number of commercial and institutional websites which do – at least partially – since open access is a legal requirement in some countries.[6] This is due to the work of associations such as the IMS Global Learning Consortium, the Equality and Human Rights Commission or the Web Standards Project.[7] The reluctance of most Humanities journals to comply with accessibility guidelines relates to the point made earlier that most online journals were initially transferred from print media to an electronic platform for enhanced dissemination but were not thought out as electronic publications. As always, it is also linked to funding issues. The online journals that do follow accessibility guidelines tend to be part of large university groups such as those published by the Cambridge and Oxford Journals, even though not all large providers offer accessibility support. For instance, Erudit's website, the platform from which *Meta* and *TTR: Traduction, Terminologie, Rédaction* (two main translation journals available online) does not offer support. Some (e.g., *Interpreting*, *Translation & Interpreting*) offer partial support such as text size options, along with bookmarking options. *JoSTrans* complies with most accessibility guidelines although not all.[8] For instance, written transcripts are not available for audio and video interviews, although plans are on the table to add them to the website. On the other hand, while most interviews are in video format, some are text-based. The journal attempts to offer a range of media that different users can choose to access.

In spite of an evident slowness to comply with official guidelines, many attempts are being made to provide clear websites and to offer multimodal communication so that translation texts are disseminated in a variety of ways for a diverse readership and viewership: audio recordings and or transcriptions, video streaming, forums, etc. As Jenny Craven reminds us:

> Access can have several meanings, including physical access to hardware and software as well as ensuring users can not only access or 'read' what is on the screen (be it using magnification, speech output or Braille output) but they can also interact with resources and services" (Craven 2003).

Although guidelines are useful in broadening our awareness and standardising practices, what matters most in the end is the dissemination of information in our discipline in the most effective and wide-ranging ways and for a diverse readership.

6. Conclusion

The five areas considered in this short account of e-publishing in the field of translation studies emphasise tensions between localisation and globalisation, which are inherent in translation principles and in today's communication exchanges.

In his work on globalisation issues in translation, Michael Cronin has shown how the drive towards a technology fully integrated into human cultures – particularly acute in translation areas – has ambivalent consequences, as "[t]ranslation partakes arguably of the generalising drive of *techne* and of the particularising drive of culture" (Cronin 2002).The use of technology can lead to a tendency "to underscore the generalising role of translation and ignore translation's commitment to particularity" (Cronin 2002).[9] It is up to us to resist this trend and use technological tools to champion cultural diversity, accessibility, and to make sure that those with less visibility are not 'lost in translation'. Perhaps it is worth remembering that the slogan voiced by René Dubos in 1972 on the occasion of the first environmental summit, "Think global, act local" can work after all, in translation as in other human affairs.

---

[1] The initial ERIH ranking of 2007 proposed three categories: A ("high-ranking international publications with a very strong reputation among researchers of the field in different countries, regularly cited all over the world"), B ("standard international publications with a good reputation among researchers of the field in different countries") and C ("research journals with an important local / regional significance in Europe, occasionally cited outside the publishing country though their main target group is the domestic academic community") (ERIH 2007). In the revised version published in 2011, the categories changed to INT1("international publications with high visibility and influence among researchers in the various research domains in different countries, regularly cited all over the world"), INT2 ("international

Lucile Desblache

publications with significant visibility and influence in the various research domains in different countries"), NAT ("international publications with significant visibility and influence in the various research domains in different countries") and W ("journals which published their first issue three years or less before the closing date for feedbacks for a given panel") (ERIH 2011)

[2] http://poeticeconomics.blogspot.com/2008/09/draft-notes-for-dramatic-growth-of-open.html. We can note that this drive towards more e-materials is also supported by librarians: "There is a strong desire among librarians to move away from print-on-paper journals. 90% of librarians who responded either strongly agreed or agreed that they would like to move more journal titles to electronic only with only 2% disagreeing" (Russell 2009: 6).

[3] "L'information est coûteuse à produire mais peu coûteuse à reproduire" (my translation).

[4] For journals by country statistics, see http://www.doaj.org/doaj?func=byCountry

[5] At present, while around 45% of pages are in English (Funredes 2007), according to Internet World Stats, 27.7% of all internet users use English (Internet World Stats: Figures updated on 31st/12/2009). See Funredes (2005): "Between the [sic] 1998 and 2005, presence of the Latin languages in the network has practically duplicated, whereas the one of the English under 75% to 45% [sic]. [...] Since 1998, can observe a constant reduction of the predominance of the English by the advance of the other languages of the planet, in particular the one of the languages of the emergent countries." http://funredes.org/LC/english/medidas/sintesis.htm

[6] The US and the UK were the first countries to enforce Web accessibility laws. For instance, in the US, "federal Web sites must comply with Section 508 of the Rehabilitation Act (29 U.S.C. §794.d). This law requires that agencies provide access to electronic information to people with disabilities. Section 508 identifies 16 specific standards for Web site accessibility." (Redish and Theofanos 2003: 38). The World Wide Web Consortium, Web Accessibility Initiative and Education and Outreach Working Group provide information pages on accessibility regulation in different countries (see W3C).

[7] Information seems contradictory on this point. While authors like David Sloan quotes results from a survey published in 2004 which describes 64% of Web developers as aware of Web site accessibility (Sloan 2006: 107), Amir A. Majid writes that in 2007, only 3% of public websites have become accessible to disabled people (Majid 2007: 76). There are of course large discrepancies in different countries, and with many transnational websites, it is difficult to process national data accurately.

[8] WCAG 2.0 Guidelines state the need for a website to be:

1 Perceivable
Provide text alternatives for any non-text content so that it can be changed into other forms people need, such as large print, braille, speech, symbols or simpler language.
1.2 Provide alternatives for time-based media.
1.3 Create content that can be presented in different ways (for example simpler layout) without losing information or structure.
1.4 Make it easier for users to see and hear content including separating foreground from background.

2 Operable
2.1 Make all functionality available from a keyboard.
2.2 Provide users enough time to read and use content.
2.3 Do not design content in a way that is known to cause seizures.
2.4 Provide ways to help users navigate, find content, and determine where they are.

3 Understandable
3.1 Make text content readable and understandable.
3.2 Make Web pages appear and operate in predictable ways.
3.3 Help users avoid and correct mistakes.

4 Robust
4.1 Maximize compatibility with current and future user agents, including assistive technologies

JoSTrans does not comply with 1.2, 2.3 (which is not relevant to the site) and 3.3. (Web Content Accessibility Guidelines).

[9] The full quote is: "Translation partakes then arguably of the generalising drive of *techne* and of the particularising drive of culture. The result is that its relationship to tools often runs the risk of being doubly misunderstood. For those committed to a technocratic view of human culture and efficiency, the tendency will be to underscore the generalising role of translation and ignore translation's commitment to particularity. Translation will be conflated with its tools so that the instantaneous, borderless use of translation will be seen as concomitant with the universality of the application of the tools. On the other hand, for those who champion cultural difference, the particularising role of, say, literary translation can be asserted as being irreducibly distinct from the technophile universalism of technical and commercial translation, ignoring the fundamental exosomatic contribution to the development of human culture and sidelining basic questions of mediation and transmission in the elaboration of specific literary polysystems" (Cronin 2002). See also Cronin (2003).

References

Altbach, Philip. 2007. 'The Imperial Tongue: English as the Dominating Academic Language' in *International Higher Education* 49. Online at http://www.bc.edu/bc_org/avp/soe/cihe/news letter/Number49/p2_Altbach.htm (consulted 27.04.2010).
Bhabha, Homi and William.J.Thomas Mitchell. 1995. 'Translator Translated: An interview with Homi Bhabha' in *Artforum* 33(7): 80-84. Online at http://prelectur.stanford.edu/lecturers/ bhabha/interview.html (consulted 10.11.2010).
Björk, Bo-Christer, Annikki Roosr and Mari Lauri. 2008. 'Global Annual Volume of Peer Reviewed Scholarly Articles and the Share Available Via Different Open Access Options' in *Proceedings ELPUB 2008 Conference on Electronic Publishing*. Toronto - June 2008. 178-186.
Boismenu, Gérard and Guylaine Beaudry (trans. Maureen Ranson). 2004. *Scholarly Journals in the Digital World*. Calgary: University of Calgary Press (French original 2002).
Cassella, Maria. 2010. Peer-review Innovations in Humanities: How Can Scholars in Arts and Humanities Profit of the 'Wisdom of the Crowds'? paper presented at the BOBCATSSS 2010 conference, 25-27 January 2010, Parma. Online at http://dspace-unipr.cilea.it/bit stream/1889/1244/1/Maria%20Cassella.pdf (consulted 27.04.2010).

Corbin, Zoëb. 2009. 'Index of Journals Scraps Controversial Grades' in *Times Higher Education* 22. Online at http://www.timeshighereducation.co.uk/story.asp?sectioncode=26&storycode=405091&c=1 (consulted 27.04.2010).

Craven, Jenny. 2003. 'Access to Electronic Resources by Visually Impaired People' in *Information Research* 8(4). Online at http://informationr.net/ir/8-4/paper156.html (consulted 17.6.2010)

Cronin, Michael. 2002. 'Babel's Standing Stones: Language, Translation and the Exosomatic' in *Crossings, The eJournal of Art and Technology* 2.1. Online at http://crossings.tcd.ie/issues/2.1/Cronin/ (consulted 27.03.2010).

Cronin, Michael. 2003. *Translation and Globalisation*. London: Routledge.

Davis, Philip. 2009. 'How the Media Frames "Open Access"' in *The Journal of Electronic Publishing* 12(1). Online at http://dx.doi.org/10.3998/3336451.0012.101 (consulted 27.03.2010).

Díaz Cintas, Jorge. 2004. 'Subtitling: The Long Journey to Academic Acknowledgement' in *The Journal of Specialised Translation* 1: 50-70. Online at http://www.jostrans.org/issue01/art_diaz_cintas.php (consulted 27.03.2010).

Eco, Umberto. 2003. *Dire quasi la stessa cosa: Esperienze di traduzione*. Milan: Bompiani.

Funredes. 2005. 'Synthesis of the Results of the Study on the Languages'. Online at http://funredes.org/LC/english/medidas/sintesis.htm (consulted 27.03.2010).

Gomez, Jeff. 2008. *Print is Dead: Books in Our Digital Age*. London: Macmillan.

Garcia, Ignacio. 2009. 'Beyond Translation Memory: Computers and the Professional Translator' in *The Journal of Specialised Translation* 12: 199-214. Online at http://www.jostrans.org/issue12/art_garcia.php (consulted 27.03.2010).

Hicks, Diana and Jian Wang. 2009. 'Towards a Bibliometric Database for the Social Sciences and Humanities'. Online at http://works.bepress.com/diana_hicks/18 (consulted 04.05.2010).

Hoffman, Eva. 1989/1998. *Lost in Translation*. London: Vintage.

Lahiri, Jhumpa. 2000/1999. *The Interpreter of Maladies*. London: Flamingo.

Linguistica Antverpiensia New Series – Themes in Translation Studies. Online at http://www.lans-tts.be/ (consulted 18.06.2010).

Majid, Amir A. 2007. 'Right of Disabled People to Accessible Internet' in *Journal of International Commercial Law and Technology* 2(2): 76-82. Online at http://www.jiclt.com/ in Maron, Nancy L.,dex.php/jiclt/article/view/22/21 (consulted 16.06.2010).

Maron, Nancy, L. and Kirkby Smith. 2009. 'Current Models of Digital Scholarly Communication: Results of an Investigation Conducted by Ithaka Strategic Services for the Association of Research Libraries' in *The Journal of Electronic Publishing* 12(1). Online at http://dx.doi.org/10.3998/3336451.0012.105, (consulted 27.04.2010).

Mitchell, William.J.Thomas. 'Translator Translated' (interview with Homi Bhabha) in *Artforum* 33(7). 80-84. Online at http://prelectur.stanford.edu/lecturers/bhabha/interview.html. (consulted 27/03/2010).

Morrison, Heather. 2008. 'Twice as much gold. OA articles in 2008 as in 2006! The Dramatic Growth of Open Access' in *The Imaginary Journal of Poetic Economics* (Sunday, 21.09.2008), online at http://poeticeconomics.blogspot.com/2008/09/draft-notes-for-dramatic-growth-of-open.html

Park, Ji-Hong (2009) 'Motivations for Web-Based Scholarly Publishing: Do Scientists Recognize Open Availability as an advantage?' in *Journal of Scholarly Publishing* (July), 343-366

Jackson, Rodhri and Catarina Walsh. n.d. 'Open Access Uptake for OUP Journals: Five years on' in *Oxford Journals*, online at http://www.oxfordjournals.org/news/2010/06/10/open_access.html (consulted 27.06.2010)

Redish, Janice and Mary Frances Theofanos. 2003. 'Guidelines for Accessible and Usable Web Sites: Observing Users Who Work With Screen Readers' in *Interactions* 10(6): 38-51. Online at http://www.redish.net/content/papers/interactions.html

Russell, Ian. 2009. ALPSP Survey of Librarians. Responding to the Credit Crunch: What Now for Librarians and Libraries?. Online at http:// www.alpsp.org (consulted 27.03.2010).

Sloan, David. 2006. 'Two cultures? The Disconnect between the Web Standards Movement and Research-Based Web Design Guideline s for Older People' In *Gerontechnology* 5(2): 106-112. Online at http://www.gerontechjournal.net/ (consulted 17.06.2010).

Suber, Peter. 2009. 'Open Access in 2008' in the SPARC Open Access Newsletter 129, 2 January 2. Online at http://www.earlham.edu/~peters/fos/newsletter/01-02-09.htm#2008 (consulted 27.04.2010).

Salaün, Jean-Michel. 2001. 'Aspects Économiques du Modèle Éditorial sur Internet' in *Communication et Langages* 130 : 47-58. Online at http://hal.archives-ouvertes.fr/docs/00/06/20/52/PDF/sic_00000047.pdf (consulted 27.03.2010).

Taler, Izabella. 2008. 'LIS Open Access E-Journal – where are you?" in *Webology* 5(4). Online at webology.ir/2008/v5n4/a62.html (consulted 27.03.2010).

Waltham, Mary. 2009. *The Future of Scholarly Journals Publishing among Social Science and Humanities Associations*. Online at http://www.nhalliance.org/bm~doc/hssreport.pdf (consulted 27.03.2010).

Wolf, Michaela. 2010. 'Translation 'Going Social,' Challenges to the (Ivory) Tower of Babel' in Fouces, Oscar Diaz and Esther Monzó (eds.), *Monti: Applied Sociology in Translation Studies 2*: 29-46.

Filmography

Lost in Translation, Sofia Coppola (2003), USA

Websites cited

Arts and Humanities Research Council, 'Research we've funded', http://www.ahrc.ac.uk/Funded Research/Pages/default.aspx (consulted 16.10.2009).

Bowker.com (2004), 'English-Speaking Countries Published 375,000 New Books Worldwide in 2004'. Online at http://www.bowker.com/press/bowker/2005_1012_bowker.htm (consulted 28.04.2010).

Budapest Open Access Initiative (BOAI). 2001/2010. Online at http://www.doaj.org/doaj?func=loadTempl&templ=about (consulted 27.03.2010).

Cambridge Journals. n.d. Online at http://journals.cambridge.org/action/stream?pageId=3720 (consulted 28.03.2010).

Directory of Open Access Journals n.d. Online at http://www.doaj.org/ (consulted 27.043.2010).

Directory of Open Access Journals. 2006. Online at http://www.doaj.org/doaj?func=load Templ&templ=060113 (accessed 30th/6/2010)

European Research Council, Scientific Council. 2006. 'Statement on Open Access'. Online at http://erc.europa.eu/pdf/open-access.pdf (consulted 28.05.2010).

European Research Council, Scientific Council. 2007. 'Guidelines for Open Access'. Online at http://erc.europa.eu/pdf/ScC_Guidelines_Open_Access_revised_Dec07_FINAL.pdf (consulted 30.06.2010).

European Reference Index for the Humanities (ERIH). n.d. Online at http://www.esf.org/research-areas/humanities/erih-european-reference-index-for-the-humanities/information-about-erih-progress.html (consulted 18.06.2010).

European Society for Translation Studies. n.d. Online at http://www.est-translationstudies.org/

European Society for Translation Studies. n.d. Resources section. Online at http://www.est-translationstudies.org/resources.html (consulted 27.06.2010).
The Imaginary Journal of Poetic Economics. 2008. Online at http://poeticeconomics.blogspot.com/2008/09/draft-notes-for-dramatic-growth-of-open.html (consulted 27.06.2010).
InTRAlinea. n.d. Online at http://www.intralinea.it/eng_open.php (consulted 27.03.2010).
Funredes, n.d. Online at http://wwww.funredes.org (consulted 10.03.2010).
Internet World Stats. n.d. Online at http://www.internetworldstats.com/stats7.htm (consulted 30.06.2010).
Interpreting. n.d. Online at http://www.benjamins.com/cgi-bin/t_seriesview.cgi?series=intp (consulted 27.03.2010).
JoSTrans, The Journal of Specialised Translation. n.d. Online at http://www.jostrans.org (consulted 30.06.2010).
Machine Translation. n.d. Online at http://www.springer.com/computer/artificial/journal/10590 (consulted 27.03.2010).
Meta. n.d. Online at http://www.erudit.org/revue/meta/2009/v54/n2/index.html (consulted 27.03.2010).
Mona Baker's Translation Studies resources. n.d. Online at http://www.monabaker.com/tsresources/callforpapers.php?id=20 (consulted 27.03.2010).
National Network for Translation (videos). n.d. Online at http://www.routesinto languages.ac.uk/translation/videos (consulted 27.03.2010).
Nature, International Weekly Journal of Science, Online videos streaming archive. n.d. Online at http://www.nature.com/nature/videoarchive/ (consulted 27.03.2010).
Open Journal Systems, Public Knowledge Project. n.d. Online at http://pkp.sfu.ca/ojs-journals (consulted 28.06.2010).
Open Journal Systems, Translating OJS. n.d. Online at http://pkp.sfu.ca/ojs-translating (consulted 28.04.2010).
The Translation Journal. n.d. Online at http://accurapid.com/Journal/ (consulted 27.03.2010).
The Translator. n.d. Online at http://www.stjerome.co.uk/periodicals/journal.php?j=72&display=volumes (consulted 27.03.2010).
TTR, Traduction, Terminologie, Rédaction. n.d. Online at http://www.erudit.org/revue/ttr/2008/v21/n2/index.html (consulted 27.03.2010).
Ulrich's Periodicals Directory. n.d. Online at http://ulrichsweb.com (consulted 16.10.2009).
Web Content Accessibility Guidelines (WCAG) 2.0. n.d.. Online at http://www.w3.org/TR/WCAG20/ (consulted 16.06.2010).
Web Standards Project. n.d. Online at Altbach, Philip. 2007. 'The Imperial Tongue: English as the Dominating Academic Language' in *International Higher Education* 49. Online at http://www.bc.edu/bc_org/avp/soe/cihe/newsletter/Number49/p2_Altbach.htm (consulted 27.04.2010).
Bhabha, Homi and William.J.Thomas Mitchell. 1995. 'Translator Translated: An interview with Homi Bhabha' in *Artforum* 33(7): 80-84. Online at http://prelectur.stanford.edu/lecturers/bhabha/interview.html (consulted 10.11.2010).
Björk, Bo-Christer, Annikki Roosr and Mari Lauri. 2008. 'Global Annual Volume of Peer Reviewed Scholarly Articles and the Share Available Via Different Open Access Options' in *Proceedings ELPUB 2008 Conference on Electronic Publishing*. Toronto - June 2008. 178-186.
Boismenu, Gérard and Guylaine Beaudry (trans. Maureen Ranson). 2004. *Scholarly Journals in the Digital World*. Calgary: University of Calgary Press (French original 2002).
Cassella, Maria. 2010. Peer-review Innovations in Humanities: How Can Scholars in Arts and Humanities Profit of the 'Wisdom of the Crowds'? paper presented at the BOBCATSSS 2010 conference, 25-27 January 2010, Parma. Online at http://dspace-unipr.cilea.it/bitstream/1889/1244/1/Maria%20Cassella.pdf (consulted 27.04.2010).

Corbin, Zoëb. 2009. 'Index of Journals Scraps Controversial Grades' in *Times Higher Education* 22. Online at http://www.timeshighereducation.co.uk/story.asp?sectioncode=26&storycode=405091&c=1 (consulted 27.04.2010).

Craven, Jenny. 2003. 'Access to Electronic Resources by Visually Impaired People' in *Information Research* 8(4). Online at http://informationr.net/ir/8-4/paper156.html (consulted 17.6.2010)

Cronin, Michael. 2002. 'Babel's Standing Stones: Language, Translation and the Exosomatic' in *Crossings, The eJournal of Art and Technology* 2.1. Online at http://crossings.tcd.ie/issues/2.1/Cronin/ (consulted 27.03.2010).

Cronin, Michael. 2003. *Translation and Globalisation*. London: Routledge.

Davis, Philip. 2009. 'How the Media Frames "Open Access"' in *The Journal of Electronic Publishing* 12(1). Online at http://dx.doi.org/10.3998/3336451.0012.101 (consulted 27.03.2010).

Díaz Cintas, Jorge. 2004. 'Subtitling: The Long Journey to Academic Acknowledgement' in *The Journal of Specialised Translation* 1: 50-70. Online at http://www.jostrans.org/issue01/art_diaz_cintas.php (consulted 27.03.2010).

Eco, Umberto. 2003. *Dire quasi la stessa cosa: Esperienze di traduzione*. Milan: Bompiani.

Funredes. 2005. 'Synthesis of the Results of the Study on the Languages'. Online at http://funredes.org/LC/english/medidas/sintesis.htm (consulted 27.03.2010).

Gomez, Jeff. 2008. *Print is Dead: Books in Our Digital Age*. London: Macmillan.

Garcia, Ignacio. 2009. 'Beyond Translation Memory: Computers and the Professional Translator' in *The Journal of Specialised Translation* 12: 199-214. Online at http://www.jostrans.org/issue12/art_garcia.php (consulted 27.03.2010).

Hicks, Diana and Jian Wang. 2009. 'Towards a Bibliometric Database for the Social Sciences and Humanities'. Online at http://works.bepress.com/diana_hicks/18 (consulted 04.05.2010).

Hoffman, Eva. 1989/1998. *Lost in Translation*. London: Vintage.

Lahiri, Jhumpa. 2000/1999. *The Interpreter of Maladies*. London: Flamingo.

Linguistica Antverpiensia New Series – Themes in Translation Studies. Online at http://www.lans-tts.be/ (consulted 18.06.2010).

Majid, Amir A. 2007. 'Right of Disabled People to Accessible Internet' in *Journal of International Commercial Law and Technology* 2(2): 76-82. Online at http://www.jiclt.com/index.php/jiclt/article/view/22/21 (consulted 16.06.2010).

Maron, Nancy, L. and Kirkby Smith. 2009. 'Current Models of Digital Scholarly Communication: Results of an Investigation Conducted by Ithaka Strategic Services for the Association of Research Libraries' in *The Journal of Electronic Publishing* 12(1). Online at http://dx.doi.org/10.3998/3336451.0012.105, (consulted 27.04.2010).

Mitchell, William.J.Thomas. 'Translator Translated' (interview with Homi Bhabha) in *Artforum* 33(7). 80-84. Online at http://prelectur.stanford.edu/lecturers/bhabha/interview.html. (consulted 27/03/2010).

Morrison, Heather. 2008. 'Twice as much gold. OA articles in 2008 as in 2006! The Dramatic Growth of Open Access' in *The Imaginary Journal of Poetic Economics* (Sunday, 21.09.2008), online at http://poeticeconomics.blogspot.com/2008/09/draft-notes-for-dramatic-growth-of-open.html

Park, Ji-Hong (2009) 'Motivations for Web-Based Scholarly Publishing: Do Scientists Recognize Open Availability as an advantage?' in *Journal of Scholarly Publishing* (July), 343-366

Jackson, Rodhri and Catarina Walsh. n.d. 'Open Access Uptake for OUP Journals: Five years on' in *Oxford Journals*, online at http://www.oxfordjournals.org/news/2010/06/10/open_access.html (consulted 27.06.2010)

Redish, Janice and Mary Frances Theofanos. 2003. 'Guidelines for Accessible and Usable Web Sites: Observing Users Who Work With Screen Readers' in *Interactions* 10(6): 38-51. Online at http://www.redish.net/content/papers/interactions.html

Russell, Ian. 2009. ALPSP Survey of Librarians. Responding to the Credit Crunch: What Now for Librarians and Libraries?. Online at http:// www.alpsp.org (consulted 27.03.2010).

Sloan, David. 2006. 'Two cultures? The Disconnect between the Web Standards Movement and Research-Based Web Design Guideline s for Older People' In *Gerontechnology* 5(2): 106-112. Online at http://www.gerontechjournal.net/ (consulted 17.06.2010).

Suber, Peter. 2009. 'Open Access in 2008' in the SPARC Open Access Newsletter 129, 2 January 2. Online at http://www.earlham.edu/~peters/fos/newsletter/01-02-09.htm#2008 (consulted 27.04.2010).

Salaün, Jean-Michel. 2001. 'Aspects Économiques du Modèle Éditorial sur Internet' in *Communication et Langages* 130 : 47-58. Online at http://hal.archives-ouvertes.fr/docs/00/06/20/52/PDF/sic_00000047.pdf (consulted 27.03.2010).

Taler, Izabella. 2008. 'LIS Open Access E-Journal – where are you?" in *Webology* 5(4). Online at webology.ir/2008/v5n4/a62.html (consulted 27.03.2010).

Waltham, Mary. 2009. *The Future of Scholarly Journals Publishing among Social Science and Humanities Associations*. Online at http://www.nhalliance.org/bm~doc/hssreport.pdf (consulted 27.03.2010).

Wolf, Michaela. 2010. 'Translation 'Going Social,' Challenges to the (Ivory) Tower of Babel' in Fouces, Oscar Diaz and Esther Monzó (eds.), *Monti:Applied Sociology in Translation Studies 2*: 29-46.

http://www.webstandards.org/ (consulted 16.03.2010).

World Wide Web Consortium (W3C), Policies relating to Web Accessibility. n.d. Online at http://www.w3.org/WAI/Policy/ (consulted 18.06.2010).

Section 2

Interpreting Sight and Sound

Quality in Live Subtitling: The Reception of Respoken Subtitles in the UK[1,2]

Pablo Romero-Fresco
Roehampton University (United Kingdom)

Abstract

The present contribution addresses the issue of quality in live subtitling – which has largely been neglected so far – from the point of view of its reception. Drawing on Romero-Fresco (2010), where the comprehension and perception of live subtitles by hearing viewers in the UK was analysed, I will go a step further in this contribution, by including also deaf and hard-of-hearing viewers. In this instance, the study tackles not only their comprehension and perception of live subtitles but also their preferences. Insights into deaf and hard-of-hearing viewers' preferences were obtained through the use of a questionnaire disseminated in collaboration with the Royal National Institute for Deaf People. The results of this study may help provide a clearer picture of how live respoken subtitles are received in the UK and what aspects may need to be reconsidered or modified.

Keywords

block subtitling, comprehension of live subtitling, perception of live subtitling, quality in live subtitling, respeaking, scrolling subtitling

1. Introduction

Most broadcasters could do without having to provide live subtitles. They are expensive, require skilled professionals and are almost invariably flawed since more often than not they contain errors and are delayed with respect to the images that they accompany. Yet, in many cases broadcasters no longer have a choice. EU legislation and national legislation set quotas for specific numbers of hours that must be subtitled (live and offline) depending on the country, type of channel, means available, etc. Indeed, from the early days of accessibility to the media, emphasis has been placed on the volume of live subtitles, which has also traditionally been the users' main concern.

However, this situation is changing. Now that respeaking seems to have become consolidated as a cost-effective method to provide live subtitles, and companies and broadcasters are beginning to meet their targets, a change of focus from quantity to quality is in order. This applies not only to the UK, where the BBC already subtitles 100% of its programmes, but also to other countries where live subtitling is still in its infancy but where it would be sensible to apply quality standards now before 'bad habits' are acquired.

The question now is how to assess quality in live subtitling and, in this case, in respeaking. The approach adopted by most subtitling companies and broadcasters nowadays seems to be that of error calculation, often carried out by in-house trainers or respeakers. This is a highly interesting topic that would merit a study in itself and that requires further research. Suffice it to say that there seems to be no consistency between the different methods used in the field, which in many ways invalidates any comparison between the live subtitles provided by the different companies (Boulianne et al. 2009). The approach adopted in this contribution for the study of quality in live subtitling in the UK is different. As part of the EU-funded project DTV4ALL (http://www.psp-dtv4all.org/), the focus here is placed on deaf, hard-of-hearing and hearing viewers. More specifically, on their comprehension, perception and preferences regarding live subtitles. Results of hearing viewers' comprehension and perception of live subtitles in the UK were already provided in Romero-Fresco (2011). The present study completes these results with data on deaf and hard-of-hearing viewers' comprehension and perception, and adds one more element: the viewers' preferences.

2. Deaf and hard-of-hearing viewers' comprehension of live subtitles

In Romero-Fresco (2011), an experiment was presented to find out how much visual and verbal information that viewers obtain from news programmes in the UK. Four clips from the *Six O'clock News* broadcast on 4 July 2007 by BBC1 were shown to 30 hearing viewers aged between 20 and 45, native or near-native speakers of English, proficient readers and habitual subtitle users. Of these 30 viewers, 15 were postgraduate students doing an MA in Audiovisual Translation at Roehampton University. The other 15 viewers were lecturers and professional subtitlers. Participants were shown two clips with two news items each and were asked to answer questions about one of them. The clips had respoken subtitles displayed at two different speeds: 180 wpm, the usual speed in the UK, and 220 wpm, so as to ascertain the effect of speed on comprehension. In order to determine how much visual and verbal information was retrieved by the viewers, the news clips were divided – drawing on Chafe's (1980) concept of idea units[3] – into 14 semi-units: 8 verbal units and 6 visual units. If participants happened to identify a semi-unit that was not included in these 14, the new unit was also considered in the final results, which are shown in percentages (0%–25% is zero to poor information retrieval, 25%–50% from poor to sufficient, 50%–75%, from sufficient to good and 75%–100% from very good to perfect). Finally, in order to have a yardstick with which to compare the results obtained by viewers watching news with respoken subtitles, a pilot test was conducted with a control group of 15 other students from the same course at Roehampton University. In this case, their comprehension without subtitles was tested, the hypothesis being that viewers under 'normal' conditions (i.e., no subtitles) do not obtain 100% of the visual and acoustic information of a news clip.

Moving on from the tests above, the study was extended to 15 deaf and 15 hard-of-hearing viewers for the present contribution. The hard-of-hearing participants were between 60 and 80 years old, the most common age range for viewers with this type of hearing loss (Ofcom 2006). Of the 15 hard-of-hearing viewers, 13 became hard of hearing after the age of 50 and were habitual users of subtitles. The 15 deaf participants were aged between 20 and 45. Of the 15 deaf participants, 13 were oralist (i.e., they used English as their first language) and only 2 were signing (i.e., they used British Sign Language as their first language). All of the participants were university students, experienced readers and frequent subtitle users. Their comprehension was tested using the same clips (with subtitles at 180 wpm and 220 wpm) and methodology (Chafe's idea units) as in Romero-Fresco (2011).

2.1. Results

Table 1 includes the results of the tests with no subtitles and with subtitles at 220 wpm and 180 wpm for hearing, deaf and hard-of-hearing viewers:

Table 1. Performance with no subtitles, subtitles at 220 wpm and subtitles at 180 wpm

	No subtitles	Subtitles at 220 wpm			Subtitles at 180 wpm		
	hearing	hearing	HoH	deaf	hearing	HoH	deaf
perfect	0%	0%	0%	0%	0%	0%	0%
very good	93.3%	0%	0%	0%	0%	0%	0%
good	6.7%	0%	0%	0%	3.3%	3.3%	0%
almost good	0%	6.7%	6.7%	6.6%	6.7%	6.7%	6.7%
sufficient	0%	13.3%	13.3%	6.6%	36.7%	36.7%	40%
less than sufficient	0%	20%	30%	26.7%	20%	20%	13.3%
poor	0%	30%	30%	26.7%	20%	13.3%	20%

| very poor | 0% | 30% | 20% | 33.3% | 13.3% | 20% | 20% |

As expected, hearing participants under 'normal' conditions (i.e., watching news clips with no subtitles) did not retrieve 100% of the visual and verbal information included in the clips. As far as the tests with subtitles are concerned, the results show very little discrepancy across the different types of viewers. The percentages are overall extremely low, with most participants information-retrieval performances being less than sufficient, poor and very poor.

2.2. Discussion

First of all, the fact that normal conditions do not yield perfect scores from the participants suggests that short-term memory may play an important role. Be that as it may, overall comprehension was very good (80% on average), particularly with respect to images (90.5% compared with 73.2% for verbal information), which makes sense considering that no subtitles were displayed. As for the similarity in the results obtained by hearing, hard-of-hearing and deaf viewers with subtitles displayed at 220 wpm and especially at 180 wpm, it may be explained by the above-mentioned familiarity of the participants with TV subtitles, whether as an object of study (hearing viewers) or as a means to access the news on a daily basis (deaf and hard-of-hearing viewers). Needless to say, this makes the overall low score with respect to comprehension even more meaningful. With subtitles displayed at 220 wpm, no one retrieved good information and only 20% of the participants retrieved sufficient information. 60% could give only a poor or very poor account of the news. While it is true that subtitles are not usually shown at this speed, it is not uncommon for presenters of debates, interviews and weather reports to speak at this rate (Uglova & Shevchenko 2005). Thus, these results may be seen as a warning against the provision of verbatim subtitles for these programmes.

However, the most surprising results were yielded in the test with subtitles displayed at 180 wpm – the usual speed of live subtitles in the UK. More than half of the participants (51%) did not obtain sufficient information. Only 3% obtained good information and 31% retrieved poor or very poor information. Furthermore, 1 out of 3 participants retrieved incorrect information, mixing up names and faces from news clips.

It must be underlined that the participants who took part in this experiment were highly literate and frequent subtitle users. Viewers who are not used to subtitles or signing deaf viewers, whose first language is not English and whose reading skills are often regarded to be poorer (Torres

Monreal & Santana Hernández 2005) can hardly be expected to obtain better results. Why do programmes with respoken subtitles trigger such mediocre comprehension results? A possible answer to this question may lie in how viewers read and process these subtitles. This can be studied with eye-tracking technology, which constitutes the basis of the second experiment included in the present contribution.

3. Deaf and hard-of-hearing viewers' perception of live subtitles

In Romero-Fresco (2011), an eye-tracking test was conducted with five hearing participants (hearing lecturers of subtitling and professional subtitlers) to discover how the participants read respoken word-for-word subtitles as opposed to block subtitles. They watched two news clips from the *Six O'Clock News* (4 July 2004) with subtitles displayed first of all in scrolling mode (word-for-word) and then in blocks of two lines, while their eyes were monitored by a non-intrusive eye tracker.[4] The aim of the experiment was to calculate the amount of time spent on the images so as this could compared with the amount of time spent on the subtitles and also the number of fixations per subtitle. A brief explanation is in order at this point to stress the importance of fixations in the reading process. As can be seen in Pictures 1 and 2, our eyes do not sweep continuously across the page (or the screen) when we read. Instead, they pause and rest for short periods of 110ms–500ms, which are called fixations. These are the moments at which we retrieve the visual information that we need (Rayner & Pollatsek 1989).

Pablo Romero-Fresco

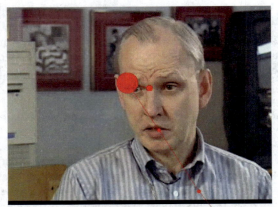

Pictures 1 and 2. Fixations and saccades

The movements between fixations are called saccades. They are ballistic movements (i.e., once started, they cannot be stopped) which may take as little as 20ms to 100ms and during which no visual information is obtained (Wolverton & Zola 1983). All visual information comes in during the fixations. Also worth highlighting is the fact that every fixation spans 8 to 10 characters. In other words, our eyes need not fixate on every word when reading a subtitle, which enables us to read faster (Rayner 1998).

While all this can be said about 'normal' lines in print and block subtitles on the screen, it remains to be seen whether it also applies to scrolling subtitles. The experiment presented in Romero-Fresco (2011) tested this with hearing participants. For the present contribution, the study was extended to 10 hard-of-hearing and 10 deaf viewers, who also took part in the comprehension study.

3.1. Results

The following table shows the results obtained in the study, namely the number of fixations per subtitled line and the time spent on images by the different types of participants, with subtitles displayed in blocks and scrolling:

Table 2. Number of fixations and time spent on images with blocks and scrolling subtitles

Viewers	Number of fixations		Time spent on images	
	blocks	scrolling	blocks	Scrolling
hearing	3.75	6.00	33.30%	11.70%
hard-of-hearing	3.75	6.50	33.20%	11.40%
deaf	3.90	6.50	31.70%	14.30%

In line with what has been described with respect to the comprehension test (see Section 2.1), the results are fairly consistent across hearing, hard-of-hearing and deaf viewers. In order to read scrolling subtitles, viewers need almost twice as many fixations than for block subtitles. The number of fixations per subtitled line in scrolling mode ranged from 3 to 10, with an average of 6 for hearing viewers and 6.5 for hard-of-hearing and deaf viewers. The number of words per line in the clips analysed was 6, which means that hearing viewers fixate on every word of every scrolling subtitle and deaf and hard-of-hearing viewers produce even more fixations than words. In contrast, the number of fixations in block subtitles ranges from 2 to 6, with an average of 3.75 fixations for hearing and hard-of-hearing viewers and 3.9 for deaf viewers. In other words, viewers manage to read block subtitles skipping almost every other word. Needless to say, this has a direct impact on the time that viewers spend looking at the subtitles and the time that they devote to the images. As shown in Table 2, in scrolling mode viewers spend most of their time bogged down in the subtitles (an average of 87.5% vs 12.5% spent on the images), whereas in block subtitles they have more time to focus on the images (an average of 67.3% on the subtitles and 32.7% on the images).

3.2. Discussion

The analysis of the reading patterns of each participant reveals some interesting elements. Rather than differentiating the participants into hearing, deaf and hard-of-hearing, the results appear to establish a distinction between fast and slow readers, which was not considered at the beginning of the experiment.[5] Besides, there seem to be two phenomena – astray fixations and regressions – that may explain the viewers' difficulty in reading scrolling subtitles and perhaps the poor comprehension results obtained in the previous experiment. As can be seen in Picture 3, fast readers often get ahead of the subtitles and cast their eyes on gaps where no word has been displayed yet. This then results in astray fixations.

Picture 3. Astray fixation

This "quicksand effect" (Romero-Fresco 2010), causes viewers to lose precious time in their reading process as they struggle to find solid ground (i.e., a word or a whole line). On average, fast readers incur two astray fixations per subtitled line. In half of the cases, they go back and re-read at least one word, which means they incur one regression per subtitled line. In the other half of the cases, they decide to continue reading the subtitle.

In contrast, slow readers do not get ahead of the subtitles (they usually lag behind them). Consequently, their patterns do not feature astray fixations and any quicksand effect. However, their eyes often land on words (in the middle of a subtitle) that are not meaningful enough for the reader to make sense of what is being said. In order to continue reading, slow readers then have to go back and re-read previous words, which happens 1.5 times per line in the participants analysed. In Picture 4, the viewers first cast their eyes on the word *have* and then go back to the beginning of the line.

Picture 4: Regression

These results seem to corroborate the view held by Rayner et al (2006) about the importance of the word to the right of the fixation for maintaining normal reading patterns. In the experiment conducted by Rayner et al., the absence of such words causes significant disruption to reading and decreases reading speeds. In scrolling subtitles, the word to the right of the fixation is often absent, which may explain the chaotic reading patterns yielded in the present experiment. On the one hand, fast readers get ahead of the subtitles and cast their eyes on gaps without words (astray fixations). On the other hand, slow readers lag behind and constantly go back to re-read words (regressions). Either way, all viewers waste time chasing subtitles which seem to be playing hide-and-seek with them, preventing them from watching the images.

Needless to say, this chaotic reading pattern and the almost non-existent time left to 'read' the images may go some way towards explaining the poor comprehension results obtained by deaf, hard-of-hearing and hearing participants in the comprehension test described above. What remains to be seen is what viewers think about this and other types of respoken subtitles. Are they happy with them? Do they realise that this display mode may hinder their comprehension of live programmes?

4. Deaf and hard-of-hearing viewers' preferences regarding live subtitles

Very often, many of the decisions adopted by broadcasters about subtitling features are based on viewers' preferences. This sounds logical and certainly preferable to adopting decisions without consulting the audience but there are some matters that merit further study. On the one hand, it may be useful to conduct comprehension studies and perhaps even eye-tracking studies – such as the ones included in this contribution – to ascertain whether (and how) viewers understand subtitled programmes. On the other hand, viewers' preferences are not set in stone, which means that surveys need to be conducted periodically.

To name but one example, the choice of scrolling versus block subtitles in the UK has traditionally been based on two arguments: (1) the fact that scrolling subtitles have less delay than block subtitles and (2) the fact that viewers prefer scrolling subtitles to live programmes because they have grown accustomed to them. As explained in Romero-Fresco (2011), the first argument can now be easily refuted. Swiss TxT in Switzerland have shown that respoken subtitles produced with Dragon NaturallySpeaking 11 (Nuance) can have a 4–6 second delay on average, very much like the scrolling subtitles produced with ViaVoice 10 (IBM).[6] As for the second argument, it may be necessary to revisit viewers' preferences, especially considering the lack of reception-studies research into live subtitling and the way in which new technology develops.

One of the most recent surveys regarding subtitling for the deaf and hard of hearing (SDH) in the UK is the one carried out in early 2009 by the Royal National Institute for the Deaf (RNID).[7] Although it focused generally on TV access, participants identified subtitling as the main issue that they wanted the RNID to campaign for. Almost 80% of the participants experienced problems with subtitles and more than half had been forced at times to stop watching programmes as a result. The two main issues were (1) the delay of subtitles with regard to the audio (25%) and (2) their inaccuracy (17%). These were identified as more important factors than having no subtitles available (7%). In other words, it would appear that viewers are now prioritising quality over quantity and – judging by their main concerns (delay and accuracy) – it is the quality of live subtitling that they are particularly worried about.

Given the absence of data about viewers' preferences with respect to live subtitling in the UK, a questionnaire was prepared as part of the DTV4ALL project and disseminated using the RNID website.[8] The following sections include information about the participants as well as a discussion of their replies.

4.1. Description of the survey

A total of 434 viewers took part in the survey. Of these 434 viewers, 259 were hard of hearing, 164 were deaf (of whom 27 were BSL users) and 11 were hearing. The results included here will focus mainly on the first two groups since the numbers are more representative. More than half of the participants (58.7%) were over the age of 60, 33% were between 35 and 59 and 8.3% were between 17 and 34. As suggested also by Ofcom (2006), this reflects the state of affairs in the UK, where the largest group of SDH viewers are hard-of-hearing people over the age of 60. With respect to the participants' educational backgrounds, most participants in the survey (72.6%) had attended university or a technical college. Finally, with respect to subtitle use, 70% of the participants stated that they used subtitles all the time, while 20% looked at them some of the time, 6.5% did so only occasionally and 2.5% never looked at them. As shown in Table 3, deaf viewers proved more likely to use subtitles as the only way to access the audio of the programmes, whereas in the case of hard-of-hearing viewers, the results were more evenly split among those who used them to understand the original soundtrack better and those who relied on them completely.

Table 3. The use of subtitles by deaf, hard-of-hearing and hearing viewers

What do you use subtitles for?	Deaf number	Deaf percentage	HoH number	HoH percentage	Hearing number	Hearing percentage
They are the only way to access the dialogue	100	61%	118	45.6%	0	0%
They help me understand	63	38.4%	133	51.3%	9	81.8%
I use them to learn English	0	0%	1	0.5%	0	0
I don't use them	1	0.6%	7	2.7%	2	18.2%
N/A	0	0%	0	0%	0	0%
Total	164	100%	259	100%	11	100%

Participants were asked 14 questions about live subtitling. The first three questions covered general aspects, namely how live subtitles are produced (questions 1 and 2) and the viewers' opinion about the quality of the subtitles (question 3). The next six questions (questions 4–9) focused on the viewers' opinion about live subtitling on the main UK channels: BBC, ITV, Channel 4, Channel 5 and Sky. The last five questions (questions 10–14) dealt with specific respeaking issues such as mistakes, delay and display mode.

4.2. Results and discussion

The data obtained from the questionnaire are reported in the sections below.

4.2.1. Awareness of how live subtitles are produced

Most participants do not know how live subtitles are produced, 26.7% claim to know but only 13.3% identify current live subtitling methods.

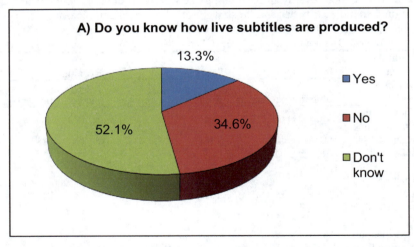

There seems to be a general belief that live subtitles are produced using automatic speech recognition, with little or mostly no human intervention. In other words, viewers' expectations of current speech recognition technology are unrealistic, which may go some way towards explaining some frequent complaints about live subtitles not being error-free or in perfect synch with the original soundtrack. As for respeaking, only 3.5% of the participants knew of this method. Overall, deaf participants proved more knowledgeable about live subtitling methods than hard of hearing, and so did frequent subtitle users. In keeping with this, the more viewers rely on subtitles, the more likely they are to know about them and perhaps to take an interest in how they are produced. In any case, the very low figures regarding knowledge about live subtitles in general and respeaking in particular send a worrying message about the visibility of this activity.

4.2.2. General opinion about live subtitles in the UK

As the pie chart below indicates, there is overall dissatisfaction with live subtitles in the UK.

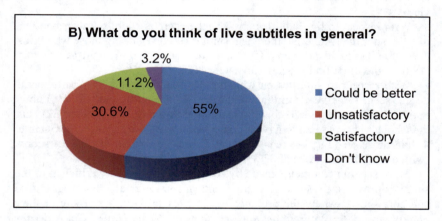

More than half of the participants (55%) think that they could be better. Many (30.6%) find them unsatisfactory and only 11.2% consider them satisfactory. Deaf viewers seem to have a more favourable opinion than hard-of-hearing viewers, and so do frequent subtitle users when compared with occasional users, 50% of whom find live subtitles unsatisfactory. In other words, it would seem that the more viewers look at – or rely on – live subtitles, the happier they are with them. However, it must be noted that this difference is only reflected in more viewers choosing the 'could be better' option rather than the 'unsatisfactory' option. The percentage of viewers who consider live subtitles satisfactory remains low at 11–12%.

4.2.3. Opinion on subtitles as shown on the BBC, ITV, Channel 4, Channel 5 and Sky

As shown in this survey, BBC live subtitles are rated slightly more favourably than those shown on other UK channels, with 28% of the participants who consider them satisfactory. Yet, in line with what was explained in the previous section, more than half of the participants (52.2%) think that they could be better and 19.7% find them unsatisfactory. In general, participants seem to be very familiar with live subtitles on the BBC and deaf viewers have a better opinion about them than hard-of-hearing viewers.

With respect to live subtitles on ITV, the score is slightly lower than that of BBC subtitles. Although there is a similar result regarding those who think that subtitles could be better (56%), fewer viewers find them satisfactory (18.6%) and more find them unsatisfactory (25.3%).

With respect to subtitles on Channel 4, Channel 5 and Sky, participants do not seem to be very familiar with them. 25.5% chose the 'I don't know' option for Channel 4, 38% for Channel 5 and as many as 62.9% for Sky. On the whole, viewers seem to have a higher opinion of live subtitles on Channel 4 than those on ITV, whereas Channel 5 and Sky obtain the lowest scores (with dissatisfaction rates of 32.3% and 38.5% respectively).

More specific comments made by some participants show criticism of the subtitles provided for some sporting events, many regional news programmes and chat shows, where the presence of subtitles seems to be erratic or their quality very poor. Programmes such as *Question Time*, *Have I Got News for You*, *Mock the Week* and *The One Show*, all chat shows, are singled out as particularly problematic. Of all the concerns voiced by viewers, the main one seems to be the delay with which the live subtitles are presented, followed by the number of mistakes that they contain. These mistakes appear to be particularly noticeable in regional news programmes. Other complaints pertain to not being able to see the speakers' faces to lip-read what they are saying, excessive editing, the volume of commercials being too loud, the intervention of unnecessary on-air corrections and the failure to indicate in the subtitles that a new topic is being introduced.

In sum, while in the past user satisfaction seemed to focus mainly on quantity, now that the different channels are meeting their targets, viewers are placing the emphasis on quality, which seems very much subject to improvement.

4.2.4. Extent to which different errors and delay are perceived to affect the comprehension and appreciation of subtitles

The results for the question related to what extent the viewers feel that errors affect their comprehension indicate that participants are split between those who think that it is often possible to understand the original meaning when there is a mistake in live subtitles (45%), and those who think it is only sometimes possible (45.5%). A noticeable difference is found here between deaf and hard-of-hearing viewers. Whereas the former struggle to restore the original meaning in more than half of the instances, the latter tend to find it easier. This makes sense considering that many hard-of-hearing viewers can mentally correct misrecognised words by thinking of the similar-sounding words that were supposed to appear. Many deaf viewers – particularly pre-lingually deaf, who have no recollection of sounds – may not be able to correct misrecognised words. Still, further research is required on this topic.

When asked about their opinions on the acceptability of current delays in presentation (considering that it is currently impossible to eliminate it), viewers tend to be rather negative.

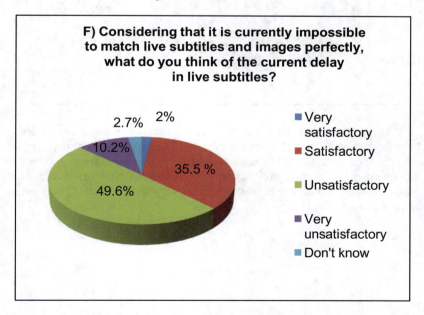

Just under half of the participants (49.6%) find the current delay of respoken subtitles on UK TV channels unsatisfactory. Although a significant percentage (35.5%) finds it satisfactory, there are more who consider it very unsatisfactory (10.2%) than very satisfactory (2%).

When asked whether it is possible to relate the subtitles to the images despite the delay, results are worse than in the question about mistakes. The distinction between deaf and hard-of-hearing viewers resurfaces. Whereas hard-of-hearing participants are evenly split between those who can often relate images and subtitles and those who can only do so sometimes, most deaf participants choose the latter option.

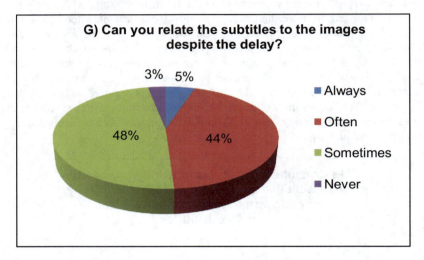

It appears that most people find it more difficult to relate the subtitles to the images than to mentally correct mistakes. This may explain why – in the next question – which was focused on whether it is more important to reduce the delay or to reduce the mistakes in respoken subtitles, 2 out of 3 participants chose delay over mistakes, with very similar results among deaf and hard-of-hearing viewers:

Quality in live subtitling

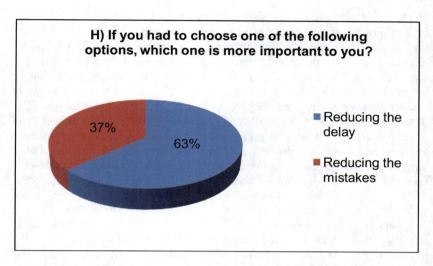

Finally, respondents were asked for their general opinion of the display mode of live subtitles.

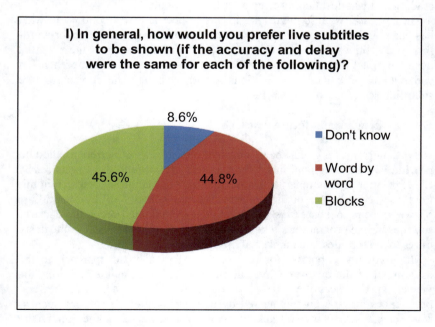

As noted in Section 4, the viewers' preference for word-for-word subtitles is often posited as one of the main reasons why live subtitles in the UK are not displayed in blocks. Yet, the results obtained in the survey under discussion question this assumption. Far from showing a clear preference for scrolling subtitles, the results are very divided and – if anything – more favourable to block subtitles (45.6% vs. 44.8%). A more thorough analysis reveals that word-for-word display is mostly preferred by deaf viewers, particularly those who use British Sign Language (BSL) or who lost their hearing at birth or in the first years of their lives. Many of them cannot hear the original soundtrack but they can see how people speak and they know language is not spoken in blocks but word for word. Some of these viewers specified in the survey that subtitles displayed in blocks look manipulated, edited or tampered with, whereas scrolling subtitles look like the real thing, giving them the impression that they are listening with their eyes in real time. Yet, this does not apply to all deaf viewers and certainly not to hard-of-hearing viewers, who seem to be more favourable to blocks. In this sense, the strongest preference for blocks is registered among those participants who may be described as 'most different' from the above-mentioned deaf viewers, that is, hard-of-hearing viewers who are not BSL users, who resort to lip-reading and who lost their hearing after the age of 50.[9]

In any case, what is interesting in this respect is that – contrary to what has been held for a long time now – there is no overall preference for word-for-word subtitles over subtitles in blocks. Taking into account the potential negative effect that scrolling subtitles may have in terms of comprehension and reading efficiency (see Sections 2 and 3 above), the choice for live subtitling seems no longer justified.

5. Final thoughts and future research

Now that respeaking has been consolidated as the preferred method to provide live subtitles, and many broadcasters are meeting the targets set by EU legislation and national legislation, the time has come for research in this field to focus on the quality rather than the quantity of live subtitling. Viewers seem to share this view as their complaints about the lack of subtitles in live programmes take a back seat to other issues such as the delay of respoken subtitles, the number of mistakes, etc.

It is equally important for research to adopt a broad approach to the assessment of the quality of live subtitling. Significant as they may be, the viewers' preferences are but one element to take into account. Viewers' preferences may be complemented by data from other approaches such as comprehension tests or eye-tracking studies, which can cast some light on the extent to which live subtitles are understood or on how they are viewed and/or perceived. In the case of the respoken subtitles currently provided in the UK, the tests included in this contribution suggest that there is much room for improvement. The results obtained from the hearing, deaf and hard-of-hearing participants in the comprehension tests are extremely low. The eye-tracking study shows that this may be due to the scrolling display mode of respoken subtitles, which causes unnatural and chaotic reading patterns, with the viewers chasing the subtitles and having no time to focus on the images.

A possible solution to this problem may be the use of non-scrolling speech-recognition software such as Dragon NaturallySpeaking (Nuance) to subtitle in respeaking units (Romero-Fresco [2011]) as opposed to word-for-word. These respeaking units can help (1) respeakers make sense of the original text, (2) the software increase accuracy by producing phrases rather than individual words and (3) viewers read commonsensical blocks and then focus on the images. As suggested by the results obtained in the opinion poll presented in this contribution, the claim that viewers are massively in favour of scrolling subtitles for live programmes may no longer apply. Furthermore, the results of the survey point to other areas that may be subject to improvement. Indeed, most viewers seem to be unaware of how live subtitles are produced. Many actually believe that they are produced using automatic speech recognition, with little or no human intervention. If companies and broadcasters gave more visibility to respeaking and the (human) difficulties involved, viewers might be more lenient in their demands.

All the same, the current view is that respoken subtitles are open to improvement, notwithstanding differences between genres, channels and viewers. The main complaint is the delay in the presentation of subtitles with regard to images, which is ranked as more important than the number of errors in texts. The reason for this may be that – as most viewers point out – it is more difficult to relate images to delayed subtitles than to understand what was originally meant in a programme despite the mistakes. Given that it is virtually impossible to eliminate the delay in respeaking, broadcasters have at least two possible solutions. The first solution could be to use automatic (speaker-independent) speech recognition, with no need for a respeaker to intervene. Here, though, more time is needed, as issues such as automatic punctuation and general accuracy still require further research and improvement. The second solution would be – as some participants have pointed out – to delay the video signal and thus provide respeakers with some seconds to respeak the original soundtrack, correct the errors and cue the subtitles live with no delay. This has already been done in the Netherlands – and with good results – to subtitle live events from English into Dutch. The issues of competition among channels and even censorship that this may bring about could be solved if the decision to have the signal delayed or not is taken at the viewers' end. Set-top boxes could feature an application allowing those viewers who wish to have synchronous subtitles to have the video signal delayed.

Future research in the field of respeaking could focus on the reception of respoken subtitles with and without delay, but also on other areas such as more in-depth analyses of comprehension in scrolling versus block subtitles, the reception of on-air corrections and – based on the different preferences expressed by deaf and hard-of-hearing participants – the possible provision of different respoken subtitles depending on the viewers' hearing impairments. The latter may not be a realistic option for TV but it may be feasible for public events where an all-hard-of-hearing audience may have a different preference regarding live subtitles (display mode, delay, error correction, etc.) to an all-deaf audience.

In all cases though, partnership between enterprise and academia, which has so far only been successful in a few countries, is a key element to render research viable and ultimately successful.

---

[1] This is an updated version of the chapter "The reception of respeaking" (Romero-Fresco forthcoming).

[2] This research is supported by the grant from the Spanish Ministry of Science and Innovation FFI2009-08027, Subtitling for the Deaf and Hard of Hearing and Audio Description: objective tests and future plans, and also by the Catalan Government funds 2009SGR700.

[3] Chafe (1985: 106) defines idea units as "units of intonational and semantic closure", which can be identified because they are spoken with a single coherent intonation contour, preceded and followed by some kind of hesitation, made up of one verb phrase along with whatever noun, prepositional or adverb phrase are appropriate, usually consisting of seven words and take about two seconds to produce.

[4] The eye tracker used was the Tobii x50, working at a frame rate of 50Hz. Viewing was binocular and the images were presented on a 17" monitor at a viewing distance of 60 cm. The computer kept a complete record of the duration, sequence, and location of each eye fixation, and Tobii Studio was used to analyse all data recorded.

[5] The details of this distinction will be the subject of further investigation focusing on the length of the saccades, the duration of the fixations and the number of characters per fixation in the different conditions. This may help to determine if and how the presence of a moving target (scrolling subtitle) affects the viewing experience. Likewise, as suggested by Duchowski (2007), it may also be useful to analyse scanpaths (eye-movement patterns) to compare how subtitles and images are viewed.

[6] Reducing the delay to less than 3 seconds is very difficult, as at least one second is necessary for the respeaker to listen and one or two more seconds are needed to speak and have the words displayed on the screen.

[7] Accessible online at: http://www.rnid.org.uk/howyoucanhelp/join_rnid/_member_community/volunteering_campaigning/volunteering_campaigning_news/tvaccessresults.htm

[8] The questionnaire can be accessed at https://rnid.wufoo.com/forms/what-are-your-views-on-tv-subtitling/

[9] A full statistical analysis of the data is still underway.

References

Boulianne, Giles, Jean-François Beaumont, Maryse Boisvert, Julie Brousseau, Patrick Cardinal, Claude Chapdelaine, Michel Comeau, Pierre Ouellet, Frédéric Osterrath and Pierre Dumouchel. 2009. 'Shadow Speaking for Real-Time Closed-Captioning of TV Broadcasts in French' in Matamala, Anna and Pilar Orero (eds.) *Listening to Subtitles: Subtitles for the Deaf and Hard of Hearing*. Bern: Peter Lang. 191-207.
Chafe, Wallace. 1980. 'The Deployment of Consciousness in the Production of a Narrative' in Wallace Chafe (ed.) *The Pear Stories: Cognitive, Cultural and Linguistic Aspects of Narrative Production*. Norwood, NJ: Ablex Publishing. 9-50.
Chafe, Wallace. 1985. 'Linguistic Differences Produced by Differences between Speaking and Writing' in Olson, David, Nancy Torrance and Angela Hildyard (eds.) *Literacy, Language, and Learning: The Nature and Consequences of Reading and Writing*. Cambridge: Cambridge University Press. 105-22.
Duchowski, Andrew T. 2007. *Eye Tracking Methodology and Practice* (2nd ed.. London: Springer Verlag.
OFCOM. 2006. *Provision of Access Services*. London: Office of Communications.
Rayner, Keith and Alexander Pollatsek. 1989. *The Psychology of Reading*. Englewood Cliffs, NJ: Prentice Hall..
Rayner, Keith, Simon P. Liversedge and Sarah J. White. 2006. 'Eye Movements When Reading Disappearing Text: The Importance of the Word to the Right of Fixation' in *Vision Research* 46: 310-323.
Rayner, Keith. 1998. 'Eye Movements in Reading and Information Processing: 20 Years of Research' in *Psychological Bulletin* 124: 372-422.
Romero-Fresco, Pablo. 2009. 'More Haste Less Speed: Edited vs Verbatim Respeaking' in *Vigo International Journal of Applied Linguistics (VIAL)* 6: 109-133.
Romero-Fresco, Pablo. 2010. 'Standing on Quicksand: Viewers' Comprehension and Reading Patterns of Respoken Subtitles for the News' in Díaz Cintas, Jorge, Anna Matamala and Joselia Neves (eds.) *New Insights into Audiovisual Translation and Media Accessibility*. Media for All 2. Amsterdam: Rodopi. 175-194.
Romero-Fresco, Pablo. 2011. *Subtitling through Speech Recognition: Respeaking*. Manchester: St Jerome.
Torres Monreal, Santiago and Rafael Santana Hernández. 2005. 'Reading Levels of Spanish Deaf Students' in *American Annals of the Deaf* 150(4): 379-387.
Uglova, Natalia and Tatiana Shevchenko. 2005. 'Not So Fast Please: Temporal Features in TV Speech'. Paper presented at the meeting of the Acoustical Society of America, Vancouver, British Columbia.
Wolverton, Gary S. and David Zola. 1983. 'The Temporal Characteristics of Visual Information Extraction during Reading' in Rayner, Keith (ed.) *Eye Movements in Reading: Perceptual and Language Processes*. New York: Academic Press. 41-52.

Applying a Punctuation-based Segmentation to a New Add-on Display Mode of Respoken Subtitles

Juan Martínez Pérez
Freelance consultant for speech recognition and respeaking (Switzerland)

Abstract
Since 1983, SWISS TXT – a subsidiary of the Swiss public broadcasting corporation (SRG SSR idée suisse) – has been providing subtitles for the deaf and hard of hearing in three of Switzerland's national languages: French, German and Italian. Speech-recognition software has been used since 2008 to subtitle live television programmes in French, German and Italian. Two issues are at stake when subtitling: (1) how to subtitle real live events such as football games, chat shows, parliamentary debates and correspondents' reports, and (2) how deaf or hard-of-hearing viewers can follow the broadcasting of these events on television. The answers to both questions lie in live subtitles. Throughout the implementation and development of live subtitling, the aim has been to improve the service. This contribution describes the challenges posed by speech-recognition systems and the technology and techniques that – in collaboration with WDR Videotext and the engineers from FAB – have been developed at SWISS TXT.[1] It focuses on ways to improve transmission speed and achieve an optimum display mode of respoken subtitles.

Keywords
display mode, live subtitling, media accessibility, respeaking, speech recognition, subtitling software

1. Introduction

Speech-recognition technology has been developed for many different applications. However, since the beginning of the new millennium it has also become a valid and economically viable solution for TV stations wishing to increase their production of subtitling in order to meet their regulatory requirements, i.e. to subtitle a certain percentage of the TV programmes that they broadcast.[2] This evolution has been made possible thanks to the constantly increasing performance of IT systems and their capacity to process huge amounts of data.

Generally speaking, there are two types of speech-recognition systems: (1) speaker-dependent and (2) speaker-independent systems. The first type is used for live subtitling by most TV stations in Europe. It could be described as a software licence that can be used only by one single user at a time and that 'learns' continually about the specific way in which a given user pronounces phonemes, the basis for recognition. In this case, 'learning' also means that the software creates a user-dependent acoustic model by storing and adapting new data constantly.

In the case of the second type of speech recognition software, the acoustic model is no longer user-specific trained, but its language model has to be adapted to the application area.[3] The implementation of this second type is not yet feasible for live subtitling, but an interesting pilot project is being conducted by speech-technology experts of the European Media Laboratory (EML), who have developed a transcription system that allows TV broadcasts to be converted into text automatically. The first results will be available by 2011.[4]

All mentions of speech recognition in the body of the article refer exclusively to Dragon NaturallySpeaking Professional version 10.1, the current speech recognition software of the first type, used for live subtitling in Switzerland. In 2008, the TV station created its first respoken subtitles using IBM's Viavoice. However, because IBM was no longer supporting or developing the software and because Dragon continued to improve their product, SWISS TXT decided to change when Dragon version 10[5] was commercialised in 2009. The main reason for doing this was that the programmers at Dragon had overcome the latency issue,[6] which affected previous versions of the software (Romero-Fresco, 2011). Also in 2009, SWISS TXT commissioned FAB – the teletext and subtitling software company – with the implementation of new tools for live subtitling. FAB Subtitler software is a Windows based program which has been used by SWISS TXT since 2000 for the preparation of subtitle files and the production of subtitles for teletext subtitling.

One of the challenges facing subtitlers producing live subtitles with speech recognition under high time pressure is how to respeak and present text on screen in a lay-out form that optimises legibility. This contribution aims to give an overview of the results obtained by an experiment conducted at Swiss TXT with a new display method, optimising the possibilities respeaking software offers, and using the above-mentioned subtitling tools, interfacing with Dragon speech recognition.

2. Challenges using speech recognition for live subtitling

The point of departure for our research was the fact that speech-recognition software has not been designed to support the type of text that is used when subtitling live, namely oral text (natural or spontaneous speech), which poses a challenge in terms of accuracy (see Section 4). All the same, speech recognition is used to subtitle live programmes or parts of programmes, when there is no time to prepare the subtitles in advance. The result of this is that they cannot be cued automatically or manually by an operator, which means that in the case of respoken subtitles, two of the main principles of 'traditional' subtitling (Díaz Cintas & Remael 2007) cannot be applied to live subtitling.

Firstly, it is not feasible to match live subtitles with the visual information because live subtitles are produced just moments before they can be transmitted. Consequently, they will always lag behind the original audio signal.[7] In other words, it becomes impossible for viewers to combine listening and viewing (e.g., lip-reading). This asynchronous mode of display leads to misunderstandings, particularly when subtitles from one TV programme item run into the next one. However, it has to be said that there is a need for perfect synergy between what viewers hear and what they see only in few TV programme formats (e.g., parliamentary debates with close-up views of the speakers' faces). This is due to the trend of using different editing approaches, that is, quick cuts, cross-fading and voice-over in TV programmes to capture viewers' attention and prevent them from switching to another channel. And this is the case for both live programmes and programmes where subtitles have been prepared in advance.

Secondly, during live subtitling it is almost impossible to pay special attention to the segmentation and display mode of the respoken text because the respeaker works under high attention demands, performing more than two intellectual activities at the same time (Arumi-Ribas & Romero-Fresco 2008). A recent study (Romero-Fresco, 2011) – which compared the scrolling word-for-word output of live subtitles nowadays prevalent in the UK and many other countries around the world with block subtitles – showed the negative effect in terms of legibility and comprehension of the usually very poor line segmentation of word-for-word subtitles. This word-for-word display mode results in chaotic reading experiences for the viewers. More important, the study showed that deaf, hard-of-hearing and hearing audiences could spend only 11 per cent of the time available on the images when watching scrolling subtitles, as opposed to 30 per cent when watching blocks.

In conclusion, the three major challenges in live subtitling through speech recognition are (1) accuracy, (2) delay and (3) display mode. In the next section, this paper first proposes a definition of both the work carried out by professionals using speech recognition for live subtitling and their mental performance. This will allow us to identify some key aspects in this complex process. Subsequently, we would like to draw attention to three studies that have been carried out on the reception of respoken subtitles and that have served as a basis for the development of a new display mode in live subtitling. Following this, we will present several approaches on how to face the challenges mentioned above from a user's and a technical point of view.

Finally, a new display mode for respoken subtitles will be put forward that seems to present numerous legibility and comprehension benefits, not only for viewers but also for the professionals who use speech recognition to subtitle live events.

3. Defining some key aspects related to live subtitling through speech recognition

With respect to the terms used to refer to the profession and the discipline, it seems that throughout Europe *respeaker* and *respeaking* are consolidated both in the industry and in academia (Arumi Ribas & Romero-Fresco 2008).[8] As far as the definition of the respeaking process itself is concerned, there have been several theoretical attempts to compare it to simultaneous interpreting. However, a detailed explanation is beyond the scope of this article. We will concentrate on Gile's Effort Model (1988), which defines four core efforts for simultaneous interpreting: (1) listening and analysis, (2) production, (3) memory, and (4) "...on top of these three core efforts comes the coordination effort, which manages attention allocation and shifts between the three ..." (Gile, 2008: 61). In addition, we will add two new aspects that are characteristic of respeaking and could therefore help define the boundary between respeaking and simultaneous interpreting: (1) a technical dimension, which applies in particular to the production effort and (2) a visual dimension, which applies to all three efforts mentioned above.

By technical dimension, we mean the highly technical environment, in which respeakers carry out their task, compared with the environment in which simultaneous conference interpreters usually operate. The respeakers' technical environment always involves dealing with speech recognition and subtitling software at once. Another fundamental difference between simultaneous interpreters and respeakers is that the latter speak to a machine – a speech-recognition engine – and not to an audience, which has specific implications for the production effort, that is, the 'ideal' dictation mode (see below). In this respect, respeaking also differs from telephone interpreting, which involves speaking to a human being more or less directly, by way of a machine. By visual dimension, we mean the flood of images (TV programme) and text (the respeaker's own subtitles) to which – in contrast to simultaneous interpreters – respeakers are exposed during their activity. Consequently, this exposure renders the process of listening and analysis, production and memory more complex still.

Respeaking could therefore be considered a highly sophisticated and multifaceted variation of shadowing.[9] Indeed, it does not exclusively consist of almost simultaneously repeating a speech word by word, using the same language,[10] but also entails intentionally decoding, recoding and producing single *idea units* (Chafe, 1980)[11] one after the other[12]. In so doing, respeakers take into account that the rates of comprehension and recall of speech are higher when the source message is not merely repeated word by word (Lambert 1993). Furthermore, a better understanding of the information that has to be respoken allows the respeaker to focus on a dictation mode that seems to lend itself better to the way in which speech-recognition engines work best in terms of accuracy, that is, not to dictate word by word but in sequences, in which the respective word order is ideally part of the language model and can therefore be included in the prediction.

In the next section, we will describe how speech-recognition software can support the various types of effort that respeakers have to make at the same time.

4. Optimising speech recognition for live subtitling

As stated in the introduction, speech-recognition software has been designed to meet a wide range of application needs. However, is has not specifically been designed to subtitle live programmes on TV. Therefore, it contains many features that not only are useless for live subtitling but also reduce the speed of dictation and affect accuracy, which poses a serious challenge with regard to the delay and quality of live respoken subtitles. Nevertheless, it has to be pointed out that speech-recognition technology has made it possible to increase subtitling significantly and to diversify the types of TV programmes subtitled, mainly real-time events. The author believes that this development does not necessarily mean that "…quality might be sacrificed for quantity …" (Luyckx et al. 2010: 7) if respeakers are properly trained to deal with the technical environment that they operate in and some basic functionality of speech-recognition engines is taken into account. The factors that need to be reckoned with are listed below.

First of all, it is of crucial importance to constrain the speech-recognition engine to interpret everything that is said as dictation and nothing as a command. In this case, 'command' refers to those commands included in the software that you do not want to use or have executed.[13] Once these functions are disabled, speech recognition will speed up dictation because the software will not waste any time distinguishing dictation from commands. Furthermore, there are some changes that can be made in the parameters of the profile configuration files to speed up dictation even more.[14]

Secondly, speech-recognition software does not automatically provide a language model that supports the type of text that is most commonly used when a TV programme has to be subtitled live, namely oral texts (e.g., word orders that contain the second person singular verb form, which are often used in chat shows). However, it does offer the possibility to adapt the language model to a certain application area, in our case to create specific language models for different TV programme categories that require live subtitling. These categories could roughly be divided into three domains: (1) news, (2) sport and (3) entertainment. Ideally, when respeakers have to subtitle football games, they will use a profile whose language model contains contextual information related to only sports, for example, respoken subtitle files from other football games characterised by their oral form and specific vocabulary. Thus, it is possible to force the engine to make its predictions based on this specific language model, and obviously to extend this approach to the other two domains mentioned above.[15]

Finally, as mentioned above, speech-recognition engines make their predictions based on data from the acoustic model and the language model, which include statistical analyses of the contexts in which the respective word forms appear. The most effective results in terms of accuracy are achieved when the engine does not have to analyse and generate words individually but in sequences, because, the prediction is based exclusively on the acoustic model – which is more likely to produce recognition errors (e.g., homophones) – if only a single word has to be predicted.

Until now, we have focused on how to optimise speech-recognition software to face the challenges of accuracy and delay from bot a user's and a technical point of view. In the next section, we would like to point out three studies carried out into the reception of respoken subtitles. These studies have served as a starting point for the development of a new display mode in live subtitling.

5. The reception of respoken subtitles

Romero-Fresco (2010) was the first scholar to suggest that the live respoken subtitles currently provided in the UK – although fast and reasonably accurate – may be subject to improvement since they appear to hinder comprehension on the part of the viewers. This is due to their scrolling display mode, in which text is added word by word on the screen and words constantly move in the subtitle (new ones coming in and old ones moving further until they disappear). This mode causes viewers to spend almost 90 per cent of their time reading the subtitles, leaving only 10 per cent for the images. In this context, Romero-Fresco's (2010: 188-189) statement is particularly interesting:

> Most viewers seemed to have problems with the absence of the word to the right of fixation[16] in scrolling, word-for-word subtitles, often casting their eyes on gaps where no word had been displayed yet, (...) a sort of quicksand that makes the viewer waste precious time in his reading process. (...) Very often, this 'quicksand effect' causes the viewer to go

back (the regressions pointed out by Rayner et al. [2006]) and fixate on previous words, thus wasting further reading time.

The conclusions of a second study, which compared the scrolling word-for-word output of subtitles and subtitles in new add-on modes (see next paragraph) corroborate the findings of the first study highlighted above.[17] When viewing word-for-word subtitles, viewers spend most of their time dwelling on the words. This may be because they are anticipating the next word and waiting for it to show up, and then rapidly switching gaze. Furthermore, results indicate that in comparison to word-for-word subtitles, the subtitles displayed in the new add-on modes seem to provide a better viewing experience since they require fewer gaze points in the subtitles and a smaller number of saccadic crossovers.[18] It follows that, when viewing subtitles displayed in new add-on modes, viewers can spend more time on the image itself.

A third study was carried out to evaluate three different display modes of respoken subtitles in an attempt to determine whether punctuation-based text segmentation (see next section) affects the viewing experience as a whole or influences comprehension.[19] The three display modes were the following:

(1) add-on phrase: phrases (or lines) showed up one by one;
(2) add-on sentence: sentences (or blocks) showed up one by one;
(3) block with no segmentation: the area for subtitles was filled with the maximum amount of text regardless of any semantic or grammatical segmentation.

The best results in terms of reception and comprehension were obtained with respoken subtitles displayed in add-on sentence mode. This mode caused the smallest number of fixations in the subtitle area. In turn, this allowed participants to spend most of their time on the image and to retain the largest amounts of textual and visual information.

In the next two sections, we will describe how subtitling software can support the different types of effort that respeakers have to make at the same time, and give an overview of the new tools for live subtitling that support interfacing to speech recognition in the FAB Subtitler software, particularly those tools focused on improving transmission speed and achieving the display mode of live respoken subtitles mentioned above.

6. Optimising subtitling software for live subtitling through speech recognition

In order to allow the respeaker to concentrate exclusively on dictation, for example, not having to pay special attention to the segmentation and display mode of the respoken text, a new line is automatically inserted (see next section) after the dictation of punctuation marks. The purpose of this is to help solve the problems with the usually poor line segmentation of respoken subtitles. Furthermore, the add-on sentence mode facilitates correction – be it on the part of the respeaker (self-correction) or someone else (downstream correction) – given that errors[20] are easier to spot in blocks than in scrolling words.[21]

Subtitles displayed *with* punctuation-based segmentation:

> In the first instance,
> following British practice,

> collective decision-making applies
> only to cabinet members.

Subtitles displayed *without* punctuation-based segmentation:

> In the first instance, following
> British practice, collective

> decision-making applies only to
> cabinet members.

The first two subtitles displayed *with* punctuation-based segmentation are easier to read than the second two subtitles *without* punctuation-based segmentation. The reason is that the information in the first two subtitles is structured in a way that makes it simpler to identify the single idea units. In the second two subtitles, we have poor line segmentation, which means that the viewers' eyes have to jump from "following" to "British practice" or to wait after "collective" for "decision making" to appear to comprehend these specific idea units.

Moreover, the new speech interface used at Swiss TXT allows a choice between two transmission modes for live subtitling: (1) automatic mode or (2) manual mode. In the automatic mode, all the recognised text is sent to the output and is transmitted automatically either when the maximum number of characters in a row (or the maximum number of defined lines) has been filled or when punctuation marks have been dictated (see below). Recognition errors can be corrected only after they are displayed on air. Correction is carried out using a functionality of the speech interface that allows retracting and placement of texts which contain errors in an editor, where it can be corrected and re-transmitted both manually and by vocal command. By contrast, in the manual transmission mode, the recognised text is first displayed in an editor, where it can be modified, corrected and subsequently transmitted manually or automatically by dictating punctuation marks (see below).

The speech interface supports special text commands such as {}[22], {NL}[23] and {1} to {8}.[24] It is possible to combine and link these commands to the dictation of punctuation marks, for example, to define that working both in the automatic and the manual mode, recognised text is automatically released on screen when a full stop or comma is dictated or a new line break is inserted. In the automatic mode, the main advantage of the command is that recognised text can be sent to the output even if the maximum number of characters in a row (or the maximum number of defined lines) has not yet been filled, which improves transmission speed as much as possible. In the manual mode, recognised text can be read, modified and corrected in case of errors, before dictating "full stop" or "comma". The main advantage of the command is that in both transmission modes a new line is inserted when dictating "full stop" or "comma". In so doing, the problems with the usually very poor line segmentation of live respoken subtitles are partially solved.

The following speech-interface settings (Figure 1) allow the respeaker to concentrate exclusively on dictation, that is, the respeaker does not have to devote any attention to the display mode of the respoken text or to the duration of subtitles.

With regard to the technical potential of the software to automate the output of respoken text as much as possible, we would like to highlight the possibilities for defining a number of actions by default (in milliseconds):

(1) how long to wait before sending an incomplete subtitle (when there is a pause in dictation);
(2) how long the subtitle stays on the screen (when there is a pause in dictation);
(3) how long the minimum subtitle duration or line duration must be to guarantee readability (when there is no pause in dictation).

Juan Martínez Pérez

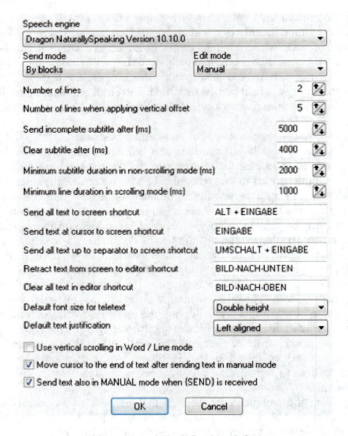

Figure 1. Actions defined by default.

7. Conclusion

Several studies have suggested that the word-by-word scrolling mode – nowadays prevalent in the UK and many other countries – may be subject to improvement since it seems to hinder comprehension on the part of viewers. Theresore, SWISS TXT started to investigate whether it was possible or reasonable to avoid this scrolling mode and to set its sights on an add-on mode, in which text appears more regularly, sentence-by-sentence on the screen (and does not move in spurts) and is additionally segmented by punctuation marks to achieve better line segmentation. In this context, the work carried out with engineers from FAB was concentrated on developing new tools for live subtitling, particularly those tools that focus on supporting the multiple operations that respeakers have to accomplish simultaneously. The ultimate aim was to improve transmission speed and to achieve an optimum display mode of respoken subtitles. As a consequence, SWISS TXT has launched a new display mode in live subtitling in an attempt to facilitate dictation for the respeaker and – at the same time – maximise readability for the viewers.

This new approach will provide a perspective for further developments and research.[25] Special importance is likely to be attached to theoretical, practical and technical approaches which take into account the significance of processing visual information, for example, constant switching between reading and scene watching, which is a result of the asynchronous mode of display of live subtitles. Another starting point could be the reduction in the number of defined characters per line to reduce the number of fixations per line in the subtitles.

The author believes that much remains to be done to define the boundary between traditional and live subtitling better. The two ways in which subtitles are created are so different that the main principles for 'traditional' subtitling cannot be applied to live subtitling, which is completely new ground.

---

[1] FAB (Teletext and Subtitling Systems): www.fab-online.com; a FAB subtitling software demo version is available on line at: www.fab-online.com/updates.htm

[2] At the time of writing this contribution, Swiss legislation on radio and television programming requires that 33% of the programmes on the eight television channels offered by the Swiss public broadcasting corporation (SRG SSR idée suisse) be subtitled by the end of 2010.

[3] Speech-recognition engines make their predictions based on data from the acoustic model and the language model including statistical analyses of the context in which the respective word forms appear.

[4] www.eml-development.de/deutsch/presse/presseberichte.php?we_objectID=371

[5] At the time of writing this contribution, Dragon version 11 was launched. This version will be tested in the coming months.

[6] A pause in dictation is required to force the speech-recognition engine to finish its calculations based on data from the acoustic modem and the language model in order to edit text and send it to the screen immediately with the shortest delay possible.

[7] A recent report (Rander & Looms 2010: 22) in Europe shows that the latency issue is perceived by deaf and hard of hearing viewers as the main disadvantage of live subtitles. From a technical point of view, it could be useful to delay the video and audio signal to resynchronise both of them with the live subtitles. However, this would have a number of editorial and legal implications for broadcasters of live programmes. This report is part of the DTV4ALL project.

[8] With the exception of Spain, where the terms *rehablador* for *respeaker* and *rehablado* for *respeaking* have become established (Romero-Fresco 2009 a).

[9] Shadowing is a technique that has been used in the initial phases of simultaneous interpreting training and that consists of simultaneously repeating a speech in the same language, using the same words (see, for example, Arumí Ribas & Romero-Fresco, 2008, for a detailed discussion).

[10] Some exceptions are BBC Wales, SF1, SF2 and SF info (3 TV channels in the German speaking part of Switzerland). At BBC Wales, live programmes are respoken from Welsh into English. At the other three, respeakers often have to translate from Swiss German into standard German.

[11] Chafe (1985: 106) defines the spurts in which speech is often produced as "units of intonational and semantic closure", which contain one verbal phrase along with whatever noun phrases, prepositional phrases, adverbs, and so on are appropriate, and are about seven words long and take about two seconds to produce (taken from Arumí Ribas & Romero-Fresco, 2008).

[12] The high speech rate of source text often makes it impossible for respeakers to follow the original soundtrack literally. This means that they have to edit the original soundtrack, thus rephrasing it rather than repeating it. (…) This explains why the most common type of live subtitling as far as editing policy is concerned is near-verbatim subtitling (taken from Romero-Fresco, forthcoming a).

[13] Some of these commands are 'Select', 'Correct', 'Spell', 'Mouse motion', 'Web search', 'Desktop search', 'Email and Calendar', 'Cut', 'Delete', 'Copy' or 'Natural Language'.

[14] https://www.knowbrainer.com/pubforum/index.cfm?page=viewForumTopic&topicId=6378&listFull

[15] Good results in terms of accuracy were also obtained when subtitling the weather forecast, a live programme with highly reduced and specific vocabulary. The language model used for the respeaking of this programme contained only respoken subtitles from previous weather forecast programmes.

[16] The visual information necessary for reading is obtained during pauses, known as fixations, which typically last about 200–250 ms (Liversedge & Findlay 2000). As shown in Rayner (1998), the overall perceptual span – the area from which useful information is obtained during a

fixation in reading – extends from the beginning of the fixated word to 14 or 15 characters to the right of fixation. The jumps between fixations are known as saccades, which take as little as 100ms and are the fastest movements that human beings are capable of making (Rayner & Pollatsek 1989). During saccades, vision is suppressed and no useful information is obtained (Wolverton & Zola 1983). This is known as saccadic suppression (taken from Romero-Fresco 2009).

[17] At the time of writing this contribution, a paper entitled 'Evaluating the Effects of Text Chunking on Subtitling: A Quantitative and Qualitative Examination' (Rajendran, Duchowski, Martínez & Romero-Fresco) was submitted to the ACM CHI Conference on Human Factors in Computing Systems (7–12 May 2011, Vancouver).

[18] A Tobii ET-1750 eye tracker was used for real-time gaze coordinate measurement. A saccadic crossover was reported when a gaze point in the subtitles was immediately followed by a gaze point in the image, or vice versa.

[19] The study involved 15 deaf and 24 hard of hearing participants from 4 different cities in the German speaking part of Switzerland. Partial results were presented at the 8th International Languages & The Media Conference (6–8 October 2010, Berlin) as part of the presentation 'The Reception of a New Display Mode in Live Subtitling' (Martínez, Romero-Fresco & Linder). The detailed results are available on line at: www.untertitelung.ch

[20] Recognition errors often occur in the middle of respoken sequences. After manual corrections it is not necessary to move the cursor to the end of the editor to continue dictating or to launch the manually corrected text on screen, because respoken text is always appended to the end of the editor. Thus, respeakers do not lose precious time by having to move the cursor.

[21] Two special modes for live subtitling are available which allow dictating, correcting and transmitting subtitles on one or two workstations: an operator on (1) the same workstation or (2) a second workstation can correct the respoken subtitles before transmitting them. Of course, this will increase the delay. Nevertheless, both modes could be used for programmes for which subtitles can be prepared in advance. Tests are being carried out on this.

[22] This command displays text up to the command even if the line or block is not full.

[23] This command inserts a new line break, displaying all new text in a new line.

[24] Colour codes; inserts colours as defined in the configuration.

[25] At the time of writing this contribution, a study is being carried out to evaluate subtitles constructed with different positioning methods to determine whether different text positioning influence comprehension or affect viewing experience as a whole. The first results will be available in 2011 on line at: www.untertitelung.ch

References

Arumi Ribas, Marta & Pablo Romero-Fresco. 2008. 'A Practical Proposal for the Training of Respeakers' in *The Journal of Specialised Translation* 10: 106-127.

Chafe, Wallace. 1980. 'The Deployment of Consciousness in the Production of a Narrative' in Wallace Chafe (ed) *The Pear Stories: Cognitive, Cultural and Linguistic Aspects of Narrative Production*. Norwood, NJ: Ablex Publishing. 9-50.
Díaz Cintas, Jorge & Aline Remael. 2007. *Audiovisual Translation: Subtitling*. Manchester: St. Jerome Publishing.
Gile, Daniel. 1988. Le Partage de l'Attention et le Modèle d'Effforts en Interprétation Simultanée in *The Interpreter's Newsletter* 1: 27-33.
Gile, Daniel. 2008. Local Cognitive Load in Simultaneous Interpreting and its Implications for Empirical Research in *Forum* 6(2): 59-77.
Kriouille, Abdelaziz, Jean-Francois Mari & Jean-Paul Haton. (1990). Some improvements in speech recognition algorithms based on HMM. In *Acoustic, Speech, and Signal Processing, 1990. ICASSP-90 1990:* 545-548 vol. 1.
Lambert, Sylvie. 1993. The Effect of Ear of Information Reception on the Proficiency of Simultaneous Interpretation in *The Interpreters Newsletter* 5: 22-34.
Liversedge, Simon P. & John M. Findlay. 2000. Saccadic eye movements and cognition in *Trends in Cognitive Science* 4: 6-14.
Luyckx, Bieke & Tijs Delbeke, Luuk Van Waes, Mariëlle Leijten & Aline Remael. 2010. Live Subtitling with Speech Recognition: Causes and Consequences of Text Reduction. Antwerpen: artesis VT working papers. Online at http://www.artesis.be/vertalertolk/upload/docs/onderzoek/Artesis_VT_working_paper_2010-1_Luyckx_et_alii.pdf
Rander, Anni & Peter Olaf Looms. 2010. DR Mature Services Evaluation Report. Online at http://dea.brunel.ac.uk/dtv4all/ICT-PSP-224994-D25.pdf (consulted 10.05.2010).
Rayner, Keith. 1998. Eye Movements in Reading and Information Processing: 20 Years of Research in *Psychological Bulletin* 124: 372-422.
Rayner, Keith and Alexander Pollatsek. 1989. *The Psychology of Reading*. Englewood Cliffs, NJ: Prentice Hall.
Rayner, Keith, Simon P. Liversedge & Sarah J. White. 2006. Eye Movements When Reading Disappearing Text: The Importance of the Word to the Right of Fixation in *Vision Research* 46: 310-323.
Romero-Fresco, Pablo. 2009. La Subtitulación Rehablada: Palabras Que No Se Lleva el Viento. In Álvaro Pérez-Ugena & Ricardo Vizcaíno-Laorga (eds.) *ULISES: Hacia el desarrollo de tecnologías comunicativas para la igualdad de oportunidades*. Madrid: Observatorio de las Realidades Sociales y de la Comunicación. 49-73.
Romero-Fresco, Pablo. 2010. 'Standing on Quicksand: Viewers' Comprehension and Reading Patterns of Respoken Subtitles for the News' in Díaz Cintas, Jorge, Anna Matamala and Joselia Neves (eds) *New Insights into Audiovisual Translation and Media Accessibility*. Media for All 2. Amsterdam: Rodopi. 175-194.
Romero-Fresco, Pablo. 2011. *Subtitling through Speech Recognition: Respeaking*. Manchester: St Jerome.
Slimane, Mohamed, Gilles Venturini, Jean Pierre Asselin de Beauville, Thierry Brouard & A. Brandeau. 1996. Optimizing Hidden Markov Models with a Genetic Algorithm in *Artificial Evolution: Lecture Notes in Computer Science* 1063: 384-396.
Wolverton, Gary S. & David Zola. 1983. 'The Temporal Characteristics of Visual Information Extraction during Reading' in Keith Rayner (ed.) *Eye Movements in Reading: Perceptual and Language Processes*. New York: Academic Press. 41-52.

Experimenting with Characters: An Empirical Approach to the Audio Description of Fictional Characters[1]

Nazaret Fresno
Transmedia Catalonia
CAIAC
Universitat Autònoma de Barcelona

Abstract

One of the most challenging aspects of audiovisual translation (AVT) is to make audiovisual media accessible to all. In achieving this aim, audio description (AD) plays an essential role, and comprehensive research in this area should be carried out. Currently, most AD research focuses largely on relevance, that is, the question that deals with what should be featured in the audio description. However, there are other important aspects still to be covered. This contribution presents a cognitive approach to the AD of fictional characters in films. In order to shed some light on the way in which we understand characters, the results of a simple empirical experiment based on viewers' recall will be presented. Finally, the possibility of applying such a perspective to AD will be discussed.

Keywords

audio description, characters, media accessibility, narratology, relevance

1. Introduction

Traditionally, characters in fiction have been defined as agents. Aristotle (trans. 1979) already considered the *pratton* (the agent, the one who performs actions) an essential element of the drama, while his *ethos* (the character, some additional qualities) played a much less important role in narrative.

Such an approach has obvious similarities with classifications and descriptions within formalism and structuralism. According to both schools of thought, characters exist only because actions do since their only function is to perform actions. As a result, it is not necessary to explore the characters themselves. The only feature that needs to be explored is what the characters do. Propp (1928) classifies characters in tales according to their spheres of action and divides them into seven categories: (1) the villain, (2) the donor, (3) the helper, (4) the sought-for-person, (5) the father, (6) the dispatcher, (7) the hero and the false hero. A similar generic distinction was proposed by Greimas (1976), who divides the characters into *actants* and *acteurs*. The *actants* consists of six general categories common to all types of narrative: (1) the sender, (2) the object, (3) the receiver, (4) the helper, (5) the subject and (6) the opponent. The *acteurs* are the specific representations that those models take in a certain literary work. Following on from this, the character is – for both Propp and Greimas – the main element in the cause and effect of storytelling.

From a more comprehensive position, Todorov (1977) supports Propp's approach though he distinguishes between apsychological and psychological narratives. For him, characters are often subordinate to the action, though some literary works may be character-centred. The psychological traits of characters certainly cause actions but they are also the effect of actions. From this perspective, characters become complex entities. As Todorov himself describes: "[A] character is a potential story that is the story of his life. Every new character signifies a new plot. We are in the realm of narrative-men" (Todorov 1977: 70).

Another interesting concept by Chatman (1978: 119) considers characters themselves to be worthy of study since "a viable theory of characters should preserve openness and treat characters as autonomous beings, not as mere plot functions". For Chatman, fictional characters boast a number of personality traits that lead them to behave in certain ways. It is their psychology that triggers their actions. Consequently, the psychology should be viewed as an essential aspect when analysing fictional characters.

The framework developed in the field of literature served to lay some of the foundations of character analysis in film studies. Balázs (1970) – more concerned with the viewer's attitude towards characters than with their construction – suggested a new dimension to film characters not discussed for characters in books, theatre or in any other form of art. According to Balázs, audiences experience films from the inside, and while they are in front of the screen, they undergo a psychological process through which they give up being themselves to become the characters. This is what Balázs calls *identification*, which he discusses as follows:

> We walk amid crowds, ride, fly or fall with the hero and if one character looks into the other's eyes, he looks into our eyes from the screen, for our eyes are in the camera and become identical with the gaze of characters. They see with our eyes. (Balázs 1970: 48)

When talking about classical Hollywood cinema, Bordwell (1990) states that characters have been traditionally understood as causal agents. However, he points out, "the narrative invariably centres on personal psychological causes: decisions, choices, and traits of character" (Bordwell 1990: 70).

All of these theories suggest the importance that characters have had in literature and cinema. Even if they were simply created as mere instruments to perform actions, some attributes must be assigned to them. In turn, this creates a deeper or narrower psychological characterisation. In this sense, they become central to an understanding of literary and filmic narrative.

2. Characters in AD

Several guidelines and similar studies have been drafted in different countries as general explanations of what AD should be like (Benecke 2004, Ofcom 2006, Orero 2007, Puigdomènech 2007, Remael 2005, Snyder 2006, UNE 153020 2007). Vercauteren (2007) has compared the existing guidelines and has noted the need for a standardised European protocol that unifies criteria. As a first step towards this protocol – and looking in particular to characters – he has provided interesting suggestions that could help harmonise one of the controversial issues when drafting an AD: the question that deals with when to mention characters' names. However, after three years no agreement has been reached and – as Orero (forthcoming a) points out – a harmonised European guideline is still not in the pipeline. Orero also states that since the existing guidelines are based on examples rather than on deep reflection, some of them are descriptive and vague, and they include truisms or even contradictions. The treatment of characters is no exception. Even though they are always included in the list of key elements for audio description, usually only general indications of how to describe them are provided.

The essential role of characters in AD has also been noted in other studies, such as McGonigle's (2007) and Palomo's (2008) unpublished MA dissertations, which focus on ADs of children's films. As McGongile points out:

> It is important in the education, socialisation and development of children for them to be able to build clear images of people, and so effective description of the main characters of a film would be very useful for the visually-impaired child. (McGonigle 2007: 25)

Ballester (2007), too, considers characters as central elements of the AD script. Through the analysis of the 1999 film *Todo sobre mi madre (All about my mother)* by Almodóvar, the author comes to interesting conclusions about how the description of aspects not mentioned in the guidelines – such as the colours or the objects decorating the characters' houses – can also provide valuable information about the way characters are and behave.

Adopting a linguistic perspective, Mascarenhas (2009) has recently analysed how the discursive strategies used in the AD of the 2006 film *Little Miss Sunshine* (Dayton) influence the construction of characters in the film. Finally, Orero (forthcoming b) has conducted a basic study of the presentation of characters in the 2001 film *Monsters, Inc.* (Docter). In her study, Orero draws attention to a random strategy used for the introduction of characters during the opening credits of the film.

Though some academic attention has been paid to the characters in AD, no systematic approach to their analysis has been observed. What seems clear is that guidelines offer a general theoretical framework that needs to be adapted to take into account the genre, the public, the narrative structure and the time restrictions of each film. This means that audio describers will necessarily have to decide which information that they wish to include in their AD, usually basing their decision on relevancy criteria. However, determining what is and what is not relevant for certain aspects of characters is not always clear and – in some cases – might end up being a subjective and personal decision. As mentioned in Section 1, the actions that characters perform are central to their construction, and it is normally easy to assess their relevancy to the plot. In contrast, when it comes to formal aspects such as physical appearance, it becomes difficult to determine which features or elements are more relevant and should therefore be included in the AD. When time is scarce, what to audio describe and what to omit ends up being a personal decision based on what the audio describer believes to be a character's most significant traits. A consequence of this is that blind and visually impaired (BVI) users may create different mental images of fictional characters depending on the features mentioned in the AD. Furthermore, those mental projections may vary in terms of accuracy, and it would be interesting to explore which traits ADs should include to help users imagine characters as precisely as possible.

The experiment described is an attempt to address an issue pointed out by Orero (forthcoming b). According to Orero, scientific studies must be undertaken to understand how to create audio descriptions which facilitate optimum reception. The purpose of the experiment presented in this contribution was to find out – by means of an empirical preliminary test – which features are best recalled by viewers, that is, which traits help them draw a mental image of fictional characters. When these have been identified, further research will be needed to assess whether their inclusion in AD contributes to the creation of more accurate mental images by BVI users.

3. The experiment

The aim of the research was to shed light on the ways in which fictional characters are understood and remembered by the audience. A simple empirical experiment was carried out. A small group of viewers was asked to watch a film fragment and to provide feedback relating to what they remembered about the characters.

3.1. Experimental design

The experimental design included three stages: (1) the choice of the test film, (2) the design of the evaluation materials and (3) the selection of the participants.

In the first phase, Burton's 2005 film *Charlie and the Chocolate Factory* was chosen as the test film because the characters in the film conform with well-known stereotypes that viewers can recognise since the film is based on the 1973 children's book by Roald Dahl with the same title. As Burton (2006) puts it, all the children appearing in the film – except for Charlie Bucket – were defined in a simple, fable manner. In addition to this simplicity, their physical and behavioural traits are emphasised throughout the film, and other features (such as their clothes) also contribute to outlining their personalities.

In the film, Willy Wonka – the eccentric owner of the most magnificent sweets factory in the world – launches a contest to find an heir to his empire of sweets. Five children are lucky enough to find the precious golden tickets that allow them to enter the world of fantasy and amusement that is Wonka's factory. Wonka's intention is to put the children to the test throughout their visit in an attempt to select one of them. However, the day comes to a close with a lesson for the chocolatier too: in order to find his heir, he will have to face the ghosts of his past.

A self-contained eight-minute excerpt was chosen for the experiment because it offered a clear portrait of the four children visiting the factory: (1) Augustus Gloop, (2) Veruca Salt, (3) Violet Beauregarde and (4) Mike Teavee (in order of appearance in the film). In the clip, the children have found Wonka's golden tickets and are interviewed by journalists on television. The four children are introduced to the viewer for the first time. Each character is on screen for around two minutes and both their physical appearance and behaviour are well illustrated through close-up shots and detailed filming of their actions. Two screen shots for each of the four characters have been included at the end of this section (Figures 1–8).

Several film critics have described the children as follows: Charlie Bucket, a good-hearted boy from a poor family living in the shadows of Wonka's factory (Levy 2005). Augustus Gloop, a gluttonous boy who thinks of nothing but stuffing sweets into his mouth all day (Scott 2005). Veruca Salt, a spoiled girl who throws fits if her father does not buy her everything she desires (Levy 2005). Violet Beauregarde, an obsessive gum chewer and a ruthlessly competitive power-pixie with a matching mum (Scott 2005). And Mike Teavee, a young boy with antisocial tendencies fed by video games (Scott 2005).

Even though the children are based on common stereotypes, the fact that they are filmed under Burton's direction gives them a special touch, which somehow makes them different. Burton's films have a personal style based on a gloomy fantasy world, in which Gothic imagery surrounds misfit characters that do not belong to the reality around them. As Solaz (1999) puts it:

> Sus héroes, perpetuamente ingenuos e infantiles, están psicológicamente asustados, son malinterpretados por la sociedad y presentan un comportamiento involuntariamente perturbador. Son figuras que trastornan la sociedad y la moralidad convencional. (Solaz 1999: 68)[2]

The exile faced by Burton's characters – sometimes geographical but always behavioural – is a trait common to all of his stories. This trait has usually been considered a reflection of the director's own experience. Some authors who have studied Burton's life and filmography – such as Hanke (1999) or Merschmann (2000) – highlight the existence of autobiographical elements and even alter egos in most of his films. In fact, both Hanke and Merschmann stress the fact that Burton does not create to explore reality, but to understand his own inner world – his biographical project, as Merschmann calls it. The director himself (2006) has contributed to this idea as follows:

> I've always felt close to all the characters in my films. I've always felt I *had* to be, because when you're doing something you're putting your life into it, and there has to be aspects to all the characters that are either a part of you, or something you can relate to, or something that is symbolic of something inside you. (Burton 2006: 44)

Figures 1 to 8 show the characters and the different physical traits tested in the experiment.

Experimenting with characters

Figures 1 (left) and 2 (right). Augustus Gloop's close-up shot (left) and characterisation (right).

Figures 3 (left) and 4 (right). Veruca Salt's close-up shot (left) and characterisation (right).

Figures 5 (left) and 6 (right). Violet Beauregarde's close-up shot (left) and characterisation (right).

Figures 7 (left) and 8 (right). Mike Teavee's close-up shot (left) and characterisation (right).

The second stage of the experimental design consisted of the creation of the evaluation materials. In order to gather data on the recall of the test group, a questionnaire was drafted. The formulation of the questions and their arrangement in the questionnaire were designed following Jackson's (2009) and Dillman's (1978) approaches respectively, that is, making sure that questions were as short and precise as possible to avoid misinterpretations and that questions were not randomised but grouped into clear subsets. The questionnaire is enclosed in the appendix. The answering time was set to a maximum of 20 minutes for all the open questions and 10 minutes for all the closed ones.

The last stage of the experimental design consisted of the selection of the participants. Twelve adult subjects (five men and seven women) – all between twenty and fifty-three years old – were selected as participants for the experiment. They had all completed intermediate or higher education and none of them had seen the film or read the book on which the film is based.

3.2. Experiment procedure

The experimental procedure comprised two stages: (1) a pilot test and the (2) experiment proper. In order to ensure that the questionnaire was clear to the participants and that the time set to answer the questions was adequate, two male participants from the sample took part in a pilot test. Their answers revealed that one of the open questions needed to be more explicit since the original 'Do you remember any other aspect?' was defined as 'unclear' by the two participants. The question was therefore changed to 'Do you remember any other aspects concerning the characterisation of the character?' The time alotted to answering the questions proved to be sufficient.

After the pilot test, the final tests were carried out in ten days and were spread over three weeks. All of the participants – the ten people in the test group who had not taken the pilot test – had correct or corrected vision, and all of the participants completed the experiment in the same room. Before watching the clip, participants were informed that they would be seeing an eight-minute excerpt from the film *Charlie and the Chocolate Factory* only once, after which they would be asked to answer some questions. For the purposes of comprehension, the clip was contextualised by means of a short summary of what had happened previously in the film. After watching the clip each participant was given a hard copy of the questionnaire with questions about the four characters. Before filling out the questionnaire, the participants were given the following instructions:

(1) Please answer the questions in the same order in which they appear in the questionnaire.
(2) Do not read one question until you have finished answering the previous one.
(3) Please complete the answers to the first four questions by writing in the boxes.
(4) For the last two questions, please tick the answers you consider to be correct.
(5) Do not add more information to this part.
(6) The time to complete the questionnaire is 30 minutes.

All of the participants watched the clip and completed the questionnaire as requested.

3.3 Data analysis

The descriptive data analysis was carried out on the raw data gathered from the questionnaires. All of the open questions focused on what the participants remembered about the behaviour, the physical description and the characterisation of the characters. The answers to the open questions were analysed by collecting all the nouns, adjectives, adverbs and the linguistic expressions with which the participants defined each character. These data were classified for every character according to the following categories:

- personality traits (different for each character).
- physical traits:
    - hair: style, length and colour
    - weight
    - eyes: glasses and colour of the eyes
- characterisation:
    - clothes

The second part of the questionnaire consisted of several multiple-choice questions aimed at measuring recall with respect to specific aspects of the characters' appearance and clothing. The answers to these questions were considered 'true' if the answers were correct and 'false' if the answers were wrong or participants had ticked the option 'I don't know'.

3.4. Results

The open part of the questionnaire included four questions per character. Each of the questions was answered by 10 participants, which would have made a total data set of 40 answers per character for any analyses to be carried out. However, one of the participants mistook Mike Teavee for Charlie Bucket, who was not studied in the experiment. Therefore, the results of the open questions will not be calculated out of a maximum of 40 answers but out of a maximum of 39 answers.

3.4.1. Open questions

(a) Describe the character
The data gathered from the replies to the general question 'Describe the character' were divided into four categories:

(1) information about personality traits;
(2) information about nationality;
(3) information about physical traits;
(4) information about the character's economic status.

The results for the open question 'Describe the character' may be found in Table 1.

Table 1. Results open question 'Describe the character'

Category	Score (max. 39)
personality traits	39 (100%)
nationality	8 (20.51%)
physical traits	5 (12.82%)
economic status	7 (17.94%)

With respect to personality traits, the results showed that all participants mentioned at least the main personality trait for each character (39/39). As far as the characters' nationalities were concerned, two participants mentioned the nationalities of all of the characters (8/39). Half of the participants included also physical traits in their descriptions. However, this was the case for only one character (i.e., Augustus Gloop) (5/39). The characters' economic status was included in 7/39 answers. However, most of those answers (4/7) referred to Veruca Salt since all of the participants mentioned her wealth in their description of the spoiled girl.

(b) What does the character look like?
In answering the question 'What does the character look like?' participants referred to the characters' weight, hair, eyes, height and skin. The characters' weight was the trait which was mentioned the most. References to the characters' weight were included in 22 of the 39 answers. However, all of the participants referred to Augustus Gloop as 'overweight', which means that 10 out of the 22 answers corresponded to the description of only one character. For the other three characters, references to weight were found in 12 out of 29 answers.

The references to the characters hair were were classified according to three subcategories: (1) hair colour, (2) hair type and (3) hair length. Information about the hair appeared in 19 of the 39 references to hair. Of those 19 references only 2 did not refer to hair colour but rather to hair type or to hair length. Of the remaining 17 references to hair, 10 references pertained only to hair colour while 7 references pertained to hair colour *and* hair length or to hair colour *and* hair type.

With respect to the characters' eyes, 13 references were found. Of the 13 references to eyes, 12 included details about eye colour and 1details about eye size. Of the 12 references to eye colour 9 references contained an exact colour while 3 references contained generic expressions such as 'light eyes' or 'dark eyes'.

With respect to the characters' height and skin, information about height and skin was less frequently recalled. 9 references to the characters' height were found and 5 to the characters' skin.

Table 2. Results open question 'What does the character look like?'

Category	Score (max. 39)	
weight[1]	22	(56.41%)
hair	19	(48.71%)
length or style	2	(10.52%)
colour	10	(52.64%)
colour and length	4	(21.05%)
colour and style	3	(15.79%)
eyes	13	(33.33%)
colour	12	(92.30%)
size	1	(7.70%)
height	9	(23.07%)
skin	5	(12.82%)

Note 1. This information refers mostly to Augustus Gloop. The results for him were 10/10 (100%), whereas for the rest of the characters the results were 11/29 (37.93%)

(c) Do you remember any other aspects concerning the characterisation of the character?

The third question provided answers relating to the characters' actions and clothing. 17/39 descriptions mentioned only the clothes, 5/39 included information only about the actions and 4/39 referred to both the clothing and the behaviour of characters. From the descriptions mentioning the clothes (21/39), 9 described the type of clothing, 5 included information on the type and the colour, 1 mentioned only the colour ("pink clothes"), 1 included information on the type of clothes and the pattern, and 5 more provided general unspecific descriptions, such as "dressed in casual clothes", "dressed like her mother" or "dressed in normal clothes".

Table 3. Results open question 'Do you remember any other aspects concerning the characterisation of the character?'

Category	Score (max. 39)	
actions	9	(23.07%)
clothing	21	(53.84%)
type	9	(42.86%)
colour	1	(4.76%)
type and colour	5	(23.81%)
type and pattern	1	(4.76%)
general descriptions	5	(23.81%)

(d) Define the characters' behaviour
The last open question was included to shed light on the participants' perception of characters. Augustus Gloop was described as "greedy" (10/10 participants) whereas Veruca Salt was described as "spoiled" (10/10 participants); Violet Beauregarde was defined as "arrogant" and/or "competitive" (10/10 participants), and Mike Teavee was considered to be a "know-it-all" and/or "hooked on videogames" (9/10 participants). All these descriptions matched the information inferred from the film, so no comprehension problem had taken place. Therefore, the data provided by all participants was taken into account for the analysis.

3.4.2. Closed questions
The two multiple choice questions in the questionnaire referred to the physical description of the four characters as well as to their clothing. The results are discussed below.

Physical description:
Participants were asked about the eyes (colour and glasses), hair (colour, type and length), height, weight, shape of the face and nose of each character. The following results were obtained:

Eyes:
-Colour: participants had to tick the correct answer among three colours. The option "I don't know" was also available.

In total, 21/39 answers were right, 7/39 answers read "I don't know" and 11/39 were wrong. From those 11/39, only 3 mentioned colours which looked similar to the actual eyes of the character (for instance, blue instead of green or vice-versa), while the rest showed no resemblance whatsoever (the answer selected was a dark colour when the character had light eyes or vice-versa).

-Glasses: participants were asked if the characters wore glasses or not. They could choose between "yes", "no" or "I don't remember".

As a result, 37/39 answers were right, 1/39 showed "I don't' know" and 1/39 was incorrect. In this case, the participant said that Mike Teavee wore glasses when in fact he did not.

Hair:
-Colour: Participants could choose between three colours. The "I don't know" option was also available.

29/39 answers were correct. Only 2/39 answers read "I don't know", whereas 8/39 were mistaken. Of the 8/39, 3 answers showed colours similar to the real ones, while the other 5 were dissimilar (dark instead of light, etc.).

-Style: Participants could choose between three styles of hair. The "I don't know" option was also available.
35/39 descriptions matched the style of hair that characters showed. The remaining 4/39 had the "I don't know" option ticked.

-Length: Participants could choose between three possible lengths. The "I don't know" option was also available.
32/39 answers were right, 3/39 answers were wrong and 4/39 chose "I don't know".

Height:
Participants could choose between "tall", "medium", "short" and "I don't know".
-Augustus Gloop was defined as "tall" by 4/10 participants, "medium" by 4/10 and "short" by 1/10 viewers. 1/10 chose "I don't know".
-Veruca Salt was defined as "medium" by 4/10 participants, "short" by 5/10 participants and 1/10 participants did not know.
-Violet Beauregarde was "tall" for 2/10 participants, "medium" for 7/10 participants and "short" for 1/10 participants.
-Mike Teavee was thought to be "tall" by 1/9 participants, "medium" by 5/9 participants, "short" by 1/9 participants and 2 more participants chose "I don't know".

Weight:
Participants could choose between "overweight", "medium", "thin" and "I don't know".
-Augustus Gloop was defined as "overweight" by all participants (10/10).
-Veruca Salt was defined as "thin" by all participants (10/10).
-Violet Beauregarde was "medium" for 4/10 participants and "thin" for 6/10 viewers.
-Mike Teavee was thought to be "medium" by 5/9 participants, "thin" by 3/9 participants and 1 participant chose "I don't know".

Shape of the face:
Participants could choose between "round", "normal", "elongated" and "I don't know".
-Augustus Gloop had a "round" face according to 9/10 participants. The other one did not know.

-3/10 participants considered Veruca Salt's face to be "round", 3/10 considered it "normal", 2/10 thought it was "elongated" and 2/10 did not know.
-Violet Beauregarde was believed to have a "round" face by 4/10 viewers, 4/10 thought she had a "normal" face and 1/10 said it was "elongated". 1/10 did not know.
-Mike Teavee's face was defined as "round" by 3/9 participants, "normal" by 3/9 participants and "elongated" by 2/9. 1/9 did not know.

Nose:
Participants could choose between "big", "normal", "small" and "I don't know".
-Augustus Gloop had a "small" nose according to 5/10 viewers, he had a "normal" nose for 3/10 participants, it was a "big" nose for 1/10 participants and 1/10 did not know.
-Veruca Salt's nose was "normal" for 4/10 viewers, "big" for 2/10 and "small" for 1/10. The other 3/10 did not know.
-Violet Beauregarde boasted a "normal" nose for 5/10 participants, a "small" nose for 3/10 and 2/10 viewers did not know.
-Mike Teavee's nose was defined as "normal" by 5/9 people and as "small" by 1/9. The remaining 3/9 did not know.

Table 4. Results of the closed questions regarding the physical description of the characters. Only the information not subject to personal interpretation is included

Category	Correct	Score (max. 39) Wrong	I don't know
eyes			
colour	21 (53.85%)	11 (28.20%)	7 (17.95%)
glasses	37 (94.88%)	1 (2.56%)	1 (2.56%)
hair			
colour	29 (74.36%)	8 (20.52%)	2 (5.12%)
style	35 (89.74%)	0 (0%)	4 (10.26%)
length	32 (82.05%)	3 (7.69%)	4 (10.26%)

Clothing:
Participants were asked about the clothes - kind, colour and pattern (whether the clothes were plain, spotted, striped, checked, etc.) - and about the kind of shoes worn by each character. The following results were obtained:

Regarding the clothes covering the upper part of the body:

-*Colour*: Participants could choose between six colours. The option "I don't know" was also available.
19/39 answers had the colour right, 11/39 chose the "I don't know" option and 9/39 answers were mistaken. None of those 9 answers included colours similar to the real ones.

-*Kind*: Participants could choose between six kinds of clothes. The option "I don't know" was also available.
23/39 answers were correct, 6/39 read "I don't know" and 10/39 answers were wrong. All those 10/39 selected clothes similar to the original (e.g. a scarf instead of a dress).

-*Pattern*: Participants could choose between six patterns. The option "I don't know" was also available.
25/39 showed the right answer for the pattern, 9/39 showed the "I don't know" option and 5/39 answers were mistaken. From those 5/39, 3 had selected a wrong kind of pattern (i.e. checked instead of striped) and 2 showed "no pattern" when there was one.

Clothes covering the lower part of the body:

-*Colour*: Participants could choose between seven colours. The option "I don't know" was also available.
17/39 answers referring to the colour were correct, 16/39 read "I don't know" and 6/39 answers were wrong. From the 16 answers showing "I don't know", 9 were related to Mike Teavee's trousers. This character appeared in the clip sitting on the floor with his legs crossed, and even though the trousers were visible, no one seemed to pay any attention to them. Lastly, concerning the 6/39 wrong answers, 5 were mistakes made when defining Augustus Gloop's trousers. In this case he appears in the clip standing up and his trousers are also visible on screen.

-*Kind*: Participants could choose between three kinds of clothes. The option "I don't know" was also available.
21/39 answers were right, 16/39 had the "I don't know option" ticked and 2/39 answers were mistaken. From the 16 which opted for the "I don't know" option, 14 referred to either Augustus's or Mike's clothes, while the 2 mistakes were divided between Mike Teavee and Violet Beauregarde.

-*Pattern*: only one piece of clothing showed patterns, so this question was not included in the questionnaire.

-*Shoes*:
The question here referred only to the kind of shoes and 19/39 answers were correct, 15/39 answers were "I don't know" and 5/39 answers were wrong. From the 15/39 which selected the "I don't know" option, 10 referred to Augustus's and Mike's shoes (5 each), whereas the remaining 5 were divided between Violet and Veruca. Of the 5 mistaken answers, 3 had to do with Augustus's sandals.

Table 5. Results of the closed question regarding the clothing of the characters.

Category	Correct	Wrong	I don't know
upper part of body			
colour	19 (48.72%)	11 (28.20%)	9 (23.08%)
kind	23 (58.97%)	10 (25.64%)	6 (15.39%)
pattern	25 (64.10%)	5 (12.82%)	9 (23.08%)
lower part of body			
colour	17 (43.59%)	6 (15.38%)	16 (41.03%)
kind	21 (53.85%)	2 (5.12%)	16 (41.03%)
shoes	19 (48.72%)	5 (12.82%)	15 (38.46%)

Score (max. 39)

3.5. Discussion

The data obtained in this relatively simple experiment provides interesting insights into viewers' attention to characters in films. When asked open questions, all of the participants mentioned the characters' personality traits. Subsequently, some of the participants completed their descriptions by adding other details, such as the characters' physical appearance, nationalities and/or economic status. The fact that this was the only question to which all of the participants provided the same information seems to indicate that characters are generally understood as a combination of specific personality traits. Of course, characters display other varying features (e.g., physical, economic, social, etc.) but the fact that the response was unanimous only when it concerned the characters' behaviour suggests the great importance of personality traits with respect to understanding a character, at least in the early phase of a film, where characters are first introduced.

Considering the results obtained in the open question, which targeted physical description, it seems clear that people tend to mention only a few features when describing characters. Obviously, if a character shows a trait which is out of the ordinary but emphasised throughout the film or which is uncommon enough to challenge the viewers' expectations, that feature will probably be better recalled. When this is not the case, the element most frequently recalled is the hair, and more specifically its colour, although often descriptions are more comprehensive and also include information about hair length or hair style. Another trait often recalled by the viewer is weight, mainly – though not exclusively – when associated with overweight characters. This indicates that characters' size is also important when creating mental images of them. The last element present in most descriptions is the eyes – mainly the colour of the eyes – though there are some sporadic allusions to their size. To finish with the open questions, let us consider the question which addresssed other elements. When asked about other elements, participants mentioned the clothes – especially the type (whether the character was wearing a t-shirt, a shirt, a jacket, etc.). Apart from the type of clothing, the colour of the clothing was also included – though not often – in some descriptions.

Considering the closed questions about the physical descriptions and clothing, memory accuracy differs from one element to another. The results show that some features – mainly a character's height, weight, face shape and nose size depend on the viewer's perception, that is, the same trait of the same character can be defined as normal or as big by different people if their standards of normality vary from one another. For the nine traits that did not depend on the viewers' subjective perception, the data were gathered, analysed and ranked for memory accuracy. The following percentages for correct answers were obtained (in decreasing rate of accuracy): personality traits (100%), glasses (94.87%), hair style (89.74%), hair length (82.05%), hair colour (74.35%), pattern of clothing (64.10%), kind of clothes (56.41%), eye colour (53.84%) and colour of clothing (46.15%).

As shown before, the recall rates are excellent when the participants are asked to remember whether characters were wearing glasses or not. In fact, there was only one mistake when we asked this specific question. This was probably due to the fact that the character erroneously thought to be wearing glasses was a young know-it-all techie and that stereotype matches the image of someone wearing glasses. The second and third elements with a fairly accurate recall rate are the style and the length of the characters' hair. However, viewers sporadically tend to get confused about the colour. After this, the recall rates are less efficient and neither the patterns nor the kind of clothes are very well remembered, though the results suggest that recall rates are much better for women's clothing than for men's clothing. The two features with the lowest recall rate are eye colour and the colour of the clothes. The fact that the participants tended to get confused by – or simply did not mention – the colour of the eyes is especially interesting because the upper part of the face is considered to play a vital role in the transmission of emotional information (Constantini et al. 2005). For this reason, it seems likely that – despite their imprecise recall – the subjects focused on the area around the characters' eyes, which supports Vilaró and Orero's (forthcoming) observation that viewers might look at certain areas when watching a film without processing all the information extracted.

Overall, these preliminary results show the importance of personality traits and viewers' preferences for such features over physical features and clothing. These findings suggest that we remember fictional characters mainly because of their behaviour and that the information about their appearance and their clothing plays a secondary role when creating a mental composition of a character.

4. Conclusion

Even though the experiment carried out was relatively simple, it has provided some interesting (albeit preliminary) information about character understanding, which might be useful for AD. Gathering substantial data that show what viewers remember could serve to indicate which traits contribute most to the creation of mental constructs of characters. In turn, this information could be relevant for audio describers, who could create their ADs relying on not only their personal impressions, but also empirical evidence.

Further cognitive research needs to be done to assess if viewers' perception can indeed help audio describers, mainly in those cases where no specific characters traits are highlighted. Similar experiments covering various film genres where different kinds of characters are presented could be carried out to obtain a comprehensive pool of data. It would be particularly interesting to test viewers' recall in the case of more realistic characters because even though these are still based on stereotypes, their traits are usually less accentuated and they tend to develop throughout the narrative plot. Thus, comparing the results obtained with flat and rounded characters could provide interesting conclusions concerning the ways in which we understand and recall those characters.

Empirical studies based on recall could also be used to determine if the mental images of characters that we create vary depending on the viewer's age. A similar kind of analysis could be undertaken with children and adults to find out if both groups remember the same details. Children's recall rates may not coincide with adults' recall rates if their attention focuses on different aspects. In turn, this may lead to the creation of user-oriented ADs.

Finally, combining recall studies with eye-tracking research could also be of interest to provide us with a more comprehensive understanding of what we remember in relation to what we see. Exploring viewers' gaze patterns in film-watching and combining those patterns with recall rates and applying the findings to AD might offer new possibilities to the question of relevancy.

To summarise, recall studies are just one of the many empirical approaches that could shed light on our understanding of film comprehension. They offer a variety of possibilities worth exploring, which could provide a complementary perspective to the current lines of research in AD. Therefore, the challenge remains to bring together theoretical and practical approaches in order to produce materials which fulfil the user's needs.

---

[1] This research is supported by the grant from the Spanish Ministry of Science and Innovation FFI2009-08027, Subtitling for the Deaf and Hard of Hearing and Audio Description: Objective tests and future plans, and also by the Catalan Government funds 2009SGR700.

[2] "His heroes, always naive and childish, are psychologically scared and misunderstood by society. They behave in an involuntarily upsetting manner and they become figures that disturb both society and the conventional morality" (my translation)

References

Aenor. 2005. *Norma UNE 153020: Audiodescripción para Personas con Discapacidad Visual. Requisitos para la Audiodescripción y Elaboración de Audioguías*. Madrid: AENOR.
Aristotle. 384 BC-322 BC. *El Arte Poética* (trans. J. Goya y Muniain). Biblioteca Virtual Miguel de Cervantes. Online at: http://www.cervantesvirtual.com/servlet/SirveObras/01338308622 026274866802/p0000001.htm#I_6 (consulted 04.03.2010).
Balázs, Béla. 1970. *Theory of the Film: Character and Growth of a New Art* (trans. E. Bone). New York: Dover.
Ballester, Ana. 2007. 'Directores en la Sombra: Personajes y su Caracterización en el Guión Audiodescrito de Todo sobre mi Madre (1999)' in Jiménez, Catalina (ed.) *Traducción y Accesibilidad. Subtitulación para Sordos y Audiodescripción para Ciegos: Nuevas Modalidades de Traducción Audiovisual*. Frankfurt: Peter Lang. 133-151.
Benecke, Bernd & Elmar Dosch. 2004. *Wenn aus Bildern Worte Werden*. Munich: Bayerischer Rundfunk.
Bordwell, David. 1990. *Film Art: An Introduction*. New York: McGraw Hill.
Burton, Tim. 2006. *Burton on Burton* (revised ed.). London: Faber and Faber.
Chatman, Seymour. 1978. *Story and Discourse: Narrative Structure in Fiction and Film*. Ithaca, NY: Cornell University Press
Constantini, Erica, Fabio Pianesi & Michela Prete. 2005. 'Recognising Emotions in Human and Synthetic Faces: the Role of the Upper and Lower Parts of the Face' in *Proceedings of the*

10th International Conference on Intelligent User Interfaces. San Diego, CA: Association for Computing Machinery. 10-27.
Dahl, Roald. 1973. *Charlie and the Chocolate Factory*. Bungay: Puffin Books.
Dillman, Don A. 1978. *Mail and Telephone Surveys: The Total Design Method*. New York: Wiley.
Foster, Edgar M. 1974. *Aspects of the Novel*. Harmondsworth: Penguin Books.
Greimas, Algirdas J. 2003. *La Semiótica del Texto: Ejercicios Prácticos: Análisis de un Cuento de Maupassant*. Barcelona: Ediciones Paidós.
Hanke, Ken. 1999. *Tim Burton: An Unauthorized Biography of the Filmmaker*. Los Angeles, CA: Renaissance Books.
Jackson, Sherri L. 2009. *Research Methods and Statistics: A Critical Thinking Approach*. Belmont, CA: Wadsworth Publishing.
Levy, Emanuel. 2005. 'Charlie and the Chocolate Factory' in *Emanuel Levy Cinema 24/7*. Online at: http://www.emanuellevy.com/Reviews/details.cfm?id=287 (consulted 15.05.2010).
Mascarenhas, Renata. 2009. 'Audio Description and Discursive Strategies: A Study on the Construction of the Characters in Little Miss Sunshine'. Paper presented at *Media for All 3* (Artesis University College Antwerp/University of Antwerp, 22-24 October 2009).
McGonigle, Francis. 2007. *The Audio Descripion of Children's Films*. MA thesis. University of Surrey.
Merschmann, Helmut. 2000. *Tim Burton: The Life and Films of a Visionary Director*. London: Titan Books. Ofcom. 2010. 'Guidelines on the Provision of Television Access Services'. Online at http://www.ofcom.org.uk/tv/ifi/guidance/tv_access_serv/guidelines/guidelines.pdf (consulted 16.02.2010).
Orero, Pilar. 2007. 'Sampling Audio Description in Europe' in Díaz Cintas, Jorge, Pilar Orero & Aline Remael (eds.) *Media for All: Subtitling for the Deaf, Audio Description and Sign Language*. Amsterdam: Rodopi. 111-125.
Orero, Pilar (forthcoming a). 'Audio Description Behaviour: Universals, Regularities and Guidelines'.
Orero, Pilar (forthcoming b). 'Audio Description for Children: Once Upon a Time There Was a Different Audio Description for Characters'.
Orero, Pilar & Anna Vilaró (forthcoming). 'Eye-tracking Analysis of Minor Details in Films for Audio Description'. To appear in *Monti 4*.
Palomo, Alicia. 2008. *Audio Description as Language Development and Language Learning for Blind and Visual Impaired Children*. MA thesis. Universitat Jaume I.
Propp, Vladimir. 2000. *Morfología del Cuento: Seguida de las Transformaciones de los Cuentos Maravillosos* (trans. L. Ortiz). Madrid: Fundamentos.
Puigdomènech, Laura, Pilar Orero & Anna Matamala. 2008. 'The Making of a Protocol for Opera Audio Description' in Pegenaute, Luis et al. (eds.) *La Traducción del Futuro: Mediación Lingüística y Cultural en el Siglo XXI*. Barcelona: PPU. 381-392.
Remael, Aline. 2005. *Audio Description for Recorded TV, Cinema and DVD: An Experimental Stylesheet for Teaching Purposes*. Unpublished lecture notes. Artesis University College Antwerp.
Scott, Anthony Oliver. 2005. 'Looking for the Candy, Finding a Back Story' in *The New York Times*. Online at http://movies.nytimes.com/2005/07/15/movies/15char.html (consulted 15.05.2010).
Solaz, Lucía. 1999. *Tim Burton y la Construcción del Universo Fantástico*. PhD thesis. Universitat de Valencia.
Todorov, Tzvetan. 1977. *The Poetics of Prose* (trans. R. Howard). Oxford: Basil Blackwell.
Vercauteren, Gert. 2007. 'Towards a European Guideline for Audio Description' in Díaz Cintas, Jorge, Pilar Orero & Aline Remael (eds.). *Media for All: Subtitling for the Deaf, Audio Description and Sign Language*. Amsterdam: Rodopi. 139-150.

Appendix

The questionnaire:

AUGUSTUS GLOOP

1. Define the character

   [ ]

   a. What elements of the film suggest it?

   [ ]

2. What does the character look like?

   [ ]

3. Do you remember any other aspect regarding his characterization?

   [ ]

4. What is the character like?

```
┌─────────────────────────────────────────────────┐
│                                                 │
│                                                 │
│                                                 │
└─────────────────────────────────────────────────┘
```

5. What does the character look like?

➢ Eyes

   Brown / Blue / Green / I don't know
   Wears glasses / Does not wear glasses / I don't know

➢ Hair

   Dark-haired / Brown-haired / Blonde / I don't know
   Straight / Wavy / Curly / I don't know
   Short / Bob / Long / I don't know

➢ Height

   Tall / Medium / Short / I don't know

➢ Weight

   Overweight / Medium / Thin / I don't know

➢ Shape of the face

   Round / Normal / Elongated / I don't know

➢ Nose

   Big / Normal / Small / I don't know

6. What is the character wearing?

➢ A:

T-Shirt / Jumper / Sleeveless sweater / Dress / Jacket / I don't know
Red / Green / Grey / Black / Pink / Yellow / Maroon / I don't know
Plain / Striped / Patterned /Checked / Spotted / I don't know

➢ Trousers:

Jeans / Corduroy / Tracksuit / I don't know
Red / Green / Grey / Black / Pink / Yellow / Maroon / I don't know

➢ Feet:

Shoes / Trainers / Slippers / Heeled shoes / Sandals

Audio Description Made to Measure: Reflections on Interpretation in AD Based on the Pear Tree Project Data

Iwona Mazur
Adam Mickiewicz University (Poland)

Agnieszka Chmiel
Adam Mickiewicz University (Poland)

Abstract
The issue of interpretation in audio description (AD) continues to divide both AD practitioners and researchers. In this contribution, we look at interpretation from the point of view of narratological behaviour of sighted viewers. To this end, we analyse data from twelve languages collected in the Pear Tree Project – a research project in which sighted viewers were asked to watch a short film and subsequently recount what they saw. Linking our findings to AD, we find in our analysis that sighted viewers interpret visual events but they avoid extremely subjective interpretations or interpretations in which they pass moral judgments. Thus, we propose that instead of applying the binary opposition of objective versus subjective, we should be using an objectivity– subjectivity scale, which can help determine which interpretive descriptions are less subjective and can consequently be used in AD without running the risk of being patronising or spoon-feeding the sense to the visually impaired.

Keywords
audio description, facial expressions, interpretation, Pear Tree Project, reception studies

1. Introduction

To date efforts in audio-description (AD) research have primarily focused on determining the specific requirements of its end users (i.e., blind and partially sighted audiences) through reception studies (e.g., in the Audetel Project and *Bollywood for all* conducted by the Royal National Institute of Blind People in the UK) to develop standards that ensure the uniformity and high quality of AD. However, no consistent guidelines have as yet been created because the preferences of the users concerned often vary from person to person and because audio description has developed on the basis of what a limited number of practitioners – as a result of their own experiences – believe to be the right way to proceed.

One issue where there is no agreement among target audiences or AD researchers is interpretation. In this contribution, interpretation is understood as the subjective treatment of reality perceived by audio describers in films and the equally subjective verbal expression of that reality in description for the blind and partially sighted. In general – and especially in early AD guidelines – subjective judgments are not welcome in AD and objectivity is favoured in order to avoid any manipulation, spoon-feeding or a patronising attitude towards the target audience. However, it is not always clear what constitutes subjective judgment and what kind of interpretation is more objective and could be included in AD.

Although we are ardent supporters of learning the preferences of visually challenged audiences through reception studies, in this contribution we suggest looking at the narrative practices of sighted viewers in general to determine whether they interpret visual events by using value judgments or evaluative words and, if so, to what extent. Such data could provide us with insights into what constitutes the objective description of events that could be included in AD, and what makes descriptions subjective and thus undesired in AD.

To this end, we reanalyse some of the data collected in the Pear Tree Project, which is briefly described below. We focus on the interpretation of three events depicted in the film used in the study. We are particularly interested in whether the descriptions of those events are interpretative. Before providing both the quantitative and qualitative analyses of the data and drawing conclusions, we present the varied – and often opposing – points of view in AD practice and research about interpretation in AD.

2. Interpretation in audio description: A bone of contention

Audio description is defined as an audio commentary accompanying films, theatre performances and the like in order to give the blind and partially sighted access to visual elements of a cultural event. Thus, AD includes descriptions of characters, settings, actions and objects appearing on the screen or stage. According to Snyder, "AD is about democracy" (2005: 16) since it offers sighted and non-sighted viewers an equal opportunity to enjoy the arts and entertainment under comparable circumstances. In this respect, it is no wonder that many AD scholars, practitioners and guidelines mention objectivity as one of the key principles of AD (Dosch & Benecke 2004, Orero 2005, Snyder 2005, Remael 2005, Vercauteren 2006). According to the ITC Guidance On Standards for Audio Description, one of the most comprehensive sets of AD best practices to date, "describers should not voice a personal opinion or interpret events" (2000: 15). Experts frequently refer to the WYSIWYG principle (What You See Is What You Get), which states that we should describe only what we can see and should avoid subjective interpretation (Snyder 2007: 4). Pfanstiehl and Pfanstiehl note that describers are cautioned "not [to] evaluate or interpret, but rather be like the faithful lens of a camera" (quoted after Udo and Fels 2009: 179, as quoted in *The Play's the Thing* 1985: 91) and instructed to describe visual stimuli without drawing any assumptions for blind audiences.

However, it is not always easy to be objective. An equally large number of publications on AD (mainly in Europe, but also in Canada) refer to the interpret-or-not problem. Udo and Fels (2009: 179) claim that the task of objective interpretation is impossible. Hyks admits that AD is highly subjective – despite the describers' efforts – and refers to this feature of AD as follows:

> [E]ven though we all agree on certain basic principles, we do see things differently and we certainly express them in very varied ways (…) [and] even though we are observers, narrators, storytellers, witnesses to what is happening on screen, what we choose to include, differs (…) from company to company and certainly from country to country. (2006: 1)

Much in the same vein, Pujol and Orero (2007) state that although audio describers may strive to be as objective as possible, their choices will nevertheless be determined by individual ways of perceiving reality.

It seems that the US tradition favours a strictly objective approach (as frequently voiced by Snyder: "The blind viewer has the right to be as clueless as the sighted one", personal communication) whereas European scholars are much more sensitive to the blurred division between what is objective and what is subjective. The previously quoted ITC Guidance states the following:

> Describers in the US are not encouraged to add anything or offer any information that is not apparent on the screen at that moment. Rather than saying a character is angry, they describe the action as they see it and let the visually impaired viewer decide what that action implies. British research seems to indicate that additional help is appreciated, as long as it is not condescending or interpretative. (2000: 15)

The same document emphasises that AD "is there to clarify what is going on but occasionally a little additional explanation can help" (ITC Guidance 2000: 15). However, interpretation is a bone of contention not only across the Atlantic but also in Europe. For instance, Holland (2009) – a long-term audio describer for the theatre in the UK – claims that although it might not be possible for audio describers to avoid interpretation altogether, they should try to be non-judgmental.

An interesting approach to objectivity and subjectivity in AD – based on Relevance Theory – is presented by Braun (2007). According to this model of communication, utterances are understood following explicatures (assumptions made explicitly by the speaker) and implicatures (assumptions implicated by the speaker). Braun presents examples from the film *The Hours* to show that audio describers have to make a whole series of inferences based on individual interpretation to understand seemingly factual content. Braun suggests that the identification of implicatures and explicatures can be useful to the audio describer when deciding the extent to which the visual stimuli should be described, and the extent to which the visual stimuli can be interpreted. She claims that the processing load of the AD audience can be reduced by verbalising "explicatures instead of the individual cues by which they are triggered" (Braun, Sabine, 2007: 10). Braun opposes the verbalisation of implicatures since it would not allow for individual interpretation (i.e., for drawing implicatures) by the blind audience.

In order to shed more light on the contentious issue of interpretation in AD, let us look at specific examples. We will first review some examples of interpretation that can be classified without any doubt as unacceptable and unnecessary. We will then proceed to discuss less obvious instances where interpretation should be carefully considered before deemed justified or undesired.

Remael (2005) presents an obvious example of unnecessary interpretation and spoon-feeding the sense of the visual material to the blind audience. A scene in which a character is tossing around in bed at night should not be interpreted as "She's having a nightmare". Movements of the character should be described instead to let the blind viewers make appropriate inferences for themselves.

Chmiel and Mazur (forthcoming) review early AD attempts in Poland and enumerate some examples of erroneous and excessive interpretation from *Ice Age 2*. A scene in which Manny and Ellie – the two leading characters – go for a walk and strike up a rather intimate conversation about their personal lives marks the beginning of a relationship that develops later in the film. In the Polish AD, the event is interpreted as a date and described as follows: "Diego i Sid, widząc, że zanosi się na randkę, oddalają się w swoją stronę" [Seeing that they are about to go out on a date, Diego and Sid leave]. In this instance, it is unlikely that such interpretation would be considered acceptable. By way of comparison, in the English AD, the event is described neutrally and objectively: "Manny and Ellie heading for the campsite".

The above examples are obviously at variance with AD guidelines and the principle of objectivity. However, the issue of interpretation in AD is most controversial in cases where the difference between objective and subjective is less obvious and where objective description is impossible due to linguistic or time constraints. These cases include the use of evaluative adjectives in describing characters, descriptions of facial expressions and the use of adverbs in order to enrich the description.

2.1. Evaluative adjectives in AD

Evaluative adjectives such as *beautiful, awful, ugly* manifest subjective interpretations of the visual material by the audio describer since viewers may have different perceptions of what is beautiful, awful or ugly. They provide concise descriptions but may be considered manipulation of the film. Surprisingly, in a small-scale AD reception study conducted by Mazur and Chmiel (manuscript in preparation) involving 18 respondents with sight dysfunction, the majority of the respondents (71%) claimed that they like descriptions with evaluative adjectives. To examine the issue further, the authors asked the same respondents to judge whether in their opinion specific evaluative adjectives are objective or subjective. More than half participants (62%) judged the phrase *sexy brunettes* as subjective. This phrase was also questioned by visually-impaired consultants who reviewed the AD script including this and other descriptions used in the survey. 46% of respondents viewed the phrase *attractive singer* as subjective, and the remaining examples (e.g., *smart clothes*) were identified as objective by the majority of participants (62% to 77%). Paradoxically, 54% of respondents claimed that, in general, they do not accept audio description with subjective interpretations. The results are inconclusive and more research is needed with larger samples to allow for generalizations.

All of the above examples may be reformulated in a more neutral way, provided there are no time constraints in the film and longer descriptions fit between dialogues. For instance, the adjective *sexy* can be replaced with more objective characteristics of those *sexy* characters such as *long legs, large bosoms*, etc. Viewers can use this information to decide if the characters are sexy or not, depending on their perception of sex appeal. Similarly, *attractive* can be described by specific features that make the singer *attractive* in the audio describer's opinion. *Smart clothes* can also be replaced with a more detailed description of individual garments. However, under time constraints, that is, when longer descriptions cannot be included in the script and the identification of such features is important for the plot, the use of such evaluative adjectives should seriously be considered by audio describers.

2.2. Describing facial expressions

Facial expressions are extremely difficult to describe objectively and briefly since the human face is able to express highly complex emotions thanks to numerous muscles (Mazur & Chmiel, manuscript in preparation). Although a subjectively interpreted emotion of joy can be described objectively by mentioning the action of smiling (the same with sadness and crying), there are many more complex emotions and facial expressions that are difficult to describe objectively without naming them subjectively (e.g., concern, confusion, self-consciousness). The audio describer can resort to describing facial expressions but emotions are always more subtle. For example, a seemingly simple act of raising eyebrows can point to anxiety, relief, surprise, wryness and many other emotions when combined with movements of other facial muscles.

Dosch and Benecke (2004: 24) also underline the tricky issue of facial expressions in AD:

> Besonders vorsichtig muss man sein, wenn es um die Beschreibung von Gesichtsausdrucken geht, die ja immer etwas über den Gefühlszustand einer Person sagen. Hier besteht die Gefahr, durch zu plumpe Erklärungen einen Film zu verflachen (...). Statt solcher 0-8-15-Begriffe (...) sollte man sich die Zeit nehmen, die wirklich wichtigen Gesichtausdrücke (und nur diese!) differenzierter zu beschreiben (...). (Beispiel: Statt "Angespannt sieht er sie an" vielleicht: "Er hat die Augen zusammengekniffen, seine Wangen sind gerötet, die Lippen zusammengepresst").

> You have to be extremely cautious when describing facial expressions that always say something about the character's emotions. The danger is that awkward explanations can distort the profoundness of the film (...). Instead of such strict and constraining notions (...) the audio describer should take time to describe those really important facial expressions (and only those!) in a more sophisticated way (...). (For example: instead of "He looks at her nervously" the following description could be used: "He squints,, his cheeks are flushed, his lips pressed together"). (our translation)

We are not convinced that such descriptions can cover the whole range of mixed and complex feelings visible on film characters' faces and be as comprehensible and as easy to interpret by a blind audience as by a sighted audience. This issue requires further research involving blind and partially-sighted participants exposed to two different AD scripts – one including detailed and objective descriptions and the other with briefer descriptions with more explicit and subjective naming of emotional states. Comprehension tests and surveys of preferences should provide valuable guidance to audio describers.

Dosch and Benecke (2004: 24) are aware of the problem of time constraints when applying lengthy descriptions of facial expressions: "Fairerweise muss man ergänzen, dass es sich angesichts der oft kurzen Dialogpausen nicht immer vermeiden lässt, einen Gesichtsausdruck auf die kurze Art zu beschreiben." [To be fair, it has to be added that because of short pauses between dialogues, the need to describe facial expressions succinctly cannot always be avoided.] (our translation). Indeed, time constraints may pose a more serious problem to the description of facial expression than the plausibility of appropriate reflecting of emotional states in objective terms. Despite acknowledging the problem, Dosch and Benecke do not offer any solutions. A good example of such a problematic scene is given by Chmiel and Mazur (forthcoming). In the Polish film *A Warm Heart [Serce na dłoni]*, two male characters are seated in a limousine that has to swerve to avoid hitting an elderly lady on a motorcycle who tries to block their way and stop the car. The two men exchange surprised looks. The surprise is only subtly visible on their faces. The sighted viewers simply interpret their looks in this way based on their experience of reading human faces, looks and body language. Additionally, there is very little time between the dialogue. Consequently, a longer description would not fit in the pause. The alternative here seems to be either to use the interpretative description and mention the 'exchange of surprised looks' or to lose some content and resort to the exchange of looks only.

Orero and Vercauteren (manuscript in preparation) tackle the issue from a cognitive and narrative perspective. They claim that AD should include subjective descriptions of emotions since various studies confirm that at least some emotions are universal and correctly identified. They provide interesting examples of such objective and subjective descriptions. The following description: *the upper eyelids and brows rise, and the jaw drops open* can simply be replaced with a subjective (yet quite universal) interpretation of this expression: *surprise*. Similarly, the following description can adequately be replaced with the word *angry*: *both the lower and upper eyelids tighten as the brows lower and draw together; the jaw thrusts forward, the lips press together, and the lower lip pushes up a little* (Orero & Vercauteren, manuscript in preparation). Apart from the obvious time saving (always an asset in audio description), the subjective descriptions do not present the listeners with a heavy cognitive processing load, which is the case when lengthy objective descriptions are used.

2.3. Adverbs

The use of expressive adverbs is encouraged since they can enrich descriptions and modify described actions. According to Rai, "adverbs are a useful shorthand to describing emotions and actions, but should not be subjective" (2009: 93). Similarly, the ITC guidelines (ITC Guidance 2000) encourage the use of verbs modified with adverbs, but warn audio describers to be cautious. The reason is that some adverbs are descriptive and specific while others can be vague and interpretative. Thus, the descriptive and specific adverbs should be used and the vague and interpretative adverbs should be avoided. The document presents examples of undesired adverbs (e.g., *arguably, characteristically, clearly, instinctively, suitably*). The meaning of such adverbs is indeed vague and they have no added value for AD. The list of descriptive and specific adverbs includes the following:

anxiously, brusquely, carefully, cautiously, eagerly, haughtily, jovially (ITC Guidance 2000: 21). Interestingly enough, adverbs such as *anxiously* and *jovially* can actually be classified as interpretative since they imply that the character feels anxious or jovial, which is inferred subjectively by the audio describer. All in all, it seems that the issue of subjective interpretations in AD is quite complex since there are contradictory views regarding not only the acceptability of interpretations under certain circumstances but also the classification of certain words and expressions as objective or subjective.

3. Analysed data

Given the opposing points of view with regard to interpretation in audio description presented above, as well as the blurred division between interpretation that is more subjective or objective, we thought it useful to investigate whether sighted viewers interpret certain events when talking about a film and, if so, how they do it. Such data could help us determine which interpretative descriptions would be considered more universal and objective, and thus more acceptable by blind and partially sighted viewers as well. To this end, we have used data collected in the Pear Tree Project (PTP) conducted as part of the EU-funded DTV4ALL project, whose primary objective was to uncover dominant narrative patterns across a number of languages to determine whether development of common European AD guidelines is possible.

Twelve languages were included in the project: Afrikaans, Catalan, Dutch, English (UK and US), French, German, Greek, Italian, Irish English, Polish, Spanish (European and US).[1] The subjects (20–25 for each language) were asked to watch a 6-minute film, in colour, with sound but with no dialogue. The film presented a chain of events related to a boy riding a bicycle and a man picking pears (for a detailed summary of the plot of the film see Du Bois 1980: xii-xiii). Having watched the film, the subjects were asked to recount what they had seen, in writing (for a detailed description of the project, including its objectives, participants, methodology, design and results see Mazur and Chmiel (manuscript in preparation). The project was modelled on an earlier project conducted by Chafe and his co-workers in the mid-1970s (Chafe 1980). However, the analysis of the data was based on that of Tannen's related to Chafe's project (Tannen 1980).

Of the thirteen aspects analysed in the Pear Tree Project, we present three aspects below that tackle the issue of interpretation in descriptions of visual events, that is, giving pears to the boys, taking the basket, and the pearpicker's discovery that the basket is gone. We thought it interesting to see whether descriptions of those events provide a neutral account of what has happened or whether they are interpretations of those events, and if so, how such interpretations come about. Therefore, what follows is both a quantitative and a qualitative analysis of the three aspects under consideration. It is important to stress that the original PTP analysis was solely quantitative and the data were compared and contrasted crosslinguistically to find both similarities and differences in the reception of visual images across all of the languages (and cultures) under consideration. However, in this contribution we are predominantly concerned with analysing the data holistically to make some general observations about the description of the visual input – irrespective of the language (or culture) concerned.

4. Interpretation of events: Data analysis

In this section, we present and analyse data with regard to three aspects of the PTP: (1) giving the pears to the boys, (2) the boy taking the pears and (3) the pearpicker's discovery that the basket is gone. First, we briefly recount a given event and the purpose of its analysis. Subsequently, we present the collected data. Finally, we analyse the data in terms of their relevance for interpretation in AD.

4.1. Giving the pears to the boys

In one of the scenes from the short film a boy falls off a bike and loses his hat, which is returned to him by three boys. Having got the hat back, the boy gives the three boys a pear each. In the analysis of this aspect, we wanted to see how many descriptions give just a basic rendering of this event, how many do not mention this event at all, in how many this event is interpreted as a gesture of thanks (e.g. *the boy gave them a pear in return for their help*) and how many provide a (moral) judgment of this event (e.g. *as he should do, the boy gave them a pear in return for their help*). The last two descriptions would indicate that there is some degree of interpretation on the part of the describers. However, it should be noted that when placed on a scale, the former would be much less subjective than the latter. Table 1 presents the results of the analysis, broken down into individual languages. What we are most interested in, however, are the overall results for all the languages combined.

Table 1. Results giving the pears to the boys (in per cent)

Language	Reference to event			
	basic	no mention	thank you	moral judgment
Afrikaans	30.0	20.0	45.0	5.0
Dutch (Belgium)	8.7	13.0	78.3	0.0
Catalan	20.0	5.0	70.0	5.0
German	27.3	36.4	36.4	0.0
English (UK)	11.8	5.9	82.0	0.0
English (US)	0.0	50.0	50.0	0.0
French	0.0	21.1	78.9	0.0
Greek	25.0	35.0	40.0	0.0
Irish	21.7	17.4	56.5	4.3
Italian	38.1	23.8	38.1	0.0
Polish	20.0	20.0	60.0	0.0
Spanish	25.0	20.0	45.0	10.0
Total	18.2	22.7	57.0	2.1

In summary, only 18.2% of the descriptions were neutral. More than half of the participants (57.0%) interpreted the giving of the pears to the boys as a thank-you gesture, whereas only 2.1% provided a moral judgment of this event (an example from Catalan: '*It seems that the boy who found the hat on the ground and didn't show much solidarity asks him for 3 pears in return for the favour*). When it comes to interpreting the event as a thank-you gesture, in most of the texts the actual verb *thank* was used or a word or phrase similar to *thanks*, such as *odwdzięczać się* 'to reciprocate', *w podzięce* 'as a thank you' in Polish, or *als dank* 'by way of thanks' in Dutch. However, in the descriptions, phrases corresponding to the English phrase *in return* or *in exchange* – such as *a canvi* (Catalan), *w zamian, w rewanżu* (Polish) or *in ruil* (Dutch) – were also common. Such descriptions were also treated as interpreting the event as a thank-you gesture.

Given the above results and examples, it can be concluded that when describing the type of behaviour such as the one in the analysed case, people tend to interpret it – if only to a limited extent (e.g., as a thank-you gesture or doing something in return).[2] Rarer are descriptions with extremely subjective interpretations or (moral) judgments. This could imply that in AD such objective interpretations may be used since they are in line with how sighted viewers perceive and describe events. However, far-fetched interpretations which involve some kind of (moral) judgment should be avoided.

4.2. Taking the pears

This analysis refers to a scene where the boy on the bike takes one of the baskets that the pearpicker has filled with pears and rides off. The categories in this analysis are similar to those included in the analysis in Section 4.1. What we were most interested in here was whether event was described in neutral terms (e.g., *the boy takes the basket*) or whether it was interpreted as stealing (e.g., *the boy steals the basket of pears*). What was also interesting was whether there was any moral judgment of the act on the part of the participants (e.g., *he takes the basket, which is wrong*). The results of the analysis are presented in Table 2.

Table 2. Taking pears – results (in per cent)

Language	Reference to event			moral judgment
	no mention	basic	stealing	
Afrikaans	0.0	76.5	23.5	0.0
Catalan	0.0	25.0	75.0	0.0
German	0.0	83.3	16.7	0.0
English (UK)	0.0	44.4	55.5	0.0
English (US)	0.0	65.0	30.0	5.0
French	0.0	36.8	63.2	0.0
Greek	15.0	60.0	25.0	0.0
Irish	0.0	55.0	40.0	5.0
Italian	0.0	44.0	52.0	4.0
Polish	0.0	90.0	10.0	0.0
Spanish	5.0	30.0	60.0	5.0
Total	1.9	54.0	42.2	1.9

The data show that the majority of the subjects (54.0%) provided a neutral description of the deed. As few as 1.9% of the participants expressed any moral judgment of this event whereas 42.2% interpreted it as stealing. However, it should be noted that some descriptions which were counted as unbiased, later on included phrases that implied the act of stealing (e.g., *the man who he has stolen from* or *the boy and the stolen pears fall on the ground* (English (UK) examples).[3] What is more, in most of the neutral descriptions of the boy taking the basket, it was often added that he makes sure that his deed will go unnoticed, which in itself could be considered interpretation. Also, in some interpretations the boy first considers taking only one pear out of the basket, but then decides to take the entire basket. In some cases, the participants even provided the rationale for stealing the basket, as in the following example from Italian: ... *a little boy with a bicycle – probably a poor boy, or maybe he's fine and simply hungry – steals one basket.*

Interestingly, although the results in the last category (moral judgment) are very similar to the results in 4.1, there is no consistency in neutral versus interpretive descriptions in the two aspects analysed so far. The difference could perhaps be attributed to the fact that interpreting the giving of the pears as a thank-you gesture does not imply any judgment about this event, whereas describing the taking of the basket as stealing is in fact a (moral) judgment in itself, which some of the participants may have wanted to avoid in their descriptions. Another reason could be the young age of the protagonist. It is possible that people are not at ease evaluating the deeds of children by the same standards as those of adults.

Given the above results, it seems that when audio describing this scene a neutral description of the boy taking the basket would probably be more appropriate than describing it as stealing. However, surmising the motivation behind the boy's action should be avoided at all costs.

4.3. The pearpicker's discovery

This analysis refers to the scene following the one analysed in Section 4.2. In this third scene, the pearpicker discovers that the basket is gone. Again, we wanted to see whether the descriptions provided were basic, neutral accounts of the event (e.g. *he notices that the basket is gone*) or whether they provided information about either emotions or a reaction of the pearpicker (e.g., *the picker is surprised/angry/sad etc. to see that the basket is gone*), or both the emotions and the reaction (e.g., *the picker is surprised to see the basket gone and looks suspiciously at the boys*). We also wanted to investigate whether the descriptions included any interpretation of the pearpicker's reaction on the part of the participants (e.g., *the picker suspects that the boys who are eating the pears stole the basket*). The results of the analysis are presented in Table 3.

Table 3. The pearpicker's discovery – results (in per cent)

Language	Reference to event no mention	basic	describe emotions or reaction	interpret	describe emotions and reaction
Afrikaans	0.0	36.8	47.4	10.5	5.3
Catalan	5.0	20.0	40.0	5.0	30.0
German	10.0	40.0	30.0	10.0	10.0
English (UK)	10.0	30.0	30.0	25.0	5.0
English (US)	0.0	30.0	30.0	25.0	15.0
French	5.3	36.8	42.1	5.3	10.5
Greek	20.0	25.0	10.0	35.0	10.0
Irish	15.0	50.0	25.0	10.0	0.0
Italian	22.2	50.0	11.1	5.6	11.1
Polish	0.0	35.0	45.0	15.0	5.0
Spanish	10.0	35.0	40.0	15.0	0.0
Total	8.8	35.0	32.0	15.0	9.2

When looked at individually, the results above suggest that the majority of the subjects provided a neutral description of the event. However, given the purpose of the analysis, it seems reasonable to combine the results for the categories 'describe emotions *or* reaction' and 'describe emotion *and* reaction' since they both pertain to some degree of interpretation of how the pearpicker responded to the basket having disappeared. If this is the case, we can therefore conclude that most of the descriptions (i.e., 41.2%) were biased and did interpret the pearpicker' behaviour in one way or another.

With regard to the actual descriptions of the emotions/reactions, most of the above-mentioned 41.2% of participants reported that the pearpicker was 'surprised' to see that the basket had gone. This result appears to be in line with Orero, Pilar,'s and Vercauteren's claim that some emotions are universal and can be correctly identified (see Section 2.2). For this reason, describing the actual emotion rather than the facial expression that underlies it is recommended for writing AD. Coming back to the case in point, it could be assumed that if this particular scene was to be audio described, the describer – irrespective of the time constraints – could actually name the pearpicker's reaction rather than describe the facial expression that points to the reaction.

When it comes to cases of more subjective interpretations, some subjects made assumptions as to why the pearpicker did not react to the taking of the basket, an example being: *However he does not say anything, so maybe the young boy who took the basket was actually supposed to collect it from the man?* (English (UK) data). Moreover, when compared with the results for the more subjective interpretations obtained in the two previous analyses (i.e., 2.1% and 1.9% respectively), the result obtained in this third analysis is surprisingly high (15.0%). This could be due to the fact that no actual moral judgment, but merely subjective assessment of the situation is given. Despite the reason for the higher result, it seems that this type of interpretation is excessive and would not be appropriate in AD since it would involve some degree of character mind-reading on the part of the audio describer.

5. Conclusions

Although we are aware that the issue of interpretation in AD will probably continue to divide AD practitioners and researchers in the years to come and may never be fully resolved, we would like to propose that instead of the binary opposition of objective versus subjective we should rather be working with a scale with objective and subjective at the two extremes and varying degrees of objectivity and subjectivity in between. We also believe that studies investigating the narrative behaviour of sighted viewers – as the one presented in this contribution – can shed more light on what types of visual stimuli tend to be interpreted universally and where to place such descriptions on the objectivity–subjectivity scale. In turn, this could help us avoid audio descriptions that are patronising and that spoon-feed the sense to the visually impaired.

The analyses have shown that sighted viewers tend to interpret visual events, but interestingly they avoid extremely subjective interpretations that include a (moral) judgment or subjective assessment of the situation. In the three aspects analysed, such descriptions constituted as little as 2.1%, 1.9% and 15.0% respectively of all the descriptions. When it comes to the prevailing descriptions in the aspects analysed, the giving of the pears was interpreted as a thank-you gesture by the majority of the subjects (57%), whereas the taking of the basket by the boy was described in neutral terms by most of the subjects (54%) rather than as stealing (42.2%), which in itself is a form of a moral judgment. With regard to the last of the aspects analysed, most of the descriptions interpreted the reaction of the pearpicker to the basket being gone as surprise (41.2%). This last example is particularly interesting from the point of view of the debate on whether to audio describe facial expressions or whether to name the emotions that are manifested through them. This result suggests that the latter should be the case, as most of us are capable of deciphering such emotions correctly and consistently.

To conclude, when it comes to interpretation in AD, we believe that not only reception research on the specific requirements and preferences of the blind and partially-sighted viewers but also studies on human perception and narrative behaviour in general can help us produce audio description of better quality.

---

[1] Please note that not all of the languages are covered in all of the discussed aspects since some countries provided data for only a number of aspects.

[2] It may be the case that such limited interpretations could be considered as interpretations of culture-bound but recognizable situations of interaction between people, for example, involving rules of politeness. In turn, this could mean that descriptions by non-Europeans might be different in this respect. This issue, however, requires further investigation.

[3] Such descriptions were nonetheless counted as neutral since what was looked at in this respect was the very act of taking the pears. However, it should be noted that the very fact that a given description of the event is neutral does not necessarily mean that it was not interpreted as, for example, the act of stealing by the describer.

References

Braun, Sabine. 2007. 'Audio Description from a Discourse Perspective: A Socially Relevant Framework for Research and Training' in *Linguistica Antverpiensia NS* 6: 357-372.
Chafe, Wallace,, Wallace (ed.). 1980. *The Pear Stories: Cognitive, Cultural and Linguistic Aspects of Narrative Production*. Norwood, NJ: Ablex Publishing.
Chmiel, Agnieszka & Iwona Mazur (forthcoming). 'Audiodeskrypcja jako intersemiotyczny przekład audiowizualny: Percepcja produktu i ocena jakości'. To appear in an edited collection to be published by Leksem publishing house.
Chmiel, Agnieszka & Iwona Mazur (forthcoming). 'Overcoming Barriers: The Pioneering Years of Audio Description in Poland". To appear in Serban, Adriana, Anna Matamala and Jean-Marie Lavaur (eds) *Audiovisual Translation in Close-up: Practical and Theoretical Approaches*.
Dosch, Elmar & Bernd Benecke. 2004. *Wenn aus Bildern Worte Werden: Durch Audio-Description zum Hörfilm*. Bayerischer Rundfunk: Munich.
Du Bois, John W. 1980. 'Introduction – The Search for a Cultural Niche: Showing the Pear Film in a Mayan Community' in Chafe, Wallace (ed.) *The Pear Stories: Cognitive, Cultural and Linguistic Aspects of Narrative Production*. Norwood, NJ: Ablex Publishing. 1-7.
Holland, Andrew. 2009. 'Audio Description in the Theatre and the Visual Arts: Images into Words' in Anderman, Gunilla and Jorge Díaz Cintas (eds) *Audiovisual Translation. Language Transfer on Screen*. Basingtoke: Palgrave Macmillan. 170- 185.
Hyks, Veronika. 2006. 'Translation versus Origination, Creativity within Limits'. On line at: http://www.languages-media.com/lang_media_2006/protected/Veronika_Hyks.pdf (consulted 15.04.2010).
ITC Guidance on Standards for Audio Description. 2000. On line at: http://www.ofcom.org.uk/static/archive/itc/uploads/ITC_Guidance_On_Standards_for_Audio_Description.doc (consulted 15.04.2010).

Mazur, Iwona & Agnieszka Chmiel (manuscript in preparation). 'Towards a Common European Quality Audio Description: Final Report on the Pear Tree Project'.
Orero, Pilar. 2005. 'Audio Description: Professional Recognition, Practice and Standards in Spain' in *Translation Watch Quarterly* 1: 7-18.
Orero, Pilar & Gert Vercauteren (manuscript in preparation). 'The Importance of Adequate Descriptions of Facial Behaviour: Cognition beyond Description'
Pujol, Joaquim & Pilar Orero. 2007. 'Audio Description Precursors: Ekphrasis and Narrators' in *Translation Watch Quarterly* 3(2): 49-60.
Rai, Sonali. 2009. Bollywood for All. On line at: http://www.rnib.org.uk/aboutus/Research/reports/accessibility/Documents/2009_09_Bollywood_AD_report.pdf (consulted 12.04.2010).
Remael, Aline. 2005. 'Audio Description for Recorded TV, Cinema and DVD: An Experimental Stylesheet for Teaching Purposes'. On line at: www.hivt.be (consulted 12.04.2010).
Snyder, Joel. 2005. 'Audio Description: The Visual Made Verbal across Arts Disciplines – across the Globe' in *Translating Today* 4: 15-17.
Snyder, Joel. 2007. 'Audio Description: The Visual Made Verbal' in The International Journal of the Arts in Society. On line at: http://www.audiodescribe.com/about/articles/ad_international_journal_07.pdf (consulted 12.04.2010).
Tannen, Deborah. 1980. 'A Comparative Analysis of Oral Narrative Strategies: Athenian Greek and American English' in Chafe, Wallace (ed.) *The Pear Stories: Cognitive, Cultural and Linguistic Aspects of Narrative Production*. Norwood, NJ: Ablex Publishing. 51-87.
Pfanstiehl, Margaret & Cody Pfanstiehl. 1985. 'The play's the thing' in *British Journal of Visual Impairment* 3: 91-92.
Udo, John Patrick & Deborah I. Fels. 2009. 'Suit the Action to the Word, the Word to the Action: An Unconventional Approach to Describing Shakespeare's Hamlet' in *Journal of Visual Impairment & Blindness* 103(3): 178-183.
Vercauteren, Gert. 2006. 'Practical Guidelines for Audio Description'. Paper presented at the Audiovisual Translation Scenarios Conference (University of Copenhagen, 1-5 May 2006).

The In-vision Sign Language Interpreter in British Television Drama

Alex McDonald
University of Leeds (United Kingdom)
Alexander Communications (United Kingdom)

Abstract

The provision of in-vision sign language interpreters in television drama is a growing area of demand in the United Kingdom. The advent of digital television has led to an increase in the number of programmes and channels available to the viewing public. This, coupled with the requirements of the Communications Bill (2003), the Broadcasting Act (1996) (OPSI), and the Code on Television Access Services (Ofcom), and that five per cent of digital, terrestrial, cable and satellite output must be accessible to Deaf[1] viewers through sign language presentation or in-vision interpreting, means that there is a continuing demand for British Sign Language (BSL) interpreters working in the audiovisual medium - the field of audiovisual translation (AVT). Sign language interpreters face unique challenges in providing the interpretation of a television drama. In British television drama, the in-vision interpreter is traditionally placed, from the viewer's perspective, in the lower right-hand corner of the screen and framed in a fixed mid-shot. The interpreter is responsible for the delivery of the interpretation of the programme from English to BSL. This responsibility includes 'playing' all characters and usually being on-screen and visible for the duration of the entire programme. This contribution explores firstly the interpreter's role in assisting the audience in negotiating the interactions of the competing visual images. Secondly, it highlights the author's own research evidence that interpreters are failing in this task. Thirdly, it aims to identify how this situation has arisen. Finally, the contribution explores how an interpreter's rendition can use the programme's visual structure, and how in-vision interpreters can become an additional element in the semiotic web of the drama.

Keywords

in-vision interpreter, new approach, sign language, television drama

1. Deaf culture

From the outset it is important to stress that the British Sign Language-using community is a distinct linguistic and cultural minority. It is a common assumption that because it uses *British* Sign Language (BSL), and because the national spoken language is English, the two languages are in some way related. In fact, the two languages are grammatically, syntactically and idiomatically very different. In addition, BSL functions spatially. It is not simply a process of switching modalities when providing BSL interpretations in any interpreter-mediated event.

Deaf people have a distinct cultural identity different from that of hearing people (Kyle & Woll 1993: 259; Wurm 2007: 117; Rocks 2011: 72), and when BSL interpreters work in any setting, they approach the task as one in which they are required to interpret between two languages and two cultures.

2. The in-vision interpreter and audiovisual translation

There are parallels to be drawn between in-vision interpreting and other areas of audiovisual translation (AVT). The issues confronting in-vision interpreters when preparing and delivering their interpretation in many ways resemble those faced by translators producing subtitles, dubbing and voice-over. Despite the similarities between the different strands of AVT, there are significant issues that are particular to the sign-language interpreter working in audiovisual media (theatre, film and television drama).

2.1 Commonalities between the in-vision interpreter and AVT

Like subtitles, the sign-language interpreter is included in the visual frame, becoming an additional semiotic element within the television drama's existing system, yet at the same time violating the image (Reimer & Davis 2008), forcing the audience to work harder to engage with the programme. This violation manifests itself in two ways: (1) the interpreter's image covers part of the screen and (2) the interpreter's image creates a competing visual image, resulting in viewers having to direct their attention away from the drama to receive the interpreter's rendition of the dialogue.

The dubbing of dialogue hides the original text by replacing the voices of the original actors with those of other actors. Although the sign-language rendition of a TV drama does not in itself replace the source text, the Deaf audience is unable to hear it and therefore relies solely on the interpreter for the dialogue. Like the translator providing subtitles, the interpreter is only one person providing the 'voices' of multiple characters from a location outside the drama. However, in the case of both subtitling and dubbing, the person or persons providing the target text attempt to match the timing of the source text (Luyken et al. 1991:31).

Along with other audiovisual translators, the in-vision interpreter must address the question of translation strategies such as omission, reduction, translating humour and metaphors, timing of utterances and so on, whilst recognising that the television drama is composed of a complex semiotic web and that there are temporal constraints placed on the delivery of the interpreted rendition.

The same conflicts arise around the idea of the domestication of audiovisual products: is the interpretation an opportunity to provide a 'window on the hearing world', or is it more important that it is familiar enough to the viewer? To what extent can interpreters domesticate the product when they are always visible and a constant reminder that the audience is watching a drama from another culture?

The interpreter is also responsible for allowing the audience members to suspend their disbelief and enter into the world of the drama. Even though the visibility of the interpreter is, in one way, a constant reminder that the programme is not in its original form, we have to accept that, as Chaume (2004: 38) indicates, "[t]he function of a fictional audiovisual text is primarily to entertain the viewer", or as Kahane maintains, "The ultimate goal is credibility, complete make believe" (Chaume 2004: 39).

2.2 Specific features of the in-vision interpreter in AVT

Interpreters are always visible to the viewers, yet do not physically exist within the narrative world of the drama. However, the target language is delivered in first person from the character's point of view: interpreters 'play' the characters as if from within the narrative world. They therefore work from a liminal space since they never 'exist' as interpreters in their own right. Since the interpreter never 'exists' in his or her own right, we can apply the notion of liminality, taken from Turner (1979), to the status of the in-vision interpreter.

The presence of interpreters creates an additional visual focus for the Deaf audience. As a result, interpreters have to work with the programme's sign system, not against it. Interpreters must negotiate the competing tensions between the essential movement of sign language and the stillness of a particular scene while maintaining the atmosphere of the drama.

Additionally, in-vision interpreters must be aware that their presence on the screen presents a second moving image, which is entirely outside the fictional world on the screen and therefore competes for the attention of the viewer.

On the surface, it appears that the interpretation of a television drama is a simultaneously interpreted dialogic event with the in-vision interpreter simply delivering the characters' conversations as they happen. Yet, we know that although the dialogue appears to be natural and unfolding, it can be over-determined in that the conversational maxims are carefully designed to have a specific effect on the viewer (Gambier 2003: 183; Wurm 2007: 124).

Although there are similarities between BSL interpreted television drama and the provision of subtitles, there are also significant differences, as mentioned above: Deaf viewers are not able to 'speed read' the interpreter's rendition since they must wait for the interpreter to deliver the signed text. Deaf viewers rely on the speed of delivery used by the interpreter, whose signed rendition is temporally bound to the character utterances. The interpreter cannot get ahead of the dialogue since BSL has spatial temporal aspects that insist on the allocation of information to respective characters; we cannot break the temporal relationship between the character's utterances and the interpreter's rendition. The spatial-temporal constraints are further enforced by the constructed world of the drama. In subtitling for the hard of hearing, the identification of which character is speaking and when can be achieved by the positioning and colour-coding of subtitles superimposed in the frame. In so doing, the spatial arrangement and orientation of the characters on screen helps viewers understand to whom the dialogue is being delivered. However, the interpreter cannot be moved around on the screen to provide interpreted utterances nearer to the speakers of the source text. The interpreter – from a fixed position at the edge of the screen – has to 'locate' the drama's characters, objects and their topographical relationships accurately, in the signing space available. If the spatial relationships between these entities in the interpreted rendition do not agree with those in the drama, the result is an inaccurate interpretation, in the same way that, for example, a source utterance 'over there' is not correctly rendered as 'over here'.

In dubbing and subtitling, actors and translators can review work and edit during the process. The BSL interpreter – presenting renditions of *all* of the characters – has to be visible to the audience and therefore has to present the rendition 'live' as the drama unfolds. The result is the interpreter's inability to stop, review and 're-do' small sections of text.

Taking these issues into account, how do in-vision interpreters provide accurate renditions that enable Deaf viewers to engage with the television drama?

3. Providing the interpretation

In BSL narrative the topographical use of signing space recreates a spatial layout representing that of the real world (Sutton-Spence & Woll 2005: 129). This allows the interpreted rendition to match the three-dimensional space of the world of the drama. Interpreters use the spatial, temporal and three-dimensional functions of BSL to recreate the physical location of the programme's characters and their spatial relationships with the other characters and objects in the drama, in the signing space.

Interpreters are able to 'play' each character through the use of *role-shift* or *character perspective* (Sutton-Spence & Woll 2005: 272; Sandler & Lillo-Martin 2006: 379; Meir & Sandler 2008: 70). This enables them to deliver the dialogue in the first person, as the character in the world of the drama. Using this shift in perspective, interpreters match the physical orientation and eye gaze of the character, and they play 'in the moment'. When another character speaks, they 'role-shift' into that character's orientation, their eye gaze, reflecting the character's spatial relationship within the narrative world that the character inhabits. By using these features, interpreters are able to recreate the physical and spatial relationships of the narrative world accurately in their interpretations.

To deliver a coherent rendition, interpreters must prepare and rehearse. In addition to learning the blocking, orientation and eye gaze of the characters, interpreters must also be competent at working with dialogue that appears to be that of everyday conversation when in fact it is not. Selby and Cowdery claim that "[f]ar from being natural, every narrative is the 'the result of manipulation and editing information together'" (1995: 30).

The interpreter, then, has to thoroughly prepare not just the spoken text, but the complete performance text in advance of the interpreted rendition (Rocks 2011: 76). In Herbst's words: "Interpreting a film [television drama] without having seen the pictures available is absurd in itself and explains why a lot of textual meaning that is not explicitly expressed in words never gets translated" (1995: 268).

Since the Sign Language interpreter has access to the finished audiovisual text, and time to make preparation, this event is 'protected' (Russo, 1995:344). The interpreter must use the complete text in order to identify where the visual elements informationally outweigh the dialogue, and find ways to naturally allow the viewer to focus on the visual frame. We have to remember that the Deaf viewer faces additional challenges by being forced to look away from the drama to see the dialogue

Although providing a BSL interpretation of a television drama is a highly complex and difficult process, like other strands of AVT it can be successfully delivered. Fortunately, the functions of BSL allow an interpreter's rendition to match the temporal and spatial relationships of the original accurately; the finished performance text is available, which means that interpreters are able to prepare and rehearse prior to the recording of the interpreted rendition.

However, analyses of interpreted television dramas show that interpreters are failing to demonstrate an awareness of the polysemiotic nature of television drama, or to show a true understanding of the genre in which they are working (McDonald 2006: 46).

4. Research

My previous MA research (in 2006) employed an adapted multimodal transcription analysis, based on those of Thibault (2000) and Taylor (2003) to analyse a selection of mainstream British television dramas (examples included domestic, medical, detective and historical dramas), each broadcast with different in-vision interpreters. The analysis involved the transcription of the drama's dialogue and arrangement of characters on screen, as well as a transcription of the interpreter activity during the drama with a special focus on the interpreted rendition's temporal relationship with the source dialogue, and on the accuracy of orientation with the characters on screen. My ongoing PhD research is the development of a multimodal annotated analysis of in-vision interpreting for TV dramas.

To date, the research has found interpreters in general using little or inaccurate role-shift, and often delivering dialogue straight to camera, although the characters never deliver their dialogue to the camera. The interpreters often sign everything that is uttered without allowing viewers the opportunity to look at the screen when there is redundancy in both dialogue and image. Thus, viewers have little time to watch the programme itself. Throughout the texts analysed, there is evidence which demonstrates that interpreters' role-shifts fail to match both the orientation of the characters on screen and the position of the character that the dialogue is addressed to, along with apparent random shifts in focus. Here, I am using the term 'focus' to refer to the direction of the gaze of a character (and that of the interpreter when rendering the dialogue of that character) towards the position (or implied position) of another character or entity in the world of the drama, that is, the direction of delivery of dialogue, and not the grammatical use of eye gaze in sign language, which includes elements such as deictic referencing, expressing subject and object agreement (Tate 2002), locus and movement of referents in space (Braffort & Lejeune 2006: 39; Bahan 1996), turn taking (Lucas 2002: 99) and the marking of present and future times (Sutton-Spence 2005: 96).

Transcription 1 (Figure 1) is of a 5-minute section of the one-off drama *Soundproof,* originally broadcast by the BBC on 12 July 2006, with the sign-language interpreted version broadcast on 19 July 2006. In the transcription, each character utterance is numbered, and at each utterance we can also see that character's direction of address, along with the parallel activity of the interpreter, demonstrating the temporal relationship between the source text and target text.

The in-vision sign language interpreter in British television drama

Transcription 1: 'Soundproof'

```
DIALOGUE:                  WOMAN: 1. Hi...        2. Hello...             3. [WOMAN Clears throat]
CHARACTER ADDRESS:         [FROM A DISTANCE TO RIGHT OF CAMERA——]          [TO LEFT OF CAMERA——]
BACK TRANSLATION:                  1.Hi.  [ADDITION]:Ignoring me.  2.Hello. [ADDITION]:Snooty. [ADDITION]:Hello.
INTERPRETER ADDRESS:       [CAMERA]   [CAMERA/LEFT][CAMERA/LEFT] [CAMERA]                      [LEFT+DOWN]

DIALOGUE:              [NO DIALOGUE]
CHARACTER ADDRESS:     [SHOT TOWARDS DEAN WITH HIS BACK TO CAMERA. WOMAN TAPS DEAN ON SHOULDER]
BACK TRANSLATION:               3.Cough.
INTERPRETER ADDRESS:        [CAMERA] [SCREEN FOCUS——]

DIALOGUE:              4. WOMAN: Sorry, sorry,... You are English aren't you?    5. DEAN [SPEAKS AND SIGNS]: I'm Deaf.
CHARACTER ADDRESS:     [TO RIGHT——————————————]                                  [TO LEFT——————]
BACK TRANSLATION:                          4. Sorry........You English? You English?
INTERPRETER ADDRESS:     ————SCREEN FOCUS——————————]    [CAMERA                 ] [SCREEN FOCUS——]

DIALOGUE:              6. WOMAN: Oh...well...I'm sorry. I'm so sorry...I didn't realise. Would you like some coffee?
CHARACTER ADDRESS:     [TO RIGHT——————————————————————————————————]
BACK TRANSLATION:               5.Speaks I'm Deaf.   6. Sorry.....  Sorry...  Didn't realise.   You want coffee?
INTERPRETER ADDRESS:        [CAMERA                ] [CAMERA——LEFT+DOWN——]        [CAMERA/LEFT+DOWN/CAMERA——]

DIALOGUE:              7.DEAN: No.   8.WOMAN: Tea?....Some tea? [DEAN SHAKES HIS HEAD]  9.WOMAN: Wh...some water?
CHARACTER ADDRESS:     [TO LEFT——]              [TO RIGHT——————————————————————]                              9.Any water?
BACK TRANSLATION:          7. [ZERO RENDITION]..                    8.Tea?                                    ] [CAMERA——]
INTERPRETER ADDRESS:   [SCREEN FOCUS————————]        [CAMERA] [SCREEN FOCUS——————]
```

Figure 1. Transcription of *Soundproof*

195

In dialogue 6 for example, the WOMAN directs her speech to the right of the screen while the interpreter is rendering utterance 5 in the back translation and addressing it to the camera.

In this section, I identified twelve separate interpreter utterances, with nine of the utterances corresponding with the spoken dialogue, and three additional ones. Of those twelve utterances, seven were directed to the camera, three were rendered with the focus moving between the camera and to the left, one was directed to the left and down, and one was a zero rendition. Not one utterance matched the alignment or direction of focus of either character on screen at any time during the segment. The observations made here were characteristic of the interpretation as a whole. Noticeable throughout the drama was firstly the interpreter's delivery of almost all the interpreted dialogue towards the camera. This was not a case of the interpreter directing his gaze to a neutral point that happened to be the camera by coincidence (which should under all circumstances be avoided as it plays against the convention of the dramatic 'fourth wall'). On the contrary, it was a direct and purposeful address of the dialogue to the viewers. This phenomenon was also observed in other examples. Also notable was the failure of the interpreter to match – at any time – the orientation and focus of the character whose dialogue was being interpreted. Similar observations were once again made in the other dramas analysed.

This lack of agreement of focus in the interpreter's version starts to break down what should be the visual agreement between the narrative world, the character uttering the source language, and the rendition received by the target audience. It also highlights that interpreters regularly breach the 'fourth wall' of the television drama by playing to the camera, although this never occurs in the narrative world of the drama.

We know that television and film use conventions and codes to manipulate the viewers' reactions and their relationships with the programme and characters (Cartmell 2000: 5). Interpreters 'playing to camera' not only cause a visual discrepancy between the two images of the programme and the respective interpreter, the habit also cuts across the conventions and codes of signing, which causes Deaf viewers to respond to the drama in a way that was not intended by the original (Burch 1982: 22). This playing to the camera also breaks the character perspective function of BSL. In all the dramas analysed, the characters never look at the camera as observed by Davies as follows:

> An actor in a play who is supposed to be speaking to another character should never in any circumstances look into the lens. If he does, realism will be lost as he will appear to be speaking to the viewer. (1966: 54)

Breaks in the temporal/visual relationship between the narrative world and the interpreted rendition were also identified. My analyses found that the interpreted rendition often and substantially lags behind the dialogue of the programme, damaging not only the perceived relationship between the characters, but that between the programme and the viewer. In simultaneous interpreting, there is always a flexible temporal relationship between the source text and target text. Yet, in the setting of television drama, interpreters are bound to the semantic relationship between spoken text and the visual element. Where there are attempts at role-shift, an interpreter's temporal lag causes the rendered dialogue to be incorrectly attributed.[2]

During a scene in *Desperate Romantics* (see Transcription 2 in Figure 2) Mrs Ruskin congratulates the artist Millais (Dialogue 1). Because of the interpreter's temporal lag, the BSL rendition has Millais congratulating Mrs Ruskin because by the time the interpreter starts to deliver the BSL rendition of Dialogue 1, the spoken dialogue has moved on, with the screen showing Millais responding with the question "For what exactly?" (Dialogue 2). This temporal/visual discordance is further compounded by the interpreter's orientation when delivering Mrs Ruskin's line "I hear that congratulations are in order…" by actually matching the orientation of Millais on screen. The interpreter's temporal lag and inappropriate orientation continues throughout the remainder of the scene.

Alex McDonald

Transcription 2: 'Desperate Romantics'

DIALOGUE: 1. MRS RUSKIN: I hear that congratulations are the order of the day. 2. MILLAIS: For what exactly?
CHARACTER ADDRESS: [To LEFT--] [TO RIGHT-----]
BACK TRANSLATION: 1. I should congratulate you.
INTERPRETER ADDRESS: [SCREEN FOCUS---------------------------------] [TO CAMERA/UP+TO RIGHT]

DIALOGUE: 3. MRS RUSKIN: For becoming an associate of the Royal Academy. 4. MILLAIS: Yes…yes
CHARACTER ADDRESS: [TO LEFT--] [TO RIGHT]
BACK TRANSLATION: 2. Me? For what? 3. Becoming an associate of the Royal Academy
INTERPRETER ADDRESS: [RIGHT/UP+TO LEFT] [UP + TO RIGHT]

DIALOGUE: …[pause]…5. Mr Ruskin is a good fellow. 6. MRS RUSKIN: Indeed.
CHARACTER ADDRESS: [DOWN+TO LEFT-----------------] [TO RIGHT-----]
BACK TRANSLATION: 4. Yes… Yes. 5. Mr R-U-S-K-I-N…….he's a good man.
INTERPRETER ADDRESS: [UP+TO RIGHT] [TO CAMERA------------------]/UP + TO RIGHT--]

DIALOGUE: 7. MILLAIS: But not of our kind – his soul always among the clouds.
CHARACTER ADDRESS: [TO RIGHT+UP--]
BACK TRANSLATION: 6. Yes 7. But not the same as us, his soul is in the clouds.
INTERPRETER ADDRESS: [UP+LEFT] [TO CAMERA-------------------------][UP+LEFT]

Figure 2. Transcription of *Desperate Romantics*

'Screen focus'[3] – although widely used in BSL interpreting – is a style that works against the audiovisual medium and seems at odds with the visual images of the programme. It appears to be a convention used by in-vision interpreters to give focus to the action on screen and at points when there are sequences without dialogue. Although not confined to in-vision interpreting, interpreters generally give focus by standing in a business-like manner, hands clasped in front, appearing to look at the drama on screen (or at the speaker in other settings) effectively closing the channels of communication (McDonald 2006: 39).

At one level, giving focus to the drama serves to inform the audience that they should be focusing on the visual action. However, at the same time it plays against the programme's own semiotic codes. To Deaf viewers, it appears as if the interpreter has 'shut down' and has disengaged from the programme. Yet, no character shuts down or disengages from the drama. This use of screen focus is not confined to sections without dialogue but also occurs during exchanges of dialogue. For example, when a character pauses during an utterance, the interpreter also clasps his or her hands and looks to the screen until the character resumes speaking. In this way the interpreter effectively edits out the characters' pauses, altering the 'flow' of the dialogue, or indicates that the conversation has ended, when in fact it continues in the original.

The examples used above are representative of the interpretations provided throughout the respective television programmes. Interpreting approaches inappropriate for the setting, such as temporal lag and breaches of the fourth wall, conflict with the messages from the drama. In addition, the target language produced serves to confuse the audience further. From my analyses it would appear that the interpretation is being carried out at word or sentence equivalence rather than at text level, without taking into account the visual context in which it is delivered. Consequently the target viewer is unable to construct a meaningful narrative world based on the interpreter's rendition.

So why do BSL interpreters play against the semiotic codes of television drama and why do they not allow the natural function of BSL to accurately match the narrative world created by the television drama?

It is, in part, due to that fact that BSL interpreting is a relatively young profession (McDonald 2006: 1) and does not have the "academic tradition of literary translators or spoken language conference interpreters" (Rocks 2011: 73). Although university postgraduate and MA interpreter training is now becoming more available to BSL interpreters, these courses still cover only the areas of dialogue and conference styles of interpreting and have no formal modules for working in the field of AVT. In contrast, translators and interpreters for other languages generally have access to courses which deal with screen translation. The vast majority of BSL interpreters working in TV are not actors, and like society in general, they are only viewers of television drama, not experts in the field. Consequently, they may tend to treat the interpretation of TV drama as a standard simultaneous interpreting assignment and neglect to make the necessary preparation that AVT clearly requires.

It appears that misguided notions are being applied to interpreting for television drama and that interpreters are attempting to use interpreting strategies that work in everyday settings such as dialogic events and conferences. Additionally, there is a mistaken assumption about the relationship between television dramas and viewers. By borrowing from conference interpreting, seemingly viewing the interpretation of television drama as a monologic communicative event, interpreters fails to understand how drama is communicated to viewers. The dialogue is written as a secondary speech genre (Bakhtin 1986: 61-62), that is, the drama is filmed with the knowledge that viewers are not participants but rather observers of the action. By playing to the camera, interpreters are, in effect, having a dialogue with the viewers, shifting the status of the target audience from that of spectators to interactants.

5. A new approach to the in-vision interpretation of TV drama

A successful approach to the in-vision interpretation of television drama must use the natural aspects of BSL (i.e., character perspective/role-shift) to match and maintain the three-dimensional space created by the drama on screen.

It is important to note that although using character perspective, interpreters do not physically exist in the narrative world. Visible to the audience, superimposed onto the drama's visual image, and although aiming to merge with its semiotic channels, interpreters are clearly not part of the narrative world, yet their role – at any time – is that of a character from the narrative world. However, the interpreter never exists as an interpreter or narrator.

As we know, there are important markers of information in non-verbal channels and although we cannot break the temporal/spatial relationship between spoken dialogue and the interpreted rendition, we can manipulate this relationship.

The manipulation of the timing of utterances in the interpreters' renditions can permit the target text to be finished a few beats ahead of the characters' dialogues so that viewers have time to focus on the screen and see vital information. It is at these moments that interpreters must maintain the feel or atmosphere of the drama, not as interpreters overtly telling viewers to 'watch now', or by using screen focus inappropriately, 'shutting down' and disengaging from the drama, but by giving focus to the drama with engagement.

It may well be the case that the visual signs of the programme are sufficient to carry the message, especially when we take into account that the most important information about characters tends to be communicated through their actions (Potter 2001: 231). By using the screen narrative to tell the story for us, it becomes apparent that interpreters provide an additional channel of the drama's communication system.

I propose that we take the scene – within the overall arc of the drama's storyline – as the starting point of this translation/interpretation process, as Herbst (1995:270) suggests as a pragmatic approach to dubbing.

The definition of a scene is described variously in film-studies literature as a narrative scene, action scene, one-shot scene, and so on. However, since the function of character perspective/role-shift in sign language is based on the actual spatial arrangement of the characters and objects in the narrative world, we must demarcate the scene by changes of location. This approach also allows interpreters to use the visual grammar of the drama, in particular the use of the opening and establishing shots (Cardwell 2002: 141), showing the spatial relationships of entities located in the scene to support those of the interpreted three-dimensional world.

This enables the interpreted rendition not only to deliver and correctly allocate the spoken text but also to work with and maintain the drama's visual grammar. Block (2001: xii) stresses the critical relationship of the visual structure and the story structure in the construction of the drama. In the same way that the story structure communicates emotions and moods, the visual image structure also portrays these aspects.

We now begin to blur the traditional borders between translating and interpreting. By having to account for the visual narrative, to identify where the informational load is being carried, and to work with dialogue that is over-determined, there has to be process of translation that has a direct bearing on the work and roles of interpreters.

How we watch the drama and which areas of the screen we focus on is directed by the structure of the visual frame. It is the manipulation and directing of the viewer's points of attention that serves to reinforce what Millerson (2001: 421) refers to as the drama's 'illusion of reality'; where the actors are in placed relation to each other, the track of their eye gaze, and so on, "we [the audience] build up a mental image of where things are located within the scene. We form these judgements from various visual clues: comparing common features, movements, the relative directions in which people are looking" (Millerson 2001). Film and television studies recognise that it is extremely easy to compromise this mental image through visual anomalies such as not maintaining the relative screen positions (Millerson

2001: 421; Thompson 1998: 9). The relative screen positions can be disrupted or destroyed by crossing an imaginary line as described by Thompson:

> The imaginary line can exist between two people looking at each other, or a person looking at an object, between a person moving to an object or a place, or even between two places. The line can even exist between an object leaning or moving in one direction to another... Without 'the line' even the simplest scene can become confusing to an audience. (Thompson 1998:16)

It is useful to determine from where the audience is looking, for clarification, and to eliminate visual complications. Thompson discusses this as follows:

> Thus 'the line', is critical as a guide for the audience. It helps to overcome the problem of credibility; it puts the audience in an idealised position so that they believe what they see. Otherwise 'reality' is not seen to be accurate. (Thompson 1998:18)

For Deaf viewers there is an additional point of attention: an in-vision interpreter in the bottom right corner of the visual frame. In order to receive the dramatic text, the viewers' attention is drawn – like readers of subtitles – to an area that is light on information (Reimer & Davis 2008). The competition for focus between the drama's visual frame and the in-vision interpreter prevents the viewer from concentrating solely on the drama; the very presence of the in-vision interpreter alters the grammar of the moving image. "Once that grammar is changed or omitted, either by design or ignorance, then many of the elements in the complex process of perception, of reading and understanding, are themselves changed" (Thompson 1998: 9).

However, the interpreters' use of character perspective replicates the relative screen positions of referents. This enables the maintenance of 'the line' and serves to underpin the visual structure of the drama. If interpreters plays against the narrative world – as the analyses show – they are in effect 'crossing the line'. Without detailed translation processes interpreters will not be equipped to provide appropriate interpretations with reference to the narrative worlds and visual structuresof dramas. It is time that BSL interpreters working in audiovisual media also become aware that the use of interpretational lag in this type of setting is counterproductive to the audience's understanding of the drama. They also need to appreciate that thorough preparation – essential in the interpreting of fixed time-bound audiovisual texts – will not only address this issue, but also serve to improve the quality of their interpretation, allowing them to move away from the word-for-sign translation often observed.

6. Conclusion

Interpreters – as well as the broadcasters commissioning signed programmes – must be aware that providing an in-vision interpretation is in fact commissioning both a translation *and* an interpretation.

The field of AVT provides sign-language interpreters with new challenges, different from those of either conference or dialogue interpreting. While some of these challenges are unique to in-vision sign-language interpreters, AVT can provide a framework from which new approaches can be developed. Initially, it may seem that television and film dialogue replicates dialogue found in everyday life. However, it has a much more complex structure with the conversational maxims designed to have a specific effect on viewers, to delineate character and to serve the plot (McDonald 2006: 44).

We need to address how interpreters can successfully negotiate the complex semiotic nature of television programmes and not work against them. Specific training for sign-language interpreters in AVT must involve the understanding of film and television, its structure and production. As Bartrina (2004: 157) highlights, past research has looked at film studies to gain a better understanding of the complexities in this genre. AVT studies can provide appropriate approaches to the translation and interpretation of television drama by working with – not against – the supporting polysemiotic codes.

---

[1] In this context the term *Deaf* relates to first language sign language users (Neves 2008: 172, Rocks 2011). It does not refer to those who have become deaf or people who are 'hard of hearing', whose first language remains English and who would access these programmes using subtitles for the hard of hearing.

[2] Cokely (1986: 341-376) compared what he terms the "lag time" of simultaneous sign language interpreters in education, and found "an inverse relationship between the amount of lag time and the number of interpreter errors'; an interpreter lag time of 2 seconds produced more miscues than a lag time of 4 seconds. The BSL interpreting community has adopted this evidence, and it is now widely accepted that having a consistent lag time [in any setting] is an interpreting strategy" (Rocks 2006: 22).

[3] When the interpreter looks to his or her right as if watching the drama, is used as a method to indicate to the target audience that they should focus upon the screen action rather than on the interpreter.

References

Bahan, Benjamin. 1996. *Non-Manual Realization of Agreement in American Sign Language*. PhD thesis, Boston University.

Bakhtin, Mikhail M. 1986. *Speech Genres and Other Late Essays* (transl. Vern W. McGee, edited by Caryl Emerson & Michael Holquist Austin, TX, University of Texas Press.

Bartrina, Francesca. 2004. 'The Challenge of Research in Audiovisual Translation' in Orero, Pilar (ed.) *Topics in Audiovisual Translation*. Amsterdam, John Benjamins. 157-167.

Block, Bruce A. 2001. *The Visual Story: Seeing the Structure of Film, TV, and New Media*. Oxford: Focal Press.

Braffort, Annelies & Fanch Lejeune, (2006) 'Spatialised Semanitc Relations in French Sign Language: Toward a Computational Modelling in Gesture in Human-Computer Interaction and Simulation Lecture Notes' in *Computer Science* 3881: 37–48.

Burch, Noël. 1982. 'Narrative/Diegesis – Thresholds, Limits' in *Screen* 23: 16-33.

Cardwell, Sarah. 2002. *Adaptation Revisited Television and the Classic Novel*. Manchester: Manchester University Press.

Cartmell, Deborah. 2000. *Interpreting Shakespeare on Screen*. London: Macmillan.

Chaume, Federico .2004. Synchronization in Dubbing: A Translational Approach in Orero, Pilar (ed.) *Topics in Audiovisual Translation*. Amsterdam, John Benjamins. 35–52.

Cokely, Dennis. 1986. 'The Effects of Lag Time on Interpreter Errors' in *Sign Language Studies* 15(53): 341-376..

Davis, Desmond. 1966. *The Grammar of Television Production*. London: Barrie & Jenkins.

Gambier, Yves. 2003. 'Introduction. Screen Translation: Perception and Reception' in *The Translator* Volume 9(2): 171-189.

Herbst, Thomas. 1995. People Don't Talk in Sentences: Dubbing and the Idiom Principle in Audiovisual Communication & Language Transfer: International Forum, Strasbourg Council of Europe 22-24 June 1995. *Translatio Nouvelles de la FIT/FIT newsletter, New Series* 3-4.

Kyle, Jim G. & Bencie Woll. 1993. *Sign Language*. Cambridge: Cambridge University Press.

Lucas, Ceil. 2002. *Turn-taking, Fingerspelling and Contact in Signed Languages*. US Gallaudet University Press.

Luyken, Georg-Michael., Thomas Herbst, Jo Langham-Brown, Helene Reid & Herman Spinhof, 1991. *Overcoming Language Barriers in Television: Dubbing and Subtitling for the European Audience*. Manchester: The European Institute for the Media.

McDonald, Alex. 2006. A Multimodal Transcription Analysis of the In-vision Sign Language Interpreter in Television Drama. Unpublished MA thesis. University of Leeds.

Meir, Irit & Wendy Sandler. 2008. *A Language in Space the Story of Israeli Sign Language*. New York: Lawrence Erlbaum.

Millerson, Gerald. 2001. *Television Production*. Oxford. Focal Press.

Neves, Josélia. 2004. 'Language Awareness through Training in Subtitles' in Orero, Pilar (ed.) *Topics in Audiovisual Translation*. Amsterdam, John Benjamins. 127-140.

Neves, Josélia. 2008. 'Training in Subtitling for the d/Deaf and Hard-of-Hearing' in Díaz Cintas, Jorge (ed.) *The Didactics of Audiovisual Translation*. Amsterdam, John Benjamins. 171-189.

Ofcom. *Code on Television Acces*. n.d. Online at http://www.ofcom.org.uk/tv/ifi/codes/ctas/ (consulted 15.04.2010).

Office of Public Sector information (OPSI). 1996. *Broadcasting Act 1996* . Online at http://www.opsi.gov.uk/acts/acts1996/ukpga_19960055_en_1 (consulted 15.04.2010).

Office of Public Sector information (OPSI). 2003. *Communications Act 2003* Online at http://www.opsi.gov.uk/acts/acts2003/ukpga_20030021_en_1 (consulted 15.04.2010).

Potter, Cherry. 2001. *Screen Language: From Film Writing to Film-making*. London: Metheun.

Reimer, Robert C. & William S. Davis. 2008. *Subtitling and Dubbing as Film Adaptation*. Paper given at Cultures of Translation: Adaptation in Film and Performance Conference. 26-28June. Cardiff. Cardiff School of Creative & Cultural Industries.

Rocks, Siobhán. 2006. *What do they do when they come to a line with no words in it?: The British Sign Language Interpreter in Mainstream Theatre*. Unpublished MA thesis, University of Leeds.

Rocks, Siobhán. 2011. 'The Theatre Sign Language Interpreter and the Competing Visual Narrative: The translation and interpretation of theatrical texts into British Sign Language' in Baines, Roger, Cristina Marinetti & Manuela Perteghella (eds.) *Staging Translation: Text and Theatre Practice*. Basingstoke: Palgrave Macmillan.

Russo, Mariachiara. 1995. Media Interpreting: Variables and Strategies in Audiovisual Communication & Language Transfer: International Forum, Strasbourg Council of Europe 22-24 June 1995. *Translatio Nouvelles de la FIT/FIT newsletter, New Series* 14(3-4).

Thompson, Roy. 1998. *Grammar of the Shot*. Oxford: Focal Press.

Sandler, Wendy & Diane Lilllo-Martin. 2006. *Sign Language and Linguistic Universals*. Cambridge: Cambridge University Press.

Selby, Keith & Ron Cowdery. 1995. *How to Study Television*. London: MacMillan.

Stoddart, Jonathan. 2000. 'Teaching through Translations' in *The Journal 11*. British Council. April. Online at http://www.britishcouncil.org/portugal/journal/j1106js.htm

Sutton-Spence, Rachel & Bencie Woll. 2005. *The Linguistics of British Sign Language: An Introduction*. Cambridge: Cambridge University Press.

Tate, Erin. 2002. Eye Gaze in American Sign Language. Online at http://www.lifeprint.com/asl101/topics/eyegaze.htm (consulted 15.04.2010).

Taylor, Christopher. J. 2003. Multimodal Transcription in the Analysis, Translation and Subtitling of Italian Films' in *The Translator* 9(2): 191-205.

Thibault, Paul. 2000. The Multimodal Transcription of a Television Advertisement: Theory and Practice in Baldry, Anthony (ed.) *Mulimodalityand Multimediality in the Distance Learning Age*. Campobasso, Palladino Editore. 311-385.

Turner, Victor. 1979. 'Frame, Flow and Reflection: Ritual and Drama as Public Liminality' in *Japanese Journal of Religious Studies* 6(4): 465-499.

Wurm, Svenja. 2007. 'Intralingual and Interlingual Subtitling: A Discussion of the Mode and Medium in Film Translation.' in *The Sign Language Translator and Interpreter* 1(1): 115-41.

Filmography

Desperate romantics (Episode 3), Paul Gray (BBC Sign Zone, 11.08.2009), UK
Soundproof, Edmund Coulthard (Broadcast BBC Sign Zone, 19.07.2006), UK

Section 3

The Discourses of Audiovisual Translation

AVT Classics Revisited (pp. 209-247)

Bilingualism, Multilingualism and Its Consequences (pp. 249-334)

AVT, Film Language and Corpora (pp. 335-425)

Voice-over or Voice-in-between? Some Considerations about the Voice-over Translation of Feature Films on Polish Television

Monika Woźniak
University of Rome La Sapienza (Italy)

Abstract

Of all the AVT techniques, voice-over has probably been the least studied and the least valued. This state of affairs can be found in not only western Europe (where voice-over is limited to mostly non-fiction programmes) but also in Poland (where voice-over remains the most widely applied technique of translation for feature films for the television and DVD markets. The aim of this contribution is to re-evaluate some of the existing academic prejudices against voice-over and to highlight its advantages in comparison with subtitling and dubbing, given that voice-over is free of some specific constraints that are present in the other two AVT techniques. The analysis – illustrated by selected examples taken from the TV science-fiction series *Star Trek* – focuses on the interaction between the key factors in successful voice-over: (1) the acoustic balance between the original film's soundtrack and the text delivered by the reader, (2) the quality and the quantity of translated text and (3) the timbre and intonation of the reader's voice, and (4) the way in which the reader synchronises the reading with the original soundtrack. In the conclusion, the author proposes that the voice-over of feature films could be improved dramatically by transforming it into a 'voice-in-between' technique.

Keywords

fiction programmes, Poland, television, voice-over

1. Introduction: Voice-over, the 'ugly duckling' of AVT studies

Orero – one of few scholars who have shown an assiduous interest in voice-over translation – rightly pointed out that within the field of audiovisual translation (AVT) studies "techniques such as voice-over have been left aside and not clearly understood […]. As a result, it comes as no surprise that reference works on AVT have not considered voice-over as a discrete entry" (2009: 130-131). The technique of voice-over – used widely in television programmes – is usually associated with only non-fiction products in western countries. Since there appears to be a common belief that "translated foreign material within non-fictional output (…) constitutes uninteresting data for the purposes of research" (Franco 2000: 3), the problem of its translation has long been considered a "straightforward, non-problematic activity" (Franco

2000: 3) that offers no stimulus for academic research. Even if the interest in this topic among scholars seems to have increased in the last few years and some important publications focusing on voice-over have recently been released (Orero, Matamala & Franco 2010), it still remains one of the lesser known AVT modes and awaits further academic scrutiny.

2. Views on the voice-over translation of feature films

But if voice-over can justly be called the "ugly duckling" of AVT (Orero 2006), the practice of using it in fictional products – although long-established in many countries in eastern Europe – has been, so far, practically ignored within the field of AVT. Scholars from western Europe, most of whom have never been exposed to this kind of translation, usually limit themselves in their essays to brief tidbits about the bizarre audiovisual practice that exotic nations seem to be fond of. They show little understanding of substantial differences existing in voice-over translation between such countries as the Baltic States, Bulgaria, Poland and the Ukraine. The peculiarity of the Polish voice-over translation strategy, which shares some characteristics with Gavrilov translation,[1] seems particularly puzzling to many foreign scholars, who even resort to negative or sarcastic comments about it. While they usually do not go as far as to suggest that Polish voice-over translation is "a particularly egregious hangover from the Communist system" and also due to the fact that "a lot of people in Poland have bad eyes and don't have enough money for glasses" as an article from *The New York Times* did some years ago (Glaser 1992), statements such as "voice-over translation is also used in countries with a high level of illiteracy, because it doesn't require the capacity of reading, and it is particularly popular in Eastern Europe" (Perego 2005) or "language transfer using this method can in no sense maintain or do justice to the quality of the original version" (Dries 1995b) are not as uncommon as one would suppose.

To a certain extent it is understandable that western scholars show little interest in the translation technique that they have not experienced first-hand and that they are uncapable of directly evaluating. It is more difficult to understand why – in spite of the fact that voice-over translation covers almost 100% of foreign fiction programmes on Polish television – most Polish scholars follow suit. In fact, Polish scholars tend to dismiss voice-over translation in fiction as "a technique without a future" (Tomaszkiewicz 2006) and therefore do not feel compelled to pursue the topic in their scientific investigations. Moreover, a bias against this "immanently imperfect" (Hendrykowski 1984) translation mode is often perceivable in opinions such as "the only positive aspect of this technique is its low cost" (Belczyk 2007), it "shouldn't be used for translation of feature films" (Tomaszkiewicz 2006), or "*Unfortunately* Polish viewers are not ready to accept subtitles in everyday practice" (Garcarz 2007, my emphasis). Among Polish film critics, journalists and some viewers who aspire to be considered the educated elite, bad-mouthing the voice-over technique is almost fashionable. Moreover, it is not rare to run into very emotional and strong negative judgments expressed in heated discussions on internet forums.[2] However, it is worth noting that the main argument used in favour of introducing subtitles instead of voice-over translation on Polish television is purely utilitarian, that is, that subtitles help viewers learn English.

Still, a huge majority of Polish viewers prefer voice-over translation on television. According to a 2002 survey, 50.2% of Poles prefer voice-over and 43.4% opt for dubbing. Subtitling supporters constitute only 8.1%. When asked which form of AVT was the worst, a staggering 72.1% of Poles chose subtitling (Bogucki 2001). Interestingly enough, the public does not appear to object to subtitles in the cinema and is also willing to accept – or even to greet with enthusiasm – dubbing, as long as it is limited to animated films such as *Shrek*[3] and feature films for children. On the other hand, Polish viewers prefer voice-over to dubbing on television. This preference is so pronounced that some private channels that tried to offer dubbed versions of TV series ultimately gave up the practice (Subbotko 2008).

To sum up, the argument about subtitles being the best method to stimulate the audience to learn English is a valid one (at least as long as we identify TV fiction with American/English production) but it has nothing to do with aesthetic aspects of the film and the voice-over translation as such. Also, negative opinions about the low quality of Polish voice-over translation are very often justified. However, this is a criticism which is directed not so much at the technique itself, but rather at the ways in which voice-over is implemented by broadcasters. This may include poor professional preparation and inadequate salaries for translators and *lektors* (individuals who read the text), hurried production, and finally – and maybe most important – the lack of standards regarding this kind of translation. Hardly any attempt has been made so far to conduct a serious analysis of the specific requirements of voice-over translation used in fiction or to establish a set of rules which could help improve the quality of voice-over translation.

While I would not go as far as to say that Polish voice-over translation for TV fiction is in fact a beautiful Cinderella living in the shadow of her two ugly sisters named subtitling and dubbing, it is indeed my intention to defend the honour of the damsel in distress. I hope to demonstrate in the subsequent sections of this contribution that many of the prejudices against voice-over are unfounded or exaggerated, and that this technique possesses qualities which could eventually be brought to fruition as an effective and unobtrusive AVT method.

3. Challenges facing studies on voice-over translation

While at this stage it would be premature to try to establish a normative set of rules regarding the voice-over translation of fiction, the discussion below highlights some salient points that – with further scrutiny – cannot only offer a significant contribution to such a model, but also prove interesting in the general context of voice-over translation research.

3.1 General remarks

The first important issue to consider pertains to the functions played by the original soundtrack in non-fiction and fiction programmes and – consequently – to the main objectives that underlie the translation strategy and its incorporation into audiovisual programmes. Once we agree that these functions are indeed essentially diverse, it becomes clear that whatever rules and strategies have been established for voice-over translation in non-fiction genres, they will probably be of little use to feature films, with one notable exception discussed below. For example, the "authenticity illusion" aims to convince the audience members that what they are "being told in their own language is what is being said in the original language" (Franco 2000: 36). This also seems to be an important factor in the perception of voice-over translation of feature films, since Polish viewers stress the fact that the voice-over version allows them to hear the original voice of the actors.[4] However, the segmentation of the soundtrack in non-fiction and fiction genres usually differs quite substantially. A discursive commentary, narration or monologue is the dominant form of communication in documentaries, news reports or political speeches. Arguably, more affinities may be found between film dialogues and interviews or – in a larger perspective – in documentaries with an interactive mode of presentation (Nichols 1991: 44-56). However, the resemblance seems rather superficial, as far as both the conversational pattern and speech functions are concerned. Interviews are a form of over-determined[5] and hierarchical structure "deriving from the unequal distribution of power, as in the confessional and interrogation" (Nichols 1991: 47). Therefore they often – if not always – follow the conversational pattern of longer utterances by the interviewees punctuated by the interviewers' questions. Film conversations tend to be shorter and favour more balanced exchanges between the characters. They are also deeply embedded in the visual context, given that in a feature film the language is a part of a "perfectly disguised fictionality" (Baumgarten 2003) with all subsequent functional implications (see Kozloff 2000: 33-63) and that film dialogue needs to work on two dimensions: On the one hand, an utterance has a function in the speech situation on-screen, on the other hand, the utterance also functions as a major constituent in the film text as a whole, whose addressees are the audience. This means – according to Baumgarten (2003: 21) that "a character's implicit or indirect communication on-screen must be made explicit in the sense that the viewer needs to be able to decode and interpret the utterance in the context of the film as a whole. [...] It is crucial for this level of communication that the viewer as indirect addressee be provided with information adequate to understanding what is meant by the on-screen exchanges, since there is, of course, no backchannel available".

Therefore, the general rule of voice-over translation – which is to begin delivery of the translated text with a few seconds delay and to end it before the original soundtrack ends – should not be automatically applied in fictional programmes, in which the translation has to take into account two parallel levels of communication and lexicalise the conversation within the frame of the visual message. However, from a purely technical point of view the dialogue structure in fictional programmes is more complicated and polyphonic (i.e., the original text is distributed among many voices) on the one hand but usually offers more possibilities to find pauses between utterances on the other hand.

3.2 Voice-over translation as a combination of three elements

In fact, one of the major difficulties in researching the voice-over translation of feature films may lie in the fact that a successful delivery of the translated text depends on three independent, yet strictly correlated factors:

(1) The acoustic balance between the original film's soundtrack and the text delivered by the reader;
(2) The quality and the quantity of translated text;
(3) The timbre and intonation of the reader's voice, and the way in which the reader synchronises the reading with the original sound.

Unfortunately, not one of these three elements has been subject to serious research so far, especially in the context of the other two. The effect of a particular reader's voice on the audience is bound to be subjective – at least to a certain extent – and since no empirical surveys in this field have been conducted, the knowledge of Polish viewers' preferences is incomplete. One of the few existing unwritten rules says that only male voices (called *lektor*) are employed to read dialogue lists of feature films, while female readers frequently deliver translation in non-fictional programmes, including cases in which a male voice is heard in the original soundtrack (Szarkowska 2009: 189). Similarly, although it is a common practice in voice-over translation to have the original sound "either reduced entirely or to a low level of audibility" (Luyken 1991: 80), it has never been established to what degree the foreign soundtrack should be lowered so as not to create too much confusion and interference with the delivery of the translated text, while simultaneously offering the audience the pleasure and the illusion of listening to the original language. As for the quality and quantity of the translated text, the belief that voice-over is "the easiest and most faithful of the audiovisual translation modes" (Luyken 1991: 80) implies that there is little to be said about it. Indeed, it was not until recently that some scholars[6] (e.g., Orero 2006, Tomaszkiewicz 2006, Garcarz 2007, Baranauskienė & Blaževičienė 2008) began to point out that this type of translation is in fact far from being an exact reproduction of the original speech and that it tends to simplify and reduce the amount of information when compared with the original verbal output. However, even if there is a general consensus that voice-over translation "is rendered in a more concise way than the original text" (Baranauskienė & Blaževičienė 2008: 20), it is not quite clear which methodological approach would best suit a detailed analysis of this condensation.

An additional hurdle in any attempt to conduct in-depth investigation into the three factors mentioned above is the nature of their mutual interaction. Low quality of one of the factors renders the whole translation unsuccessful. If the original soundtrack is barely audible (for example, because it is set on very low volume or because there is too much overlap with the *lektor's* voice), the audience cannot hear the voices of actors and compensate for the reductions and condensations in the translation. If the *lektor* has a disagreeable timbre of voice or if he delivers the text too emotionally, he becomes too "visible" (this point will be discussed in Section 3.3) and distracts the viewers from following the film's plot. Finally, a low-quality translation obviously damages the overall perception of the film and can also become too "visible". Furthermore, if the translation is not skilfully condensed, it does not allow enough time for audiences to hear larger portions of the original soundtrack. For this reason, it is not possible to analyse any of these factors without taking into account all the possible implications of their mutual interaction. Additionally, the fact that their effectiveness hinges on the subjective perception of the viewers makes the research even more difficult.

3.3. Voice-over translation versus dubbing and subtitling

It may be easier to approach the problem from a different angle, by first identifying the most important similarities and differences between dubbing, subtitling and voice-over. Many definitions – such as "partial dubbing"

(Hendrickx 1984), "non-synchronized dubbing" (Dries 1995b), "half-dubbing" (Gambier 2004) – tend to treat voice-over translation as a type of lower quality pseudo-dubbing.[7] Arguably, this kind of approach can be justified in the case of voice-over translation of feature films in some eastern European countries, such as Belarus, Bulgaria and the Ukraine, where voice-over translation consists of dividing the delivery of the script between at least two (male and female), but more often four or five actors, who perform it imitating emotions and intonation expressed in the original version, while the 'real' foreign-language soundtrack is virtually inaudible. However, the Polish voice-over translation of fictional programmes is based on a different principle. To criticise it for the fact that "[t]he viewer simply gets the dialogue 'read' [...] most of the time without any difference in intonation or acting attempts" (Dries 1995b) is to misunderstand the way in which it works. While the channel of transmission is in this case the only similarity between Polish voice-over and dubbing, the task of the *lektor* by no means involves any attempt to imitate the intonation and emotional expressions of the original voices. On the contrary, the Polish tradition requires the *lektor* to remain as discreet as possible to make the audience 'forget' his existence. The Polish audience expresses a distinct preference for the 'invisible' reader, that is, someone skilful enough to create the illusion that viewers are listening to and are able to understand the original voice track. Krzyżaniak describes the situation as follows:

> The best *lektor* is the one we do not hear after a couple of minutes so we do not lose anything from original actors' timbre and intonation of voice. [...] For a Polish viewer it is more acceptable to hear Robert de Niro in the background rather than to hear him speak Polish with the voice of a known actor (Krzyżaniak 2008: 6).

Since access to the original soundtrack appears to be a top priority for most Polish viewers, the comparison with subtitling seems more useful. Like subtitling, voice-over in Poland does not replace the original voice track but is superimposed upon it. Therefore, it acts not as an alternative but as a support to the original. The tendency to reduce and simplify the translated text, which is a general characteristic of voice-over, is therefore valid for the Polish practice because it allows increasing the audibility of the original soundtrack. The main difference between subtitling and voice-over lies in the channel of transmission: visual in the case of subtitling, auditory in the case of voice-over. The auditory channel of transmission in voice-over potentially eliminates some disadvantages relative to the written nature of subtitling: the constraining factors are less rigid than in a written language; there is no need for viewers to divide their attention between visuals, the original soundtrack and subtitles. Thus, there is no need to compensate for the probable losses in the perception of the original sound and visual elements of the film. But is it truly possible for voice-over to be as unobtrusive as subtitling? Since there is no research in the area, no specific data can be consulted to address this question. Therefore, the proposal concerning guidelines for the voice-over of feature films presented below is bound to be speculative and subject to further verification and correction.

3.4 Voice-*over* or voice-*in-between*?

The main premise of this proposal is that in order to achieve maximum invisibility and unobtrusiveness of voice-over, the principle of superimposition should be replaced with that of juxtaposition. In other words, voice-*over* should be transformed into voice-*behind* or voice-*in-between*.

It is important that the original soundtrack should be clearly audible. However, at the same time it should not compromise the audibility of the reader's voice. Fortunately, the acoustic adjustment of the two soundtracks does not pose significant difficulties anymore from a technological point of view. It is possible to leave the original soundtrack clearly audible and to reduce it only when a *lektor*'s superimpositions are necessary. Hence, the *lektor* becomes the key figure for the whole process of translation. The *lektor* not only needs to possess an 'invisible' voice but he should also be able to deliver the text in pauses and gaps in the original dialogue, or – if this is not possible – to reduce the impact by leaving whole sentences or coherent parts of them audible. However, to be able to do so, he should be given a transcript translated with such an objective in mind. Hence, the translator's focus – as is the case for subtitling – should be on a suitable reduction of the original dialogue. It has already been claimed that voiced-over versions can be even more reduced than the subtitled ones (Grigaraviciuté & Gottlieb 2000). This is a topic that deserves further study to establish if the rules of condensation for voice-over differ from those used in subtitling. Some preliminary observations based on the analysis of the materials presented in Sections 4.1 and 4.2 suggest that it is indeed so.

4. Empirical investigation of existing voice-over translations

Unfortunately, the quality of the voice-over of feature films in Poland is generally very low. With no precise rules and parameters, translators and readers depend on their own instincts. For example, even very experienced readers often simply follow the guidelines applied in the voice-over of non-fiction programmes, trailing the original soundtrack by a second or two or even covering it completely. What is more, it is not uncommon – especially on private channels – to come across the voice-over of an American western, in which the soundtrack audible in the background is Italian.[8] Another frequent and unfortunate solution – especially used in DVD versions of feature films – is to have the *lektor* simply read out the subtitles, so there is no need to pay separately for voice-over. However, this means that the *lektor* has to work with a text which is prepared without taking into consideration the oral channel of transmission and which is segmented in accordance with the rules of distribution of the written words on the screen. As a result, in such cases the original soundtrack is usually covered almost completely by the voice-over.

However, in the plethora of Polish voice-over translations on television and in DVD releases there are some that seem to be heading – even if imperfectly and probably intuitively – towards the model of the voice-*in-between* proposed above. The samples presented below come from science fiction programmes, namely from selected episodes of the *Star Trek* TV series. The choice of the material was motivated by the notoriously repetitive and conventional language typical of this filmic genre (Sobchack 2002: 149). This type of language allows us to focus the analysis on the purely technical problems of voice-over strategies.

4.1 The voice-over translation of short dialogues

The first two dialogues are examples of a standard exchange of short parts of pseudo-military speech between the officers on the bridge of a space ship. In spite of a considerable time gap between the two series (*Star Trek: The Original Series* (henceforth *TOS*) was produced in 1966–1969, *Star Trek Enterprise* (henceforth *Enterprise*) in 2001–2005), the situation in both samples is very similar and so are the dialogues: brave captains (Kirk in *TOS*, Archer in *Enterprise*) and their faithful crew come across a dangerous alien-of-the-week and try to figure out what the strange creature/object that they have to face actually is. The utterances are extremely short and it would seem that there is no need to condense them in translation. Nonetheless, both translations are considerably shorter than the original versions.

1. Star Trek – The Original Series: *Carbomite Maneuver*

Original script	Polish voice-over	Back-translation into English
SPOCK: Reporting, sir. Sensors show it is solid, but its composition is unknown to us.	SPOCK: Stan obiektu stały. Skład nieznany.	SPOCK: A solid object. Composition unknown.
KIRK: Lieutenant Uhura.	KIRK: -	KIRK: -
UHURA: Hailing	UHURA: Nadal nikt nie	UHURA: I still get no

frequencies still open, sir. I get no message from it.	odpowiada.	message.
KIRK: Navigation.	KIRK: Nawigacja?	KIRK: Navigation?
BAILEY: Distance from us, fifteen hundred ninety-three meters, position constant.	BAILEY: Odległość 1593 metry.	BAILEY: Distance 1593 meters.
SULU: Each of its edges measures one hundred seven meters. Mass, a little under eleven thousand metric tons.	SULU: Bok 107 metrów, masa 11 tysięcy ton metrycznych.	SULU: Edge 107 meters, mass 11 thousand metric tons .
KIRK: Scotty.		
SCOTT: Motive power? Beats me what makes it go.	KIRK: Scotty?	KIRK: Scotty?
	SCOTT:. Sam nie wiem, na co chodzi.	SCOTT: I don't know what makes it go.
KIRK: I'll buy speculation.		
	KIRK: Przypuszczenia?	KIRK: Suppositions?
SCOTT: I'd sell it if I had any. That's a solid cube. How something like that can sense us coming, block us, move when we move, well it beats me. That's my report.	SCOTT: Chciałbym. Sześcian. Nie mam bladego pojęcia jak się porusza i kontruje nasze manewry.	SCOTT: I would like. A cube. I have no idea how it moves and controls our maneuvers.
KIRK: Life signs?	KIRK: Oznaki życia?	
MCCOY: Same report.	MCCOY: Powtórzę za Scottim	KIRK: Life signs?
BAILEY: Sir, we going to just let it hold us here? We've got phaser weapons. I vote we blast it.	BAILEY: Będziemy tak siedzieć? Rozwalmy go.	MCCOY: I will repeat after Scotty.
		BAILEY: We will just sit? Let's blast it.
KIRK: I'll keep that in mind, Mister Bailey, when this becomes a	KIRK: Wezmę to pod	

218

Voice-over or voice-in-between?

democracy.	uwagę, kiedy przyjmiemy demokrację.	KIRK: I'll keep that in mind, when this becomes a democracy.

Star Trek: Enterprise: *Harbinger*

Original script	Polish voice-over	Back-translation into English
HOSHI: Captain, I'm picking up an intermittent signal. Very faint.	HOSHI: Wykryłam słaby sygnał	HOSHI: I picked a faint signal.
T'POL: An object, approximately five meters in length.	T'POL: Obiekt. Pięć metrów długości.	T'POL: An object. Five meters in length.
ARCHER: Let's see it.	ARCHER: Ekran.	ARCHER: Screen.
T'POL: It's just a few hundred meters from the edge. I'm reading one biosign. Humanoid.	T'POL: Kilkaset metrów od krawędzi. W środku jest humanoid	T'POL:. Few hundred meters from the edge. A humanoid inside.
REED: Could be an escape pod.	REED: Może to kapsuła.	REED: Could be an escape pod.
ARCHER: Are there any other ships in the vicinity?	ARCHER: Statki w okolicy?	ARCHER: Any ships in the vicinity?
T'POL: None. The biosigns are very erratic.	T'POL: Brak. Biosygnały słabną.	T'POL: None. The biosigns weaken.
ARCHER: Bring the grappler online. Try again.	ARCHER: Harpun. Jeszcze raz.	ARCHER: Grappler. Once again.
REED: I'll see if I can compensate.	REED: Wyrównam.	REED: I'll compensate.
ARCHER: Travis.	ARCHER: -	ARCHER: -
REED: We're losing	REED: Padają kolejne	REED: We are losing

systems all over the ship.	układy.	systems.
TRAVIS: Helm's not responding.	TRAVIS: Ster nie reaguje.	TRAVIS: Helm's not responding.
T'POL: There are rising levels of ammonium sulphide in the atmosphere.	T'POL:. Rośnie stężenie siarczku amonu.	T'POL:. Levels of ammonium sulphide are rising.
ARCHER: Archer to Engineering.	ARCHER: Maszynownia.	ARCHER: Engineering.
TUCKER [OC]: Commander Tucker.	TUCKER: -	TUCKER: -
ARCHER: The helm's not responding. We need full reverse	ARCHER: Ster nie reaguje. Dajcie całą wstecz.	ARCHER: The helm's not responding. Full reverse.
TUCKER: I'm on it.	TUCKER: -	
		TUCKER: -

It is obvious that the reductions in the examples above are due not so much to what *must* be simplified in terms of the time available, but rather to what *can* be simplified. In the first example, the number of words is reduced from 134 to 53. In the second, from 103 to merely 40.[9] In addition, the strategies followed by the translator are similar – but not identical – to those usually used in subtitling, that is, dialogues are far less coherent grammatically and stylistically, relying heavily on the visual and original verbal context. Moreover, some lines are eliminated altogether.

A drastic reduction of the original script is without doubt a condition sine qua non to make the transformation of voice-*over* into voice-*in-between* possible. However, to make it work it must be matched with another indispensable factor: the *lektor*'s manner of delivering the translated text. Although the two dialogues quoted above underwent a roughly similar amount of reduction (in fact, they were both translated by the same person),[10] they were read by different *lektor*s. The difference in the degree of the original soundtrack's audibility is evident (audible sections of original dialogues are highlighted in bold):

Star Trek TOS: *Carbomite Monouver*	Star Trek Enterprise: *Harbinger*
SPOCK: **Reporting, sir. Sensors show**	HOSHI: **Captain, I'm picking up an**

it is solid, but its composition is unknown to us. KIRK: **Lieutenant Uhura.** UHURA: **Hailing frequencies still** open, sir. I get no message from it. KIRK: **Navigation.** BAILEY: **Distance from us,** fifteen hundred ninety three meters, position constant. SULU: **Each of its edges** measures one hundred seven meters. Mass, a little under eleven thousand metric tons. KIRK: **Scotty.** SCOTT: **Motive power?** Beats me what makes it go. KIRK: **I'll buy speculation.** SCOTT: I'd sell it if I had any. **That's a solid cube. How something** like that can sense us coming, block us, move when we move, well it **beats me. That's my report.** KIRK: **Life signs.** MCCOY: **Same report.** BAILEY: **Sir, we going to just let** it hold us here? We've got phaser weapons. **I vote we blast it.** KIRK: **I'll keep that** in mind, Mister Bailey, when this **becomes a democracy.**	**intermittent signal. Very faint.** T'POL: **An object, approximately five meters** in length. ARCHER: **Let's see it.** T'POL: **It's just a few hundred meters from the edge. I'm reading one biosign. Humanoid.** REED: **Could be an escape pod.** ARCHER: **Are there any other ships** in the vicinity? T'POL: **None. The biosigns** are very erratic. ARCHER: **Bring the grappler online. Try again.** REED: **I'll see if I can compensate.** ARCHER: **Travis.** REED: **We're losing systems all over** the ship. TRAVIS: **Helm's not responding.** T'POL: **There are rising levels on ammonium sulphide** in the atmosphere. ARCHER: **Archer to Engineering.** TUCKER [OC]: **Commander Tucker.** ARCHER: **The helm's not responding. We need full reverse** TUCKER: **I'm on it.**

While in *Harbinger* an impressive 90% of the original dialogue is clearly audible, in *Carbomite Maneuver* the audibility decreases to no more than about 42% of the original soundtrack. It also seems that the less audible the original soundtrack becomes, the more 'visible' and – as a result – obtrusive the *lektor*'s voice seems. This observation is supported by results from tests carried out with the participation of about thirty students, further confirmed by opinions expressed in numerous Internet discussions on the topic.[11] It can be assumed that when the viewers' attention is drawn to the original dialogue, they hear the translation almost automatically, just like experienced subtitle users read subtitles unconsciously. On the contrary, if access to the original sound is reduced, the *lektor*'s voice becomes unavoidably more noticeable. Therefore, it appears undeniable that skilful delivery of the translated text is of vital importance to the successful voice-over translation of a film.

4.2 Voice-over of long utterances

The examples quoted above are very simple exchanges of short lines, with numerous pauses in which the *lektor*'s voice can be fitted. However, what happens when the dialogue is very rapid or less fragmented? Will the *lektor* still be able to find enough pauses in the dialogue to avoid covering the original soundtrack? Here is yet another sample of *Star Trek* dialogue, which seems to be considerably more challenging a task for the translator and the *lektor* in this regard. The captain of the spaceship (Archer) is interrogated by a menacing alien (Grat). Grat is talking fast, while Archer refuses to collaborate with him and remains mostly silent.

3. Star Trek Enterprise: *Detained*

Original script	Polish voice-over	Back translation into English
GRAT: I admire your spirit of exploration, but in this case it could get you into trouble. Keep to yourself.	GRAT: Podziwiam pańskiego ducha, ale proszę zachować powściągliwość.	GRAT: I admire your spirit, but be careful.
ARCHER: I'll do my best. Unless you have any more advice?	ARCHER: Postaram się. Jeszcze jakieś rady?	ARCHER: I'll do my best. Any more advice?
GRAT: No, but I do have a question. Have you ever been to Oklahoma? I guess you could say I'm a curious man myself. After you mentioned that you were familiar with the Cabal I decided to speak with our intelligence agency. They've uncovered some interesting facts. Apparently two Suliban soldiers crash-landed near a town called Broken Bow, Oklahoma. They were chasing a Klingon, of all things. I was wondering if you could provide some	GRAT: Nie, ale mam pytanie. Był pan w Oklakomie? Sam jestem ciekawski. Kiedy wspomniał pan o Kabali, skontaktowałem się z wywiadem. Odkryli, że dwóch sulibańskich żołnierzy rozbiło się pod miastem Broken Bow w Oklahomie. Gonili Klingona. Wie pan, co tam robili?	GRAT: No, but I have a question. Have you been to Oklahoma? I'm a curious man myself. After you mentioned the Cabal I spoke to our intelligence. They've uncovered that two Suliban soldiers crash-landed near a town called Broken Bow, Oklahoma. They were chasing a Klingon. Do you know what they were doing there?

Voice-over or voice-in-between?

insight into what they were doing there. ARCHER: I wouldn't know. You'd have to talk to my superiors. GRAT: Oh, I think you know a great deal. Enterprise took the Klingon back to his homeworld. Isn't that right? Rigel Ten. You made a detour there. From what I'm told, you contacted a woman named Sarin. You remember her? Well, I'll remind you. She was the head of a Suliban resistance cell. She was killed by the Cabal in a firefight at the trade complex. Several of our people saw you there, Captain. I believe you were injured, a shot in the leg. Do I have to ask your superiors about that as well? ARCHER: What exactly do you want?	ARCHER: Musi pan pomówić z moimi przełożonym GRAT: Założę się, że wie pan bardzo dużo. Enterprise odwoził Klingona. Po drodze zatrzymaliście się na Rigel 10. Nawiązaliście kontakt z niejaką Sarin. Przypomnę panu. Kierowała komórką ruchu oporu, zginęła w potyczce z Kabalą. Nasi ludzie widzieli pana. Został pan ranny w nogę. O to też mam pytać pańskich przełożonych? ARCHER: Czego pan chce?	ARCHER: You have to talk to my superiors. GRAT: I think you know a great deal. Enterprise took the Klingon back. You made a detour on Rigel 10. You contacted a certain Sarin. I'll remind you. She was the head of a resistance cell, she was killed in a firefight with the Cabal. Our people saw you. You were injured in the leg. Do I have to ask your superiors about that as well? ARCHER: What exactly do you want?

Here we have a dialogue of 219 words with two long, informative and rather fast utterances by Grat. The exchange takes 1 minute 38 seconds.[12] The translator managed to reduce the script by half, to 110 words, which is still a lot of speech to be delivered in this short screen time without covering the original soundtrack. The *lektor* did his best (highlighted in bold are the audible parts of the original dialogue).

3. Star Trek Enterprise: *Detained*: Audibility of the original soundtrack

GRAT: **I admire your spirit of exploration**, but **in this case it could get you into** trouble. **Keep to yourself.**
ARCHER: **I'll do my best. Unless you have** any **more advice?**
GRAT: **No, but I do have a question. Have you ever been to Oklahoma? I guess**

223

> you could say I'm a curious man myself. After you mentioned that you were familiar with the Cabal I decided to speak with our intelligence agency. They've uncovered some interesting facts. Apparently two Suliban soldiers crash-landed near a town called Broken Bow, Oklahoma. They were chasing a Klingon, of all things. I was wondering if you could provide some insight into what they were doing there.
> ARCHER: I wouldn't know. You'd have to talk to my superiors.
> GRAT: Oh, I think you know a great deal. Enterprise took the Klingon back to his homeworld. Isn't that right? Rigel Ten. You made a detour there. From what I'm told, you contacted a woman named Sarin. You remember her? Well, I'll remind you. She was the head of a Suliban resistance cell. She was killed by the Cabal in a firefight at the trade complex. Several of our people saw you there, Captain. I believe you were injured, a shot in the leg. Do I have to ask your superiors about that as well?
> ARCHER: What exactly do you want?

While the *lektor* was not able to avoid some superimpositions on the original soundtrack, he still managed to make about 80% (177 words) of the English dialogue audible. It also seems evident that he placed the necessary superimpositions on less important parts of the original speech and left whole sentences or at least coherent segments of the English soundtrack accessible. Interestingly enough, in order to achieve this goal he did not limit himself to a post-synchronised reading of the text. At some points he actually resorted to anticipating the original dialogue, a technique that mertis further investigation.

Detained: Distribution of Polish translation through the dialogue. The pieces of information that anticipate the original are shown in italics.

> GRAT: **I admire your spirit of exploration,** *Podziwiam pańskiego ducha* **in this case it could get you into** *ale proszę zachować powściągliwość.* **Keep to yourself.**
> ARCHER: **I'll do my best.** *Postaram się.* **Unless you have** *Jeszcze jakieś rady?* **more advice?**
> GRAT: Nie, **No, but** *ale mam pytanie.* **I do have a question. Have you ever been** *Był pan w Oklahomie?* **to Oklahoma? I guess you could say I'm a curious man** *Sam jestem ciekawski.* **After you mentioned that you were familiar with the Cabal** *Kiedy wspomniał pan o Kabali, skontaktowałem się z wywiadem.* **agency. They've uncovered some interesting facts.** *Odkryli, że dwóch sulibańskich żołnierzy* **Apparently two Suliban soldiers crash-landed near** *rozbiło się pod miastem Broken Bow w Oklahomie.* **Broken Bow, Oklahoma. They were chasing a Klingon,** *Gonili Klingona.* **I was wondering if you could provide some insight** *Wie pan, co tam robili?*
> ARCHER: **I wouldn't know.** *Musi pan pomówić z moimi przełożonymi.* **You'd have to talk to my superiors.**
> GRAT: **Oh, I think you know a great deal.** *Założę się, że wie pan bardzo dużo.* **Enterprise took the Klingon back** *Enterprise odwoził Klingona.* **Isn't that right?**

> **Rigel Ten.** Po drodze zatrzymaliście się na Rigel 10. **From what I'm told,** *Nawiązaliście kontakt z niejaką Sarin* **contacted a woman** named **Sarin. You remember her? Well, I'll remind you.** Przypomnę panu. **She was the head of a Suliban resistance** Kierowała komórką ruchu oporu, **She was killed by the Cabal** zginęła w potyczce z Kabałą **at the trade complex.** *Nasi ludzie widzieli pana.* **Several of our people** *Został pan ranny w nogę.* **I believe you were injured, a shot in the leg.** *O to też mam pytać pańskich przełożonych?* **Do I have to ask your superiors about that as well?**
> ARCHER: **What exactly do you** Czego pan chce? **want?**

It seems that the anticipation technique not only helps to find more pauses between the lines of the original speech, but can also help viewers – among other things – to *understand* the lines of the dialogue that follow. If one looks carefully at the distribution of the Polish translation in the course of the dialogue quoted above, it can be noticed that the *lektor* divided the text into small sections so that particular sentences immediately follow or precede their English equivalents. Consequently, at some points in the dialogue, the viewers are offered the Polish translation of an expression or a sentence read discreetly by the 'invisible' *lektor*, and a split second later they distinctly hear the same sentence or expression in the original language. The length of these anticipations may vary. Some are very short (*Jeszcze jakieś rady?* [more advice?] "more advice?"), but sometimes they can be more elaborate sentences (*Musi pan pomówić z moimi przełożonymi.* [You have to talk to my superiors.] "You'd have to talk to my superiors."). Of course, such a strategy can help viewers understand the original dialogue only if they already have some knowledge of the language spoken.

5. Conclusion

While the samples of Polish voice-over presented in this contribution were quite successful in maintaining a balance between the two voice tracks, they could be improved further if they were prepared on the basis of precise standards rather than the translator's and *lektor*'s intuitive strategies. Nonetheless, in spite of their imperfections, they do seem to demonstrate that the voice-*over* of feature films could be transformed into a voice-*in-between* with all the potential benefits of such a strategy such as better access to the original soundtrack and to information in the voice-over, more comfort in the reception of the film and even support in foreign-language learning. However, it will not be possible to create a model of such a translational mode without further extensive studies based on reliable empirical data.

Also, since the Polish model of voice-over appears to bear many similarities with such AVT techniques as audio subtitles on the one hand and audio description on the other, a comparative study of these three modes could be mutually beneficial for improving their standards and for opening up new interesting perspectives for research. In fact, it seems that certain audio description principles could be applied successfully to voice-over to make it more unobtrusive and to reduce interference with the original soundtrack, while an in-depth analysis of Polish voice-over practices might have a positive impact on the study of audio subtitles and generally on media accessibility. Last but not least, one has to remember that the voice-over of fiction programmes is a daily experience for millions of viewers in Europe. Serious research on this topic is urgently needed not only because it might result in new discoveries in the field of theoretical AVT studies, but also because it could lead to a public debate on standards for voice-over translation and have an impact on improving the quality of this AVT technique in everyday practice.

---

[1] http://en.wikipedia.org/wiki/Gavrilov_translation (consulted 21.10.2010)

[2] www.dubbing.fora.pl, www.dialogista.pl but also many other: advantages and disadvantages of subtitles, dubbing and voice-over translation are a recurrent topic of discussion among Polish Internet users.

[3] The Polish version of *Shrek,* radically domesticated by Bartosz Wierzbięta and dubbed by very popular actors (Jerzy Stuhr, Cezary Pazura and others) was immensely successful and initiated a new trend in Polish dubbing. However, it seems that viewers' enthusiasm for dubbed films does not exceed beyond the realm of animated productions.

[4] No exact data can be given here since no in-depth research into Polish audience preferences has been conducted so far. However, such is the general opinion that emerges from many heated discussions about this topic held on internet forums. Subtitles may be preferred over voice-over, but dubbing is unanimously considered the worst solution.

[5] That is, they follow a set pattern in which the role-taking has been determined beforehand.

[6] See: *A commented bibliography on voice-over translation,* in: Franco, Matamala & Orero (forthcoming).

[7] "No doubt, simplification and a lack of understanding of the media and its process have made voice-over to be seen in the same light as dubbing, which is certainly a different mode, subject to different translation and production processes" observes Pilar Orero (Orero 2009: 131).

[8] The reason is, of course, purely pecuniary: to purchase a dubbed Italian version from Italy costs less than to acquire the original film.

[9] Since in Poland the *Star Trek* series is not available on DVD, there are no subtitled versions of the show; as a matter of comparison it is interesting to note, however, that for example in the Italian subtitled version, the dialogue from the second sample (*Harbinger*) counts no less than 87 words.

[10] Due to external political factors, *Star Trek,* the old *Original Series* included, arrived in Poland only after the fall of the communist regime in the early 1990s. Only in the last ten years have all six series of the *Star Trek* franchise begun to appear regularly on private TV channels.

[11] See for example: http://pytamy.pl/question/lektor-czy-dubbing/1; http://www.movieforum.pl/temat/8592/60/; http://forum.blogowicz.info/topics16/napisylektor-czy-dubbing-vt2275.htm; http ://www.e-mlodzi.com/napisy-lektor-czy-dubbing-vt12064,45.htm; http://www.torrentmania.nfo/f-filmy-i-seriale-14/t-napisy-lektor-czy-dubbing-168/page28.html; http://forum.pobierz.pl/temat, dubbing-vs-lektor-vs-napisy,40,595; http://forum.interia.pl/watek-chronologicznie/co-lepsze-lektor-dubbing-napisy,1086,1086818,,c,1,62,0,0; http://www.movieforum.pl/temat/8592/60/ (consulted 20.06.2010)

[12] As a matter of comparison: 103 words of *Harbingers* dialogue, quoted before, were distributed over one minute and 40 seconds of screen time.

References

Baumgarten Nicole. 2003. 'Shaken and Stirred: Language in Film in a Cross-Cultural Perspective' in Baumgarten, Nicole, Claudia Böttger, Markus Motz & Julia Probst (eds.) *Übersetzen, Interkulturelle Kommunikation, Spracherwerb und Sprachvermittlung - Das Leben mit mehreren Sprachen: Festschrift für Juliane House* (Sonderausgabe der Zeitschrift für Interkulturellen Fremdsprachenunterricht) [Online] 8 (2/3).
Belczyk Arkadiusz. 2007. *Tłumaczenie filmowe.* Witkowice: DLA SZKOŁY.
Bogucki, Łukasz. 2001. 'The Constraint of Relevance in Subtitling'. Online at http://www.jostrans.org/issue01/art_bogucki_en.php (consulted 16.09.2011).
Dries, Josephine. 1995a. *Dubbing and Subtitling: Guidelines for Production and Distribution.* Dusseldorf: European Institute for the Media.
Dries, Josephine. 1995b. 'Breaking Eastern European Barriers' in *Sequentia* 2(4): 6-7.
Franco Eliana. 2000. *Revoicing the Alien in Documentaries: Cultural Agency, Norms and the Translation of the Audiovisual Reality.* PhD thesis, Catholic University of Leuven.
Gambier, Yves. 2003. 'Screen Transadaptation: Perception and Reception' in *The Translator* 2(9): 171-189.
Garcarz, Michał. 2007. *Przekład Slangu w Filmie: Polskie Przekłady Filmów Amerykańskich na Język Polski.* Kraków: Tertium.
Glaser, Gabrielle. 1991. 'Why Marylin Monroe is a Polish Baritone?' *The New York Times* 24.02.1991.
Grigaraviciuté, Ieva & Gottlieb, Henrik. 2000. 'Danish Voices, Lithuanian Voice-over: The Mechanics of Non Synchronous Translation' in Gottlieb, Henrik (ed.) *Screen Translation 2000: Six Studies in Subtitling, Dubbing and Voice-Over.* Copenhagen: Centre for Translation Studies, Department of English, University of Copenhagen: 75-114.
Hendrickx, Paul. 1984. 'Partial dubbing'. *Meta* 2(29): 217-218.
Hendrykowski, Marek. 1984. 'Z Problemów Przekładu Filmowego' in Balcerzan, Edward (ed.) *Wielojęzyczność Literatury i Problemy Przekładu Artystycznego.* Wrocław: Ossolineum. 243-259.
Ivarsson, Jan. 1992. *Translating for the Media.* Stockholm: TransEdit.
Kozloff, Sarah. 2000. *Overhearing Film Dialogue.* Berkeley, CA: University of California Press.
Krzyżaniak, Wojciech. 2008. 'Głosy z Ekranu'. *Gazeta Wyborcza. Gazeta Telewizyjna* 11.01.2008: 6.

Luyken, Georg-Michael., Thomas Herbst, Jo Langham-Brown, Helene Reid & Herman Spinhof, 1991. *Overcoming Language Barriers in Television: Dubbing and Subtitling for the European Audience*. Manchester: The European Institute for the Media.

Nichols, Bill. 1991. *Representing Reality: Issues and Concepts in Documentary*. Bloomington, IN: Indiana University Press.

Orero, Pilar. 2006. 'Voice-over: A Case of Hyper-Reality'. Online at http://www.euro conferences.info/proceedings/2006_Proceedings/2006_Orero_Pilar.pdf (consulted 16.09.2011).

Orero, Pilar. 2009. 'Voice-over in Audiovisual Translation' in Díaz Cintas, Jorge and Gunilla Anderman 130-139.

Orero, Pilar, Anna Matamala & Eliana Franco. 2010. *Voice-over Translation: An Overview*. Bern: Peter Lang.

Perego, Elisa. 2005. *La traduzione audiovisiva*. Roma: Carocci

Sobchack, Vivian. 2002. *Spazio e tempo nel cinema di fantascienza* (English ed. 1980) Bologna: Bononia.

Subbotko, Donata. 2008. 'Kapitulacja BBC prime'. *Gazeta Wyborcza*. 11 January 2008.

Szarkowska, Agnieszka. 2009. 'The Audiovisual Landscape in Poland at the Dawn of the 21st Century' in Goldstein, Angelika & Biljana Golubović (eds.) *Foreign Language Movies: Dubbing vs Subtitling*. Hamburg: Kovač.

Tomaszkiewicz, Teresa. 2006. *Przekład audiowizualny*. Warsaw: PWN.

Tveit, Jan-Emil. 2009. 'Dubbing vs Subtitiling' in Díaz Cintas, Jorge & Gunilla Anderman (eds.) *Audiovisual Translation: Language Transfer on Screen*. Palgrave: Macmillan. 85-96.

Surtitling for the Stage and Directors' Attitudes: Room for Change

Anika Vervecken
Independent surtitler

Abstract

Providing surtitles for live performances such as opera or theatre is complex at best. One might argue even impossible in some cases. This contribution explores the obstacles encountered in producing this new translation mode and also challenges the belief that many directors hold that surtitles are disruptive and undermine the quality of their work. To some extent, this belief is based on facts but it is also due to ignorance about the versatility of this young translation mode and directors' unwillingness to work with the surtitlers or the surtitling team (Griesel 2008). The present contribution will first provide an introduction to the main features of surtitles. This will be followed by an outline of the specific challenges that surtitling poses. Finally, a brief overview of the people involved in the production process will provide additional insights into the main focus of the contribution: the production process of surtitles. How can this process be optimised? And what is the role of the director in the production process?

Keywords
audiovisual translation, director, opera, performance, subtitling, surtitling, theatre

1. Introduction

In opera as well as the theatre, directors tend to dislike surtitles because they are distracting and may contaminate the visual image, the aesthetic composition that they have so carefully designed.[1] In opera, opposition has diminished significantly since surtitles were first introduced in the early 1980s (Burton 2009). However, even though most opera directors now see surtitles as "a necessary element" (Sario & Oksanen 1996: 186), many of them still fail to understand to what degree surtitles influence their work and how they themselves can use surtitles to their advantage, that is, turn negative impact into positive influence on the play. Since "spoken theatre relies much more heavily and directly upon language, accessibility to that language is distinctly more important" (Carlson 2000: 83), surtitles were accepted more readily in theatre. All the same, in both types of surtitling there still is a tendency to consider surtitles a mere technicality. This attitude is common among directors as well as other professionals in the performing arts such as the organisers of festivals.[2] Finally, even those directors who do show great interest in surtitles sometimes lack a basic understanding of their nature and many directors do not want to involve themselves with the production process of the surtitles at all, leaving all the responsibility with the opera house, (host) theatre or festival.[3] Consequently, the people in charge of the task of producing surtitles are often faced with a situation which is far from ideal, whether they are in-house personnel or surtitlers hired to provide translations for a visiting production. The result, too, is often far from ideal, and manages only to reinforce the director in question's negative or indifferent attitude towards surtitles. In other words, a vicious circle ensues.

This contribution wishes to contribute to developing an understanding of surtitles and of their production process. It will also address the question of what can be done to improve surtitle quality and the efficiency of the production process and it will discuss specific key issues that are of interest to directors wishing to ensure that their work is properly represented in the surtitles.

2. Situating surtitles

Since little academic research on surtitles has been done, a definition is in order, as is a brief overview of a number of important variables affecting the functioning of surtitles.

2.1. Surtitles: A working definition

A consultation of the Bibliography of Interpreting and Translation (BITRA) yields only seven articles on surtitling.[4] However, it should be noted that the academic research that does exist has resulted in some very interesting findings, as is demonstrated in the publications of, for instance, Griesel (2000, 2005, 2007, 2008), Mateo (2002, 2005, 2007) and others, discussed below. In spite of the relatively short existence of surtitles, Mateo (2002: 51-53) provides a brief but thorough history of surtitling in opera, as does Burton (2009: 58-59). Carlson's article (2002: 78-80) on surtitles includes a historical account of how international theatre dealt and deals with the problem of language accessibility.

One indicator of the newness of the 'surtitle' is how difficult it is to find an accurate definition in most modern dictionaries. Several English dictionaries now include the word *surtitle* (or *supertitle*) but their definitions are not always comprehensive. For instance, the Oxford Dictionary Online describes a surtitle as "a caption projected on a screen above the stage in an opera, translating the text being sung."[5]

I propose the following adaptation to this definition:

a caption displayed on a screen that is usually suspended above the stage during a live performance or event such as opera or theatre, translating or transcribing the text that is being vocalised, generally in a concise or summarising manner

The word *displayed* is favoured over the word *projected* since there are several ways in which surtitles can be displayed, and not all of them necessarily involve projection. (see Section 2.3). The addition referring to surtitles often being 'concise' translations was made because this is an extremely important characteristic.

One last important observation is that the word *surtitle* is not the only word used to describe this phenomenon. Carlson (2000) talks of "supertitles", whereas Matamala and Orero (2007: 264) mention the use of the word "overtitle". However, when looking at the most recent articles, it is safe to say that the use of the word *surtitle* is widespread today. This is also evident in the equivalents used in other languages such as Dutch (*boventitel* (Vanattenhove & Van Kerkhoven 2002)), French (*sur-titrage* (Lavolee 2008)), German (*Übertitel* (Griesel 2007)) and Spanish (*sobretítulo* (Mateo 2002)).

2.2. Different types and functions of surtitles

In only a few decades, the use of surtitles has expanded. Surtitles were first used for opera in the early 1980s (Burton 2009: 58) but have since migrated not only to the theatre, but also to conferences, political meetings, concerts etc. Today, surtitles are used both interlinguistically and intralinguistically, the latter usage being most common in opera. Though it is still a rare practice, surtitles have been adapted for the deaf and hard of hearing to S^{r}DH. (Matamala & Orero 2007). It is important to note that S^{r}DH and other types of intralinguistic surtitles are very different. Nonetheless, it is not uncommon for standard intralinguistic surtitles to be marketed under the label of accessibility in spite of the fact that they do not provide the same support as S^{r}DH.

At times, surtitles are also used for artistic purposes not related to translation. Sometimes a character exists merely in the surtitles, in which case these surtitles cease to be a translation (i.e., an intermediary information channel) but act as a direct source of information for the audience. This was the case in the opera *The Woman Who Walked into Doors* by Guy Cassiers and Kris Dufoor, a production by the Toneelhuis of Antwerp (2001). In other cases, the actors comment on the surtitles or ask for them to be turned off altogether, which happened during *Revue 2008* produced by the Brussels company KVS in December 2008 because something was not "meant for Walloon ears" (Vervecken 2009: 84), causing amusement among both the

Flemish and Walloon audience members. One minor use of surtitles is for commercial purposes. Opera houses often use them to display their sponsors before or after the performance. Interestingly, the habit of displaying the name of the surtitler or surtitlers at the end of the performance, a fairly common practice in subtitling, has not yet been adopted everywhere.[6]

Finally, it should also be noted in passing that surtitling for opera and surtitling for theatre are two disciplines that differ significantly. There are two major differences: (1) the way in which the subtitles are segmented differs considerably from the way in which surtitles are segmented since the timing is much more subject to variability in theatre than in opera, where it is dictated by the music and (2) the translation strategies are very different.

By contrast, the production process shows significant similarities and – unfortunately – the issues relating to 'surtitle prejudice' discussed in this contribution are shared as well. This explains my discussion of standard interlingual surtitles in a general sense.

2.3. Displaying surtitles

There are various ways to display surtitles and this choice is based on technical requirements, the features of the performance space and the performance itself, the available budget and the function of the surtitles.

The most common place to display surtitles in both opera and theatre is at the top of the proscenium or somewhere above the heads of the performers, hence the name *surtitle*. For surtitles displayed at the top of the proscenium there are two further options: (1) displaying them on a LED screen or (2) projecting them onto a screen or on the back wall of the stage with a beamer. Though opera houses tend to favour LED screens, neither option is considered qualitatively superior to the other. Both have their advantages and disadvantages and are consequently more desirable in certain circumstances (Vervecken forthcoming). However, neither LED screens nor projections have to be positioned at the top of the proscenium. In Asian countries, it is common for surtitles that run vertically to appear to one or both sides of the stage. At times, surtitles are displayed below the stage. There are even examples of performances where the surtitles are constantly displayed in different places or move around. This was the case in *The Woman Who Walked into Doors* (see Section 2.2).

A recent development in the display of surtitles is the use of individual screens, such as screens mounted on the back of the seats (Mateo 2007b) or on handheld devices (Wise 2009). The advantage of individual screens is that the surtitles can – in theory – be customised to the needs and preferences of each individual audience member, for instance, by offering a variety of languages. It is also a a technique which can be used to offer S^{r}DH without distracting the regular audience members with the additional information for the hearing impaired.

When different display modes are available, choosing the most appropriate mode is important, as is deciding where the surtitles will be displayed. If a director leaves this up to the theatre, opera house or technicians, the selection is generally motivated by means of economic or practical concerns, rather than features relating to how the physical appearance and placement of the surtitles interact with the artistic performance, or how this will influence the comprehensibility of both the surtitles and the performance.

3. Translating an unfinished product

Surtitlers are usually the last people in a line of professionals working with and modifying the text of a performance. In spite of this, their source text is never a 'finished product'.

3.1. Is a libretto an unfinished product?

It may seem odd to consider a libretto or theatre script as an unfinished product. For a surtitler they are unfinished products since surtitles are the translation of the performance; the text as it is performed, as it is put into context. Thus, the "production as a whole" becomes the 'source text' (Griesel 2005: 2) and the target text is constituted by the surtitles as they are combined with this performance. In the case of surtitles, both the source text and the target text are completed at the same time, that is, when the curtain falls

In order to be able to translate, one has to interpret. However, in the case of theatre or opera, the translator is not the only person interpreting. The actors are interpreting as well, as are the director, the set designer and everyone else involved in the production. If the surtitler or translator simply starts interpreting the written text without looking at how the other agents involved have interpreted it, the result could be catastrophic. The outcome could be – at best – acceptable but never exceptional. The famous line *Get thee to a nunnery* from Shakespeare's *Hamlet* is a perfect example. The word nunnery can be interpreted literally or as a reference to a brothel. It is essential for the surtitler to understand the director's interpretation.

In opera, it is not unusual for there to be a disparity between what is being sung and what is being performed on stage. In the surtitles, this disparity should be avoided as much as possible to prevent confusing the audience. Take the fictitious example of someone singing *I am sitting at my desk thinking of my darling*, while there is no actual desk. In this case, it might be desirable to omit the desk from the surtitles. However, such omissions are only possible when the surtitler is familiar with the production. Moreover, in opera there are often two or even three casts and simply because of their physical appearance, the surtitles might need to be adapted for each.

Some elements of a performance that are not in the original text (i.e., anything related to the director's vision and the staging) can be provided to the translator beforehand. Other elements such as improvisations, unexpected occurrences and the exact timing cannot be provided. Even though the music score of an opera provides a great deal of information on rhythm, there is never any certainty as to the pace of a performance because the conductor can always accelerate or decelerate a sequence and a performer can always miss a line or alter the order of delivery. However, in theatre surtitling, the timing tends to pose a greater challenge still because the rhythm of a performance is subject to constant change. Consider the extreme example of an actor who unexpectedly speaks twice as fast as in any rehearsal. There is a likely possibility that the surtitles will then disappear before the audience has been able to read them. Consequently, the surtitles will fail to meet their purpose (even if the translation is a good translation) because the translator will have had no way of knowing this was going to happen and would have been working with only a partial performance, that is, an unfinished product.

These observations are not meant to support the argument that good surtitles are impossible because surtitlers do not receive a finished product to translate. In fact, the opposite is true. Many misconceptions and bad surtitles result from the lack of understanding of the specific production process of surtitles for a theatrical production.

3.2. How to translate an unfinished product

If it is impossible for surtitlers to work with a finished product, the question of what they should do to overcome this handicap remains. A good surtitler anticipates, the best method being by communicating with the director. The director knows the intended end result and that is what a surtitler should work towards. Like the set designer, the lighting designer, the stage manager and the actors, the surtitler should have the same end result in mind as the director. This is important because – as Carlson (2000: 85) has highlighted – for many audience members the surtitles "will operate (…) as another element in the multi-channeled reception experience". Like everyone involved in a theatrical performance, surtitlers should use their knowledge, abilities and creativity to work towards the same goal, as part of the same team.

One of the elements that ultimately makes or breaks a production is whether everyone involved in the performance is on the same wavelength. In order to sweep an audience off its feet, all the elements that make up the production: the acting, music, lighting, surtitles etc. need to converge seamlessly. They should flow together, making the audience forget that the actors are acting, while imagining themselves in Africa or Othello's court rather than in a comfortable theatre seat, not noticing the lighting or music changes unless they were meant to be noticed. Likewise, in an ideal situation, surtitles are integrated so well that the audience forgets that they are there (Burton 2009: 63) and afterwards quotes the performance without realising that they are quoting the surtitles.[7]

This need for communication and cooperation is not exclusive to surtitling. According to Gambier and Gottlieb (2001: xi – xii), teamwork is a fundamental characteristic of audiovisual translation, and Mateo (2002: 53) already pointed out that this is indeed the case for surtitling. Likewise, Udo and Fels (2009: 1) stress how important it is that the creator of an audio description for the visually impaired is able to communicate with the director of a film.

Creating that perfect emulsion, where the surtitles blend in perfectly, is not easy. Only if everyone involved in the process understands that surtitling is a unique form of audiovisual translation, will the option of using them to facilitate extensive touring and multilingual performances (See Section 4, Needcompany) outweigh any perceived disadvantages.

4. The production process

4.1. Surtitling: A shared responsibility

This chapter discusses all the agents involved – directly and indirectly – in the surtitle production process. Figure 1 provides an overview of the different steps in the production process, designating to what part of the organisation specific agents belong. Furthermore, Figure 1 shows the information and materials which are or should be provided by the creative team and/or host theatre as well as those producing the surtitles.

Anika Vervecken

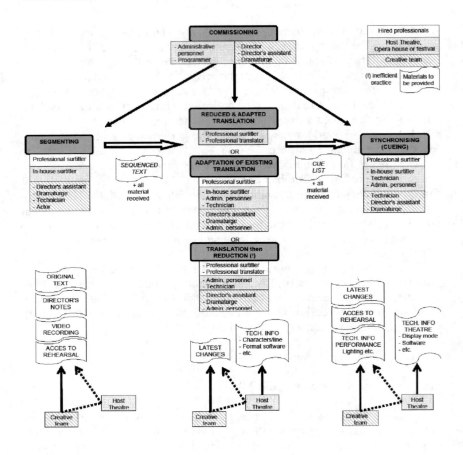

Figure 1. People involved in the production process of surtitles and the materials provided.

One extremely important agent shown at the top of figure 1 is not always taken into account, namely the person who commissions the surtitles. Many directors regard surtitles as a practicality and will leave it up to the theatre or an assistant to make choices. However, the importance of this stage in decision-making should not be underestimated since this is the point in the process when the decision is taken about which of the three stages in the production process are to be outsourced and which will be completed in-house. There is no single solution ideal for every production, but if directors are not involved in this decision, they take a risk.

Another important responsibility is that of providing the right materials to the people in charge of each phase of the production process since each segment of the creation process requires different materials and information. Direct communication between the creative team and the agents involved in producing the surtitles is always favoured. The chart misleadingly suggests that this is one-time and one-way communication. In an ideal world, however, this is a constant exchange where the producing agent is able to ask questions and the creative team provides updates.

4.2. The different stages of the production process

This section will discuss how surtitles are created, what practices deliver the best results and how directors can influence this process. As Figure 1 demonstrates, the process of creating surtitles can be divided into three major components: (1) segmenting, (2) translating and (3) rendering during the performance. Sometimes one person performs all of these tasks but they may also be carried out by two or three different people.

4.2.1. Segmenting

Before any translation takes place, the original text is segmented, thereby delimiting the portions of text that will have to be translated into one single surtitle. The division of the text is based on two elements: (1) the rhythm of the play or opera and (2) the speed of speech. The rhythm is observed to establish where blank surtitles are needed and where the text will be segmented, based on where the actors tend to put the emphasis or take small pauses. The speed of speech is important to know how much reduction is needed. If the actors speak or sing very fast, the portions of the source text to be conveyed in one surtitle will be bigger, forcing the translator to condense the text further to enable the audience to read the surtitles while following the action. The degree of reduction required for theatre or opera can be as high as almost 50 per cent (Griesel 2005: 10) whereas in subtitling this precentage tends to be lower (Díaz Cintas & Remael 2007).

The practice of text reduction sounds quite straightforward and is consistent with general subtitling practices (Díaz Cintas & Remael 2007). However, as theatre and opera are live performances, the rhythm is different for every performance and has the ability to evolve. Therefore, the ideal person to segment the text is someone who is very close to the actual production and has been closely involved with the rehearsal process from the beginning. The director's assistant may be an appropriate person to be involved, as is the case with the Belgian theatre company KVS and the international theatre company Needcompany (Vervecken 2009: 66). One of the actors could also perform this task. This is sometimes the case with the

Dutch theatre collective Dood Paard (Vervecken 2009: 66). Since they have been part of the creative process from the outset, these people know the rhythm of the play or opera very well and will not base the segmenting on one single rehearsal or performance but on their understanding of the performance, which is alive and constantly changing. For instance, they may be aware of one of the actors' tendency to speed up a particular section.

Because opera houses have a consistent need for surtitles, they tend to have an in-house person in charge of the surtitles who is able to attend the rehearsals. In theatre, surtitles are often used only when a performance goes on tour in a foreign country.[8] The use of in-house personnel for the segmenting or any other part of the surtitle production process is therefore much rarer here. It is also much more common in theatre to contract someone who is not connected to the theatre or theater company.[9] In that case, the segmenting is often based on a video recording,[10] often a low resolution recording made by a small camera rendering the entire performance from one angle. This practice is not ideal but may be the best or easiest solution at hand. The reason why the use of a recording of a performance is not recommended as a basis for the segmenting is because it is an extremely limited source of information. Indeed, a video shows only the rhythm and speed for a single performance and contains no information about changes made to the performance after the recording was made. By contrast, an in-house person will be able to take the 'average performance rhythm' and the likelihood of changes to the speed into account.[11]

To conclude, when it comes to segmenting the text, the choice of who performs this task can make a tremendous difference, as do the materials that are provided to this person. Recordings are not ideal as a sole source of information. However, they can still be used to create high-quality surtitles if the recording is recent and accompanied by notes, and provided that the surtitler is able to communicate with the creative team and has at least one rehearsal to trial-run the prepared surtitles.

4.2.2. Translating

Surtitling has difficulties in common with literary translation. However, like subtitling, surtitling is faced with additional challenges: the need for reduction, spatial limitation and the fact that surtitlers translate a performance, not a script.

The most important reason for text reduction is to try to minimise the time that the audience spends on reading the surtitles. As the pace of speech on stage accelerates, especially when several performers talk or sing simultaneously, the need to condense increases. If there is not enough reduction, there is a greater chance that the audience will spend the whole time reading the surtitles without being able to watch the action or – in the case of several performers speaking – the audience might not be able to follow who is saying what (Skantze 2002: 26). Attending numerous performances of a single Argentinean play which contained an argument about politics, I was still unable to discern who was in favour and who was against Peron's policy because there was not enough time to read all of the surtitles. After a reworking of the surtitles, omitting repetitions and some details, and adapting the translation to make it more concise, the audience was able to follow the argument with ease.[12]

However, convincing the producers of a performance of the need for reduction in surtitling can be challenging. It is not uncommon for directors to refuse any reduction for fear that some of the meaning will be lost or because they feel it is 'sacrilege' to change anything in an existing translation or text. Sometimes, it is argued that the metre of a canonical translation used as a basis for the surtitles has to be retained. This makes reduction virtually impossible while it is improbable that the audience will be able to appreciate this metre in the surtitles. Ironically, directors often complain that surtitles are too distracting while at the same time resisting any form of reduction, which is the most important means of minimising this distraction.

The spatial limitations in surtitling are much more liberal than in subtitling because there is not the same physical limitation of the width of the screen, although there may be restrictions due to the size and/or type of screen or projection space. The variety of possibilities is much broader as is the potential for creativity. Surtitles can often be spread over three lines or even different screens. In addition, different fonts, sizes and colours can be used. Nevertheless, even if it is physically possible to display more text, this does not mean that it is a good idea to do so. For this reason, many professional surtitlers impose their own limitations on the number of characters and lines. The general consensus for opera as well as theatre is 40 characters per line and a maximum of two lines (Burton 2009: 64), even though it is quite easy to find examples that do not comply with this consensus.

Another important challenge is determining how to distribute a surtitle over the two available lines. Analogous to practices in subtitling (Díaz Cintas & Remael 2007), the distribution of the text on the screen has a significant influence on how comprehensible the text is. At times, a distribution that is easier to comprehend – because it does not separate the subject and verb for instance – requires more reduction in either the top or bottom line. Directors who dislike the idea of reduction will argue that there is enough space anyway or will suggest a distribution that might confuse the audience because the sentence is no longer logically divided.

As mentioned above, surtitles should not be a rendering of the script but a rendering of the text within the context of the production (Griesel 2007: 13).

Imagine a passage where a man on stage is furious and talking very fast and the following is part of his discourse: *I am so angry because my wife promised to cook me steak tonight and now I am supposed to eat steamed cod.* Because of the speed, significant reduction is needed and a very obvious omission would be to leave out the *I am so angry* because the audience can deduce this from his tone of voice and gesturing. For example:

> *My wife promised to cook me steak
> and now I am supposed to eat steamed cod.*

Now consider the same scene, but instead of ranting, though still speaking very fast, the actor is smiling and adopting the mannerisms of a newsreader. In that case, the reference to his state of mind should not be dropped as that is the indication the audience needs to understand the intention and create irony. For example:

> *I am angry because my wife promised me steak
> and we are having cod.*

Every performance contains many such nuances, often much more subtle and therefore hardly noticeable. Incorporating them often makes the difference between surtitles that are merely acceptable and surtitles which keep the audience enthralled.

4.2.3. Cueing

The projection of surtitles is not an automated process. There is always a human being involved. A list of surtitles is prepared beforehand. This document is similar to a cue list for subtitling but without time codes and with blank captions for silences. During the performance the cue master is responsible for synchronising the surtitles with what is being vocalised on stage. This is also referred to as *cueing*. Claiming that this person simply pushes a button whenever the next line is said/sung or the next silence occurs would be oversimplifying matters, but it does help to create a visual image. Depending on the software used, the cue master may or may not be able to insert a blank caption quickly when there is an unforeseen silence or jump in the list when a performer skips a line or entire section. Some software also allows the cue master to insert short improvisations quickly.

Opera houses tend to have an in-house cue master, often more than one. Theatre companies that travel a lot and have a great need for translation tend to delegate this responsibility to a technician or other person involved in the production (e.g., the director's assistant). Wayn Traub, for instance, put a sound technician in charge of synchronising the surtitles for his last production *Maria-Magdalena*, a multilingual and multimodal production featuring seven languages including Chinese and 16th-century English (Vervecken 2009: 58).

4.2.4. Evolution after the opening night

The curtain falls. The audience applauds. We are done. Tomorrow we just come back and do the same thing. This is probably how people tend to think about a theatrical production and the accompanying surtitles. Reality, however, proves to be different. A live performance is never the same as the night before, the speed and rhythm will be at least slightly different. Although these generally subtle changes may not seem that important, over time they will evolve and the differences will become bigger as the performance develops. That is why some surtitlers take notes while they cue the surtitles. It goes without saying that this action can be performed only if it does not distract the surtitler from the actual act of cueing, which is why the notes generally consist of the numbers of the captions that need adaptation, at times accompanied by a symbol specifying the required adaptation. These symbols are different for almost every cue master. These are, by way of example, some symbols used by the writer:

X	remove (blank) surtitle
O	insert blank surtitle
//	split into two captions
+	join two captions
↺	surtitle can be/needs to be reduced
⊥	problem with alignment/distribution over two lines

Notes such as these provide surtitlers with an account of how the performance evolves and enables them to make decisions about which surtitles should be adapted, as it is impossible to remember all of these minute details.

In opera surtitling, there is much less need for adapting the surtitles after the opening night. The rhythm does not change as it is dictated by the music, but the general speed of the performance can change.[13] However, a change in pace affects the entire performance and will generally not require many changes to the surtitles. Indeed, most surtitlers will take the possibility of this occurring into account and provide ample reduction to cope with these slight accelerations.

By contrast, many of the ongoing changes made in surtitles for theatre are likely to be due to a change in the rhythm of speech. Consider an actor who says the following with a slight pause exactly where the two surtitles are split:

Anika Vervecken

I went to the market on Sunday.

I saw Mark at the fruit stand.
I think he is using again.

Should the actor – after several performances – shift the pause to follow, for example, the second sentence, it is essential to change the surtitles. Not doing so would give the audience the information about Mark too early and if this information provokes a strong emotional reaction from another character on stage, it would cause the audience members to believe that the synchronisation is off. Such subtleties in timing are also important when working with humour.

In opera, the conductor is in charge of the speed. In theatre, the actors are and they often start speaking more quickly in the course of a tour as a result of their becoming more comfortable with the text.[14] Let us consider again the example shown above, where the actor says the same thing but without any pause and a little faster. In such a situation, the surtitler would need to reduce the text to be able to fit the discourse into one caption. Assuming that Mark's location at the fruit stand is not relevant information, one possibility would be:

I saw Mark at the market on Sunday.
I think he is using again.

The person translating and the cue master are not always the same person, nor do they need to be. Cue masters may be professionals hired by either the hosting theatre or the producers of the production. However, cueing can also be done by in-house personnel who may or may not have any training or talent for the task. Cueing surtitles requires intense concentration, a feel for rhythm and timing, and an eye for last-minute changes. As the performance evolves and changes, so should the surtitles.

4.2.5. Needcompany

The international theatre company Needcompany is a perfect example of teamwork when it comes to surtitling. Therefore, their work merits special mention. Since the 1980s Needcompany has been producing multilingual and multimodal performances, in which surtitles are almost always the means of translation. For each production, someone from the company – usually the director's assistant or dramaturge – takes on the responsibility of the surtitles. This person segments the text and works with a professional translator to translate and reduce, that is, to create the company's surtitles. For every production, a 'checklist' is also drawn up. This list consists of all the potentially problematic passages that contain essential information or are prone to misinterpretation (Vervecken 2009: 72). For every new set of surtitles that is created in another language, someone from the company will proofread the translation. If no one at the company knows the target language, the director's assistant will go through the checklist with the translator. During the performances, the same person is in charge of cueing and adapting the surtitles as the performance evolves. These adaptations are frequently sent to the translator to ensure that they do not contain errors. The surtitles not only enable the company to tour abroad, they have become an essential part of most of the company's performances. Without surtitles the company would not be able to have three languages or more spoken on stage. This multilingualism has now become one of the company's trademarks. Moreover, in some productions, the surtitles surpass their mere informative function and become part of the performance as the actors comment on them or the surtitles take on various fonts, colours and sizes as in *King Lear* (Carlson 2000: 88) and *The Ballad of Ricky and Ronny*[15] respectively.

5. Conclusion

This paper was not written in defence of surtitles. Like all forms of translation, surtitles have certain disadvantages and in some cases it may be better not to have any translation at all or to have a different form of translation.[16] It is unquestionable that surtitles have undesirable side effects. However, when they are used, their negative impact can be reduced to a minimum. Therefore, I oppose substandard surtitling, in particular when its flaws can be prevented. The director or producers of a production are not the only agents who have an influence on how surtitles are produced, but they are key agents in the production process. If they decide to become involved and make it clear that they want high quality, then the likelihood of achieving this increases dramatically. Alternatively, if the host theatre wants high quality, they may still fail if the theatre company provides dated material only and refuses to hold rehearsals with surtitles.

The first step towards first-rate surtitles is a basic understanding of how surtitles work. Directors need not be experts but they should have enough insight into surtitling to realise what is and what is not feasible and which material and instructions need to be provided. In addition, having some insight will also enable the director to become an active participant in the process of finding the right people for the job. Directors carefully choose those who are to perform, to conduct the orchestra or to cue the lighting. This should be no different for the surtitler. By being involved in the process, directors not only have more influence over the outcome, they also build up a network of people who they know will deliver high quality. In so doing, they

Anika Vervecken

will also realise that providing at least one rehearsal with surtitles can make a tremendous difference. Directors who are not interested in becoming acquainted with surtitling practices need only to provide accurate and up-to-date materials, making themselves or others in the company available for questions to ensure better results in the translation of their work.

---

[1] In some theatre productions, the director may not be that 'directive' or there may not be a director at all as is the case for the Flemish 'actor-oriented theatre collective' tgSTAN. For the sake of simplicity, however, we will assume that there always is a director supervising the production of the play, though in reality this role may be assumed by the producer or a group of actors. Moreover, a director in theatre environments is not quite the same as a director in opera environments. For instance, an opera tends to have two directors: a musical director and a mise-en scene director. Again, in this contribution the term *director* refers to the person or people in charge of the overall artistic production.

[2] All surtitlers who I spoke to confirmed that a large number of directors will never comment on the surtitles on any level other than a grammatical or practical level.

[3] Griesel (2000: 69) provides a perfect example of a director who insisted on very literary surtitles that may not have been the best choice, considering issues of reading speed and legibility.

[4] https://aplicacionesua.cpd.ua.es/tra_int/usu/buscarresultados.asp (consulted 09.11.2010)

[5] Source: www.askoxford.com (consulted 06.03.2010)

[6] Neither are surtitlers always mentioned in the programme, even when the person translating the play for performance is mentioned.

[7] For instance, when a review quotes the surtitles without any mention of the surtitles except for a short note in the paragraph with the practical information. This was the case with several reviews for the 2009 French tour of Julius Caesar, created at the American Repertory Theatre in Boston and directed by Arthur Nauzyciel. Such as a review was published in L'express on 22 October 2009 by L.L.

[8] In multilingual countries or regions, surtitles may be used systematically in theatre, as is the case for the KVS in Brussels. Nevertheless, these theatres are quite rare.

[9] This information is based on my own research in Flanders (2009) and interviews with several professional surtitlers from Belgium, Germany, Greece, the Netherlands, Spain, the US and several international theatre festivals.

[10] This was confirmed by professional surtitlers in Belgium, the Netherlands, France, Germany and Spain.

[11] Changes in rhythm and speed can be the simple result of how the performance naturally evolves and changes over time. They can also be the result of circumstances or a deliberate decision on the part of the director or the actors. A perfect example of the devastating effect a

change in circumstances can have is the performance of *Quand j'étais Révolutionnaire* (8 April 2009), for which the Zuiderpershuis in Antwerp (Belgium) hired a professional surtitler (Vervecken 2009: 86-87). On the night of the performance, the rhythm of speech was much slower than it was on the recording that the surtitler had received because the actor had not performed this monologue in over a year. Therefore, some surtitles remained visible for a very long time and the level of reduction was too high. This left the audience frustrated, feeling as if it was cheated out of some information because of the obvious disparity of the amount of text on stage and the amount in the surtitles but also due to the "gossiping effect", where "the cohabitation of source and target texts allows the viewers to immediately compare both messages" (Díaz Cintas & Remael 2007: 55). Of course, this is possible only when most of the audience members have a notion of the language spoken on stage (Skantze 2002: 27), which was almost unavoidable in this case since most Flemish-speaking people have some notion of French. While it was not the case for this example, it is a perfect illustration of an occasion where a director could complain about the surtitles destroying his work, even though the director provided dated material that was not representative of the performance.

[12] As I had witnessed the illegibility before, resolving this problem was important to me. Therefore, this specific section was tested on several people and after the performances the opinions of several audience members were consulted as well.

[13] One surtitler spoke of an instance where the conductor significantly increased the pace of the music "so he could finish in time to see the second half of the football finals". Obviously, this is an anecdote, but it does prove that tempo changes occur, even if these are not usually intentional.

[14] When Arthur Nauzyciel came back to Boston in 2007 after leaving his crew to perform a production of *Julius Caesar* without him for over a month, he was surprised to find a performance that lasted almost twenty minutes less than the one he had left. In a two and a half hour performance that is a significant reduction, one which would have had considerable influence on the legibility of the surtitles (had there been any). This information is based on conversations with Arthur Nauzyciel in November of 2009.

[15] Technically, this is a production by MaisonDahlBonnema, a "name adopted by the duo Hans Petter Dahl and Anna Sophia Bonnema", two performers of Needcompany. Source: www.needcompany.org (consulted 24.06.2010).

[16] In *Translation im Theater*, Griesel (2000) analyses several possible ways to deal with the language accessibility problem in theatre: synopsis, surtitling, interpreting and bilingual parallel texts.

References

Burton, Jonathan. 2009. 'The Art and Craft of Opera Surtitling' in Anderman, Gunilla & Jorge Díaz Cintas (eds.) *Audiovisual Translation: Language Transfer on Screen*. Basingstoke: Palgrave Macmillan. 58-69.
Carlson, Marvin. 2000. 'The Semiotics of Supertitles' in *Assaph* 16: 77-90.
Desblache, Lucile. 2004. 'Low Fidelity: Opera in Translation' in *Translating Today* 1: 28-30.
Desblache, Lucile. 2007. 'Music to My Ears, but Words to My Eyes? Text, Opera and Their Audiences' in *Linguistica Antverpiensia NS* 6: 155-70.

Dewolf, Linda. 2001. 'Surtitling Operas, with examples of translations from German into French and Dutch' in Gambier, Yves and Hendrik Gottlieb (eds.) *(Multi)Media Translation. Concepts, Practices and Research.* Amsterdam: John Benjamins. 179-188.
Díaz Cintas, Jorge & Aline Remael. 2007. *Audiovisual Translation: Subtitling.* Manchester: St. Jerome.
Durastanti, Sylvie. 2004. 'Surtitrer: Enjeux, Licences et Contraintes' in Marschall, Gottfried. R. (ed.) *La traduction des Livrets: Aspects Théoriques, Historiques et Pragmatiques.* Paris: Presses de l'Université Paris-Sorbonne. 623-628.
Gambier, Yves & Hendrik Gottlieb (eds) 2001. *(Multi)Media Translation. Concepts, Practices and Research.* Amsterdam: John Benjamins.
Griesel, Yvonne. 2000. *Translation im Theater: Die Mündliche und Schriftliche Übertragung Französischsprachiger Inzsenierungen ins Deutsche.* Frankfurt am Main: Peter Lang.
Griesel, Yvonne. 2005. 'Surtitles and Translation: Towards an Integrative View of Theatre Translation' in *Conference Proceedings of MuTra 2005: Challenges of Multidimensional Translation.* Online at http://www.euroconferences.info/proceedings/2005_Proceedings/ 2005_Griesel_Yvonne.pdf (consulted 14.04.2010).
Griesel, Yvonne. 2007. *Die Inszenieruing als Translat: Möglichkeiten und Grenzen der Theaterübertitelung.* Berlin: Frank and Timme.
Griesel, Yvonne. 2008. 'Theatre surtitles: Possibilities and Limits'. Paper presented at the symposium *Boventiteling, Daar kijk je van op.* [Surtitling: Something to look up to]. (Artesis University College Antwerp, 6 March 2008).
Hurt, Christina. 1996. 'Übertitel als Teil einer Operninszenierung am Beispiel von Wagners Siegfried', in Heiss, Christine & Rosa Maria Bollettieri Bosinelli (eds.) *Traduzione Multimediale per il Cinema,la Televisione e la Scena.* Bologna: CLUBEB. 85-94.
L.L. 2009. 'Les Mains Sales' in *L'Express* (22 October 2009).
Lavolee, Bruno. 2008. 'Les Systèmes de Sur-titrage' in *La Scène: Cahier technique* 6: n.p.
Matamala, Anna & Pilar Orero. 2007. 'Accessible opera in Catalan: Opera for all.' in Díaz Cintas, Jorge, Pilar Orero & Aline Remael (eds.) *Media for All: Subtitling for the Deaf, Audio Description, and Sign Language.* Amsterdam: Rodopi. 201-214.
Matamala, Anna & Pilar Orero. 2008. 'Opera Translation: An Annotated. Bibliography' in *The Translator* 14(2): 492-453.
Mateo, Marta. 2002. 'Los Sobretítulos de Ópera: Dimensión Técnica, Textual, Social e Ideológica' in Sanderson, John (ed.) *Traductores para Todo: Actea de las III Jornadas de Doblaje y Subtitulación.* Alicante: Universidad de Alicante. 51-57.
Mateo, Marta. 2005. 'La traducción de 'Salomé' para Distintos Públicos y Escenarios' in Merino Alvarez, Raquel, Eterio Pajares & José Miguel Santamaría López (eds.) *Trasvases Culturales: Literatura, Cine y Traducción 4.* Bilbao: UPV/EHU. 225-242.
Mateo, Marta. 2007a. 'Reception, Text and Context in the Study of Opera Surtitles' in Gambier, Yves, Miriam Shlesinger & Radegundis Stolze (eds.) *Doubts and Directions in Translation Studies: Selected Contributions from the EST Congress, Lisbon 2004.* Amsterdam: John Benjamins. 169-182.
Mateo, Marta. 2007b. 'Surtitling Nowadays: New Uses, Attitudes and Developments' in *Linguistica Antverpiensia NS* 6: 135-154.
Nisato, Catherine. 1999. 'What's in an Opera? Wouldn't a Translation Sound as Sweet?' in *ATA Chronicle* 28(6).
Sario, Marjatta & Susanna Oksanen. 1996. 'Le Sur-titrage des Operas à l'Opéra National de Finlande' in Gambier, Yves (ed.) *Les Transferts Linguistiques dans les Medias Audiovisuels.* Villeneuve d'Ascq (Nord): Presses Universitaires du Septentrión. 185-193.
Skantze, P.A. 2002. 'Watching in Translation, Performance and the Reception of Surtitles' in *Performance Research* 7(2): 26-30.
Udo, John Patrick & Deborah I. Fels. 2009. 'The Rogue Poster-Children of Universal Design: Closed Captioning and Audio Description' in *Journal of Engineering Design* 21(2-3): 1-15.

Vanattenhove, Miel & Marianne Van Kerkhoven. 2002. 'Wat Denkt een Vrouw die Beneveld voor zich uit Zit te Staren?' in *Etcetera* 80: 50-54.
Vervecken, An. 2009. *Surtitles: The Making of.* MA thesis. Department of Translators and Interpreters, Artesis University College Antwerp.
Vervecken, An. (forthcoming). *The Types and Functions of Surtitles* (provisional title).
Wise, Louis. 2009. 'West End Translates for Foreign Theatre Goers' in *The Sunday Times* (20 December 2009). Online at http://entertainment.timesonline.co.uk/tol/arts_and_entertainment/ stage/theatre/article6959351.ece (consulted 14.10.2010).

Old Films, New Subtitles, More Anglicisms?[1]

Henrik Gottlieb
University of Copenhagen (Denmark)

Abstract
The focus of this contribution is on paving the way for systematic diachronic studies of screen translation. It develops a methodology for comparing translations – more specifically subtitles – from different periods and focuses on the topical language-political issue of anglification. Based on a comprehensive taxonomy of anglicisms, the degree of anglification is calculated for contemporary and 'original' Danish subtitles for three classic English-language movies. The results of this small-scale investigation indicate that although Danish and other languages are increasingly influenced by widespread anglocentric globalisation, subtitles may not act as motors in this anglification process. The individual translational choices made by subtitlers may in fact go against the grain and introduce or maintain renderings that are less anglified than original domestic texts.

Keywords
anglicisms, diachronic screen translation research methodology, film subtitling, language politics.

1. Background and aim of the study

In the study reported on in this contribution, two phenomena related to translation will be analysed from a predominantly diachronic point of view. These two phenomena are interlingual subtitling (as defined in Gottlieb 2001a) and linguistic influence from English, the 'visible' results of which will be referred to as anglicisms.

Whereas anglicisms have incessantly been seen as linguistic entities entering various languages in waves – a simile used in the last hundred years in both public discourse and scholarly debate (Dunger 1909, Stiven 1936, Gottlieb 2005: 175ff.) – translation scholars and others have treated subtitles as something almost devoid of change. The pros and cons of subtitling – often contrasted with those of dubbing (Koolstra et al. 2002, Díaz Cintas 2003, Nornes 2007, He 2009, Tveit 2009) – have been considered fixed properties unanchored in a historical context. To my knowledge, of the hundreds of analyses and comparative studies of subtitles made so far, only one has focused on the historical developments of subtitling (Pedersen 2007).[2]

In an attempt to investigate at least one aspect of the historical development in subtitling, the present study looks at translational choices, and especially the use or non-use of anglicisms – then and now – in Danish subtitles for English-language feature film classics.

As a linguistic phenomenon, anglicisms have been eagerly discussed for more than a century.[3] As France was the first speech community in which the English influence was felt to be a challenge to the domestic language, French works on the subject often discuss the original wave of *Anglomanie* in the late 18th century (Mackenzie 1939), and since that period, French has found itself in a downward spiral. This is reflected both in the declining international prestige vis-à-vis English and in the increasing import of English loanwords into French. An interesting case study of the early penetration of English into French literature is found in the monograph *Proust's English* (Karlin 2005).

Still, translations are also common subjects for discussions of English influence abroad. German encountered the 'onslaught of English' some hundred years later than French, partly due to the already existing fascination with things French (Dunger 1909). Today, another century later, German is experiencing an unprecedented influence from English (Onysko 2007), not least via the media, and – ironically – through dubbing, still the prevalent form of screen translation in Germany (Herbst 1994, 1995, 1997). Italian and Spanish have been markedly influenced by English, too. As many as 93 Italian and 139 Spanish titles on anglicisms were recorded in the *Annotated Bibliography of European Anglicisms* (Görlach 2002b).

The pro-subtitling Nordic countries constitute "a well-suited 'laboratory' for research into the contexts and consequences of today's globalisation and the general advance of English" (Kristiansen & Sandøy 2010: 1). Several Nordic studies have dealt with the English influence attested in translated texts, resulting in translationese (e.g., Tirkkonen-Condit 2002, Gellerstam 2005). A few titles have focused on the English influence found in and disseminated via subtitles (Sajavaara 1991; Gottlieb 2001b, 2001c).

Whereas previous studies (e.g., Gottlieb 2001b, 2001c) looked at anglicisms in different films subtitled and dubbed into Danish within a very short time span (i.e., the 1990s), this contribution sets out to compare the same films subtitled in two periods: when they were released in the mid-20th century and some 50 years later, around the year 2000.

As the title of this contribution reveals, the working hypothesis of the study was that with the passing of time and the augmented English impact on Danish (Sørensen 1997; Jarvad 2001; Gottlieb 2004b, 2009b), more anglicisms – including morphosyntactic calques, loan translations, etc. – would be found in the 'new' subtitles than in the 'old' ones. As we shall see, the results point to a more complex relationship between the two sets of subtitles.

Before we take a closer look at the notion of anglicism, let us turn to the historical development of screen translation in general and of subtitling in particular (see Gottlieb 1997).

2. The backdrop of subtitling

Early in the 20th century, the printed word found itself confronted with two serious rivals: radio and motion pictures. While radio meant that people no longer had to decode an abstractly phrased (written) message, it still required that audiences understood the language spoken. Bypassing this problem, the new film medium – with its silent visual form – was thought to transcend all educational and linguistic borders: cinema was regarded as a 'universal language', conceived of as a new means of expression and characterised by its universality. It promised the abolition of national barriers, a notion that in France in the 1920s was coined 'esperanto visuel' (Brant 1984: 11).

Esperanto – the artificial language – never gained worldwide acceptance. Films did, but not quite without words. Already in 1903, we saw the first silent movie with so-called 'subtitles' – which after the appearance of sound film were renamed 'intertitles' (Marleau 1982: 272).

But with the invention of the 'talkies' in 1927, film distributors could not just settle for replacing a couple of foreign intertitles. The entire dialogue had to be translated. To this end, two methods were developed: subtitling and dubbing (the latter also known as post-synchronisation). France soon became the land of film translation par excellence. Numerous French and foreign movies were dubbed or subtitled into a vast number of languages, but neither method was flawless. Many film buffs felt that a translated film was a ruined film: a dubbed film was an insult to the actors, and a subtitled version was a violation of the picture.

However, foreign-language films soon comprised a major part of what was shown in cinema theatres worldwide. Even today, domestic film production in most European countries does not match anglophone imports when it comes to box-office revenue (Gottlieb 2009a). In short, ever since the introduction of sound film around 1929, foreign-language movies – and later, TV programmes – have constituted a major part of domestic cultures worldwide. Together with voice-over, the 'poor cousin' of screen translation (Orero 2009), dubbing and subtitling are still the dominant types of screen translation, in spite of their innate limitations.

Yet, some things have changed since the infancy of subtitling. When subtitles first appeared on the silver screen in European cinema theatres, they represented little more than a gist translation, while at the same time the typical audience knew very little English, let alone other foreign languages.

In the 1950s, subtitles represented a larger part of the dialogue. In Danish cinemas, subtitles were presented at a rate of some 12 characters per second (cps), and shot changes were respected, so that no subtitles were found 'hanging' over a cut. With the successful introduction of films on DVD in the late 1990s, presentation rates of up to 16 cps became common in the home cinema environment as well as in movie theatres. On Scandinavian public-service TV, the last three decades have seen a shift from a maximum of 10 cps to 12 cps (Pedersen 2007). Commercial stations often operate with rates in the 14–16 cps range. Far from constituting trivial technical details, these figures represent a shift from the 'condensed translation' label of traditional subtitling to the status closer to that of 'full' translation, on a par with literary or technical translation.

This decreasing condensation is testified in the material of this study, as exemplified by the following excerpt from the film *Sabrina* (Wilder 1954)

Table 1. Degrees of condensation in subtitling

Film dialogue	Danish film subtitle (1954)	Danish DVD subtitle (2001)
I'm not very bright. It took me until this morning to add two and two together	Jeg lagde 2 og 2 sammen	Det varede indtil i morges, før jeg havde lagt to og to sammen
	[I added 2 and 2 together]	[It lasted until this morning, before I had added two and two together]

Today, people in many European subtitling countries are functionally bilingual. As many as 86% of the Danish population, 87% of the Swedish population and 89% of the Dutch population – as opposed to a mere 56% of the population in pro-dubbing Germany – claim to be able to speak English "well enough in order to be able to have a conversation" (European Commission 2006: 13; see also Preisler 2003). This means that for hearing audiences, subtitlers may no longer need to translate obviously transparent dialogue elements such as terms of address and exclamations. Conversely, as a result of the feedback effect from the original dialogue comprehensible to most of the audience, it may also lead to a preference for somewhat unidiomatic renderings in the target-language (TL) subtitles.

Another result of the feedback effect on semibilingual audiences – including hard-of-hearing people – is that such audiences often want everything translated, and this – in connection with American and British anti-condensation norms – means increased reading speeds in subtitling. This increased presentation rate means that subtitling audiences go from being underinformed of the original verbal content to being 'overinformed', that is, being served an almost complete written translation literally on top of a verbal anglophone dialogue, which they understand almost completely. [4]

With anglophone productions, the function of subtitling is now shifting away from replacing the original dialogue to supplementing it – a development already demonstrated in Denmark in the late 20th century (Neesbye-Hansen 1983).

3.1. Anglicisms then and now

As discussed in the introduction, anglicisms and the fear of English influence have been around for generations. In Denmark, an early warning against Anglicisms was found in the following passage from a Danish sports magazine, *Dansk Sportstidende*, issue 44, 1888. The journalist, with the byline "Spectator", says:

Sport er et engelsk Begreb, og et Ord der ligesom saa mange andre fremmede Ord er uoversættelige paa Dansk. Fremmed, som det er, har det først faaet Borgerret i vort Sprog ved en altfor hyppig og kritikløs Anvendelse, og brugt i Flæng snart om *enhver Beskjæftigelse, som ligger uden for det daglige Slid og Slæb,* er dets Betydning efterhaanden bleven ligesaa vag som meningsløs.

[Sport is an English term, and a word which as many other foreign words cannot be translated into Danish. Foreign as it is, it has only acquired citizenship in our language through much too frequent and uncritical use, and when used indiscriminately of *almost any activity beyond the daily toil and chores,* its meaning has now become both vague and futile.] (my translation and emphasis)

This quote is interesting in three ways:

(1) Accidentally, it reveals the very reason why anglicisms now and then have their way with speakers of other languages; English borrowings are associated with leisure and pleasure, cf. the italicized sequence.
(2) Unintentionally, the text proves the fact that Danish – as many other languages – relies heavily on foreign borrowings, *in casu* German loanwords (Winge 2000). All the words underscored are (fully

integrated) Germanisms, something that the journalist most likely would not have realized.

(3) Both the name of the magazine and the byline of the journalist represent English loans ('sports-' and 'spectator' are both Anglicisms), an ironical demonstration of the point our "Spectator" was trying to make.

In scholarly discourse on linguistic influence, anglicisms are often defined as words borrowed from English, adapted according to receptor language norms, and integrated into that language (e.g., Filipović 1996: 45).[5] However, as is obvious from the taxonomy below, regarding anglicisms merely as lexical and integrated items of language is no longer tenable – if it ever was. Today, English influence is found at all levels of language, and any thorough investigation of the phenomenon will have to include features such as grammar, orthography, stylistics, etc.

For this reason an anglicism is defined in this contribution as follows:

> Any individual or systemic language feature adapted or adopted from English, or inspired or boosted by English models, used in intralingual communication in a language other than English.

This broad definition is relevant in this study since subtitles would be expected not only to retain certain English words spoken on screen, but also to echo various syntactic constructions. To a large extent, this echoing is triggered by the aforementioned feedback effect from the soundtrack, which may encourage subtitlers to phrase their translations in such a way that the discrepancy between what is said in English and what is read in the domestic language will not be too marked.

Before presenting a taxonomical overview of the various structural types of anglicisms, let us first have a brief look at the typical nature of anglicisms in the centuries discussed in this contribution:

Table 2. Scope of anglicisms

Time	Scope	Examples
18th–19th centuries	foreignism	gentlemen
20th century	borrowings	TV
21st century	globalisms	blogger

Worldwide, the scope of anglicisms has expanded from the 18th and 19th centuries, in which the typical English loan referred to social customs and other phenomena found in Britain (and, occasionally, the British colonies or the US). Such loans included words like *Lord, poker, tennis, whisky* and *tomahawk*. Not only did such words sound English on foreign lips, they also referred to entities that originated in the English-speaking world, hence the label *foreignisms*.

In the 20th century, as the number and scope of anglicisms increased, more and more borrowings referred to phenomena that were introduced along with their English-sounding terms. This included words such as *start, jazz, know-how* and *computer*.

Beginning in the 20th century, but accelerating in the 21st century, new anglicisms often redefined already existing phenomena in receptor languages. The domestic terms were already there, but the competing English-sounding words and constructions contributed to the attraction of the phenomena in question. This explains their frequent usage in commercial lingo. Examples of such modern borrowings are *make-up, cool, dating* and *coach*.

The ousting of existing words and pragmatic expressions has been lamented by several observers, for instance in Spain, where poor dubbing from English is often claimed to play a major part (Gómez Capuz 2001). Also in a subtitling context, some concern has been voiced. In reference to specific Spanish subtitles displaying syntactic calques from English, these subtitles are condemned as being not only lexically and syntactically incorrect in Spanish, but also nonsensical. With their peculiar grammar, such subtitles are an attack on the Spanish language and do very little to educate their readers. Prolonged contact with this peculiar Spanish, riddled with interferences from English, is not only threatening the Spanish language, but is also harmful to the viewer's brain (Díaz Cintas 2005: 21).

While some scholars may get emotionally involved, others – at times labeled by their opponents as laissez-faire – maintain a strictly descriptive attitude towards the anglification generated by screen-translation practices: For some, of course, the fear is that the older established terms will be progressively eliminated by the new forms. Some academics believe that it is possible to stop the flow of these changes (Munday 2005: 67).

However, there is only a slim chance that such linguistic tides can be turned by language-political actions from above. Not even Iceland, perhaps the world's most homogenous nation, renowned for its purist language policies, is highly successful in its attempt to keep Icelandic free from anglicisms. (Svavarsdóttir 2004: 164).

In addition to the established terms often losing ground to seemingly synonymous English-inspired competitors (Gottlieb forthcoming), we now see English – and English-inspired – coinages for everything that belongs to the global community, that is, all non-local entities. Most speech communities have already generally accepted terms like *computer* – albeit spelled in various ways – and globalisms such as *outsourcing*, *benchmarking* and the verb *google*. Although one would be naïve to say that such expressions – most of them based on American practices – are truly international, they still penetrate most languages spoken today and may affect people's mindsets in the process. This brings us to Table 3, which illustrates the development in the structure and the effects of anglicisms:

Table 3. Penetration of anglicisms

Time	Depth	Danish examples
19th century	shallow: lexical imports	strejke ('strike'), lockout
20th century	medium: semantic loans & loan translations	kernefamilie ('nuclear family')
21st century	profound: syntactic and pragmatic loans	eg elsker dig ('I love you')

In a relatively open speech community like Denmark with five million speakers of Danish, a language related to both German and English, we witness a steady and seemingly unproblematic integration and – more interestingly – wholesale adoption of anglicisms. Already in the 19th century, the twin concepts of (industrial) strike and lockout were introduced in Danish, in both cases using the English words, yet with a modified spelling which made the most frequent of the terms, *strejke*, look and sound completely Danish to the lay observer.

In addition to such lexical imports already frequent in the previous century, the 20th century saw a vast variety of loan translations and 'reactive' types of anglicisms (see Tables 4 and 5). Again, only some expressions were easily identifiable as anglicisms. The word *kernefamilie*, a direct translation of *nuclear family*, is thus totally inconspicuous to the Danish layperson.

In the 21st century, we see more and more examples of anglicisms that creep in under the lexical carpet, thus resulting in altered semantics and syntax (Gottlieb forthcoming). As an illustration of this new trend, the Danish expression *Jeg elsker dig* (I love you) – normally used very sparingly and intimately – is now often seen in Danish subtitles, as a direct calque of the inflated American good-bye formula 'I love you' so often encountered in Hollywood movies.

Also semantic loans are still common and do not always generate new shades of meaning in the affected language. In Danish subtitles and other translated texts, the English word *morning* is often mistranslated into Danish as *morgen*, which in Danish means early morning – even when the time of day it refers to is close to noon. In Danish, as in English in days gone by, the word *formiddag* (forenoon) conveniently refers to the time from the beginning of the working day, that is, around 8am or 9am to noon. This distinction – as many other distinctions not maintained or found in English – is at stake in speech communities that enter the third phase outlined in Table 3, as the impact of English is becoming more profound.

After this perhaps somewhat proscriptive diagnosis, let us turn to the general taxonomy announced above (based on Gottlieb 2004a).[6]

3.2. An international typology of anglicisms

This taxonomy, based on the definition in Section 3.1, operates with three main structural categories of anglicisms:

(1) active anglicisms, in which English features are adapted or adopted;
(2) reactive anglicisms, which represent English inspiration;
(3) code shifts, which represent texts with embedded English discourse.

Table 4. Active anglicisms

Category	Type	Examples	English trigger
(1) overt lexical borrowings	**single-word unit**	branding (Danish)	branding
	multi-word unit	Learning by Doing (German)	learning by doing
	sub-word unit	-minded (Norwegian)	-minded
(2) covert lexical borrowings	**single-word unit**	keks (Slovene)	cakes
	multi-word unit	Stop en halv! (Danish) [literally: 'stop one half']	Stop and haul!

257

(3) loan translations	**compount substitute**	involtino primavera (Italian)	spring roll
	multi-word substitute	Tað er at siga (Faroese)	that is to say
(4) Hybrids	**partial loan translation**	Computerkunst (German)	computer art
(5) Pseudo-anglicisms	**archaism**	butterfly (Danish)	butterfly tie (= bow tie)
	semantic changes	overhead (Norwegian) (= slide, OPH transparency)	overhead
	contamination	after-ski (Swedish)	after + ski (English: après-ski)
	morphological change	fit for fight (Swedish)	fighting fit
	jocular derivation	webmaster (Danish) [literally: 'web auntie']	webmaster
(6) Phonetic borrowings	**phonetic loan**	brand [introducing an English *r*] (Danish)	brand

Table 5. Reactive anglicisms

Category	Type	Anglicism	Standard	Trigger
(7) Semantic loans	**Extension**	*lernen* = find out (German)	*lernen* = be taught	*learn*
	Reversal	*overhøre* = hear (Danish)	*overhøre* = ignore	*overhear*
	Limitation	*skudt og dræbt* (Danish)	*skudt* = killed by gunfire	*shot and killed*

Old films, new subtitles, more anglicisms?

	Double	*spotte* = detect (Danish)	*spotte* = mock	*spot* (verb)
(8) Ortho-graphic deviations	Changed spelling	*literatur* (Danish) *N8* (German)	*litteratur* *Nacht*	*literature* *sk8* (=skate)
	Changed punctuation	Michael*'s* Køreskole (Danish)	Michael*s* køreskole	Michael*'s* [Driving School]
(9) Phonetic deviations	Phonematic change	*unik* pronounced as [you'nik] (Danish)	[oo'nik]	*unique*
	Prosodic change	falling intonation in exclamations (Brazilian Portuguese)	slightly rising intonation	American intonational pattern
(10) Morpho-syntactic calques	Inflectional	*autobahns* (Danish)	plural *–er*	*-s*
	Morphological	*disrespekt* (Danish)	*despekt*	*disrespect*
	Phraseological	*Hier sind Sie.* (German)	*Bitte sehr.*	*Here you are.*
	Grammatical	*Jan is 'n dosent aan die POK* (Afrikaans)	*Jan is dosent aan die POK*	*(Jan is) a professor (at the POK)*
	Syntactic	*Dog, han vil ikke ...* (Danish)	*Han vil dog ikke ...*	*However, he ...*
	Valency	*Ring en ekspert* (Danish)	*Ring til en ekspert / Tilkald en ekspert*	*Call an expert*

	Prepositional	*ud af vandet* (Danish)	*op af vandet* [op = up]	*out of the water*
(11) Intensified usage	**Favored single-word cognate**	*còpia* [... of a book] (Catalan)	*exemplar*	*copy*
	Favored multi-word cognate	*Hun gav mig denne her.* (Danish)	*Jeg har fået den af hende.* [I've gotten it from her]	*She gave me this one.*
	Default equivalent	*anlända* (Swedish)	*komma*	*arrive*
	Pragmatic calque	*Jeg elsker dig!* [used as a greeting] (Danish)	*Hav det godt!* [Have a nice time]	*I love you!*

Table 6. Code-shifts

Category	Example	Pragmatic context
(12) Tags	*, okay?*	Danish post-sentence standard oral interpersonal assurance formula
(13) Intrasentential shifts & foreignisms	Wer wird *Germany's next* Top-Modell?	Headline in German car magazine
(14) Bilingual wordplay	"De Frygtløse – *The Muuhvie*" [Danish title for the American animated movie (featuring cows) "Home on the Range" from 2004]	Common linguistic device in commercial punchlines and political slogans in semi-bilingual speech communities
(15) Sentence-shaped shifts	*Way to go, girl!*	The final words in a (Danish) music review

(16) Total shifts  Website of major Danish company (www.maersk.com/Pages/default.aspx) unavailable in Danish

(17) Domain loss *Product Carbon Footprint Memorandum Position statement on measurement and communication of the product carbon footprint for international standardization and harmonization purposes* Title of an academic paper written by two German scientists at the *Öko-Institut e.V.* (December 2009)
[In some countries up to 90% domain losses in scientific papers, computer games, pop lyrics and certain business documents; more moderate losses in domains like advertisements, commercial brands and film titles.]

3.3. No end of Anglification?

Including the initial French wave of *anglomanie,* with its permanent effects on the French language, the (linguistic) influence from English-speaking countries has now lasted almost a quarter of a millennium. In all likelihood, the following five factors will contribute to the perpetuation of this state of affairs:

(1) English enjoys *overt prestige* in all powerful countries – not least the two largest nations in the world, both emerging economies: China and India. In addition, influential corporations, organisations and individuals all use English in international communication. This choice of language naturally rubs off on local vernaculars, from Japanese in the east to (Latin American) Spanish in the west (Viereck and Bald 1986).

(2) English also enjoys global *covert prestige.* Hip subcultures worldwide use English in international communication – and disempowered third-world people will often code-switch into English or use English elements in their internal communication. In Senegal, for instance, the urban youth's preference of stigmatised English words is indicative of their rejection of the overt prestige of French

and Arabic, and their acceptance of the covert prestige of English as sign of group solidarity and membership (Ngom 2003: 360).
(3) English is the first foreign language taught in probably all UN member states in which English is not already used in domestic communication.
(4) While in relative terms English is now losing ground online (Graddol 2006: 44-45), it is still the dominant language in the entertainment industry. English-language lyrics, computer games and software are often used overseas untranslated, while – as we mentioned above – dubbed or subtitled anglophone films and TV productions tend to enhance the global dominance of English.
(5) English triggers and benefits from diminishing cross-border understanding. A recent phenomenon relates to the fact that young people (e.g., in Scandinavia) tend to know only one foreign language (English). Feeling uncomfortable with the language of their neighbours, no matter how close that language may be, they switch into English, thus further increasing the importance and influence of that language (Gregersen 2009).

4. Methodology and material

The aim of the study reported on in this contribution was to find a suitable methodology for investigating linguistic anglification in present-day subtitles, compared with subtitles from a generation or two ago. With this aim in mind, at least two research designs presented themselves: (1) comparing modern subtitles for contemporary anglophone productions with 'classic' subtitles for anglophone film classics, and (2) comparing today's subtitles for anglophone film classics with their original subtitles.

For this explorative pilot study, the second – more 'naked' – research design was chosen since that specific design limited the variables to two: (1) potential change in technical subtitling standards and (2) potential change in the linguistic choices made by subtitlers. The films were the same, all spoken lines were identical. Only the wording in the subtitles differed.

To begin with, a 1962 British caper comedy, *The Wrong Arm of the Law* (Owen 1963) was analysed. The original subtitles were compared with the modern Danish public-television subtitles, with special focus on solutions that displayed anglicisms (of any of the types listed in Tables 4 to 6). 36 relevant dialogue sequences were selected (somewhat idiosyncratically) in this way and as we will see, the results 'behaved' well. In accordance with the research hypothesis, the modern Danish version contained significantly more anglicisms than did the 'original' Danish version.

In order to eliminate the risk of continued idiosyncratic compilation of data – which is hard to avoid when trawling through any text looking for certain linguistic features – two measures were taken. First, additional materials were randomly selected by picking the first two pre-1970 English-language films whose titles begin with S (the letter in English dictionaries with the largest number of words that have it as their beginning letter), which were available on DVD with Danish subtitles, and – most important – whose original (cinema) subtitles could be acquired from the archives of the Danish Film Institute. Second, each of the two films that presented themselves for investigation – *Sands of Iwo Jima* (Dwan) from 1949 and *Sabrina* (Wilder) from 1954 (both American productions) – was subsequently analysed by comparing the old and new subtitles found at exact 5-minute intervals throughout the film. By including two subsequent subtitles at each 5-minute 'stop', the amount of data for each film was comparable to the data from *The Wrong Arm of the Law*.

While the selective anglicism search in the British film produced 36 pairs of relevant hits, the systematic stop-and-go modus operandi in dealing with the American films yielded 40 and 42 analysed film excerpts respectively (reflecting the difference in duration between these movies), most of which contained no anglicisms.

To be able to compare the different versions and the different films, the degree of anglification represented by the translational strategy found in a given subtitle was rated according to the following criteria:

Table 7. Degrees of anglification in subtitling

Rating	Strategy	Anglicisms involved
-2	Purist translation (anti-English hypercorrection)	none
-1	Substitution (Danish intra-cultural solution)	none
0	'Neutral' translation; no English-language features	none
1	Favoring cognate Danish expressions	category 11
2	Use of established English loanwords	categories 1, 2, 3, 4, 5 & 12
3	Use of syntactic calques (semantically transparent)	category 10
4	Use of foreignisms and/or non-transparent calques	categories 13 & 10

| 5 | Total transfer) | code-shifting | (complete categories 14 & 15 |

It is perhaps worth noticing that, as we will see in the *Sabrina* data, purist or pronouncedly domesticating solutions in subtitling may outweigh English-inspired wording found elsewhere in the subtitles to a certain extent.

To obtain a general picture of the anglification displayed in the material, four potential levels of anglification were established, based on the average score for the subtitles in the selected sequences of each film version:

Table 8: Levels of anglification in subtitling

Level	Type
-2.00 - 0.00	Counter-anglification (*domesticated solutions; unauthentic language*)
0.00 - 0.99	Neutral solutions (*idiomatic language*)
1.00 - 2.99	Light anglification (*English-flavored solutions*)
3.00 - 5.00	Heavy anglification (*foreignized solutions; unidiomatic language*)

5. Results and discussion: Does time mean anglification?

In the following section, we will look at whether the modern subtitles for the three films represent a higher degree of anglification than did the original subtitles. The original cinema subtitles will be referred to as the A subtitles, while the more contemporary subtitles will be labeled B subtitles.

1) ***WRONG ARM OF THE LAW*** (Owen, 1962, featuring Peter Sellers) **Danish cinema subtitles c. 1963; Danish TV subtitles 1991**

Perhaps somewhat unexpectedly, several A subtitles display anglification in situations where the B subtitles are neutral. This proves to be the case in 9 out of the 36 instances investigated. In a further 11 instances, we find anglification in both sets of subtitles, while 13 B subtitles express anglification in contexts where the A subtitles do not. This adds up to 20 anglified subtitles in version A, against 24 in B.

Counter-anglification is found in only one instance in either version of the film. In version A, the subtitler renders the colloquial *Look, mate, just because you ...* as *Bare fordi De ...*, demonstratively using the polite form of address, *De*, instead of the more idiomatic *du* – the equivalent of French *tu* and German *du*. In version B, the nickname of the undercover policeman, *Big Time*, is conspicuously replaced by *Fætter Højben*, aka *Cousin Gander* from Disney's cartoon universe. Table 9 sums up the differences between the two versions.

Table 9: *Wrong Arm of the Law*	Version A (c. 1963) 36 instances		Version B (1991) 36 instances	
Anglification	20 instances	55.6 %	24 instances	66.7 %
Counter-anglification	1 instance	2.8 %	1 instance	2.8 %
Neutral solutions	15 instances	41.7 %	11 instances	30.6 %
Average degree of anglification	1.11		1.81	
Increase in anglification	**63 %**			

The average degree of anglification is calculated as the accumulated anglification figures – according to the rating principles listed in Table 7 – divided by the number of instances in the respective version. Because all of the segments from this film were selected based on the presence of anglicisms, the average degree of anglification of the film as a whole will be lower than the figures in Table 9 indicate. However, it remains a fact that the anglification represented in version B is markedly higher than that of version A, which is in perfect concert with the hypothesis of this study. The increase in anglification – calculated as the average degree of anglification in version B minus that of version A divided by the latter figure, *in casu* (1.81 – 1.11) / 1.11 – is 63 %.

A considerable part of this increased anglification is due to the fact that, except for the *Cousin Gander* example that was highlighted above, the English nicknames (for the gangsters and coppers in the film) are retained in version B, whereas the original subtitler translated them. In this way, *Brassknuckles*, for instance, became *Knojern* in 1963 but stayed *Brassknuckles* in 1991. Another interesting feature is the tendency – even in version A – to copy English idioms and sayings which often results in downright unidiomatic translations, as version A's incomprehensible *Man ved aldrig, om man kommer eller gaar!*, a literal translation of the idiom in the line *You never know whether you're comin' or goin' on this job*.

We will now look at the two films in which random data selection was made.

2) *SANDS OF IWO JIMA* (Dwan, 1949, featuring John Wayne)
Danish cinema subtitles c. 1960; Danish DVD subtitles 2004

Table 10: *Sands of Iwo Jima*	Version A (c. 1960) 46 instances	Version B (2004) 48 instances

Henrik Gottlieb

Anglification	15 instances	32.6 %	5 instances	10.4 %
Counter-anglification	1 instance	2.2 %	0 instances	0 %
Neutral solutions	30 instances	65.2 %	43 instances	89.6 %
Average degree of anglification	0.72		0.23	
Increase in anglification	**-68 %**			

Since all of the instances in this film were found randomly, the results shown in Table 10 should be representative of the total population, that is, the approximately1000 subtitles in each version of the film. As it turns out, the 'modern' Danish subtitler favours neutral solutions and manages to keep anglification to a minimum while not resorting to counter-anglification, that is, extremely 'conservative' translation strategies.

In stark contrast with the previous set of data (see Table 9), the degree of anglification in version B of *Sands of Iwo Jima* is down by 68 % when compared with version A. While version A uses, for example, the word *Marinekorpset* for *the Marine Corps*, version B translates it as *Marineinfanteriet*, the standard Danish term. Similarly, the line *What's your problem, son?*, which in version A was translated word-by-word as *Hvad er dit problem?* was rendered more idiomatically as *Hvad er der los, knægt?* (literal translation: *What is wrong, boy?*) in version B. Interestingly, while version A's calque would have sounded unidiomatic in 1960, it was widely used by 2004, while version B's solution is slightly old-fashioned – probably as a result of a conscious effort on behalf of the translator not to come up with anachronistic (i.e., too modern-sounding) subtitles for a now-classic movie.

In passing, it should be noted that as a result of faster presentation rates – partly to do with the 'fast' DVD medium and partly caused by the general present-day subtitling standards discussed earlier – more of the dialogue is represented in the 2004 version than was the case in 1960.[7] However, this should not in itself influence the degree of anglification.

3) *SABRINA* (Wilder, 1954, featuring Audrey Hepburn and Humphrey Bogart)

Danish cinema subtitles 1954; Danish DVD subtitles 2001

Table 11: *Sabrina*	Version A (1954) **48 instances**		Version B (2001) **50 instances**	
Anglification	11 instances	22.9 %	14 instances	28.0 %
Counter-anglification	6 instances	12.5 %	0 instances	0 %
Neutral solutions	31 instances	64.6 %	36 instances	72.0 %
Average degree of anglification	0.38		0.46	
Increase in anglification	**21 %**			

With this film, the original hypothesis fares better. Still, the increase in anglification is modest and mostly due to subtitler B's being less inclined to using counter-anglification than her predecessor.

An example of this shift of strategy is Bogart's line *What's wrong with the kind of an urge that gives people libraries, hospitals, baseball diamonds*. In 1954, it was rendered as *Folk faar biblioteker, hospitaler, boldbaner* (*People get libraries, hospitals, ball parks*), while in 2001, it was rendered as *Hvad er der galt med en indre drift der giver folk biblioteker, hospitaler, baseballbaner* (*What is wrong with a inner urge that gives people libraries, hospitals, baseball diamonds*). Notice here that the all-American term *baseball diamonds* is counter-anglified by subtitler A using the hyperonym *boldbaner*, whereas subtitler B opts for the solution *baseballbaner*, which keeps the original reference. Again, this strategy is accompanied by a lesser degree of condensation. Bogart's 16-word line – although represented by two consecutive subtitles in both Danish versions – occupied 15 words in the 2001 subtitles, against only 5 words in the 1954 subtitles.

6. Increasing anglification through subtitles?

As is obvious when looking at the accumulated data in Table 12, the three subtitled films investigated yield conflicting evidence regarding anglification over time. Two conclusions can be drawn from this. The material is too limited to produce valid evidence, which again is due to the quite comforting fact that the strategies chosen by individual translators differ now as they did 50 years ago.

Table 12: Anglification in all films

Material Film	Excerpts	Anglification score Version A	Version B
Wrong Arm of the Law (UK 1963)	36; selected	Anglification: 42 Counter-anglification: 2 Average degree: 1.11	Anglification: 66 Counter-anglification: 1 Average degree: 1.81 Increase: 63 %
Sands of Iwo Jima (USA 1949)	40; randomly chosen	Anglification: 34 Counter-anglification: 1 Average degree: 0.72	Anglification: 11 Counter-anglification: 0 Average degree: 0.23 Increase: -68 %
Sabrina (USA 1954)	42; randomly chosen	Anglification: 25 Counter-anglification: 7 Average degree: 0.38	Anglification: 23 Counter-anglification: 0 Average degree: 0.46 Increase: 21 %

In a future larger-scale empirical study based on the methodology developed in this contribution, an increase in anglification of the magnitude represented by the *Sabrina* data might be expected. A quantitative increase of some 20 per cent over a half-century seems to constitute a conservative estimate, taking into consideration the lexical and pragmatic changes that have taken place in the Danish speech community and in other speech communities since the Second World War. Thus, in the Nordic countries, the share of modern import words – predominantly anglicisms – in (untranslated) newspaper texts has tripled from the year 1975 to the year 2000 (Graedler & Kvaran 2010: 34). For this reason alone, even 'classic' texts – as the mid-20th century film dialogue studied in this contribution – ought to be more anglified in the 21st century than when they were first translated.

Results may be even more pronounced with a different research design, for example, the alternative one mentioned in Section 4, in which aged texts with aged translations would be compared to modern texts (e.g., 21st century Hollywood movies) in contemporary translation. If, however, a study along those lines shows substantial evidence of increasing anglification in subtitling, it will still remain to be seen whether this is a result of increased anglification in the surrounding speech community or vice versa. In other words, are subtitles – and other types of translation, including dubbed film dialogue – motors of change, or do they simply reflect anglification trends generated by 'original' text production in non-anglophone speech communities? Although some studies point to the latter explanation (Gottlieb 2000, Gellerstam 2005), until a series of macrostudies are made, the jury is still out.

---

[1] A Spanish translation of an earlier version of this paper was published in 2008 (see Gottlieb 2008).

[2] Another study (Martínez Tejerina 2008) compares an old dubbed film version with a modern subtitled one.

[3] For recent studies of Anglicisms across Europe, see Görlach 2002a and 2002b, Aijmer and Melchers 2004, Anderman and Rogers 2005, and Fischer and Pułaczewska 2008.

[4] The aesthetics and reader perception of subtitling are discussed at length in Gottlieb 2010.

[5] On borrowing in general, see Haugen 1950, Weinreich 1963, Poplack et al. 1988, Gottlieb 2006 and Szubert 2006.

[6] All examples in Tables 4–6 are authentic, and in order to avoid inconsequential instances of mistranslation, all examples come from original sources – not from translations from English.

[7] A typical example of this decrease in condensation is the line: "And I won't insist that he be tough. Instead, I'll try to make him intelligent." In 1960, it went "Han skal ikke være barsk, men intelligent" [He need not be tough, but intelligent]. In 2004, it became "Og han behøver ikke være sej. Jeg vil forsøge at gøre ham klog." [And he does not have to be tenacious. I will try to make him clever.]

References

Aijmer, Karin & Gunnel Melchers (eds.). 2004. *The Influence of English on the Languages in the Nordic Countries. Special issue of Nordic Journal of English Studies* 3(2).
Anderman, Gunilla & Margaret Rogers (eds.). 2005. *In and Out of English: For Better, For Worse?* Clevedon: Multilingual Matters.
Brant, Rosemary. 1984. *The History and Practice of French Subtitling*. Unpublished MA thesis. Austin, TX: University of Texas at Austin.
Díaz Cintas, Jorge. 2003. *Teoría y Práctica de la Subtitulación: Inglés – Español*. Barcelona: Ariel.
Díaz Cintas, Jorge. 2005. 'The Ever-Changing World of Subtitling: Some Major Developments' in Sanderson, John (ed.) *Research on Translation for Subtitling in Spain and Italy*. Alicante: Publicaciones de la Universidad de Alicante. 17-26.
Díaz Cintas, Jorge & Gunilla Anderman (eds.). 2009. *Audiovisual Translation: Language Transfer on Screen*. Basingstoke: Palgrave Macmillan.
Dunger, Hermann. 1909. *Engländerei in der Deutschen Sprache* (2nd ed.). Berlin: Verlag des Allgemeinen Deutschen Sprachvereins. (Reprinted in 1989 by Georg Olms Verlag, Hildesheim.)
European Commission. 2006. Europeans and Their Languages. *Special Eurobarometer* 243. Online at http://ec.europa.eu/education/languages/pdf/doc631_en.pdf. (consulted: 19.11.2010).
Filipović, Rudolf. 1996. 'English as a Word Donor to Other Languages of Europe' in Hartmann, Reinhard (ed.) *English Language in Europe*. Exeter: Intellect Books. 37-46.
Fischer, Roswitha & Hanna Pułaczewska (eds.). 2008. *Anglicisms in Europe: Linguistic Diversity in a Global Context*. Newcastle upon Tyne: Cambridge Scholars.
Gellerstam, Martin. 2005. 'Fingerprints in Translation' in Anderman, Gunilla & Margaret Rogers (eds.) *In and Out of English: For Better, For Worse?* Clevedon: Multilingual Matters. 201-213.
Gómez Capuz, Juan. 2001. 'Diseño de Análisis de la Interferencia Pragmática en la Traducción Audiovisual del Inglés al Español' in Sanderson, John (ed.) *¡Doble O Nada! Actas de las I y II Jornadas de doblaje y subtitulación*. Alicante: Publicaciones de la Universidad de Alicante. 59-84.
Görlach, Manfred (ed.). 2002a. *English in Europe*. Oxford: Oxford University Press.
Görlach, Manfred.(ed.). 2002b. *An Annotated Bibliography of European Anglicisms*. Oxford: Oxford University Press.
Gottlieb, Henrik. 1997. 'The History of Subtitling: From Cardboard Signs to Electronics' in *Subtitles, Translation & Idioms*. University of Copenhagen: Center for Translation Studies and Lexicography. 49-68.
Gottlieb, Henrik. 2000. 'Sample Chapters on the Web as a Basis for Empirical Studies of Translationese'. Research paper. University of Copenhagen: Center for Translation Studies and Lexicography.
Gottlieb, Henrik. 2001a. 'Subtitling: Visualising Filmic Dialogue' in Lorenzo García, Lourdes & Ana Maria Pereira Rodríguez (eds.) *Traducción Subordinada (II): El Subtitulado (Inglés-Español/Galego)*. Vigo: Servicio de publicacións da Universidade de Vigo. 85-110.
Gottlieb, Henrik. 2001b. 'Anglicisms and TV Subtitles in an Anglified World' in Gambier, Yves & Henrik Gottlieb (eds.) *(Multi)Media Translation*. Amsterdam: John Benjamins. 249-258.
Gottlieb, Henrik. 2001c. ''In Video Veritas': Are Danish Voices Less American than Danish Subtitles?' in Chaume, Frederic & Rosa Agost (eds.) *La Traducción en los Medios Audiovisuales*. Castelló de la Plana: Universitat Jaume I. 193-220.
Gottlieb, Henrik. 2004a: 'Language-Political Implications of Subtitling' in Orero, Pilar (ed.) *Topics in Audiovisual Translation*. Amsterdam: John Benjamins. 83-100.

Gottlieb, Henrik. 2004b. 'Danish Echoes of English' in Aijmer, Karin & Gunnel Melchers (eds.) *The Influence of English on the Languages in the Nordic Countries*. Special issue of *Nordic Journal of English Studies* 3(2). 39-65.
Gottlieb, Henrik. 2005. 'Anglicisms and Translation' in Anderman, Gunilla & Margaret Rogers (eds.) *In and Out of English: For Better, For Worse?* Clevedon: Multilingual Matters. 161-184.
Gottlieb, Henrik. 2006. 'Linguistic Influence' in Encyclopedia of Language and Linguistics (2nd ed.) vol. 7: 196-205. Oxford: Elsevier Ltd. Online at http://www.sciencedirect.com/science-/referenceworks/9780080448541 (consulted 19.11.2010).
Gottlieb, Henrik. 2008. 'Películas Antiguas, Subtítulos Nuevos, ¿Más Anglicismos?' (translated by Dulcinea Tomás) in Sanderson, John (ed.) *Películas Antiguas, Subtítulos Nuevos: Análisis Diacrónico de la Traducción Audiovisual*. Alicante: Publicaciones de la Universidad de Alicante.
Gottlieb, Henrik. 2009a. 'Subtitling against the Current: Danish Concepts, English Minds' in Díaz Cintas, Jorge (ed.) *New Trends in Audiovisual Translation*. Bristol: Multilingual Matters. 21-43.
Gottlieb, Henrik. 2009b. 'Parallelism or Convergence? The English Influence on Danish' in Harder, Peter (ed.). English in Denmark: Language Policy, Internationalization and University Teaching. Special issue of Angles on the English-Speaking World. University of Copenhagen: Museum Tusculanum. 68-94.
Gottlieb, Henrik 2010. 'Subtitles: Readable Dialogue?' in d'Ydewalle, Géry & Elisa Perego (eds.) *Research in Accessibility in Audiovisual Translation*. Amsterdam: John Benjamins.
Gottlieb, Henrik (forthcoming). 'Phraseology in Flux: Anglicisms beneath the Surface' in Pulcini, Virginia & Christiano Furiassi (eds). *The Anglicization of European Lexis*.
Graddol, David. 2006. English Next: Why Global English May Mean the End of 'English as a Foreign Language'. British Council. Online at http://www.britishcouncil.org/learning-research-english-next.pdf (consulted 19.11.2010)
Graedler, Anne-Line & Guðrún Kvaran. 2010. 'Foreign Influence on the Written Language in the Nordic Speech Communities' in *International Journal of the Sociology of Language* 204: 31-42.
Gregersen, Frans. 2009. 'Scandinavian Language Policy: Its Problems and Possible Perspectives for the rest of Europe: Is there a regional alternative to English?' in Harder, Peter (ed.) English in Denmark: Language Policy, Internationalization and University Teaching. Special issue of Angles on the English-Speaking World. University of Copenhagen: Museum Tusculanum. 95-108.
Harder, Peter (ed.). 2009. English in Denmark: Language Policy, Internationalization and University Teaching. Special issue of Angles on the English-Speaking World. University of Copenhagen: Museum Tusculanum.
Haugen, Einar. 1950. 'The Analysis of Linguistic Borrowing' in *Language* 26(2): 210-231.
He, Yuanjian. 2009. 'A Functional Gap between Dubbing and Subtitling' in Fong, Gilbert C.F. & Kenneth K.L. Au (eds.) *Dubbing and Subtitling in a World Context*. Hong Kong: The Chinese University Press. 63-78.
Herbst, Thomas. 1994. *Linguistische Aspekte der Synchronisation von Fernsehserien*. Tübingen: Niemeyer.
Herbst, Thomas. 1995. 'People Do Not Talk in Sentences: Dubbing and the Idiom Principle' in Gambier, Yves (ed.) *Audiovisual Communication and Language Transfer*. Translatio – FIT Newsletter 14(3-4): 257-271.
Herbst, Thomas. 1997. 'Dubbing and the Dubbed Text – Style and Cohesion: Textual Characteristics of a Special Form of Translation' in Trosborg, Anna (ed.) *Text Typology and Translation*. Amsterdam: John Benjamins. 291-308.
Jarvad, Pia. 2001. *Det Danske Sprogs Status i 1990'erne med Særligt Henblik på Domænetab*. Copenhagen: Dansk Sprognævn.

Karlin, Daniel. 2005. *Proust's English*. Oxford: Oxford University Press.
Kristiansen, Tore & Helge Sandøy. 2010. 'The Linguistic Consequences of Globalization: The Nordic Laboratory' in *International Journal of the Sociology of Language* 204: 1-7.
Koolstra, Cees M., Allerd L. Peeters & Herman Spinhof. 2002. 'The Pros and Cons of Dubbing and Subtitling' in *European Journal of Communication* 17 (3): 325-354.
Mackenzie, Fraser. 1939. *Les Relations de l'Angleterre et de la France d'après le Vocabulaire. I: Les Infiltrations de la Langue et de l'Ésprit Anglais. Anglicismes Français.* Paris: Librairie E. Droz.
Marleau, Lucien. 1982. 'Les Sous-Titres... Un Mal Nécessaire' in *Meta* 27(3): 271-285.
Martínez Tejerina, Anjana. 2008. 'La Traducción de la Paronimia en las Versiones Doblada (1965) y Subtitulada (2003) de Sopa de Ganso (Duck Soup,1933)' in Sanderson, John (ed.) *Películas Antiguas, Subtítulos Nuevos. Análisis Diacrónico de la Traducción Audiovisual.* Alicante: Publicaciones de la Universidad de Alicante.
Munday, Jeremy. 2005. "E-mail', 'Emilio', or 'Mensaje de Correo Electrónico'? The Spanish Language Fight for Purity in the New Technologies' in Anderman, Gunilla & Margaret Rogers (eds.) *In and Out of English: For Better, For Worse?* Clevedon: Multilingual Matters. 57-70.
Neesbye-Hansen, Nicolai. 1983. *En Undersøgelse af Danske Undertekster til Engelsksprogede Udsendelser i TV, med Særligt Henblik på Seernes Brug af – og Holdning til – dem.* Unpublished MA thesis. University of Copenhagen: Department of English.
Ngom, Fallou. 2003. 'The Social Status of Arabic, French, and English in the Senegalese Speech Community' in *Language Variation and Change* 15: 351–368.
Nornes, Abé Mark. 2007. 'Loving Dubbing: The Translator as Ventriloquist'. Chapter six of *Translating Global Cinema*. Minneapolis; MN: University of Minnesota Press. 188-228.
Onysko, Alexander. 2007. *Anglicisms in German: Borrowing, Lexical Productivity, and Written Codeswitching*. Berlin: Walter de Gruyter.
Orero, Pilar. 2009. 'Voice-over in audiovisual translation' in Díaz Cintas, Jorge & Gunilla Anderman (eds.) *Audiovisual Translation: Language Transfer on Screen*. Basingstoke: Palgrave Macmillan. 130-139.
Pedersen, Jan. 2007. *Scandinavian Subtitles: A Comparative Study of Subtitling Norms in Sweden and Denmark*. Stockholm: Acta Universitatis Stockholmiensis.
Poplack, Shana, David Sankoff & Christopher Miller. 1988. 'The Social Correlates and Linguistic Processes of Lexical Borrowing and Assimilation' in *Linguistics* 26: 47-104.
Preisler, Bent. 2003. 'English in Danish and the Danes' English' in *International Journal of the Sociology of Language* 159: 109-126
Sajavaara, Kari. 1991. 'English in Finnish: Television Subtitles' in Ivir, Vladimir & Damir Kalogjera (eds.) *Languages in Contact and Contrast: Essays in Contact Linguistics*. Berlin: Mouton de Gruyter. 381-390.
Sanderson, John (ed.). 2008. *Películas Antiguas, Subtítulos Nuevos: Análisis Diacrónico de la Traducción Audiovisual*. Alicante: Publicaciones de la Universidad de Alicante.
Sørensen, Knud. 1997. *A Dictionary of Anglicisms in Danish*. Copenhagen: The Royal Danish Academy of Sciences and Letters.
Stiven, Agnes Bain. 1936. *Englands Einfluß auf den Deutschen Wortschatz*. Inaugural-Dissertation. Zeulenroda: Bernhard Sporn Verlag.
Svavarsdóttir, Ásta. 2004. 'English in Icelandic: A Comparison between Generations' in Aijmer, Karin & Gunnel Melchers (eds.) *The Influence of English on the Languages in the Nordic Countries. Special issue of Nordic Journal of English Studies* 3(2). 153-165.
Szubert, Andrzej. 2006. 'Lingvistisk Klassificering af Låneord' in Jørgensen, Merete K. & Henrik Blicher (eds.) *Danske Studier*. Copenhagen: Reitzel.
Tirkkonen-Condit, Sonja. 2002. 'Translationese: A Myth or an Empirical Fact? A Study into the Linguistic Identifiability of Translated Language' in *Target* 14(2): 207-220.

Tveit, Jan-Emil. 2009. 'Dubbing versus Subtitling: Old Battleground Revisited' in Díaz Cintas, Jorge & Gunilla Anderman (eds.) *Audiovisual Translation: Language Transfer on Screen.* Basingstoke: Palgrave Macmillan. 85-96.

Viereck, Wolfgang & Wolf-Dietrich Bald (eds.). 1986. *English in Contact with Other Languages.* Budapest: Akadémiai Kiadó

Weinreich, Uriel. 1963. *Languages in Contact: Findings and Problems.* Den Haag: Mouton. [Original edition: New York 1953].

Winge, Vibeke. 2000. *Pebersvend og Poltergejst: Tysk Indflydelse på Dansk.* Copenhagen: Gyldendal.

Filmography

Sabrina, Billy Wilder (1954), USA.
Sands of Iwo Jima, Allan Dwan (1949), USA.
The Wrong Arm of the Law, Cliff Owen (1963), UK.

Audiovisual Information Processing by Monolinguals and Bilinguals: Effects of Intralingual and Interlingual Subtitles

Dominique Bairstow
University of Montpellier III (France)

Jean-Marc Lavaur
University of Montpellier III (France)

Abstract
This contribution explores the effects of language fluency and different types of subtitles (intralingual and interlingual) on film comprehension. In a first experiment, we examine the role of interlingual subtitles in two experimental conditions (with and without French subtitles). In this experiment, comprehension is assessed by a test just after viewing the sequence (images, dialogues and understanding of the situation). The results show facilitating effects of subtitling for the monolinguals and inhibitory effects for bilinguals. In a second experiment, the participants are divided into three groups depending on their knowledge of the oral language of the film (English). Subsequently, the participants are shown three versions of the sequence (non-subtitled, with English (intralingual) or French (interlingual) subtitles). The results indicate an interaction of both experimental factors. This implies an overall facilitating effect of subtitles for the beginner group (particularly when the subtitles are presented in the participants' first language), which is in contrast with a distracting effect for the advanced group (more so when both known languages are on-screen). A third study seeks to evaluate the opportunities that these different types of subtitles may provide in foreign language acquisition or consolidation.

Keywords
audiovisual information, information processing, language fluency, subtitles

1. Introduction

It is now established that audiovisual translation (AVT) studies have spread worldwide – since 1990 especially – with a proliferation of international conferences and the publication of numerous papers on the subject (Díaz Cintas 2003). Audiovisual studies have also become interdisciplinary, extending beyond the boundaries of translation and incorporating psychology, sociology, film studies as well as linguistics (Remael & Neves 2007).

Research in cognitive psychology has widely investigated technical aspects of subtitled film reception since the very presence of subtitles can modify the viewer's audio and visual integration processes as a result of competition between the different sources of information (Roskos-Ewoldsen, Yang & Lee 2007). Indeed, a film contains various types of information that can be either audio, video or situational (combining information from the film with the viewer's previous knowledge). All these types of information can be either linguistic or non-linguistic. The competition between these can occur particularly if the information is considered "disparate but simultaneous" (Möttönen & Sams 2008) as is the case with audio information in one language and written information in another (interlingual subtitles). Initial studies focused mainly on font, colour, size and number of lines (and words per line) in a subtitle, using eye-tracking devices for attention issues or post-viewing questionnaires to investigate comprehension (Wang & Kan 2003; d'Ydewalle & DeBruycker 2007). Furthermore, most research studying the cognitive processing of movies used the most common type of subtitling (interlingual), although some did take into account other types of subtitling such as intralingual, subtitles for hearing-impaired viewers and – more recently – reversed subtitling.

Although these studies have yielded some very interesting results, they do not systematically compare the effects of each type of subtitling on film comprehension. Moreover, the psychological approach of subtitling includes various dimensions, not only technical considerations, but also comprehension and memory processes when more than one language is involved. Therefore, on the same level as the type of subtitles presented on-screen, studies must focus on the characteristics of the audience members, not only their language skills but also their familiarity with different translation methods, as pointed out by Koolstra, Peeters and Spinhof (2002).

This contribution aims to deal with the influence of languages in the media and their reception by the audience. Many factors can influence audiovisual processing, some of which are linked to the characteristics of the population and others to the various versions of one movie. The issue of this contribution is to understand how these factors can interact during film processing. With this end in view, the results of two experimental studies (see Bairstow 2011 and Lavaur & Bairstow 2011, for a complete description) that aimed to measure the relative effects of different types of subtitling on film comprehension, depending on the viewer's knowledge of the on-screen languages, will be presented below. In addition, in a third study, based on the findings of the earlier two, we attempt to evaluate the opportunities that these different types of subtitling may provide with respect to foreign language acquisition or consolidation. All three studies used post-viewing questionnaires to evaluate comprehension (Wang & Kan 2003; Lavaur & Nava 2008).

2. The role of interlingual subtitles in three aspects of film comprehension

This first study followed the results of two experiments previously run in our laboratory. To begin with, Lavaur and Nava (2008) showed that when a film is presented in the viewers' native language and the subtitles are unnecessary to the understanding of the sequence, the subtitles have a negative effect on the perception of visual information, compared with situations in which viewers watch silent and dubbed versions of the same film. Secondly, interlingual subtitles were also shown to be distracting in a study by Grignon, Lavaur and Blanc (2007), but only as far as image processing was concerned. With regard to linguistic information, as expected, subtitles proved to be a great help for viewers with a low fluency level in the spoken language of the film. These results led us to imagine a new situation that would enable us to measure the effects of subtitles on three different aspects of film comprehension (visual, linguistic and situational), depending on the degree of subtitle necessity for the viewers' proper understanding (thus depending on language-fluency levels). As shown in the studies referred to above, the negative effect attributed to subtitles for fluent viewers, as well as the positive effect for non-fluent viewers, was expected to become evident in the overall comprehension scores. In contrast, with regard to the different types of information, subtitles were expected to have an all-round distracting effect for bilinguals, whereas they were thought to be of great help for the monolinguals' linguistic integration. As for the situation-based questions, it was thought that effects could vary since the understanding of a situation depends on the integration of both information from the film (perceptual data) and the viewers' previous knowledge. The experiment is described below.

2.1. Participants

A total of 32 participants were recruited from the first- and second-year students of the University of Montpellier (France). They were divided into four groups, reflecting their fluency (high or low) in the spoken language of the movie (English) and the version (subtitled in French or not) of the film they were going to be shown. Thus, two high fluency groups (in English) of eight participants each saw either the original (English) or the subtitled version of the film and two low fluency groups (also in English) of eight participants each also saw either of the two versions.

2.2. Materials

The selection of material consisted of two stages: (1) the choice of the film sequence and (2) the selection of different versions of the film.

In research on film comprehension, it is obvious that the choice of the sequence is crucial since it forms the basis of the whole experimental setting. Therefore, we shall briefly list the selection method used in the first two studies.

In order to limit the risk of the film having been seen by our participants, we limited the choice to films produced between 1950 and 1980. A second criterion was based on the film content. Care was taken to ensure that an equal amount of action and dialogue occurred (for the comprehension questionnaire) and that the number of characters appearing in the clips was enough to create interest but not so many as to create difficulty in following the story. Finally, the dialogues needed to be rich enough for the viewer to make inferences from the situation (context understandable independently from the rest of the film), but also to be adaptable in another language (as subtitles).

The extract which was finally selected was an 8-minute, 36-seconds sequence from Alfred Hitchcock's *North by Northwest* (1959), for which we also had the bilingual scenario including all the dialogues in both English and French.

Having extracted the sequence onto a separate DVD, we proceeded to adapt the subtitles to make them as compatible as possible with the spoken dialogues (while following the recommendations set forth by Ivarsson and Carroll (1998) regarding oral and written language modes). Two versions of the film were used: (1) English with French subtitles (interlingual version) and (2) non-subtitled English (original version). Furthermore, a comprehension questionnaire was drawn up.

The understanding of a film is based on three essential types of information: (1) visual, (2) audio and (3) situational data (see above). A first questionnaire was created, which consisted of eighty multiple-choice questions about information representing any of these three factors in the sequence. The questionnaire was administered to a group of twelve native French participants, who had watched the French dubbed version of the excerpt (for optimal comprehension). The items for which the success rate was too far from the mean (too easy or too complicated) were eliminated, giving us a questionnaire with 45 questions (15 for each type of information) distributed evenly throughout the film (see appendix A). Each question had one correct answer, three wrong answers and one *I don't know* option.

2.3. Design

In this experiment, participants were divided into four groups based on the language that they were most fluent in (English or French) and on the version of the film viewed (English or English with French subtitles). All participants had to answer the comprehension questionnaire, which consisted of all three types of question (visual, dialogue, situational). Therefore, the independent variables were (1) Language Fluency, with the two levels *bilingual* and *monolingual*, (2) Version of the Film, with the two levels *English* and *English with French subtitles*, and (3) Type of Question, with the three levels *visual, dialogue, situational*. The dependent variable was the number of correct answers to the items in the comprehension questionnaire.

2.4. Procedure

All of the participants saw one version of the film and replied to the questionnaire individually on a computer by using a set of headphones to reduce interference from the environment. They were asked to watch the film attentively. In addition, they were warned that they would have to answer a series of questions afterwards.

2.5. Results

The data were analysed using a 2 (Version of the Film) x 2 (Language Fluency) ANOVA design with a .05 level of significance (α). The effect size used was Cohen's *d*. The main results of this experiment show a significant interaction between Version of the Film and Language Fluency, $F(3, 28) = 27.84$, $p < .0001$. As expected, after seeing the non-subtitled version of the film, the bilinguals obtained a significantly higher global comprehension score than the monolinguals. On the other hand, the monolinguals achieved a higher level of comprehension than the bilinguals after watching the subtitled version, showing the negative effect of subtitles for bilinguals (Figure 1).

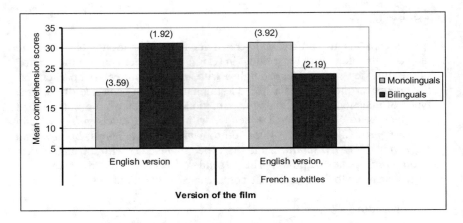

Figure 1. Mean comprehension scores (standard deviations in parentheses) showing an interaction between the Version of the Film (English or English with French subtitles) and Language Fluency (monolingual or bilingual)

Detailed analysis of the comprehension scores also showed a significant effect of both version and language fluency on the answers to each type of question (see Figure 2). With the original version, the bilinguals obtained higher scores than the monolinguals for both visual data, $F(1, 14) = 7.45$, $d = 1.37$, and dialogue data, $F(1, 14) = 44.21$, $d = 3.33$, whereas the opposite occurred with the subtitled version for both visual information, $F(1, 14) = 12.53$, $d = 1.77$, and dialogue information, $F(1, 14) = 6.66$, $d = 1.29$. As for the questions about the situation, the result of the analysis was only barely significant, following the same general pattern as the other two other types of information, but with much smaller differences between scores (best score for bilinguals watching the non-subtitled version; best score for monolinguals when subtitles are on-screen). For a more detailed statistical analysis, see Bairstow 2011.

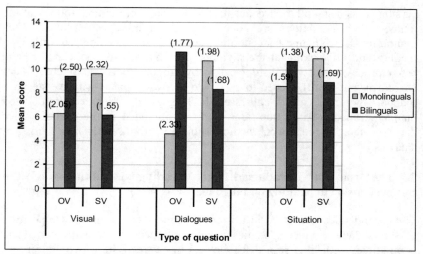

Figure 2. Mean scores (standard deviations in parentheses) for each Fluency Level (monolingual or bilingual) depending on the Type of question (visual, dialogue or situational) after watching the non-subtitled version (OV) or the subtitled version (SV)

2.6. Discussion

The aim of this first study was to examine the effects of subtitles on film comprehension, depending on the viewers' fluency level in both the spoken and written languages on-screen. The overall results confirm the effects generally associated with subtitles, a distracting effect when they are unnecessary, against a facilitating effect when the viewers do not master the film's spoken language. However, the partial results reveal a more unexpected finding: subtitles seem to help monolinguals to understand the linguistic information. They also seem to facilitate the processing of visual information for monolinguals. This last result is rather confusing since subtitles are generally associated with a loss of visual information perception (this is indeed the case for the near-bilingual sample of this study).

A possible explanation for this visual information processing facilitation could lie in the composition of our groups. The very nature of the 'foreign language' used in this study (English) means that there is very little chance of finding – in a European country – participants who have no knowledge of English whatsoever. Therefore, our French monolinguals must have had at least a low level of fluency in English. This means that they might have tried to use this limited knowledge to understand dialogues in the non-subtitled version (thus using all their concentration to listen, rather than to look at the images). When subtitles are added, one could imagine that the French monolinguals were not concentrating so much on listening, but more on reading and on looking at the pictures. This hypothesis could explain the better processing of visual information by monolinguals when subtitles are on-screen, but it still needed to be put to the test. That is why we set up a second experiment, which addressed the language levels in a more detailed manner. Situation-based questions were not included in the analysis since they seemed, in retrospect, far too subjective for a satisfying statistical analysis.

3. The role of intralingual and interlingual subtitles in film comprehension depending on language levels

The second study presented in this contribution focused on the composition of the audience. Indeed, studies usually compare fluent with non-fluent populations, with little regard for viewers in between these two 'extremes'. That is why we set out to investigate the effects of subtitles on the comprehension of films by viewers with three different levels of fluency. This decision was taken to shed light on the progressive evolution of comprehension as a function of language fluency. What is more, the effects were measured depending on the type of subtitles – interlingual or intralingual – so as to examine their relative effects on the perception and integration of visual and linguistic elements. Both types of subtitling can be expected to be distracting for viewers who are fluent in the two languages of the film, whereas only interlingual subtitles can be expected to help monolingual viewers. For those viewers with a fluency level considered medium, the different types of subtitling should have variable effects since they would be presented in either their dominant or their non-dominant language. Furthermore, these effects should vary depending on the type of information on which the questions are based (visual or linguistic data).

A summary of the second experiment and general results are presented below. For a full description and detailed results, the reader is referred to *Languages on the screen: is film comprehension related to the viewers' fluency level and to the language in the subtitles?* (Lavaur & Bairstow, in Press). The methodology is also explained below.

3.1. Participants

For this second study, 90 participants comprising an international cross-section were selected from a French secondary school. Using a lexical test (translation task), elaborated according to the Laxen, Aparicio and Lavaur

(2008) lexical database, we were able to separate the participants (from both the French and the international sections) into three groups depending on their language fluency level (in English): (1) beginners, (2) intermediate and (3) advanced. In addition, the participants were asked to fill in a personal data questionnaire regarding their familiarity with English and their film-viewing habits. Finally, the participants were invited to take part in an auto-evaluation task to determine their English and French fluency levels.

3.2. Materials

Again, the film fragment and film versions had to be determined. The film used for this experiment was the same as the one used in the previous experiment since it still met our requirements about content, length and flexibility in the dialogues (*North by Northwest*, Hitchcock 1959).

Three different versions of the film clip were prepared: (1) the original version (in English), (2) the original version with English subtitles (intralingual) and (3) the original version with French subtitles (interlingual). Each participant saw only one of the three versions of the film depending on the group that the participant was assigned to (see Section 3.3, Design).

In order to create a questionnaire that would evaluate comprehension as accurately as possible, a group of twelve native French participants was asked to watch a silent version of the sequence, followed by a version dubbed into French. After each viewing, the participants in this group were asked to recall as much information as possible in five minutes and to write down the information on a sheet of paper. This setting led to a majority of visual-based information for the first recall (since the film was silent) and dialogue-based information for the second recall (since the participants in this group were asked to recall different information this time). After excluding erroneous and inferential information, we analysed the recalled information in terms of frequency of utterances. The most frequently mentioned data were considered to represent the most prevalent information in the film and that information was used in the making of the experimental questionnaire. In order to balance the proportion of visual and dialogue-based questions – but also to ensure that visual and dialogue-based questions would be distributed equally throughout the sequence – some questions used in the previous study were integrated into this new questionnaire. The final version of the questionnaire for the second study contained 42 items (see appendix A). Half of items concerned visual information, the other half dialogue data.

3.3. Design

In the second experiment, two independent variables were combined: (1) Language Fluency, with the three levels *beginner, intermediate* or *advanced*, and (2) Version of the Film, with the three levels *English* (original), *English with English subtitles* (intralingual) or *English with French subtitles* (interlingual). Language Fluency and Version of the Film are both between-subject variables while the Type of Question (with the two levels visual or dialogues) is a within-subject variable. As previously, the dependent variable was the number of correct answers to the comprehension questionnaire.

3.4. Procedure

All of the participants took part in the experiment individually and in three distinct phases. They began by filling in the personal data questionnaire (with the auto-evaluation task) and the translation test. Next, they were asked to watch the film sequence, having been warned beforehand as to which version they would see. Finally, the participants had to fill in the comprehension questionnaire, presented with the *Sphynx Lexica* software on the same computer as the one used for watching the film.

3.5. Results

The first analysis set out to estimate the linguistic proficiency of each of the three groups, using both the translation task and the auto-evaluation scale (included in the personal-data questionnaire). An overall positive correlation was found between both tasks (Bravais Pearson r (88) = .90 $p < .001$). This meant that participants who achieved the best scores also rated themselves as having high fluency levels in the auto-evaluation scale. The same correspondence between scores applied for the intermediate and beginner groups.

The analysis of the general comprehension scores revealed an overall significant interaction between Version of the Film and Language Fluency, $F(4, 81) = 21.22$, $\eta^2 = .512$. The beginners' comprehension significantly increased when interlingual subtitles were added. However, for the advanced group, the presence of any kind of subtitles on-screen had a detrimental effect on information processing (see Figure 4).

Audiovisual information processing by monolinguals and bilinguals

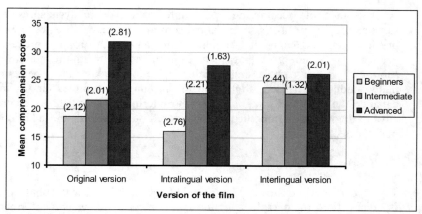

Figure 3. Mean global comprehension scores (and standard deviations) (experiment 2) showing an interaction between Version of the Film (original, intralingual, interlingual) and Fluency Levels (beginner, intermediate, advanced)

The detailed analysis (see Lavaur & Bairstow, in press, for complete statistical data), taking into account the language fluency levels, revealed a significant effect of the presence of subtitles for two groups (beginner and advanced) out of three (no significant difference for the intermediate group).

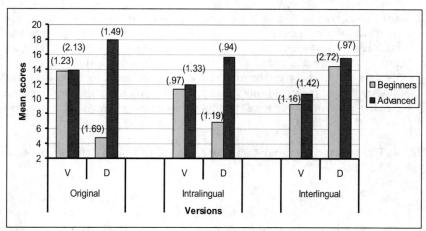

Figure 4. Mean scores (and standard deviations) for two Fluency Levels (beginners, advanced) depending on the Version of the Film (original, intralingual, interlingual) for visual questions (V) and dialogue questions (D)

If we take into account the type of information, the analysis showed the same result patterns as those for global comprehension. As already shown in previous studies, both the beginner and advanced groups' processing decreased – when processing visual information – with the addition of subtitles. When processing dialogue information, the beginners' understanding increased slightly with intralingual subtitles and almost equalled the advanced group's score with interlingual subtitles. By contrast, advanced viewers' comprehension decreased steadily with the addition of both types of subtitles.

3.6. Discussion

The second study confirmed the general effects associated with subtitles, that is, distraction of overall attention with respect to visual information processing and a source of help for linguistic information comprehension for viewers who have not fully mastered the language spoken in the film. These effects are visible with both types of subtitling (intra- and interlingual) and for both linguistic groups (beginners and advanced viewers), although no significant effect was found for the intermediate group. The fact that the members of this group auto-evaluated their fluency level in a high manner (very close to the advanced group's evaluation) might be a clue as to this absence of effect. This shall be considered in more detail in the general discussion. Moreover, intralingual subtitles seemed to provide a certain amount of help for the beginners, which led us to believe that these viewers read the subtitles – even though they were in a foreign language – and tried to use their limited knowledge of this language to understand the film. Bearing this in mind, we decided to set up a new experimental study to check whether viewers would still pay attention to foreign subtitles if the film were in their mother tongue (reversed subtitling) and, if so, whether this could be used for language learning purposes (compared with a situation of conventional/ standard subtitling).

4. The effects of standard and reversed subtitling on film comprehension and lexical retrieval

The third and last experiment aimed to link comprehension and language acquisition research. Indeed, it has to be taken into consideration that more and more language learning courses – in schools or with home learning software – use audiovisual programmes for language acquisition in general and vocabulary acquisition in particular (Yuksel & Tanriverdi 2009). The reason for this is that a film provides a large semantic and cultural context that can help learners understand the meanings of certain words or expressions. Various cognitive studies have demonstrated that watching subtitled films can induce a certain amount of incidental learning and that viewers can actively use subtitles for vocabulary acquisition if they have been taught appropriate and intentional viewing strategies (Danan 2004). Once again, little comparison has been made of the various types of subtitles available, which led us to look into two different types of subtitling (standard and reversed) to see which type of subtitling induced both the best comprehension and the best memorisation of vocabulary. By comparing the comprehension scores and the number of items correctly memorised for each version, we hoped to determine which type of subtitling induces the best form of incidental vocabulary acquisition and optimum comprehension.

Only preliminary results are presented in this contribution. The complete study will be presented at ISB8 (Oslo, 2011). The methodology for the experiment is explained below.

4.1. Participants

For the third (and last) experiment, we will show the preliminary results for 24 participants, who were all native French-speaking university students with levels of English-language proficiency which ranged from poor to medium. Their language levels were established with a translation task and a personal data questionnaire (see Section 4.2, Materials).

4.2. Materials

In this study, the film chosen was different from the film used in the first and second study. Since we were interested in evaluating only dialogue comprehension, a film with next to no action (yet not totally static so as not to run the risk of boring the participants) but with relatively complex dialogues was needed. Using the same selection method as before – but adding these last two requirements to the list of constraints – we ended up choosing a 6-minute, 43-second excerpt from Alfred Hitchcock's 1951 film *Strangers on a Train*.

The third experiment aimed to study the relative effects of different types of subtitles on film dialogue comprehension and memorisation. In order to do this, we used four different versions of the film sequence: two non-subtitled versions (the original English and a French dubbed version) and two subtitled versions (standard subtitles with dialogues in English and subtitles in French; and reversed subtitles with French dialogues and subtitles in English). Finally, two questionnaires, a recall task and a translation task were devised. The translation task consisted of six sentences to be translated from English into French and six from French into English. The sentences were extracted from an English learning CD-ROM (one half of the sentences from the medium level and the other half from the advanced level) and were used to measure the participants' fluency level in English. A personal data questionnaire was used to ensure that all of the participants could be considered as equal with respect to features such as age, education and even their film-watching habits. Subsequently, a comprehension questionnaire was created to assess dialogue comprehension only with the items shared out evenly throughout the length of the sequence. This questionnaire consisted of 40 multiple-choice questions (one correct answer, three wrong answers, and one possibility of answering *I don't know*). Finally, a vocabulary memorisation test was created using twelve extracts from the film's dialogues (in English), in which a missing word had to be recalled by the participants. These twelve extracts were chosen on the basis of several qualities: the sentences were contained in a string of dialogue, not isolated; they contained a noun or an adjective (which was the word which had been removed); this word could be guessed only with great difficulty by using the context provided by the rest of the sentence. Of the twelve missing words, four were considered fairly easy (if the viewer was normally attentive to the film - *easy*) and eight were considered indicative of memorisation (four words were rather old-fashioned, rarely used nowadays - *outdated*; the other four words were misleading because many other words could fit in the sentences - *ambiguous*).

4.3. Design

All of the participants had similar levels of fluency in English. They saw only one of the four versions of the film and answered only dialogue-based (linguistic) questions. Therefore, the experimental design had only one between-subjects variable, which was Version of the Film, with the four levels *English, French, English with French subtitles* or *French with English subtitles*. Two dependent variables measured the number of correct answers to the comprehension questionnaire for the first, and the number of correctly recalled words from the dialogues for the second.

4.4. Procedure

All of the participants took part in the experiment individually and in two phases. First, the participants were asked to fill in the personal data questionnaire with the auto-evaluation task. Subsequently, the participants were asked to watch the film clip, having been warned as to which version they would be shown, and using a set of headphones so as not to be distracted. Following this first viewing, the participants had to answer the comprehension questionnaire (presented on the same laptop as the film). For the second part of this last study, the participants were first asked to perform the translation task, which was printed on a sheet of paper to optimise results. Finally, the participants were warned that they were going to see the same version of the extract as before, after which they would have to answer a final questionnaire. This was the vocabulary recall questionnaire and was administered to all of the participants, even those who had seen the French dubbed version.

4.5. Results

The preliminary results of half the sample (24 participants, 6 per version) will be presented below.

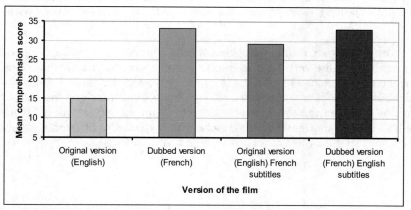

Figure 5. Comprehension of the dialogues depending on the version of the film (original, dubbed, standard subtitles or reversed subtitles)

As far as the comprehension scores are concerned, the preliminary results seem to indicate that the original version is the least well understood while the dubbed version gets the highest score, a result that we expected considering the viewers' low fluency level in English. What is more, the value of subtitles is demonstrated as the addition of French subtitles brings the comprehension score almost level with that of the dubbed version. Finally, the addition of English subtitles to the dubbed version does not seem to have a negative effect on the understanding of the film. For complete results and statistical data for the full sample, see Baisrtow and Lavaur (2011).

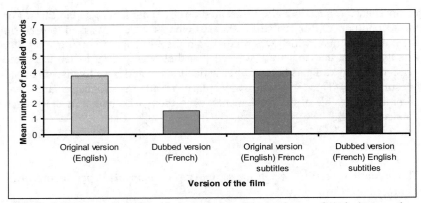

Figure 6. Mean number of words (out of a possible maximum of twelve) correctly recalled depending on the version of the film (original, dubbed, standard or reversed subtitling)

The preliminary results for the recall task (completion of twelve dialogue extracts in English missing one specific word) show that viewers watching the French version with English subtitles (reversed condition) obtain the highest number of recalled items, as opposed to those watching the dubbed version, who get the lowest score (since the film was presented in French only). As for the original version, global recall appears to be approximately the same as for the English version with French subtitles.

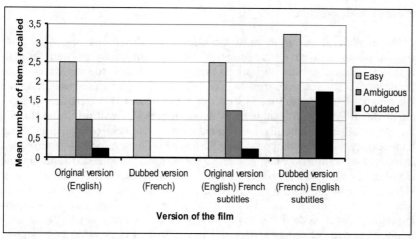

Figure 7. Mean number of words (out of a possible maximum of four) correctly recalled depending on the version of the film (original, dubbed, standard subtitling, reversed subtitling) and the type of item (easy, ambiguous, outdated).

These results are clearer when looking at the type of words recalled after seeing each version of the film. Indeed, the dubbed version provided the viewer with only the possibility of guessing some of the easy words, as was mostly the case with the original version too. The viewing of the original version with French subtitles led to much the same recall pattern as the original version, whereas the dubbed version with English subtitles gave the best recall, especially for the outdated words.

4.6. Discussion

These preliminary results seem to indicate that reversed subtitling is the best scenario as far as incidental memorisation (and maybe learning) of vocabulary is concerned. This could mean that reading rather than hearing a language is easier for both the comprehension and memorisation of a foreign language (as scores were high for both comprehension and memorisation) when a translation is available (auditorily in this case).

5. General discussion

This contribution set out to study the effects that different types of subtitles may have on film comprehension and the role they may play in foreign-language vocabulary memorisation. In order to do this, the results of three experimental studies were reported. The first experiment aimed to investigate the role of standard subtitles in the comprehension of two treatment groups, either fluent in only one language or fluent in both. Overall results confirmed the two effects generally associated with subtitles (distracting when unnecessary, helping comprehension if needed). These effects were extended to individual results depending on the type of information tested (although no significant effect was found for situation-based questions) for the bilingual viewers, but not for the monolinguals, for whom subtitles appeared to help with both linguistic and visual comprehension. This last result was hypothetically linked to the composition of our treatment groups as they might have had better knowledge of English than was assessed (see Section 2.6, Discussion for more in-depth explanations of this hypothesis). This idea was put to the test in a second experiment, which focused on the viewers' fluency levels, but also took into consideration the type of subtitling.

The second set of results showed an overall interaction between the version of the film and language fluency. Indeed, the higher the fluency level, the more superfluous the subtitles were, and therefore the lower the comprehension scores for subtitled clips was. Furthermore, the distracting effect proved to be stronger when two known languages were on-screen simultaneously (audio dialogues and written subtitles). This effect was also apparent for visual information processing by both the intermediate and the beginner groups, which means that the effect found in the first experiment was not repeated. Moreover, no particular effect was found for the intermediate group, meaning that either the participants in the intermediate group were not sensitive to the presence, absence or type of subtitles, or that the effects of the subtitles were not measurable with the means that we used to test them. Either way, further research is needed to come to a satisfying conclusion.

Another interesting result showed that beginners were helped by not only interlingual subtitles. They were partly helped even when the subtitles were intralingual, meaning both linguistic information sources were in a foreign language. This result led us to conclude that viewers pay attention to written text even if it is in a foreign language. This finding also led us to verify whether this would still be the case when the audio language was their own.

In the third and last experiment, two subtitling types (standard and reversed) were compared to two non-subtitled versions (original version and French dubbed) of one and the same film. The aim of this study was to find out whether one scenario was better than another to achieve both a good understanding of the film and good memorisation of the vocabulary that was used. The viewers were all native French speakers and had a poor to medium fluency level in English. Effects were estimated following two main lines: (1) the level of comprehension achieved after viewing each version and (2) the number of words recalled from a selection of vocabulary from the film. The preliminary results of this research seem to indicate that reversed subtitling constitutes a situation in which both high comprehension levels and good memorisation can be achieved. Although standard subtitles gave better results than both non-subtitled versions, reversed subtitling clearly seemed to offer more opportunities for a non-fluent viewer.

The three studies yielded some very interesting results for cognitive psychology but also for audiovisual translation (AVT) studies. Bearing in mind that a great number of Europeans today are at least bilingual (Media Consulting Group 2007) – with many being actually multilingual – studies taking into account fluency levels and the role the levels can play in film reception are very much needed to meet the audience's needs. Moreover, depending on the type of audiovisual product, the information can be of primary importance to any given film-maker since translation methods might need to vary too, depending on whether the linguistic information is there only to accompany the images or the other way round. This is why it is extremely important to study the ways in which various types of AVT (types of subtitling in this contribution) affect the processing of all the different types of information contained in a film.

In the same way, audiovisual productions do not have a purely informational or recreational use anymore. They are also used in learning and are invading more and more classrooms and homes. Indeed, the merits of subtitles have already been highlighted in various studies (Yuksel & Tanriverdi 2009; Koolstra & Beentjes 1999) but have yet to be evaluated in greater detail. For example, future research must look into the pros and cons of each type of subtitling with regard to language learning to find the most efficient approach for viewers, measuring 'costs' both in terms of attention (using eye-tracking) and cognitive load (with event-related potentials). Another interesting line of research would be to investigate the various viewing strategies offered to viewers (see Danan 2004) so as to check whether some are better than others and whether it depends on the type of programme and subtitling being viewed.

All in all, this field of research is vast and ever-changing. The tools to investigate it are numerous, which promises a long future of exchange on the subject.

References

Bairstow, Dominique. 2011. 'Audiovisual Processing while Watching Subtitled Films: A Cognitive Approach' in Serban, Adriana, Anna Matamala & Jean-Marc Lavaur (eds.) *Audiovisual Translation in Close-Up: Practical and Theoretical Approaches*. Bern: Peter Lang. 205-219.

Bairstow, Dominique & Jean-Marc Lavaur. 2011. 'Standard vs. Reversed Subtitling: Effects on Movie Comprehension and Lexical Retrieval'. Oral communication presented at *International Symposium on Bilingualism* (ISB8), Oslo, Norway, 15-18 June 2011.

Danan, Martine. 2004. 'Captioning and Subtitling: Undervalued Language Learning Strategies' in *Meta* 49(1): 67-77.

Díaz Cintas, Jorge. 2003. 'Audiovisual Translation in the Third Millennium' in Anderman, Gunilla & Margaret Rogers (eds.) *Translation Today: Trends and Perspectives*. Clevedon: Multilingual Matters. 192-204.

d'Ydewalle, Géry & Wim DeBruycker. 2007. 'Eye Movements of Children and Adults while Reading Television Subtitles' in *European Psychologist* 12(3): 196-205.

Grignon, Pamela, Jean-Marc Lavaur & Nathalie Blanc. 2007. 'The Effect of Subtitles on Film Understanding'. Paper presented at *Seventeenth Annual Meeting of the Society for Text and Discourse*, Glasgow, July 2007.

Ivarsson, Jan & Mary Carroll. 1998. *Subtitling*. Simrishamn: Transedit.

Koolstra, Cees & Johannes Beentjes. 1999. 'Children's Vocabulary Acquisition in a Foreign Language through Watching Subtitled Television Programs at Home' in *Educational Technology Research and Development* 47(1): 51-60.

Koolstra, Cees, Allerd L. Peeters & Herman Spinhof. 2002. 'The Pros and Cons of Dubbing and Subtitling' in *European Journal of Communication* 17(3): 325-354.

Lavaur, Jean-Marc & Dominique Bairstow (in press). 'Languages on the Screen: *Is Film Comprehension Related to the Viewers' Fluency Level and to the Language in the Subtitles?*' in *International Journal of Psychology*. DOI: 10.1080/00207594.2011.565343.

Lavaur, Jean-Marc & Sophie Nava. 2008. 'Interférences Liées au Sous-Titrage Intralangue sur le Traitement des Images d'une Séquence Filmée' [Interferences due to Intralingual Subtitling on the Processing of Images from a Filmed Sequence]. In Hoc, Jean M. & Yves Corson (eds.) *Proceedings of the French Society of Psychology Congress*. France. 59-64.

Laxen, Janika, Xavier Aparicio & Jean-Marc Lavaur. 2008. 'Base Lexicale Trilingue ESF: Mesure du Partage Orthographique et du Recouvrement Sémantique Interlangue [ESF Trilingual Lexical Base]'. Paper presented at the *French Society of Psychology*; Bordeaux, France, September 2008.

Media Consulting Group. 2007, September. *Study on Dubbing and Subtitling Needs and Practices in the European Audiovisual Industry: Final Report*. London: Peaceful Fish.

Remael, Aline & Josélia Neves (eds.). 2007. Introduction. *A Tool for Social Integration?: Audiovisual Translation from Different Angles*. Special Issue of *Linguistica Antverpiensia NS* 6: 7-22.

Möttönen, Riikka & Mikko Sams. 2008. 'Audiovisual Interaction' in Havelock, David, Sonoko Kuwano & Michael Vorländer (eds.) *Handbook of Signal Processing in Acoustics*. New York: Springer. 731-745.

Roskos-Ewoldsen, Beverly, David Roskos-Ewoldsen, Moon hee Yang & Mina Lee. 2007. 'Comprehension of the Media'. Paper presented at *The Annual Meeting of the International Communication Association*. San Francisco, May 2007.

Wang, An-Hsiang & Yun-Feng Kan. 2003. 'Effects of Display Type, Speed, and Text/Background Colour-Combination of Dynamic Display on Users' Comprehension for Dual-Task in Reading Static and Dynamic Display Information' in *The International Journal of Advanced Manufacturing Technology* 23(1): 133-138.

Yuksel, Dogan & Belgin Tanriverdi. 2009. 'Effects of Watching Captioned Movie Clips on Vocabulary Development of EFL Learners' in *The Turkish Online Journal of Education Technology – TOJET* 8(2): 48-54.

Filmography

North by Northwest, Alfred Hitchcock (1959) USA.
Strangers on a Train, Alfred Hitchcock (1951). USA.

Appendix A. Examples from the comprehension questionnaires.

Experiment 1:

Visual question
The first scene takes place:
At the bottom of a staircase; In front of a building; In front of an elevator; Near the subway entrance; I don't know.
Dialogue question
After getting in a taxi, Thornhill asks the driver to stop at:
The theatre; The Ritz hotel; His apartment; The Plaza hotel, I don't know.
Situational question
Thornhill starts joking in order to:
Amuse his abductors; Divert their attention; Hide his anxiety; Make them feel ridiculous; I don't know.

Experiment 2:

Visual question
While crossing the building hall, the man speaks to:
The porter; A colleague; A girlfriend; His mother; I don't know.
Dialogue question
In this way, we learn the man's name:
Kaplan; Taylor; Townsend; Thornhill, I don't know.

Heterolingualism in Audiovisual Translation: *De Zaak Alzheimer / La Memoria del Asesino*

Anna Vermeulen
University College Ghent (Belgium)

Abstract

This contribution focuses on the problem of translating heterolingualism in audiovisual translation (AVT). At first sight, AVT seems to offer the perfect opportunity to maintain the use of different languages in a film. In the subtitled versions, the other languages always remain present since the original soundtrack is not replaced and translations are rendered in the subtitles, whereas in dubbed versions the other languages can be rendered by the dubbing actor or narrator in the foreign language and also be translated in subtitles. Thus, viewers who can distinguish between foreign languages and who are not distracted from listening by reading the subtitles can easily notice code switching. However, as this case study shows, it is not as simple as that. Depending on the meaning and the relevance of heterolingualism in the context on the one hand, and the target audience's views on foreign languages and cultures on the other, the translators/adaptors of the Spanish subtitling and dubbing of the Belgian (Dutch spoken) film De zaak Alzheimer / La memoria del asesino resorted to different strategies to overcome the problem. The aim of this case study is to identify the different functions that heterolingualism performs in the film and to summarise the translation strategies that were used to maintain (or to neutralise) heterolingualism. In fact, this film is no exception. Given the linguistic situation of Belgium, heterolingualism is a feature of many of its film productions.

Keywords
audiovisual translation, code switching, heterolingualism, interlingual language variation, intralingual language variation

1. Introduction

The successful 2003 Flemish thriller *De zaak Alzheimer*, (*The Alzheimer Case*, also called *The Memory of a Killer*), directed by Erik Van Looy and produced by *MMG Film&Television Production* tells the story of a hit man, Angelo Ledda, who suffers from Alzheimer's and does not remember whether or not he has committed a number of murders. When he realises that he has to kill a twelve-year-old girl, Ledda turns against his clients, who try to eliminate him. Furious over the attempt on his life, he kills the middleman, Seynaeve. When the leading Detectives Erik Vincke and Freddy Verstuyft arrive at the crime scene, a policeman reads out loud the number plate of Seynaeve's car: IAM469. The fact that the first part of the license plate is pronounced in English ('I am for') and the second part in French (*soixante-neuf*) creates a special, comic, effect, that is noticed by his superior, the Detective Chief Inspector, who replies saying 'he is even more of a pervert than you'. This is one of the many examples of heterolingualism in this particular film that without any doubt proved a major challenge for the Spanish translators / adaptors who provided the translation for the subtitled and the dubbed versions on the DVD of *La memoria del asesino*, which was distributed in Spain by Paramount Home Entertainment in 2006.

2. Heterolingualism in (audiovisual) translation

The term 'heterolingualism' was first introduced by Rainier Grutman in 1997 and refers to the use of foreign languages or social, regional, and historical language varieties in literary and (later on also non-literary) texts. The term is interchangeable with plurilingualism and multilingualism and offers a more neutral alternative to the ideologically loaded 'bilingualism' and 'diglossia'. As Grutman himself stated, it is

> [...] a phenomenon I labelled *heterolingualism* in order to avoid unnecessary confusion with real-life situations stemming from language contact, such as societal bilingualism or diglossia [...]. (2006: 18)

It comes as no surprise that in a multilingual country such as Belgium, the use of different languages is reflected in the films that are produced there. Nonetheless, Grutman warns that even in texts whose fictional universes claim to portray society, realism largely remains a matter of skilfully crafted illusionism. It is and will always be a construction, and

> [...] because of its varying manifestations, heterolingualism is too multifarious a phenomenon to be easily subsumed under the heading of 'realism'. Mimetic readings do not explain how languages interact with each other within the boundaries of texts whose use of foreign tongues quite often goes beyond mirroring society or supposedly 'translating' reality. (2006: 19)

Still following Grutman (1993: 209), a text, or a script for that matter, may only be called heterolingual if code switching plays an essential role in it. That is certainly the case in *De zaak Alzheimer* where the use of different language varieties (both intralingual and interlingual) cannot be explained simply by reference to a plurilingual environment, the fact that Belgium is a multilingual state where the Flemish people speak Dutch, the Walloons French, and a minority German. The use of different languages in the film has a particular function and is interpreted as such by the primary Flemish speaking audience. The fundamental question that the translator faces here is how to determine the relevance of these other languages in the target text, since each audience will interpret the use of heterolingualism according to their own experience (Valdeón 2005). As for dialects and accents, according to House (1973), Langeveld (1986) and Berman (1985) they tend to disappear in translation, be it audiovisual translation or not. In Baker (1993), normalization of language variety has even been presented as a translation universal. Similarly, Venuti (1995) observes that domestication smoothens out many social and ideological functions of heterolingualism. Talking about film translation, Heiss (2004) remarks that as a result of the widespread practice of trying to meet the presumed expectations of the target audience, examples of flattening out and of the formalisation of authentic-sounding spoken language are to be found in almost all dubbed versions. Assis Rosa concluded from her study on features of oral communication in subtitling that:

> [...] the phonetic, morphological and syntactic features of sub-standard varieties are a) omitted, b) sometimes lexicalised. As for informal and colloquial registers, slang and taboo words (often occurring in speech), they are usually levelled to less informal standard discourse. (2001: 216)

Similarly, Díaz Cintas & Remael state that:

> Whether or not languages, or dialects, are subtitled in the ST and in the translated version, will depend on the expectations one has of the average viewer in any particular country. (2007: 60)

They recommend to correct dialectical grammar, or, where it is a crucial feature (as in *My Fair Lady*), to render the accent or poor pronunciation by using an improvised phonetic transcription. Generally speaking, since non-standard varieties rarely have an established written form, there is a tendency to use the standard variety in subtitles, although Lopes Cavalheiro (2008) and Ramos Pinto (2009) detected a difference in the preservation of non-standard features in Portuguese subtitling depending on the television channel. Subtitles produced for the public channel by its own translation department tend to be more normalized (thus promoting the use of standard, written Portuguese) than the subtitles on a private channel which were produced by freelance translators who preserved some features perceived as reflecting a low educational level and low social status.

This case study is based on a corpus containing the transcripts of the original dialogue list of *De zaak Alzheimer* and the Spanish dubbing and subtitling of *La memoria del asesino*. It focuses on the way the language varieties are embedded within the original discourse and are represented in both translations. The corpus is divided into 1181 dialogue units, according to the number of subtitles. In the original version, 54 of these units are rendered in French and in 25 units an English word or expression is used.

3. Heterolingualism in the original version

The main language of the film is the informal variant of Dutch spoken in various parts of Flanders (the Northern part of Belgium), which, according to Geeraerts (2001), is a variety of Dutch, one of the three official languages of Belgium and also the national language of the Netherlands[1]. Whereas in formal registers Belgian Dutch has converged towards Netherlandic Dutch (Goossens 2000), in informal, more personal situations of everyday life, Flemish people increasingly use a register between standard Dutch and the Flemish dialects, called 'interlanguage' (De Caluwe 2004), that comprises different variants according to the region and the social status of the speaker. The most dominant and trendsetting regiolect is the one spoken in the Brabant dialect area (Vandekerckhove 2005, Taeldeman 2005), that is in the central provinces of Flemish-Brabant and Antwerp, the biggest city in Flanders, and also the place where the film in question is set. In order to add to the *couleur locale* the characters use the Antwerp regiolect[2] to different degrees, depending on their social status. This is clearly a manifestation of heterolingualism, since – more generally speaking - in film as on the stage (Ladouceur 2006), heterolingualism not only manifests itself at the level of vocabulary but also at the level of accent.

According to De Caluwe (2004), the informal variant of Belgian Dutch is not only marked by strong dialectical variation, but also by rampant French influence. Foreign translators trained in the Netherlands will indeed be surprised by the significant amount of lexical and syntactical interference of the French language on Belgian Dutch. So, another striking manifestation of (intralingual) linguistic variation in the film are the many French loanwords that are used: *allez, au fond, bon, coiffeurs, colère, content, dedju, dju, gazet, madame, motard, nondedju, patron, piste, plateauke, soigneren, tuyau, voilà*. These words are very common in informal Belgian Dutch of the type defined above and they are definitely not used in this film for reasons of foreignisation or comic relief[3]. The reason why the characters in the film have adopted the typical local and socially marked way of speaking is to enhance the film's realism, to make it sound more spontaneous, although, as Chaume states (2006), a film story always remains a construction and a film script is an intentionally fabricated text.

Besides the informal variant of Belgian Dutch, Netherlandic Dutch is also used, since one of the characters (Mrs Seynaeve, the middleman's wife) comes from the Netherlands and therefore speaks with a noticeable Northern accent, which, in this particular case is mainly a reference to a certain stereotype: Dutch people in Flanders are sometimes known for their arrogance or for expressing themselves in a coarse way.

The second language spoken in this film is French. One of the main characters, the hired assassin, Angelo Ledda, lives in Marseille. His mother tongue is French, but he was raised in Antwerp and went to school in Flanders, so he also speaks the Belgian variant of Dutch. At the beginning of the film he is contacted in Marseille by a client who wants to hire him to assassinate two people in Belgium. This dialogue, announced by an insert (*Marseille, 5 dagen later*, 'Marseille, five days later') is rendered entirely in French and translated in the original version into Dutch subtitles. Apart from one small dialogue that can easily be understood by the Flemish audience (see example 9), all French utterances are translated into Dutch subtitles in the original version.

The third language used in the film is English. As a result of the influence of the film and music industries on linguistic usage, the use of English words and expressions has become very common in Dutch, so the young detective Verstuyft uses English swearwords (*bullshit, djeezus, fuck*) and discourse markers (*forget it, shoot*). The other examples of English words and expressions in the film belong to a technical register and refer to police jargon (*all units, clean, deal, feedback, it's a go, lock-in, repeat, stand-by, target, tracer*). None of them needed Dutch subtitles in order to be understood by the primary audience. It is clear that the English argot and jargon are not used in the film to introduce some kind of foreignisation, but as a token of identity, to enhance the realism of the situation.

4. Heterolingualism in the audiovisual translations

Depending on the meaning and the relevance of heterolingualism in the context and the target audience's view of foreign languages and cultures, the translators / adaptors of the Spanish dubbing and subtitling of the Belgian Dutch language film *De zaak Alzheimer / La memoria del asesino* resorted to different strategies to re-create (or not) the linguistic variation.

4.1. Preservation of the heterolingualism

When code switching is significant and forms an integral part of the dialogue, it is the translator's task to find a strategy that reflects the change of language. That is the case when the characters refer explicitly to the use of another language. In the examples below I present the original version (O.V.) including the subtitles in Dutch in the first column (all spoken parts are in italic), the second and the third column contain the Spanish dubbing (SP DUB) and the Spanish subtitling (SP SUB), and the fourth column provides a back translation of the source text (EN TR) into English (the translation is mine).

During Ledda's first meeting with the Flemish middleman, Seynaeve, the latter assumes that the assassin, Ledda, does not understand Dutch – after all he hails from Marseille. Accordingly, he addresses him in French. Ledda (using another name) has Seynaeve believe that he does not speak Dutch by replying in French. In the original version (1.1.), as in the Spanish subtitled version (1.3.), the French lines are subtitled (misinterpreted in Spanish: instead of 'are you mister…? It says 'Are you okay, mister…?). In the Spanish dubbed version (1.2.), the French lines are dubbed by a Spanish actor (who speaks French with a Spanish accent) and remain untranslated:

Example 1: French in O.V. (+ subtitle) → French in DUB (no subtitle) / Spanish in SUB

	1.1.	1.2.	1.3.	
	O.V	SP DUB	SP SUB	EN TR
S L	Vous êtes bien monsieur... U bent toch.../ Casoni Casoni./	Vous êtes bien monsieur... Casoni	-¿Se encuentra bien, señor.... ?/ -Casoni.	Are you mister…? -Casoni.
S	Le voyage s'est bien passé? Is uw reis goed verlopen ?/	Le voyage s'est bien passé?	¿Ha tenido buen viaje ?/	Did you have a safe trip?
	J'ai les dossiers que vous avez demandés Ik heb de dossiers/ die u gevraagd heeft.	J'ai les dossiers que vous avez demandés.	Tengo los informes que me pidió./	I have the files that you asked for.
	Tout est là-dedans. Alles zit erin./	Tout est là-dedans.	Todo está en ellos./	Everything is in there.

This conversation is interrupted by a call on Seynaeve's mobile phone, which he takes in Dutch. In this call he refers to the assassin as being stupid:

	O.V.	SP DUB	SP SUB	EN TR
S	Pardon.	Pardon.	Disculpe.	Sorry.

Heterolingualism in audiovisual translation

Ja, Hallo ?	¿Sí, diga ?	¿Sí, diga ?	Yes ? Hello ?
Ja, ja ik ben d'r volop mee bezig	Sí, ya estoy con él.	Sí, ya estoy con él.	Yes, I'm working on it.
Nee, hij zegt nie veel.	No, no habla mucho.	No, no habla mucho.	No, he doesn't say much.
En zijne kop heeft precies een jaar of twee onder nen tram gelegen.	Parece como si un tranvía le hubiese pisado el cerebro.	Parece como si un tranvía/ Le hubiese pisado el cerebro./	His head appears to have lain under a tram for a year or two.

Then he returns to the conversation in French. As before, the French lines are subtitled into Dutch in the original version, rendered in Spanish in the dubbing and subtitled into Spanish in the subtitled version:

	O.V.	SP DUB	SP SUB	EN TR
S	Mon client veut savoir quand. Mijn klant wil weten wanneer./	Mon client veut savoir quand.	Mi cliente quiere saber/ cuándo.	My client wants to know when.
L	Si vous avez bien préparé vos dossiers... Als alles goed voorbereid is,/	Si vous avez bien préparé vos dossiers,	Si ha preparado bien	If all the files are well prepared
	Ça sera vite fait. zal het snel gaan./	ce sera vite fait.	los informes será pronto./	it will be done soon.
S	Vite c'est trop lent. Snel is te traag./	Vite, c'est trop long,	"Pronto" es mucho tiempo./	"Soon" is too late.
	On veut savoir quand. We willen weten wanneer./	on veut savoir quand.	Quiere saber cuándo.	We want to know when.

At the end of the conversation in French, Ledda repeats, in Flemish, the insulting remarks the contact person made about him, so that Seynaeve realises that the hit man also speaks Dutch:

	O.V.	SP DUB	SP SUB	EN TR
L	Ik ga eerst nog een jaar of twee met mijne kop onder den tram liggen.	Uno o dos años, luego que me aplaste un tranvía.	Uno o dos años, luego que/ me aplaste un tranvía.	I will first lain my head under a tram for a year or two.

In view of the coherence of the dialogue, the lines had to remain in French in the dubbed version. The use of subtitles, as in the original version, could have solved the loss of meaning for the Spanish viewers.

Similarly, when Ledda arrives in Antwerp and checks in at his hotel, the receptionist addresses him in French (2.1.) until Ledda specifies that he speaks Dutch (*Ik spreek Nederlands* / 'I speak Dutch'). Due to this remark, the translator had to maintain code switching. So, in the Spanish dubbed version (2.2.) the receptionist speaks French (without subtitles) until Ledda's remark, translated by a hypernym into *Hablo su idioma* ('I speak your language'):

Example 2: French in O.V. (+ subtitle) → French in DUB (no subtitle) / Spanish in SUB

	2.1.	2.2.	2.3.	
	O.V.	SP DUB	SP SUB	EN TR
R	S'il vous plaît, monsieur Ledda./ Je vous ai donné la 633. Alstublieft, Mr. Ledda / U heeft kamer 633.	S'il vous plaît, Monsieur Ledda, je vous ai donné la 633.	Señor Ledda, Su habitación/ es la 633.	Mr. Ledda, I've given you room number 633.
	C'est votre première fois Ici dans l'hôtel? Is dit uw eerste verblijf / in ons hotel?	C'est votre première fois ici dans l'hôtel ?	¿Es la primera vez Que se hospeda en el hotel?/	Is this your first visit to our hotel?
L	Ik spreek Nederlands.	Hablo su idioma.	Hablo su idioma.	I speak Dutch..

After the criminal who went after Ledda is killed when his car explodes in the garage of the hotel, the hit man presents himself to the police as a hotel guest, Bernard Casoni, who witnessed the incident. Once again, the dialogue starts in French (3.1.), until Ledda / Casoni says "*U mag Vlaams spreken*" ('You can speak Dutch'), translated as before with a hypernym (3.2.), into *Hablo su idioma* ('I speak your language'). The viewers of the subtitled version (3.3.) are supposed to notice code switching from the soundtrack.

Example 3: French in O.V. (+ subtitle) → French in DUB (no subtitle) / Spanish in SUB

	3.1. O.V.	3.2. SP DUB	3.3. SP SUB	EN TR
F	Monsieur Casoni. Mijnheer Casoni,	¿Monsieur Casoni?	¿Sr. Casoni?	Mr Casoni.
	Votre passeport. Uw paspoort.	Votre passeport. Por favor.	Su pasaporte, por favor./	Your passport.
L	Merci. Dank u.	Merci.	Gracias.	Thank you.
V	Bonjour. Goeiendag,	Bonjour. Vincke, commissaire.	Buenos días.	Hello.
	Vincke, commissaire. Vincke, commissaris.		Vincke, comisario.	Chief Inspector Vincke
L	U mag Vlaams spreken commissaris.	Hablo su idioma, comisario.	Hablo su idioma, comisario./	You can speak Dutch,, Chief Inspector

The dialogue below (4) provides another example of a reference made to code switching. It is routine for Belgian policemen to pass a French test as part of their training, so the young detective Verstuyft is studying and reading aloud some sentences from a manual (4.1.). When he makes a mistake in the pronunciation, his chief, Vincke, corrects him (*'Eu', un oef, des 'eu'*). Due to the complaint about this requirement ('why do policemen have to study French') the French lines had to remain in French in the Spanish dubbing (4.2.) in order to make sense. In the original version and in the Spanish dubbing, the French lines remained without subtitles, probably because the content of the utterance is not relevant, only the poor pronunciation matters. In the Spanish subtitling (4.3.), the lines are translated into Spanish, but the error is transposed to a typical Spanish error in pronunciation: the pronunciation of the 'h' in 'huevos' that some people pronounce as 'gü'.

However, the simultaneous presence of the original French lines may provoke confusion in the minds of those who also rely on the original soundtrack.

Example 4: French in O.V.(no subtitle) → French in DUB (no subtitle) / Spanish in SUB

	4.1.	4.2.	4.3.	
	O.V.	SP DUB	SP SUB	EN TR
F	*Nous avons invité*	*Nous avons invité*	Hemos invitado	We have invited
	des amis très chers.	*des amis très chers.*	A amigos muy queridos./	some good friends.
	On ne peut pas faire une omelette	*On ne peut pas faire une omelette*	No se puede hacer una tortilla/	You cannot make an omelette
	sans casser des eufs...	*sans casser des eufs...*	sin romper los "güevos"./	without breaking eggs.
V	*Eu.*	*Eu.*	¿"Güevos"?	[Vincke corrects the French pronunciation error]
	Un euf (oeuf), des eu (oeufs)	*Un euf (oeuf), des eu (oeufs)*	Huevos.	
F	*Dju, g'hebt gelijk.*	*Tienes razón.*	Tienes razón.	You are right.
	Vincke, waarom moet ge nu Frans kennen voor een examen van commissaris?	*Vincke,¿ por qué tengo que aprender francés para ser comisario?*	Vincke,¿ por qué tengo que aprender / francés para ser comisario?/	Vincke, why do I have to study French to pass an exam to become a Chief Inspector?

A very special case of retaining code switching in the translation is shown by the following example (5): at the end of the film, Ledda, who realises that there is no escape, keeps repeating the same line in French which contains a cryptic clue to finding the final piece of the puzzle: *néant* sounds like 'neon' and refers to a neon light where the hit man hid a cassette with evidence against the corrupt baron. In the original version (5.1.), the French line is not only subtitled into Dutch (*op weg naar het* niets), but the cue word (*'le néant'*) is even repeated in French, between quotation marks, drawing too much attention to the wordplay. In the Spanish dubbed version (5.2.) the lines

Heterolingualism in audiovisual translation

are dubbed in French by the dubbing actor, with a Spanish accent, without subtitles. In the Spanish subtitled version (5.3.) the lines also remain in French (in italics), because of the allusion to the neon light, which would be lost by the translation into '*nada*'. The content of the utterance ('on the road to nowhere') is explained in the context (*'el gran vacío'*):

Example 5: French in O.V. (+ subtitle) → French in DUB (no subtitle) / French in SUB

	5.1.	5.2.	5.3.	
	O.V.	SP DUB	SP SUB	EN TR
L	... *En route pour le néant.* Op weg naar het niets,/ '*le néant*'.	*En route pour le néant.*	*En route pour le néant./*	On the road to nowhere.
	Niewaar schutter?	¿No es cierto, tirador?	¿No es cierto, tirador?/	Right, shooter?
	Of verstade geen Frans?	¿Sabes francés?	¿Sabes francés?	Or don't you understand French?

	O.V	SP DUB	SP SUB	EN TR
F	*le néant.* Het niets.	*le néant.*	*le néant*	Nowhere.
	Nirvana. Het grote niks hè.	Nirvana, el gran vacío.	Nirvana, el gran vacío./	Nirvana. The big nowhere.

4.2. Non-preservation of heterolingualism

The intralingual variation in the original version has no function other than to raise the degree of credibility of the story depicted. The use of intralingual variants is an obvious sign of identity, and therefore significant, but, since the plot is set in Flanders and all the cultural references are definitely Belgian, it was no doubt thought inappropriate to render the dialogues in one of the Spanish regional variants. The dialogues were therefore translated into standard Spanish. The Spanish viewers of the dubbed version, like the viewers of the subtitled version, who have no knowledge of Flemish, have to deduce the identity of the characters by other means, relying on the other two channels that offer information, the audio and visual channel. The loss of linguistic variation and accent can be compensated for by the voice, the intonation, age of the characters, the way they are dressed, the body language, and so on.

Anna Vermeulen

As a result of the decision to translate the Antwerp regiolect into standard Spanish, no difference can be made between the informal variant of Belgian Dutch and Netherlandic Dutch. That becomes a problem when Mrs Seynaeve, who is Dutch and speaks with a noticeable Northern accent, makes her appearance. Offended by the rejection of the young policeman, she calls him names: *vuile Belgische kutflik*, which literally means 'dirty Belgian fucking cop'. In the Spanish dubbing she speaks exactly the same way as the Flemish characters, i.e standard Spanish, but since she refers to 'Belgian' in her utterance, the Spanish viewers may deduce that she is not Flemish. So, the content of the utterance partially compensates for the loss of meaning. Besides the linguistic variation, the national stereotype is lost as well, but since prejudices vary from one people to another (Valdeón, 2005), the Spanish viewers would not have understood the sneer anyway. However, there is not only loss here. The translator has also added meaning, since both the dubbing and the subtitle (*Todos los belgas sois unos reprimidos* which means 'You Belgians are all so frustrated') have a sexual connotation which is much less prominent in the original version. In order to compensate for the loss of the Netherlandic Dutch accent and the implied national prejudice, it seems that the translator has chosen to be more specific, respecting the semiotic cohesion: Mrs Seynaeve, in a bathing suit and a robe, reacts furiously when the young policeman refuses to oblige her.

At the beginning of the film, there is a substantial dialogue in French that is wholly rendered in Spanish in the dubbed version, without any traces of French. However, since the setting is announced by a text on screen, an insert, that indicates that the conversation takes place in Marseille (*Marsella 5 días después* / 'Marseille, five days later'), dubbing audiences tend to suspend their linguistic disbelief and accept the illusion that what they hear in their own language is actually being said in a foreign tongue (Romero-Fresco 2009).

When, later on in the film, Ledda remembers this dialogue, the French lines in the original version are treated in the same way (6.1.): subtitled in Dutch (the spoken parts are in italics) and dubbed into Spanish (6.2), the latter with a total loss of code switching. Since the subtitles offer exactly the same translation as the dubbing, they are not repeated in the examples below.

Example 6: French in O.V. (+ subtitle) → Spanish in DUB / SUB

	6.1.	6.2.	
	O.V.	SP DUB / SUB	EN TR
Gilles	Et merde! Verdomme.	¡Mierda!	¡Shit!
Ledda	T'avais raison	Tenías razón, Gilles.	You were right,

Heterolingualism in audiovisual translation

	Gilles: Je had gelijk, Gilles,		Gilles.
	pour des gars *comme nous,* mensen zoals wij	*Los tipos como* *nosotros*	Guys like us
	il n'y a pas de *retraite* gaan niet met pensioen.	*nunca descansan.*	do not ever retire.

French being his mother tongue, Ledda occasionally inserts a French line in the Dutch dialogues. These single lines are subtitled in the original version (7.1.) and always dubbed in Spanish (7.2) by the dubbing actor so that the viewers of the dubbing do not notice code switching:

Example 7: French in O.V. (+ subtitle) → Spanish in DUB / SUB

	7.1.	7.2.	
	O.V.	SP DUB / SUB	EN TR
Ledda	*Elle était un ange.* Ze was een Engel.	*Era un ángel.*	She was an angel.

	O.V.	SP DUB / SUB	EN TR
Ledda	*Rien que ma tête.* Alleen m'n hoofd.	*Excepto la cabeza.*	Except my head.

Sometimes the lines are misinterpreted in the Spanish dubbing (and subtitling), as in the example below, translated into Spanish as 'see you soon' instead of 'till the next one':

	O.V.	SP DUB / SUB	EN TR
Ledda	*Au suivant!* Tot de volgende.	*Hasta pronto.*	Till the next one.

On two occasions Freddy uses French swearwords (*cochon, ta gueule*), to insult his colleagues when they make fun of him because he has to study French to pass an exam. Only one of them (*ta gueule*) has been subtitled into Dutch in the original version (8.1.a), the other insult (8.1.b.) was not subtitled. In the Spanish dubbed version, both insults are rendered in Spanish (8.2.):

Example 8: French word in O.V. (+ subtitle / no subtitle) → Spanish in DUB / SUB

	8.1.	8.2.	
	O.V.	SP DUB / SUB	EN TR
Freddy(a)	Coemans, ta gueule! Coemans, kop dicht.	Coemans... La boquita	Coemans... mouth shut!
(b)	En stopt met naar Linda te loeren, cochon.	Y deja de perseguir a Linda, cerdo.	And stop harassing Linda, pig..

A very brief French dialogue is not subtitled into Dutch in the original version (9.1.), since in the Belgian variant of Dutch it can also be said in French without loss of meaning for the Flemish audience. In the Spanish dubbed version the dialogue is totally rendered in Spanish (9.2.):

Example 9: French in O.V. (no subtitle) → Spanish in DUB

	9.1.	9.2.	
	O.V.	SP DUB / SUB	EN TR
Vincke	Ça va?	¿Todo bien?	Are you okay?
Ledda	Ça va.	Todo bien.	I'm okay.
	Merci.	Gracias.	Thanks.

All the English words and expressions have been neutralised as well in the Spanish subtitling and dubbing, and replaced by their correlates in Spanish where possible: *all units / a todas las unidades; deal / trato; feedback / informe; forget it / Olvídalo; fuck / mierda; it's a go / adelante; target / el sospechoso*. As is common in audiovisual translation, the swearwords are sometimes censored by omission, both in the dubbing and the subtitling. In all these cases, the Spanish viewers of the dubbing do not notice any code switching, but the narrative is not affected.

And what about the translation of the number plate mentioned in the introduction? The car appears twice in the film, on both occasions the plate is spelled out in a heterolingual way in the original version: once as 'India Alfa Mike', in English, and '*vier zes negen*' ('four, six, nine') in Dutch. In that case, the Spanish subtitle contains an addition: *con matrícula IAM 469,* and in the dubbing it is heard as *con matrícula India Alfa Mike,* in English, and *cuatro seis nueve* in Spanish. In the second case (10.1.) the number plate in the original version is spelled out as 'I am for', in English, and *soixante-neuf,* in French. Code switching is obviously used here to obtain a comic effect and therefore should not be ignored. Moreover, the reaction of the Detective Chief Inspector (*nog ne ziekere mens dan gij, Freddy,* which means 'He is even more of a pervert than you, Freddy') makes no sense if the number plate is not spelled out as such. In the dubbed version (10.2.) it is spelled out in Spanish letters and numbers: I A EME CUATRO SEIS NUEVE. Not only is the comic effect lost, but also the coherence of the dialogue. The Spanish viewers of the dubbed version will have some difficulty to understand the reaction of the Detective Chief Inspector through the dubbed soundtrack when he replies: *Este anda más perdido que tú*, which means 'He is more lost than you'. In the subtitled version (10.3.) the number plate is written as IAM469, but the viewers can always rely on the original soundtrack, if they have knowledge of English and French and if they are not distracted from the sound track by the subtitles.

Example 10: English and French in O.V. (no subtitle) → Spanish in DUB / letters and numbers in SUB

	10.1.	10.2.	10.3.	
	O.V.	SP DUB	SP SUB	EN TR
V	I am for soixante-neuf.	i-a-eme-cuatro-seis-nueve	IAM 469.	I am for sixty nine.
V	Nog ne ziekere mens dan gij Freddy.	Este anda más perdido que tú.	Anda más perdido que tú./	He's even more of a pervert than you, Freddy.

5. Conclusion

The original version of the Belgian film *De zaak Alzheimer* is strongly heterolingual. In addition to the main language, the informal Belgian variant of Dutch with different degrees of Antwerp influence, also Netherlandic Dutch, French and English are spoken. The heterolingualism in this particular film performs four different functions. The first being a token of identity of the main characters: the use of the Antwerp regiolect (Vincke), the use of English slang (Verstuyft), the use of French (Gilles Resnais, Angelo Ledda). Secondly, it creates the illusion that the story is real (in Marseille they speak French, in Antwerp Flemish, in police interventions many English terms are used). Thirdly, it creates a comic effect (IAM469), and finally it is used as a reference to a stereotype (Dutch people are arrogant and rude).

In the original version most of the French interventions are subtitled into Dutch. Only in a few cases, when a very brief dialogue can be understood easily because of the context (*Ça va? Ça va. Merci*) or when lines don't have a narrative function (the young detective makes a pronunciation error while studying French), are the French lines not translated.

Both Spanish translations, the subtitling and the dubbing, are much less heterolingual than the original version. The intralingual variations ranging from Antwerp regiolect to Netherlandic Dutch are totally lost, since they have been translated into standard Spanish. This loss of meaning is sometimes compensated for by a more explicit translation, adding meaning to the context, or by the information that the viewer can deduce from the other two channels of the audiovisual production: the audio (by means of the voice, the intonation, the rhythm and the volume of speech) and the visual (by means of inserts, gestures, body language, the way the characters are dressed).

As for the interlingual variants, the use of French and English, the treatment in both modes of audiovisual translation is different, partially due to the presence of the original soundtrack, in case of the subtitling, or substitution of the original soundtrack in case of the dubbed version, and partially because of the function the other languages perform.

In the subtitling, almost all of the 54 original French dialogue units are translated into Spanish. Since the original soundtrack remains present, the Spanish viewer who is able to distinguish between foreign languages and who is not distracted from listening by reading the subtitles, can easily notice code switching and rely on the translation to understand the utterances. On three occasions the French utterance is copied in French in the subtitles (written in italics). In all of them it concerns a line that contains the word (*néant*) that phonetically approximates the word 'neon', one of the cue words of the puzzle. The word (*néant*) is also explained in the context. On one occasion, the reference to poor pronunciation of French (the plural of *oeuf* / *oeufs*) in the original version is replaced by poor pronunciation of the same word in Spanish (*huevo* / *güevo*) in the subtitling - a confusing substitution for those who rely on the soundtrack and read the subtitle at the same time. It also has to be said that for those who rely solely on the subtitles, without listening to the soundtrack, the explicit references to the other language ('I speak Dutch' or 'Don't you understand French?') might come as a surprise if they did not notice code switching in the original version.

In the Spanish dubbed version, only 22 of the 54 original French dialogue units remained in French. The switch to French has been neutralised in the long dialogues (the conversation between the hit man and the contact person at the beginning of the film) and the very short lines (occasional utterances serving as a reminder that the character is French). In the lengthy dialogue the loss of the other language is compensated for by an insert (Marseille), which reminds the viewers that what they hear in Spanish is in fact being said in French. Only when there is an explicit reference to code switching ('I speak Dutch', 'Don't you understand French'), is the use of the other language maintained. To render the reference to the other language, the same translation strategy is used: substitution by a hypernym. *Ik spreek Nederlands*, which means 'I speak Dutch', is translated as *Hablo su idioma* /

'I speak your language'). None of the French spoken lines (spoken by the Spanish dubbing actor) is translated through subtitles. The Spanish viewers of the dubbed version are supposed to understand French.

The English parts are mostly restricted to words and expressions that belong to police jargon (technical terms) and juvenile slang (swearwords and discourse markers). Meeting the expectations of the viewers, they have been replaced with their Spanish correlates or left out both in the dubbing and in the subtitling.

It would be interesting to investigate whether the Spanish viewers really detect code switching in subtitled versions. Or are they so focused on reading the subtitles that they forget to listen? And it would also be worth exploring whether Spanish viewers, who much prefer dubbing to subtitling, appreciate subtitles as a means of overcoming the problem of heterolingualism in a dubbed version.

---

[1] As Dirk Geeraerts states in his paper 'Everyday language in the media: the case of Belgian Dutch soap series', everyday informal Belgian Dutch is very much a substandard variety, often much closer to dialect than Netherlandic Dutch. The standardisation process of the language in Flanders began much later than in the Netherlands, since the Spanish, and later the Austrian and French rule did not really favour the development of Dutch in the southern part of the Low Countries as a language of high government and higher education. The foundation of Belgium in 1830 did not change that situation as the new state was politically dominated by the French-speaking bourgeoisie. Round 1900, a consensus was reached that standardised Dutch in Belgium should be identical to the Dutch standard that existed in the Netherlands, but there still exists a significant distance between informal spoken everyday language used in Flanders (with its own phonetic, morphological, lexical and syntactic peculiarities) and the standard Dutch of the Netherlands. In writing the differences between the two languages are far less important.

[2] According to Vandekerckhove et al. (2009) it has become rather common nowadays to use regiolectical rather than standard speech, both in fiction (films, series, soaps) and in non-fiction programmes that are meant to entertain, rather than inform.

[3] As is often the case in the Dutch dubbing of Disney films, where the informal Belgian Dutch variant is often used to portray comic characters, in the same way the Cuban or southern accent is sometimes used in Spanish dubbing.

References

Assis Rosa, Alexandra. 2001. 'Features of Oral and Written Communication in Subtitling' in Gambier, Yves, Henrik Gottlieb (eds.) *(Multi)Media Translation*. Amsterdam: John Benjamins. 213-221.
Baker, Mona. 1993. 'Corpus Linguistics and Translation Studies: Implications and Applications' in Baker, Mona, Gill Francis & Elena Tognini-Bonelli (eds.) *Text and* Technology. Amsterdam: John Benjamins. 233-250.

Berman, Antoine. 1985. 'La Traduction comme Épreuve de l'Étranger' in *Texte* 4: 64-81.
Chaume Varela, Federico. 2004. 'Discourse Markers in Audiovisual Translation' in *Meta*, 49(4): 843-855.
De Caluwe, Johan. 2004. 'Conflicting Language Conceptions within the Dutch-Speaking Part of Belgium' in *TRANS, Internet-Zeitschrift für Kulturwissenschaften* 15. Online at http://www.inst.at/trans/15Nr/06_1/caluwe15.htm (consulted 19.09.2011).
Díaz Cintas, Jorge & Aline Remael. 2007. *Audiovisual Translation: Subtitling*. Manchester: St Jerome.
Geeraerts, Dirk. 2001. 'Everyday Language in the Media: The Case of Belgian Dutch in Soap Series' in Kammerer, Matthias, Klaus-Peter Konerding, Andrea Lehr, Angelika Storrer, Caja Thimm & Werner Wolksi (eds.) *Sprache im Alltag: Beiträge zu Neuen Perspektiven in der Linguistkc Herbert Ernst Wiegand zum 65. Geburtstag Gewidmet*. Berlin: Walter de Gruyter. 281-291.
Goossens, Jan. 2000. 'De Toekomst van het Nederlands in Vlaanderen' in *Ons Erfdeel* 43 (1): 2-13.
Grutman, Rainier. 1993. 'Mono versus Stereo: Bilingualism's Double Face' in *Visible Language* 27(1-2): 206-226.
Grutman, Rainier. 2006. 'Refraction and Recognition: Literary Multilingualism in Translation' in *Target* 18(1): 17-47.
Heiss, Christine. 2004. 'Dubbing Multilingual Films: A New Challenge?' in *Meta* 49(1): 208-220.
House, Juliane.1973. 'Of the Limits of Translatability' in *Babel* 4(3): 166-167.
Ladouceur, Louise. 2006. 'Write to Speak: Accents et Alternances de Codes dans les Textes Dramatiques Écrits et Traduits au Canada' in *Target* 18(1): 49-68.
Langeveld, Arthur.1986. *Vertalen Wat Er Staat*. Amsterdam: De Arbeiderspers.
Lopes Cavalheiro, Lili. 2008. 'Linguistic Variation in Subtitling for Audiovisual Media in Portugal: Case Study of the film *Gone with the Wind*' in *Linguistica Antverpiensia NS7*: 7-27.
Ramos Pinto, Sara. 2009. 'How Important Is the Way You Say It ?' in *Target* 21(2): 289-307.
Romero-Fresco, Pablo. 2009. 'Naturalness in the Spanish Dubbing Language: A Case of Not-So-Close *Friends*' in *Meta* 54(1): 49-72.
Taeldeman, Johan. 2005. 'The Influence of Urban Centres on the Spatial Diffusion of Dialect Phenomena' in Auer, Peter., Frans Hinskens & Paul Kerswill (eds.) *Dialect Change: Convergence and Divergence Languages*. Cambidge: Cambridge University Press. 263-283.
Valdeón, Roberto. 2005. 'Asymmetric Representations of Languages in Contact: Uses and Translations of French and Spanish in *Frasier*' in *Linguistica Antverpiensia NS4*: 279-294.
Vandekerckhove, Reinhilde, Annick De Houwer & Aline Remael. 2009. 'Between Language Policy and Linguistic Reality: Intralingual Subtitling on Flemish Television' in *Pragmatics* 19(4): 609-628. New York: Routledge.

"You Fancying Your *Gora* Coach Is Okay with Me": Translating Multilingual Films for an Italian Audience

Vincenza Minutella
University of Turin (Italy)

Abstract
This contribution aims to investigate how multilingual films are translated for an Italian audience. The study presented in this contribution focuses on three films directed by South Asian diasporic directors (*Bend it Like Beckham*, *Bride and Prejudice* and *The Namesake*), in which communication takes place in more than one language. In addition, the films portray linguistic and cultural diversity. A small bilingual parallel corpus containing transcriptions of the original, dubbed and subtitled film dialogues is tagged for some of the main aspects of multilingual films, that is, instances of cultural references, code-mixing, code-switching and ethnolects. Taking into account both dubbing and subtitling, this contribution describes how such features are rendered in audiovisual translation (AVT) and in the different films. Several examples illustrate how the two AVT modes tackle the challenges posed by multilingual films. The translation strategies chosen by the translators are illustrated and commented on in an attempt to assess what the translators convey and whether they give priority to domestication or foreignisation.

Keywords
code-mixing, code-switching, cultural references, ethnolect, multilingual films

1. Introduction

Since multilingual films often portray multiethnic contexts and mixtures of cultures and languages, an important feature of such works is their linguistic and cultural variation. Culture-specific traits, sociolinguistic varieties, shifts from one language to another or the use of a specific language are meaningful aspects of multilingual films strictly linked to culture and among the most challenging features for audiovisual translators. The aim of this contribution is to explore how multilingual films are translated in Italy. More specifically, this contribution aims to answer the following questions: how is multilingualism dealt with by different audiovisual translators and in different films? How are cultural references (CRs), multiple languages, code-switching (CS), code-mixing (CM) and the presence of ethnolects (E) rendered in audiovisual translation? Are these different linguistic and cultural nuances transferred through translation? Is there a tendency towards domestication or foreignisation (Venuti 1995)? Although Italy is a dubbing country, in recent years there has been an increase in the number of audiovisual products subtitled for satellite TV and DVD. Therefore, another goal of this contribution is to investigate how both translation modes tackle the new difficulties presented by polyglot films. How does dubbing deal with the challenges posed by multilingualism? How do subtitles deal with such challenges? What kinds of translation strategies are adopted?

2. Corpus compilation and methodology

The films chosen for analysis are three multilingual films directed by female directors of Indian origin living in Britain or the USA: (1) *Bend it Like Beckham* (2002) and (2) *Bride and Prejudice* (2004), both directed by Gurinder Chadha and (3) *The Namesake* (2006), directed by Mira Nair. They are South Asian diasporic films portraying multiethnic contexts. They are set in contemporary Britain, the USA and India, and contain characters belonging to different ethnicities and speaking different languages, that is English, some Indian languages (Hindi, Punjabi, Bengali) and Indian English. *Bride and Prejudice* (*BAP*) is a Bollywood-style, 'Indianised' transposition of Jane Austen's novel, while *The Namesake* (*TN*) is an adaptation of the novel by the South Asian diasporic writer Jhumpa Lahiri.

The empirical study was carried out on a small, bilingual parallel corpus containing the original, dubbed, and subtitled film dialogues, which were transcribed orthographically and subsequently tagged. The orthographic transcription follows the conventions adopted by the compilers of the Pavia Corpus of Film Dialogue (Freddi & Pavesi 2009, Bonsignori 2009). Square brackets are used to indicate languages other than English spoken by the characters. The transcription conventions are the following: (1) if the foreign language is maintained both in original and dubbed dialogues (ST and TT) without subtitles, the name of the language is inserted in square brackets, with no added explanation (example 1 below), (2) if the foreign language is maintained in the ST and TT, but translated through subtitles, the square brackets contain the name of the language spoken, followed by the subtitles in English or Italian, in italics (example 2) and (3) if the foreign language is maintained in the original dialogues, but dubbed into Italian, square brackets are used only for the ST while the Italian dialogues are orthographically transcribed (example 3). When the words spoken in the foreign language can be understood, they are fully transcribed in lower-case letters, not in italics, and placed in square brackets, after the name of the language (Bonsignori 2009: 192-193). In the subtitled versions, the texts are transcribed orthographically without brackets or italics. The excerpts below from *Bend it Like Beckham* (*BILB*) and *TN* illustrate these conventions:

Table 1. Transcription conventions

Character	English version	Dubbed version	Subtitled version
(1) MRS BHAMRA	Football shoes! [Punjabi]	Scarpe da pallone.[1] [Punjabi]	Scarpini da calcio.[2]
(2) ASHOKE	You won't believe it. [Bengali: *In comparison to the professors here, even our street vendors dress well.*]	Non ci crederai [Bengali: *I nostri conducenti di risciò vestono meglio dei professori di qui.*][3]	Non ci crederai. In confronto ai professori di qui, anche i nostri venditori ambulanti sono eleganti.[4]
(3) WOMAN:	[Punjabi]	Andiamo è tardi.[5]	Andiamo, è tardi.[6]

The original dialogues were subsequently tagged for culture-specific references [CRs], code-switching [CS], code-mixing [CM] and ethnolects [Es]. Tagging these features made it easier to retrieve all the occurrences when using a concordance program.

3. Some definitions

Before the findings of the study are discussed, some definitions of the linguistic issues under analysis will be provided.

Cultural references (CRs) are "entities that are typical of one particular culture, and that culture alone" (Chiaro 2009: 156). They are words that refer to concepts or objects specific to the source culture and perhaps unknown in the target culture. Examples are words related to fields such as food and drinks, institutions, educational/political systems, place names, names of famous people, names of books, films, TV programmes, holidays and festivities, units of measurement/monetary systems, sports and objects. In the films under analysis, we will call CRs those words referring to American, British and Indian cultures. Words derived from Indian culture will also be considered instances of code-mixing when they belong to Indian languages.

Code-switching (CS) consists of "alternations of linguistic varieties within the same conversation" (Myers-Scotton 1993: 1). It is a change of language within discourse among bilinguals. Different forms of code-switching have been identified: turn-specific (switches between different speakers' turns), intersentential (switches between sentences), intrasentential (switches within the sentence), from single-morpheme to single lexical items to clause level (Myers-Scotton 1993: 4; Monti 2009: 167).

The term code-mixing (CM), also called 'nonce borrowing', will be used in this contribution to describe intrasentential code-switching, which "involves inserting alien words or constituents into a clause" (Muysken 2000: 69). Changes are to be found at the morpheme, word or constituent level, that is, only a single lexical unit or phrase from another language is inserted in a clause (Baker 2004: 68; Berruto 2002: 261; Muysken 2000).

Ethnolects (Es) are ethnic varieties of the majority language, that is, specific accents signalling that the speaker was not born in that country, or was born there but belongs to a specific ethnic group with a different native language (Salmon Kovarski 2000: 68-69). Ethnolects usually differ from the standard variety of a language in terms of accent, but variation may also occur at morphological, lexical and/or syntactic levels. Since Indian English is a non-native variety of English (Kachru 1983: 66), we will consider it an ethnolect. In the films under investigation, it is represented by the English spoken by first-generation Indian migrants or Indian people.

4. Analysis

4.1. Cultural references

Cultural references (CRs) are difficult to translate since they have no equivalents in other languages. Translators resort to various strategies, ranging from the most foreignising to the most domesticating: they can use a loan word (direct transfer or retention); loan word plus explanation; literal translation (calque); more generic word (superordinate); explanation (paraphrase); cultural substitution (adaptation); omission (Baker 1992). Not all of these procedures can be adopted in AVT due to media constraints. Gottlieb (2009: 31) proposes a taxonomy of strategies for tackling CRs in subtitling: retention, literal translation, specification, generalisation, substitution and omission.

As far as the CRs in the corpus are concerned, the main semantic fields are those of food, clothes, measurements/money, objects, people, places and taboo language. The films contain several words that denote Indian food and dishes (e.g., *achar, aloo gobi, curry, dhal, dhania, gulab jaman, ladoo, langar, paneer tikka, ras malai, round chapattis, samosas*). The translation tendency in both dubbing and subtitling and in all the films is to retain the foreign terms as loan words. Thus, a foreignising strategy is preferred in both AVT modes when Indian food is mentioned, even if the meaning of the words may remain unknown. This implies that the Italian versions maintain the original films' portrayal of Indian culture in terms of culinary traditions.

In *BILB*, references to Indian food abound and are always retained in Italian, since traditional cooking is an important aspect of the film (Jess's mother believes that Jess should learn how to cook traditional food rather than play football). An example is the following excerpt from *BILB*, where *dhal* is a dish made from cooked lentils:

Table 2. Indian food in BILB

Character	English version	Dubbed version	Subtitled version
(4) MRS BHAMRA	I was married at your age! You don't even want to learn how to cook [CR] [CM] **dhal**!	Io ero già sposata alla tua età e tu non vuoi imparare a cucinare il **dhal**.[7]	Io ero sposata alla tua età e tu non sai nemmeno cucinare il "**daal**"![8]

Another example of this foreignising strategy applied to food is the retaining of the loan word *gulab jamans* (a very sweet Indian dessert) in *BAP*:

Table 3. Indian food in BAP

Character	English version	Dubbed version	Subtitled version
(5) LAKHI	I'm going to take him for [CR] **Amritsari fish**, fruit cream and hot [CR] [CM] **gulab jamans**.	Ah ah. Menù a base di **pesce alla brace**, crema di frutta e **gulab jamans**.[9]	Volevo portarlo a mangiare il **pesce**, la crema di frutta e il **gulab jamans**.[10]

However, in the same sentence the CR *Amritsari fish* (fried fish named after the Indian city where it originated) is translated by means of adaptation in dubbing, and by means of generalisation in the subtitles. In other words, a domesticating and a foreignising approach coexist in the same utterance. Of all the culture-specific Indian food terms mentioned in the corpus only four are domesticated, all in the film *BAP*: *Amritsari fish, ras malai, aloo gobi* and *ladoo*. *Ras malai* and *ladoo* are Indian sweets, while *aloo gobi* is an Indian dish made with potatoes (*aloo*), cauliflower (*gobi*) and spices. In the Italian versions, *ras malai* and *aloo gobi*, which are uttered in songs, are replaced with more generic words (*dolce* 'dessert'; *tu cucini* 'you cook'), while for *ladoo* the translator resorts to cultural substitution in dubbing (*biscotto* 'biscuit') and omission in the subtitles (the line is omitted since we do not see the speaker).

Words referring to Indian clothes such as *dupatta* ("a long scarf of flimsy material worn by women" (Muthiah 1991: 66)); *choli* ("a tight-fitting blouse worn with a saree or skirt" (Muthiah 1991: 49)); *sari* ("a 5 to 5½-metre-long cloth wrapped round the body by the women of India as their main clothing" (Muthiah 1991: 137)) are also present in the films. The translation tendency in both dubbing and subtitling is to retain them in Italian as borrowings, as in the original English dialogues. See, for instance, the following example from *BILB*:

Table 4: Indian clothes

Character	English version	Dubbed version	Subtitled version
(6) PINKY	No, Mum, I want my [CR] [CM] **choli** more fitted.	No mamma, io il **choli** lo voglio attillato.[11]	Voglio un **"choli"** aderente.[12]

This foreignising approach contributes to giving an exotic touch to the films and portraying features of Indian culture.

References to Indian places and traditions (*Amritsar, Agra, Taj Mahal, Varanasi*) also abound in the three films, and are mostly retained. An exception is the word *Garbha* (in *Bride and Prejudice*), which denotes "a lively folk-dance from Gujarat" (Muthiah 1991: 73). It is wrongly rendered in the Italian versions and although the images make it clear that it is a kind of dance, the Italian translations opt for *temple*:

Table 5: the word 'Garbha'

Character	English version	Dubbed version	Subtitled version
(7) LAKHI	I think we can take him to the [CR] [CM] **Garbha** tonight. No, Mama?	Potremmo portare Johnny al **tempio**, no mama?[13]	Stasera potremmo portarlo al **Tempio**.[14]

Most of the names of famous people mentioned in the original dialogues are retained in the Italian versions (*Guru Nanak, Sporty Spice, Beckham, George Michael, Wham!, Posh and Becks, Tagore, Gogol*). The only exception is the name *MC Hammer* (an American rapper and dancer), which becomes *John Travolta* in the dubbed version.

The films also contain specific references to British and American culture, such as *Heathrow, High Street, As, Bs, HMV, London Eye, Match of the Day, MFA, AAA maps* and *American Idol*. The translation tendency for such items in both AVT modes and in all the films is domestication, by means of cultural substitution, neutralisation, omission or superordinates. For instance, *Heathrow* becomes its superordinate *aeroporto* in dubbing and is omitted in the subtitles. The British grades *As* and *Bs* are simplified into the more general *essere ammessa all'università* ('to get into university'). *High Street* is omitted and the music store *HMV* is eliminated, becoming *lavoro, lavoro per l'estate* ('job, summer job'). *MFA* (*Master of Fine Arts*) is replaced with the more generic words *storica dell'arte* ('art historian') in dubbing and *dottoressa* ('graduate') in subtitles. *London Eye* is generalised as *ruota panoramica* ('big wheel'). An interesting example from *BAP* is the reference to *American Idol*, a popular American reality show, which is turned into *Grease* in the dubbed version, while the subtitles maintain the original CR. The adapter probably thought that an Italian audience would be more acquainted with the American musical starring John Travolta than with the reality show, which is almost unknown in Italy. Moreover, by replacing *American Idol* with *Grease*, the dubbed version can replace MC Hammer with John Travolta as an example of a good dancer. This scene, in which a white American and two second-generation Indians living in London are at an engagement party in India, also contains another rather curious CR, the expression *Delhi belly*, a colloquial nickname for traveller's diarrhoea, used by British and Americans to refer to Westerners suffering from diarrhoea as a result of the food and water in India. It is translated with a more generic word in the Italian versions (*dissenteria*):

Table 6. Anglo-Saxon cultural references

Character	English version	Dubbed version	Subtitled version
(8) DARCY	Are you sure this is safe to eat? I don't wanna be getting [CR] **Delhi belly** on my first day. What's happening now?	Sei sicuro che posso mangiarlo? Ci manca solo che mi becco la **dissenteria** il primo giorno. Che succede adesso?[15]	Posso mangiarlo? Non vorrei prendere la **dissenteria**. Che sta succedendo?[16]
KIRAN	The Indian version of [CR] **American Idol**. I hope you've brought earplugs.	È la versione indiana di **Grease**. Spero che tu ti sia portato i tappi.[17]	È la versione indiana di **"American Idol"**. Ti sei portato i tappi?[18]
BALRAJ	This is where the girls tease the boys, and the boys tease the girls.	È fantastico vedrai. I ragazzi puntano le ragazze e loro sfuggono.[19]	È bellissimo! I ragazzi corteggiano le ragazze e viceversa.[20]

| KIRAN | Brace yourself, Darcy. He's about to transform into the Indian [CR] **MC Hammer**. | Tieniti pronto Darcy, adesso si trasforma nel **John Travolta** indiano della situazione.[21] | Tieniti pronto, Darcy. Ora si trasforma nell'**MC Hammer** indiano.[22] |

The dubbed version explains and adapts all the Anglo-Saxon CRs, while the subtitles maintain a more foreignising, distancing approach.

One last example of CR is the word *Paki*, which is "an extremely offensive word for an Asian person" (*MacMillan English Dictionary* 2006), a noun used only in British English. It belongs to British culture and is neither common nor easily understood by other cultures. Monti explains that in contemporary British racist discourse "the term Paki indicates a South Asian (or better, a subcontinental) migrant at large. [...] One should not minimise the original emphasis of the Muslim background which is definitely implied by Paki" (2008: 262). It is uttered by a football player to insult Jess (who is not Pakistani but Indian, not Muslim but Sikh) in *BILB*:

Table 7. The word 'Paki'

Character	English version	Dubbed version	Subtitled version
(9) GIRL	Piss off, [CR] **Paki**!	Vaffanculo, **brutta indi**![23]	Vaffanculo, **brutta indi**![24]
(10) JESS	She called me [CR] **a Paki**.	Mi ha chiamato **brutta indi**.[25]	Mi ha detto: "**Brutta indi**".[26]

The Italian translations resort to the word *indi*, which means nothing in Italian, since the equivalent for *Indian* is *indiano/a*, and that for *Hindi* is *Hindi*. Thus, both dubbing and subtitles adopt an invented, meaningless word, coupled with *ugly* (*brutta indi*). However, it should be noted that this 'translation mistake' is influenced by the English subtitles of the film, which actually contain the word *Indi* – which is similarly non-existent in English. The Italian versions translate the English subtitles rather than the spoken dialogues: *Fuck off, ugly Indi*; *She said ugly Indi to me*.

CRs are treated in similar ways in the three films, while they seem to be translated differently according to the type of reference. The translation strategies adopted to deal with Indian CRs are mostly foreignising when food and clothes are concerned, while for other elements they are more domesticating in dubbing and foreignising in subtitles. When CRs are related to British or American culture, there is a tendency to omit or domesticate them in both AVT modes. This might be because of a willingness to highlight the Indianness of the films rather than their British or American aspects.

4.2. Code-mixing

The films contain several instances of code-mixing, where single words, phrases or morphemes belonging to Hindi, other Indian languages or Indian English are inserted into English discourse. Particularly frequent is the use of Indian vocatives. Familiarisers such as *baba* ('father, grandfather, an elderly man, little boy'), *ma* ('mother'), *didi* ('elder sister'), *masi* or *massi* ('a sister or a cousin-sister of one's mother, an aunt'), *beti* ('daughter, or used to address any young girl'), *putar* ('son, daughter'), *auntie* ("the way most Westernized children address any lady older than them" (Muthiah 1991: 29)), often occur. They are usually maintained as foreign words in the Italian versions, as can be seen in the following table:

Table 8. Indian familiarizers

Character	English version	Dubbed version	Subtitled version
(11) GOGOL	Gogol's your favourite author. I know, [CM] **baba**.	Sì, è il tuo scrittore preferito, lo so **baba**.[27]	Sì. Gogol è il tuo autore preferito. Lo so, **baba**.[28]
(12) GOGOL	Hey, Mira [CM] **masi**.	Ciao Mira **masi**.	Ciao Mira **Masi**.

The only exceptions to this foreignising trend are *putar*, which is either omitted or translated literally with *figliolo/figliola*, and *didi*, which is translated literally as *sorella* in dubbing, and left untranslated in the subtitles. The suffix *-ji*, which is attached to a person's name as a sign of respect (Muthiah 1991: 88), is added to words signalling family relations such as *babaji*, *auntieji*, *uncleji*, *massiji* and *mamaji*. In translation, both dubbing and subtitles omit the suffix. In so doing, the translations lose an important aspect of the films' expressive meaning. *Uncleji* and *auntiji,* which are forms of address "applied to a person who is not a blood relation" (Mahal 2006: 50), and who belongs to "the generation older than oneself" (Mahal 2006: 103), are simplified to *zio* and *zia* ('uncle' and 'aunt'). In this case, *zietto* and *zietta* could be the equivalent Italian affectionate vocatives, which are also used for adult friends of a child's parents who behave like relatives.

Other frequent vocatives are *saab/sahib* ('gentleman, officer') and *babu* ('gentleman, clerk, Mr, a master, a landlord'). They are usually maintained in dubbing and subtitles, with the exception of *BAP,* where the subtitles omit all the occurrences of *saab*. The following excerpts illustrate this type of code-mixing and the translation strategies adopted:

Table 9. Other Indian vocatives

Character	English version	Dubbed version	Subtitled version
(13) MRS BAKSHI	Oh, Kholi, Kholi [CM] **saab**. Where are you going? Listen to me, Kholi [CM] **saab**.	Kholi, Kholi **saab**, dove vai? Ascoltami Kholi **saab**.[29]	Kholi, dove vai? Ascoltami, Kholi. Ti prego, non andare via così.[30]
(14) ASHIMA	Why don't you get in, my American [CM] **sahib**?	Perché non sali, mio **sahib** americano?[31]	Perché non sali, mio **sahib** americano?[32]
(15) CHOTU	Gogol, [CM] **babu**! [CS] [Bengali: *Move, move.*] Gogol! Gogol, [CM] **babu**! [CS] [Bengali: *I'm a fat man.*] Stop. Stop. Stop.	Gogol, **babu**! [Bengali: Fate largo, fate largo. Gogol! Sono grasso! Abbi pietà.][33] [Bengali]	Gogol, **babu**! Fate largo, fate largo. Gogol! Gogol, **babu**! Sono un povero grasso. Fermati. Fermati.[34]

An interesting case of code-mixing is the insertion of the noun *gora*, feminine *gori*, plural *gore* or *goras*, feminine plural *gore* or *goris*. It is an Indian English derogatory noun derived from Hindi and is used in several Indian languages with the meanings *a white person* and *a person with fair skin* (Mahal 2006: 45). It often carries negative connotations. There are five occurrences in *BILB*. *Gora* (2) is translated as *bianco* ('white'); the feminine *gori* (2) is rendered with *bionda* ('blonde') and *stronza* ('bitch'); the plural *goras* (1) is translated as *bianchi* ('white people'). As illustrated in the following examples, there is no difference in the translation choices made for dubbing and subtitles:

Table 10. The noun 'gora'

Character	English version	Dubbed version	Subtitled version
(16) TONY	Yeah. Well, you fancying your [CM] **gora** coach is okay with me.	Grazie...e se ti piace il tuo allenatore **bianco**, non lo dirò, fidati di me.[35]	Grazie. Io non dirò che ti piace il tuo allenatore **bianco**.[36]
(17) JESS	Pinks, do you think Mum and	Pinky....secondo te mamma e papà mi	Mamma e papà mi perdonerebbero se

"You fancying your gora coach is okay with me"

		Dad would still speak to me if I ever brought home a [CM] **gora**?	perdonerebbero se sposassi un **bianco**?[37]	sposassi un **bianco**?[38]
(18)	GIRL	Hey, who's that [CM] **gori** watching her?	Ehi, chi è la **bionda** che la sta guardando?[39]	Chi è la **bionda** che la guarda?[40]
(19)	PINKY	What the bleedin' hell's going on, eh? What's that [CM] **gori** going on about you being a lezbo, eh?	Si può sapere che cavolo succede? Eh? Perché quella **stronza** dice che sei lesbica?[41]	Che cavolo succede? Perché quella **stronza** dice che sei lesbica?[42]
(20)	MR BHAMRA	I was not allowed to play in any of the teams, and these bloody [CM] **goras** in their clubhouses made fun of my turban and sent me off packing!	Ma quando arrivai in Inghilterra, niente. Non mi fu permesso di giocare in nessuna squadra. I maledetti **bianchi** dei circoli sportivi mi sfottevano per il mio turbante. E mi cacciarono via.[43]	Ma quando sono venuto qui, non ho potuto giocare in nessuna squadra. I maledetti **bianchi** nei club prendevano in giro il mio turbante e mi cacciarono via.[44]

While *bianco* and *bianchi* convey the propositional meaning of *gora* and *goras*, the derogatory tone is lost in the Italian translation of examples 16, 17 and 20. On the other hand, the translation equivalent chosen for example 19 is definitely negative and quite strong, and it manages to convey the character's anger. *Bionda* in example 18 has no connection with the source dialogue, but it is linked to the images (the girl referred to is blonde). It is worth noting that the Italian versions are influenced not by the English spoken dialogues, but by the English subtitles, of which they are literal translations. For instance, example 16 translates *I won't say you like your white coach*; example 18 corresponds to *Who's that blonde looking at her?*, and example 19 derives from *Why does that bitch say you are lesbian?*

Other instances of code-mixing involve words from Indian languages and Indian English. *Chal/chalo/challo* ('go; leave; let's go'), which are uttered by several Indian speakers, are either rendered with equivalent Italian imperatives such as *su muoviti, andiamo* ('hurry up, let's go') or omitted:

323

Table 11. 'chal/chalo'

Character	English version	Dubbed version	Subtitled version
(21) WOMAN	All I know is that children are a map of their parents. [CM] **Chalo**, eh?	Io so solo che i nostri figli sono come i nostri specchi. Capite? **Su muoviti.**[45]	I figli sono lo specchio dei genitori. **Andiamo!**[46]
(22) MRS BHAMRA	[CM] **Chal**. Get back into bed.	Jess, torna subito a letto.[47]	Torna a letto.[48]

Chi chi, an interjection expressing disgust or disapproval, is usually retained in the Italian versions since its meaning is clear from the character's facial expression and intonation. The Bengali words *daknam* and *bhalonam*, used in *TN*, are retained in the Italian versions. However, their meanings are partly explained in the dialogue since it is important for the development of the plot:

Table 12. Bengali words in TN

Character	English version	Dubbed version	Subtitled version
(23) ASHOKE	We all have two names - one pet name, [CM] **daknam**, one good name, [CM] **bhalonam**.	Noi abbiamo due nomi. Un vezzeggiativo, **daknam** e un nome vero, **bhalonam**.[49]	Abbiamo tutti due nomi: un vezzeggiativo, **daknam**, e un nome ufficiale, **bhalonam**.[50]

This follows the novel's strategy of clarifying Bengali words, and Bengali culture, for western readers. The film condenses Lahiri's description:

> a practice of Bengali nomenclatures grants, to every single person, two names. In Bengali the word for pet name is *daknam*, meaning, literally, the name by which one is called, by friends, family, and other intimates, at home and in other private, unguarded moments. [...] Every pet name is paired with a good name, a *bhalonam*, for identification in the outside world (2003: 25-26).

Code-mixing is dealt with in various ways in the Italian versions. Indian vocatives tend to be retained as loan words in all the films, while for other words there does not seem to be a norm. The approach in *TN* seems more foreignising, while in *BILB* more domestication takes place, and in *BAP*

"You fancying your gora coach is okay with me"

code-mixing is less frequent but it is mostly retained. Dubbing and subtitling appear to opt for similar solutions. An interesting strategy found in the subtitles of *BILB* is to add double inverted commas to highlight the foreignness of some Indian terms for food and clothes.

4.3. Code-switching

All the films contain several instances of code-switching, especially among first-generation Asian immigrants. UK/US-raised children use English but sometimes switch to Indian languages, resorting to turn-specific, intrasentential and intersentential code-switching only when speaking with their elders. For instance, in example 26 below, from *BILB*, the second-generation Asians Jess and Pinky meet their friend Tony with his mother, an older Indian woman. As a sign of respect, they switch language to address her. They utter the Sikh greeting *Sat shri akal* – which means 'God is the supreme truth' – to which they add the respectful vocative *massiji*. After the woman's reply in Punjabi, the conversation switches back to English. In examples 24 and 25, first-generation Indian immigrants resort to intersentential code-switching. The original versions vary in their rendering of such linguistic diversity, since in *BILB* Punjabi dialogue is not subtitled in English, while in *TN* (see example 25) all the utterances in Bengali are subtitled. The following table shows the function of code-switching and its treatment in translation:

Table 13. Code-switching in the films

Character	English version	Dubbed version	Subtitled version
(24) WOMAN	[E] English people always complaining when we're having functions. [CS] **[Punjabi]** Why did she take Jesminder's shoes?	Questi inglesi protestano sempre quando noi facciamo festa. **[Punjabi]** Perché ha levato le scarpe a Jesminder?[51]	Gli inglesi protestano sempre quando diamo una festa! **[Punjabi]** Perché ha levato le scarpe a Jesminder?[52]
WOMEN (VOICES)	[CS] **[Punjabi]**	Chi può sapere? Non ho capito bene....[53]	Chi lo può sapere? Non l'ho capito.[54]
(25) ASHOKE	[CS] **[Bengali: *These have all shrunk.*]** I mean, who asked you to	**[Bengali: *Si sono ristrette.*]** Chi ti ha detto di lavare la mia roba? **[Bengali:**	Si sono tutti ristretti. Chi ti ha detto di lavarmi i vestiti? Non

325

	wash my clothes? [CS] **[Bengali: Couldn't you have waited till I got back? Here, one dollar means eight rupees.]** We don't have so much money to buy... Where are you going? ... Ashima? Ashima? Open the door, Ashima. ... I'm sorry, Ashima. [CS] **[Bengali:** *It was my mistake.***]**	*Perché non hai aspettato che tornassi io? Un dollaro sono otto rupie.***]** Non abbiamo tanti soldi per ricomprare...dove vai? Ashima! Ashima! Apri la porta Ashima. Scusami tanto Ashima. **[Bengali:** *è colpa mia.***]**[55]	potevi aspettare che tornassi io? Un dollaro sono otto rupie. Non abbiamo tanti soldi per comprare... Dove vai? Ashima? Apri la porta, Ashima. Scusami, Ashima. È tutta colpa mia.[56]
(26) TONY	All right, Jess? Hiya, Pinky.	Come va Jess? Pinky![57]	Ciao, Jess. Ciao, Pinky.[58]
JESS AND PINKY	[CS] **[Punjabi: Sat shri akal Massiji]**	**[Punjabi: Sat shri akal Massiji]**	**[Punjabi: Sat shri akal Massiji]**
TONY'S MOTHER	Ah, [CS] **[Punjabi]** May you have a long life, my daughters!	**[Punjabi]** ... possiate vivere a lungo figlie mie.[59]	**[Punjabi]** Lunga vita, figlie mie.[60]
(27) JOHNNY WICKHAM	Better single than unhappy. [CS] **[Hindi: Thīk hai na?]**	Meglio soli che infelici, **giusto?**[61]	Meglio sola che infelice. **Giusto?**[62]

Various solutions can be adopted to deal with multiple languages (Heiss 2004; Bartoll 2006; Díaz Cintas & Remael 2007; Chiaro 2009; Sanz 2009; De Higes Andino 2009). Different translation strategies convey code-switching in the Italian versions of the films analysed. As far as *BILB* is concerned, the strategies of monolingual dubbing, monolingual subtitling and 'no translation' are the preferred options, while a combination of dubbing and subtitling (Heiss 2004) is avoided. Exchanges in Punjabi or Hindi in the original film are either maintained in dubbing and subtitles, with no translation (see examples 24 and 26), or are dubbed and subtitled into Italian (example 24). The latter option is a strategy of full explicitation which adds "meaning elements to favour the Italian audience's understanding" (Monti 2009: 169), but which alters the film's overall meaning. In *TN*, on the other hand, all the utterances in Bengali are subtitled in the Italian dubbed version.

The main language, that is English, is dubbed while the second language is conveyed through subtitles. In the subtitled version both languages are subtitled in the same way. Thus, the translation approach for code-switching in *TN* is foreignising. This choice preserves the original film's spirit and atmosphere, and the central role played by multilingualism in the film. In *BAP* code-switching is less frequent, but when it occurs various strategies are adopted. It is neutralised through dubbing and subtitling into standard Italian, as is the case in example 27, where the Hindi expression *Thīk hai na?* ('Right?/Don't you agree?') is translated with *Giusto?* ('right?'). In other cases, CS is left untranslated. For example, the speech of Indian people in the streets is not translated since it helps to convey the Indian setting but has no narrative function. On the other hand, songs in Hindi, which create the Bollywood atmosphere of the film, are not dubbed but subtitled into Italian.

4.4. Ethnolects

The films contain several examples of ethnolects, which are an important linguistic trait defining characters and their cultural environment. Features of Indian English are found in the speech of first-generation migrants or older people living in India, but are absent from the utterances by the younger characters, who are UK- or US-born or educated in English. Indian English shows some 'deviations' from Standard English (Kachru 1983). Apart from obvious variations in pronunciation and in lexis, such as the presence of borrowings from various Indian languages, or the different meanings given to some English lexical items, the most striking deviations affect syntax. Typical syntactic features of Indian English are the arbitrary use of the articles *a* and *the*, and of the zero article, and the use of reduplication to give emphasis. Other signs of Indian English grammar are the use of the progressive aspect to refer to habitual actions and the formation of interrogative clauses, where there is no subject-verb inversion (Kachru 1983: 76-81; Baldridge 2002). The speech of some Indian characters in the films contains some of these features: *25th is only available date* (omission of *the*), *he was not there for emergency* (omission of *an*), *these mosquito bites will look like juicy juicy mangoes* (reduplication) and *English people always complaining when we're having functions* (omission of the auxiliary and use of the progressive aspect). It is also worth noting that it is mostly the older women (mothers) who use ethnolects to a great extent, since they tend to be "the keeper[s] of the Asian background values" (Monti 2009: 171), are more attached to their origins and traditions, and have less contact with the western world.

Dubbing and subtitles deal with ethnolects in different ways. The translation strategy in dubbing is one of compensation, since Indian English in the original is sometimes rendered with standard Italian, but ungrammatical constructions and foreign pronunciation are inserted elsewhere in speech. Prosodic features are stressed with the omission of double consonants (e.g., *atentamente* rather than the correct *attentamente*; *dirite* rather than *diritte*; *sorela* rather than *sorella*) and the use of incorrect Italian syntax, such as the elimination of articles (e.g., *Ho detto a genitori*;[63] *Anche se sue ceneri sono sparse in Gange*)[64] or the wrong conjugation of verbs (*Tua sorela sta per sposare*[65]; *E come fa tu a respirare?*)[66]. Subtitles, on the other hand, always use standard Italian so that everyone speaks in the same way and ethnolects are erased. The following excerpts illustrate the features referred to above:

Table 14. Ethnolects in the films

Character	English version	Dubbed version	Subtitled version
(28) MRS BAKSHI	I completely forgot [E] **groom** is bringing **guest** from England.	Avevo dimenticato che lo sposo aspettava degli ospiti dall'Inghilterra.[67]	Avevo dimenticato che lo sposo avrebbe avuto ospiti dall'Inghilterra.[68]
(29) MRS BAKSHI	And what will Kholi [CM] saab say? He is staying here in a house full of young unmarried women.	Che cosa penserà Kholi saab? [E] **Altro uomo** che dorme qui [E] **in casa** di giovani ragazze nubili.[69]	Cosa penserà Kholi? Un altro uomo che dorme in una casa di giovani non sposate?[70]
(30) ASHIMA	It is a mistake. He was not there [E] **for emergency**. Only [E] **for stomach ache**.	Lei si sbaglia. Non era lì per qualcosa di grave. Aveva solo mal di stomaco.[71]	C'è un errore. Non era lì per un'emergenza. Aveva solo mal di stomaco.[72]
(31) ASHIMA	And though his ashes are scattered in the Ganges, it is here in this house, in this town, amongst all of you, that he will continue to dwell in my heart.	E anche se [E] **sue** ceneri sono sparse [E] **in** Gange, è qui dentro, in questa casa, in questa città, in mezzo a tutti voi, che lui continuerà a vivere nel mio cuore.[73]	E anche se le sue ceneri sono disperse nel Gange, è qui in questa casa, in questa città, in mezzo a tutti voi, che continuerà a vivere nel mio cuore.[74]
(32) MRS BHAMRA	Am I asking you to make it?	Ho forse [E] **chiesto fare** a voi due?[75]	Ho chiesto a voi di farlo?[76]

| (33) MRS BHAMRA | What bigger honour is there than respecting your elders? | Unico vero onore è rispettare [E] **genitori**.[77] | Onore è rispettare i genitori.[78] |

The absence of articles and plurals in example 28 from *BAP* is rendered with standard Italian in dubbing and subtitles. This is compensated for in example 29, where the dubbed version introduces ungrammaticalities such as the omission of articles, while the subtitled version is correct. Example 30 from *TN* contains ethnolect in the original version, which is neutralised in the Italian translations, while in excerpt 31 standard English is turned into non-standard Italian in dubbing (omission of articles), and correct Italian in subtitles. In the original version of *TN*, Ashima speaks good English, making very few mistakes, whereas in the dubbed dialogues she often speaks non-standard Italian. This turns the educated and cultured Indian woman into quite a different person. The last two excerpts, from *BILB*, show ungrammaticalities in dubbing which do not correspond to Indian English deviations in the original. On the whole, the Italian dubbed versions of the three films contain more 'deviations' than the source versions and they tend to exaggerate these traits, making the characters (mostly women) sound uneducated and rather funny. The translation choices in *BILB* in particular create an exaggeratedly caricatural portrayal of Mrs Bhamra in the dubbed Italian version. Thus, we can actually talk of 'overcompensation' in dubbing for all the films. Conversely, in the subtitled versions standard Italian prevails. The result of this neutralising translation choice is a levelling-out of variation, and a loss of meaning and characterisation. In other words, both audiovisual translation modes change the original films' characters to a certain extent, and do so in opposite ways.

5. Conclusions

The study presented in this contribution has highlighted several translation issues. As far as CRs are concerned, the translation strategies in dubbing and subtitling are quite similar. References to Indian food and clothes tend to be retained as borrowings in the Italian versions, the only exception being *BAP*, where food terms are sometimes domesticated. References to British and American culture, on the other hand, tend to be omitted or domesticated in all the films. However, no claims can be made about the existence of a norm or a common Italian attitude in treating CRs.

When code-mixing occurs, both dubbing and subtitling tend to maintain foreign words when they are vocatives and food terms, while for other words there is a certain balance between domesticating and foreignising strategies.

TN and *BAP* retain more foreign words, while in *BILB* domestication is more frequent.

The translation strategies adopted to deal with the phenomenon of code-switching appear to be linked to the type of film and the role of the second/third language in the film or scene rather than to the translation mode. Code-switching is prominent in *TN*, where the second language (Bengali), which covers up to 40% of the film (Nair 2007), plays an important role in defining the characters and their culture. By choosing a mixture of AVT modes, that is, dubbing for the main language and subtitles for Bengali, the Italian dubbed version retains the linguistic and cultural richness of this film, so that the characters' bilingual, bicultural identities emerge. The subtitled version opts for monolingual subtitles but retains linguistic diversity in the soundtrack. Code-switching in *BILB* is less prominent: the second language seems to have no narrative role and appears to be "part of the setting" (Dìaz Cintas & Remael 2007: 59). Switches to and from Punjabi stress Indianness and highlight difference, give an exotic flair, but what the characters actually say is not important or can be understood from the context and the images. The Italian versions sometimes opt not to translate Punjabi utterances, but often choose monolingual dubbing (or monolingual subtitling in the subtitles). They never combine dubbing and subtitling and consequently erase linguistic diversity and alter the film's "internal coherence" (Monti 2009: 183). In *BAP*, code-switching rarely occurs but three strategies are used: code-switching is (1) dubbed and subtitled into Italian, (2) left untranslated or – in the case of songs – (3) subtitled.

As for ethnolects, it is possible to discern some patterns. Indian English is always flattened out and standardised in subtitles, which is in line with the tendency of subtitling to neutralise non-standard grammar (Díaz Cintas & Remael 2007: 192). Conversely, dubbing not only conveys ethnolects, it also emphasises them by inserting several ungrammaticalities, especially in the speech of Indian women belonging to the older generation. This strategy might indicate their attachment to India and perhaps their difficulty to integrate into western society. However, it also conveys a caricatural image of these women in the dubbed versions, which does not correspond to their identities in the source films.

The examples described in this contribution indicate that although the dubbed versions resort – to some extent – to domestication and adaptation, thus diminishing the importance of multilingualism, foreignising strategies are also chosen and sociolinguistic variation is often conveyed. As argued by Heiss (2004: 218), "in multilingual films a meaningful element is represented by the fact that the viewers are confronted with what is foreign to them, and this must not be lost in the translation". The analysis presented in this contribution suggests that Italian audiovisual translators try to relay the foreignness of the societies portrayed in the films and to transfer different linguistic and cultural nuances for their audiences.

---

[1] Football shoes.
[2] Football shoes.
[3] You won't believe it! Our rickshaw drivers dress better than professors here.
[4] You won't believe it. In comparison to the professors here, even our street vendors dress well.
[5] Let's go it's late.
[6] Let's go, it's late.
[7] I was already married at your age and you don't want to learn how to cook dhal.
[8] I was married at your age and you don't even know how to cook 'daal'.
[9] Ah ah. The menu includes grilled fish, fruit cream and gulab jamans.
[10] I wanted to take him for fish, fruit cream and gulab jamans.
[11] No, Mum, I want the choli tight-fitting.
[12] I want a tight 'choli'.
[13] We could take Johnny to the temple, couldn't we, mama?
[14] We could take him to the temple tonight.
[15] Are you sure I can eat this? All I need now is for me to get diarrhoea on my first day here. What's happening now?
[16] Can I eat this? I wouldn't want to get diarrhoea. What's happening?
[17] It's the Indian version of Grease. I hope you've brought earplugs.
[18] It's the Indian version of "American Idol". Have you brought earplugs?
[19] It's fantastic, you'll see. The boys hit on the girls and the girls run away.
[20] It's great. The boys court the girls and viceversa.
[21] Brace yourself, Darcy, now he's about to transform into the Indian John Travolta.
[22] Brace yourself, Darcy. Now he's about to transform into the Indian MC Hammer.
[23] Fuck off, ugly Indi!
[24] Fuck off, ugly Indi!
[25] She called me ugly Indi.
[26] She said: 'Ugly Indi' to me.
[27] Yes, he's your favourite writer, I know baba.
[28] Yes. Gogol is your favourite author. I know, baba.
[29] Kholi, Kholi saab, where are you going? Listen to me, Kholi saab.
[30] Kholi, where are you going? Listen to me, Kholi. Please, don't go away like this.
[31] Why don't you go upstairs, my American sahib?
[32] Why don't you go upstairs, my American sahib?
[33] Gogol, babu! Make way, make way. Gogol! I'm fat. Have mercy.
[34] Gogol, babu! Make way, make way. Gogol! Gogol, babu! I'm a poor fat man. Stop. Stop.
[35] Thanks. And if you like your white coach I won't say anything. Trust me.
[36] Thanks. I won't say you like your white coach.
[37] Pinky…do you think Mum and Dad would forgive me if I married a white man?
[38] Would Mum and Dad forgive me if I married a white man?
[39] Hey, who's that blonde looking at her?
[40] Who's that blonde looking at her?
[41] Could you tell me what the hell's going on? Eh? Why does that bitch say you're lesbian?
[42] What the hell's going on? Why does that bitch say you are lesbian?
[43] But when I arrived in England, nothing. I was not allowed to play in any of the teams. Those bloody whites in their clubhouses made fun of me because of my turban. And they sent me away.

[44] But when I arrived here, I couldn't play in any of the teams. Those bloody whites in their clubs made fun of my turban and sent me away.
[45] All I know is that our children are like our mirrors. Do you understand? Come on, hurry up.
[46] Children are their parents' mirrors. Let's go!
[47] Jess, go immediately back to bed.
[48] Go back to bed.
[49] We have two names. A petname, daknam, and a real name, bhalonam.
[50] We all have two names: a pet name, daknam, and an official name, bhalonam.
[51] These English people always complain when we celebrate. Why did she take off Jesminder's shoes?
[52] English people always complain when we have a party! Why did she take off Jesminder's shoes?
[53] Who knows? I didn't understand very well.
[54] Who knows? I didn't understand.
[55] They have shrunk. Who told you to wash my clothes? Why didn't you wait till I got back? One dollar means eight rupees. We don't have so much money to buy again…where are you going? Ashima! Ashima! Open the door, Ashima. I'm really sorry Ashima. It's my fault.
[56] They've all shrunk. Who told you to wash my clothes? Couldn't you have waited till I got back? One dollar means eight rupees. We don't have so much money to buy …where are you going? Ashima? Open the door, Ashima. I'm sorry, Ashima. It's all my fault.
[57] What's up, Jess? Pinky!
[58] Hi, Jess, Hi, Pinky.
[59] May you have a long life, my daughters.
[60] Long life, my daughters.
[61] Better alone than unhappy, right?
[62] Better alone than unhappy, right?
[63] I've told parents.
[64] And though his ashes are scattered in Ganges
[65] Your sister getting married.
[66] How you going to breathe?
[67] I had forgotten that the groom expected guests from England.
[68] I had forgotten that the groom would have guests from England.
[69] What will Kholi saab think? Other man that sleeps here in house of young unmarried women.
[70] What will Kholi think? Another man that sleeps in a house of young unmarried women?
[71] You're wrong. He wasn't there for something serious. He only had stomachache.
[72] There is a mistake. He wasn't there for an emergency. He only had stomachache.
[73] And though his ashes are scattered in Ganges, it is here, in this house, in this town, amongst all of you, that he will continue to dwell in my heart.
[74] And though his ashes are scattered in the Ganges, it is here, in this house, in this town, amongst all of you, that he will continue to dwell in my heart.
[75] Have I perhaps asked you two do it?
[76] Have I asked you to do it?
[77] The only real honour is to respect parents.
[78] Honour means to respect your parents.

References

Baker, Colin. 2004. 'Bilingualism and Multilingualism', in Malmkjaer, Kirsten (ed.) *The Linguistics Encyclopedia*. London: Routledge. 64-75.

Baker, Mona. 1992. *In Other Words. A Coursebook on Translation*. London: Routledge.
Baldridge, Jason. 2002. 'Linguistic and social characteristics of Indian English' in Language in India, 2 (4). On line at: http://www.languageinindia.com/junjul2002/baldridgeindianenglish. html (consulted 15.03.2010).
Bartoll, Eduard. 2006. 'Subtitling Multilingual Films' in Carroll, Mary, Heidrun Gerzymisch-Arbogast & Sandra Nauert (eds*.) Proceedings of the Marie Curie Euroconferences MuTra: Audiovisual Translation Scenarios*. Online at http://www.euroconferences.info/proceedings/ 2006_Proceedings/2006_Bartoll_Eduard.pdf (consulted 20.09.2010).
Berruto, Gaetano. 2002. *Fondamenti di sociolinguistica*. Roma: Laterza.
Bonsignori, Veronica. 2009. 'Transcribing film dialogue: from orthographic to prosodic transcription' in Freddi, Maria & Maria Pavesi (eds.) *Analysing Audiovisual Dialogue: Linguistic and Translational Insights*. Bologna: Clueb. 185-200.
Chiaro, Delia. 2009. 'Issues in Audiovisual Translation' in Munday, Jeremy (ed.) *The Routledge Companion to Translation Studies*. London: Routledge. 141-165.
De Higes Andino, Irene. 2009. *El Doblaje de los Filmes Plurilingües de Migración Contemporáneos: El Caso de la Película 'En un mundo libre...' de Ken Loach*. MA dissertation, University of Valencia.
Díaz Cintas, Jorge & Aline Remael. 2007. *Audiovisual Translation: Subtitling*. Manchester: St. Jerome Publishing.
Freddi, Maria & Maria Pavesi (eds). 2009. *Analysing Audiovisual Dialogue: Linguistic and Translational Insights*. Bologna: Clueb.
Gottlieb, Henrik. 2009. 'Subtitling against the Current: Danish Concepts, English Minds' in Díaz Cintas, Jorge (ed.) *New Trends in Audiovisual Translation*. Bristol: Multilingual Matters. 21-43.
Heiss, Christine. 2004. 'Dubbing Multilingual Films: A New Challenge?' in *Meta* 49(1): 208-220. Online at http://id.erudit.org/iderudit/009035ar (consulted 15.03.2010).
Kachru, Braj B. 1983. *The Indianization of English: The English Language in India*. Oxford: Oxford University Press.
Lahiri, Jhumpa. 2003. *The Namesake*. London: Flamingo.
Mahal, Baljinder K. 2006. *The Queen's Hinglish: How to Speak Pukka*. Glasgow: Harper Collins.
Monti, Alessandro. 2008. 'Londoni Husbands and the Forgotten *Wives'* in Monti, Alessandro (ed.) *Society, Culture, Diaspora: A Reading of Indian Literature*. New Delhi: Prestige Books. 261-270.
Monti, Silvia. 2009. 'Codeswitching and multicultural identity in screen translation' in Freddi, Maria & Maria Pavesi (eds). 2009. *Analysing Audiovisual Dialogue: Linguistic and Translational Insights*. Bologna: Clueb. 165-183.
Muthiah, Subbiah. 1991. *Words in Indian English: A Reader's Guide*. New Delhi: Indus.
Muysken, Pieter. 2000. *Bilingual Speech: A Typology of Code-Mixing*. Cambridge: Cambridge University Press.
Myers-Scotton, Carol. 1993. *Social Motivations for Code-Switching: Evidence from Africa*. Oxford: Clarendon.
Nair, Mira. 2007. 'Cinema Diaspora: A Discussion with Mira Nair and UC Davis Faculty. May 21 2007.' Online at http://www.youtube.com/watch?v=tXJmT-zDbH8 (consulted 15.10. 2010).
Salmon Kovarski, Laura. 2000. 'Tradurre l'Etnoletto: Come Doppiare in Italiano l'Accento Ebraico' in Bollettieri Bosinelli, Rosa Maria et al. (eds.) *La Traduzione Multimediale: Quale Traduzione per Qquale Testo?* Bologna: CLUEB. 67-84.
Sanz, Elena. 2009. *Audiovisual Translation Modality and Non-Verbal Information in Multilingual Films: A Case Study: Spanglish*. Master's thesis, University of Edinburgh.
Venuti, Lawrence. 1995. *The Translator's Invisibility: A History of Translation*. London: Routledge.

Dictionaries

MacMillan English Dictionary for Advanced Learners. 2006. London: MacMillan.
Yule, Henry, Arthur C. Burnell & William Crooke. 1995. *Hobson-Jobson: A Glossary of Colloquial Anglo-Indian Words and Phrases* (2nd ed.). Richmond, VA: Curzon. Online at http://dsal.uchicago.edu/dictionaries/hobsonjobson/ (consulted 20.03.2009).
Bengali-English Dictionary. Online at http://dsal.uchicago.edu/dictionaries/biswas-bengali/ (consulted 05.03.2010).
Hindi-English Dictionary. Online at http://dsal.uchicago.edu/dictionaries/caturvedi/ (consulted 05.03.2010).
Indian English Dictionary. Online at http://www.amritt.com/IndianEnglish.html (consulted 05.03.2010).
Punjabi-English Dictionary. Online at http://dsal.uchicago.edu/dictionaries/singh/ (consulted 05.03.2010).

Filmography

Bend it Like Beckham, Gurinder Chadha (2002) UK.
Bride and Prejudice, Gurinder Chadha (2004). UK, USA.
The Namesake, Mira Nair (2006). India, USA.

The Enriching Functions of Address Shifts in Film Translation

Maria Pavesi
University of Pavia (Italy)

Abstract

Address modes such as vocatives and second-person pronouns express social roles and interpersonal relationships while their shift indexes mutations in interactants' attitudes or status. Film provides a challenging context for the translation of these socio-pragmatic features since audiovisual dialogue is supposed to imitate spontaneous interaction while at the same time creating characters' identities and advancing narration. With reference to a selection of contemporary American and British films dubbed into Italian, this contribution focuses on the specific issue of transitions from formal to informal address in the target texts. English and Italian differ markedly in this respect, with the tu-Lei pronominal contrast in Italian forcibly making explicit what may be left implicit or undefined in English. It is shown that, far from simply deriving from linguistic features of the source text or conventions of the target community, the address strategies in translated texts may be motivated by attitudinal and diegetic changes expressed contextually and paralinguistically in the original audiovisual texts. Hence, pronoun shifts are shown to code a change in characters' mutual positioning linguistically, and to anticipate or amplify the emotional intensity of key narrative moments. However, they can also result from dubbing translators' creative interpretation of the developing action and interpersonal dynamics.

Keywords
address shifts, explicitation, film narrative structure, socio-pragmatic meanings, translators' creativity

1. Introduction

Address modes linguistically express interpersonal relationships and social roles and when they undergo a change or a shift, they index crucial transitions in the mutual positioning of the interactants involved. As audiovisual dialogue is supposed to imitate spontaneous conversation, while at the same time advancing narration and offering a condensed representation of individual and social identities, film provides a challenging context for the selection of address forms, especially when the text is being transferred from one culture to another. More precisely, the complexity inherent in such translation choices in films significantly depends on the systematic socio-pragmatic contrasts across different languages and communities (Pavesi

1996), on the co-deployment of several semiotic codes on-screen (Chaume, Frederic, 2004a), as well as on the dramatic and teleological structures of mainstream film narrative (Remael 2008).

Using a descriptive approach to film translation (Díaz Cintas 2004), this contribution will focus on the specific issue of address shifts in the dubbing from English into Italian, with the aim of exploring the phenomenon in relation to the norms of the source and target communities, together with the semiotic and narrative functions of films. It will be shown that, far from simply deriving from linguistic features of the source text or mimetically reflecting the socio-pragmatic conventions of the target community, address modes in translated texts may be motivated also by the diegetic developments expressed paralinguistically and contextually in the original audiovisual texts. Address in films will thus emerge as a dynamic feature which can be negotiated in dialogue as a means for disclosing, imposing and reaffirming personal and interpersonal identities. In addition, it can also contribute to alerting viewers about decisive moments in the story architecture.

1.1. Address

Address is a fundamentally relational phenomenon whose motivations and underpinnings are intricate and multifaceted. Starting from seminal works from the 1960s on this socio-pragmatic phenomenon (Brown & Gilman 1972), two major dimensions – or sets of norms – have been identified to account for the use and variation of address systems: (1) power and (2) solidarity. The first dimension underlines the hierarchical and asymmetrical relationships between people. When the dimension of power is active, the social inferior receives familiar or informal address – a T form – whereas the superior receives formal or respectful address – a V form. The second dimension prevails within an ideology of social equality when people exchange symmetrical forms of address in response to the degree of perceived similarity or social proximity. Distant relationships entail reciprocal formal address, close relationships entail reciprocal informal address.

Although Brown and Gilman's (1972) model has been widely influential, criticisms have been levelled against the essentially monolithic distinction between T and V pronouns that it presents. Several studies have in fact shown that languages vary widely in terms of address modes, both interlinguistically, depending on the actual distinctions made and the lexical or grammatical strategies available (e.g., Helmbrecht 2003), and intralinguistically, depending on the different communities and networks involved (e.g., Clyne et al. 2009).

English and Italian contrast markedly when expressing address, with the distinction between formal and informal second-person pronouns in Italian forcibly making explicit what can be left implicit or undefined in English (e.g., McCarthy & O'Keefe 2003; Murray 2002; Renzi 1995; Scaglia 2003). In Italian the T–V distinction extends to all verb forms and is thus obligatorily codified in the grammatical system of the language. At a first level of generality, the *tu* pronoun is used for informal or familiar address, and the *Lei* pronoun for formal or respectful address. Other devices – namely vocatives[1] – are available in English to mark similar interpersonal positioning in address (Ervin-Tripp 1986), with first names, endearments, familiarisers and kinship terms marking an informal relationship, and honorifics and title plus surname a formal one (Biber et al. 1999). However, vocatives do not constitute obligatory systemic options. In particular, whereas avoidance in English is a strategy readily available to allow interlocutors to opt for neutral forms without any significant losses in communication (Formentelli 2009; Clyne et al. 2009), in Italian evading the choice between *tu* and *Lei* forms results in contrived and artificial exchanges.

Shifts of address mode occur in both English and Italian. Normally they involve a transition from formal to informal address to express a closer, more egalitarian or less respectful relationship. Since Italian possesses an absolute system of address (see Hickey 2003), pronominal transitions tend to occur only once in the course of a relationship and are typically realised as transitions from reciprocal *Lei* or asymmetric *tu-Lei* to a symmetrical and egalitarian *tu*. In common experience, the actual shift is often preceded by an explicit request and may be accompanied by a period of fluctuation if interactants do not feel at ease with the interpersonal implications brought about by the pronominal change (see Morford 1997; Renzi 1995). In English, shifts characteristically involve a transition from formal address or no use of vocatives to first name address. However, they may also entail a period of negotiation (see Clyne et al. 2009).

In the dubbing of English into Italian, transitions of second-person pronouns and verb morphology represent critical moments during the translation and adaptation process as a reflection of the role that they perform in real life relationships (Pavesi 1996; Ulrych 1996). More specifically, translation can be hypothesised to rely on and exploit both the sociolinguistic and pragmatic functions inherent in address. These may vary in response to macrosociological variables such as interlocutors' kinship relationships, gender, relative age, authority and socioeconomic status, as well as interactional variables which include the formality of the setting and the emotional tone between participants in the interaction (Marford 1997).

The remainder of this contribution is organised into two main parts. In Section 2, the various contextual motivations for transitions in pronominal forms in dubbing will be explored in relation to the predictability of address shifts, the interacting semiotic codes on-screen and resultant intersemiotic and linguistic explicitations. In Section 3, the functions of address in film translation as narrative will be discussed by showing how shifts resourcefully highlight the diegetic dimensions of films, convey further intensity to crucial moments in the storyline and contribute to character development. Thus, address will emerge as being strongly mediated by translators' creativity.

This explorative analysis of address shifts in dubbing will rely on a selection of 15 American and British films dubbed into Italian dating from 1991 to 2008. The selection includes the films contained in the *Pavia Corpus of Film Dialogue* (Freddi & Pavesi 2009), to which two earlier and one later film have been added to widen the time span considered. The full list of films is provided in the filmography at the end of this contribution.

2. Contextual motivations for address shifts in film translation

As a rule, there is more than one occasion in a text to switch from V to T forms when translating English into a language which codifies address grammatically (Horton 1996). Besides the difficulties connected with the differences in linguistic behaviour between the two cultures, film dubbing poses special problems because of the compression of narration in audiovisual texts and the interplay between the various semiotic codes co-deployed on screen (Paolinelli & Di Fortunato 2005; Pavesi 1996; Ulrych 1996; see also Guillot 2010). At first, two source-text-bound motivations will be discussed which are context-dependent and result from clearly discernible features of film scenes: (1) linguistic motivations deriving from specific choices of address in the original text and (2) semiotic and linguistic motivations which are rooted in the overall fabric of the film. Address-related shifts do not entail substantial variations in the dubbed vis-à-vis original version since the target audience witnesses the same plot development – though through formally different means – as the original audience. On the other hand, when address shifts cannot be ascribed directly to the corresponding pragmatic and sociolinguistic levels in the original dialogue but relate to other semiotic resources, depth is conferred to the translated film as the meanings inherent in pronoun change in the target culture are transferred onto the screen. Such additions are possible given the mismatch between a language that expresses address modes only through lexical means and a language that obligatorily codifies address by means of a specific grammatical apparatus.

In this contribution, translation strategies will be shown to be strongly dependent on verbal as well as non-verbal cues, with the dimensions of multimodality being paramount for the choice of pronouns in films. It will emerge that, address – being triggered by crosslinguistic transfer –represents not only an all-embracing translation problem but also a translational resource.

2.1. Address-related interlinguistic motivations

It must be pointed out from the beginning that when dubbing Anglophone films into Italian, the level of (in)formality of nominal address is generally transferred from the source text to the target text, and vocatives in the form of first-name and other familiar appellatives, title or title plus surname are normally maintained (Hirvonen & Sutinen 2005; Pavesi 1996). These are the two prototypical choices of nominal address available in English taken to parallel the choice between T and V pronouns in other languages. If the first name appears in English, the same vocative will also appear in the dubbed Italian version. Similarly, if the title plus surname are employed as a form of address in English, the title (usually translated and sociolinguistically adapted) plus the surname will be reproduced in Italian.[2] Alternatively, vocatives can simply be omitted in the target text or transferred through a translation shift from the lexical to the grammatical level (see Pavesi 1996).

As for the selection of address pronouns, the analysis of the films in the corpus shows that a transition from a formal to an informal vocative in the source text will often correspond to a shift of address pronoun in translation, from a formal *Lei* to an informal *tu*. For example, in the original version of *Ae Fond Kiss*, when Rukhsana (Casim's sister) meets Roisin (Casim's Irish girlfriend) for the first time, she addresses her with a title plus surname: Miss Hanlon – cf. (1) *infra*. Later on, in a café, Rukhsana switches to Roisin's first name. In the Italian version, the same shift of vocatives occurs, accompanied by a shift from formal *Lei* to the informal pronoun *tu*[3].

(1)
In the street

→	rukhsana	excuse me?. are-are you **miss-- hanlon?**	mi scusi?.. **lei** è la **professoressa hanlon? ((V form))** [Excuse me, are you miss Hanlon?]
	roisin	yeah	sì [yes]
	rukhsana	erm--, my name's rukhsana khan, I'm casim's older sister	eh--, io mi chiamo rukhsana khan, sono la sorella maggiore di casim [I'm called rukhsana khan, I'm Casim's older sister]
	roisin	hi!	salve! [Hi!]

	rukhsana	erm--. is it possible to have a-have a chat with you?	eh--. le posso parlare solo un attimo? [Erm, can I speak to you just for a second?]
	Later in a café		
	waitress	tea?	il tè? [Tea?]
	rukhsana	thanks	per me, grazie [For me, thanks]
	waitress	here you are	ecco [Here]
	roisin	thanks	grazie [Thanks]
	waitress	this is great, thanks ((leaves))	grazie a lei ((leaves)) [Thank you]
→	rukhsana	**roisin**, you must be wondering why-- I've asked to--, well, I've come to see you […]	**roisin**, io penso che-- **tu** possa immaginare?--, il motivo per il quale ho deciso di incontrar**ti** […] **((shift to T))** [Roisin, I think you can imagine the reason why I have decided to meet you]
→	roisin	I love your brother. why can't you accept that?	io amo **tuo** fratello. perché non riuscite ad accettarlo? **((shift to T))** [I love your brother, why can't you accept it?]

Similarly, the lexical and lexico-pragmatic reliance on the source texts is also obvious in the calqued formulas used in the dubbed Italian versions to encourage the shift from formal to familiar address. In no dubbed translation do we find the negotiation strategies (e.g., invitations, requests to opt for T forms, suggestions) which typically lay the ground for a transition of address mode in Italian (Renzi 1995; see also Hickey 2003 for a similar pattern in German). Fixed sequences in English involving first names and introductions are regularly reproduced in Italian translations and transferred quite literally (Paolinelli, Di Fortunato 2005: 69-70, see also Pavesi 1996). In the same film, Casim at first addresses Roisin formally as *Miss Hanlon* (Italian *professoressa Hanlon*). At one point, however, Roisin encourages him to establish a closer relationship by inviting the young man to use her first name by saying *It's Roisin*. The English formula is translated quite literally into Italian as *Mi chiamo Roisin* ('My name's Roisin') and the repaired vocative becomes the trigger for a reciprocal T in the Italian dialogue which follows.

There is further evidence that the original selection of nominal address is carried over into the dubbed Italian text as the negotiations of address

Enriching functions of address shifts in film translation

revolving around the choice of vocative often represented in Anglophone films are regularly transferred to the Italian translation. An example of the repeated use of such interpersonal strategies can be found in *Gran Torino*, in which the relationship between a young priest (Father Janovich) and an older, recently widowed protagonist (Walt Kowalski) is negotiated throughout the film by means of exchanges about how the two parties should address each other. The device is functional to the development of the plot and the characterisation of the widower, who at first rejects the intimacy and spiritual guidance that the priest is offering him, or rather is trying to impose on him, with the choice of the familiarised first name *Walt*. Thus, Walt Kowalski asserts his self-sufficiency and moral independence by requesting to be addressed with a more formal and distant appellative. The Italian version reproduces the same dynamic negotiation of vocatives, intensified by a shift in address pronoun from the familiar *tu* accompanying the familiar vocative to the respectful *Lei* coupled with title plus surname *Mr Kowalski*. The following extract (2) illustrates the first encounter between the priest and Walt Kowalski at Mrs Kowalski's funeral:

(2)
At Mr Kowalki's

→	father janovich	how you holding up. walt?	Come **te** la passi, walt? **((T form))** [How you holding up. Walt?]
	walt kowalski	mister kowalski!	mister kowalski! [Mr. kowalski!]
	father janovich	huh?	eh? [Huh?]
	walt kowalski	mister kowalski. that's my name	mister kowalski. è questo il mio nome [Mr Kowalski. This is my name]
→	father janovich	right! mister kowalski. your wife and I became quite close these last few months. she asked I watch over you when she passed on	d'accordo, mister kowalski.. **sua** moglie e io eravamo amici negli ultimi tempi. prima di morire mi ha chiesto di vigilare su di **lei ((shift to V))** [Alright, Mr Kowalski. Your wife and I were quite close in this last period. Before she died, she asked me to watch over you]

341

In Italian film dubbing, however, the equivalence often designated between first name and familiar pronoun on the one hand and title plus surname and respectful pronoun on the other hand does not automatically occur. Similarly to what Horton (1996: 76) reports for translations from English into German, "translators universally follow the [source language text] in the selection of [title plus surname name] vs. [first name] [...]. This leaves, then, the difficult question of pronominal differentiation". More precisely, Italian dubbing may resort to the fairly restricted combinations of first name plus formal pronoun of address (Hirvonen & Sutinen 2005; Pavesi 1996), sociolinguistically intermediate forms employed by Italian speakers to encode nuances of social and affective meanings that the two poles of the *tu* and *Lei* scale do not readily allow (Renzi 1995; Scaglia 2003).

In the original version of the film *Thelma and Louise*, for example, the shift to first name corresponds to the increasing sympathy and understanding that a police officer (played by Harvey Keitel) feels towards two women escapees. At the end of the film, Keitel, after having systematically adopted title plus surname (*Miss Sawyer*), addresses the woman on the other end of the telephone with her first name (*Louise*):

police officer   it is as if I knew you, louise

The Italian version predictably reproduces the transition of vocative in English whereas it preserves the formal pronoun used on previous occasions:

police officer   mi sembra di conoscer**la**, louise **((V form))**
                        [I seem to know you, Louise]

The resulting pattern is a combination of first name and *Lei* pronoun, an intermediate mode (Clyne et al. 2009) which indexes the police officer's greater power over Louise's actions but simultaneously conveys respect and warmer feelings towards the woman. With such shifts involving a change in vocative but no transition of pronoun, the target text is kept close to the source text (to the benefit of synchronisation), while the relatively unusual combination of first name plus *Lei* contributes to the characterisation of dubbing as a third norm (Pavesi 1996).

To summarise the translational behaviour taking place in relation to shifts of address mode in the Anglophone source text, as a rule a similar shift of vocative can also be observed in the Italian target text: if characters start exchanging first names in English, they will do the same in Italian. However, even though the interlinguistic correspondence between first name in English and informal pronoun in Italian is quite productive, a shift of nominal address does not necessarily correspond to a shift in pronominal address, with the pattern of first name plus formal pronoun representing a clearly recognisable feature of the language of dubbing from English into Italian.

2.2. Address shifts as intersemiotic and linguistic explicitation

So far the transition of address modes in dubbed Italian has been viewed as strictly bound to a change of vocative in English. Nevertheless, there are instances in which address shifts are restricted to the target text since no clear linguistic motivation can be identified in the English source text. In many such cases, translation appears to rely on other semiotic codes in the film, thus adding an enriching extra dimension to the target dialogues (see Paolinelli & Di Fortunato 2005: 69-71). In particular, two situations stand out as situations that trigger transitions to T address; these occur in films, and do not necessarily mirror what happens in spontaneous interaction. First, a shift to T forms typically occurs when intimacy is represented on-screen by means of paralinguistic traits such as intonation and voice quality, as well as body language, physical proximity, kinetic features, gaze and posture. The linguistic alteration in the dubbed version hence corroborates and strengthens what is expressed by means of different semiotic modalities on-screen.

At the beginning of the film *Notting Hill*, an American actress (Anna) has been invited by William – whom she has just met – to clean herself up in his house after he has spilt coffee over her by mistake. On her way out, after a few awkward exchanges, Anna kisses William, shifting from the formal *Lei* they have been exchanging up to that moment to a familiar *tu* – cf. (3) *infra*. It would be unquestionably very unnatural for two Italians to keep using formal address after experiencing physical intimacy. However, it would be equally odd to wait for a kiss before shifting to informal address.

(3)
At William's

william ((in the hall)) so--.. it was nice to meet you. surreal but, erm--, but nice.. sorry. ((opens the door to let her go)) ((anna leaves))...=

((in the hall)) allora--.. è stato bello conoscerla. surreale, ma--. ma bello.. oh, mi scusi ((opens the door to let her go)) ((anna leaves))...=
[So, it was nice to meet you. Surreal but nice. Oh, I'm sorry]

[...]
anna I forgot my other bag

ho dimenticato l'altra busta
[I forgot the other bag]

william oh, right!... ((hands her the bag))

ma certo!, certo... ((hands her the bag))

→	anna	thanks... ((kisses him))...	[But right, right!] grazie... ((kisses him))... [Thanks]
	william	I'm very sorry about the--. "surreal but nice" comment. disaster!	m-mi dispiace molto per--. il commento "surreale ma bello". un disastro! I [I'm very sorry about the comment "surreal but nice". A disaster!]
→	anna	that's ok, I thought the--. apricot and honey thing was the real low point	non fa niente, direi che--. con le albicocche e il miele avevi già toccato il fondo **((shift to T))** [That's ok. I'd say that with the apricots and honey you had already reached the lowest point]

Another typical situation which frequently calls for a shift from V to T forms in Italian dubbing occurs in episodes which contain aggressive behaviour, bursts of rage, quarrels or fights. Shifts to the "T of contempt or anger" (Brown & Gilman 1972: 277) may occur reciprocally or unilaterally when a character is accusing, psychologically intimidating or physically overpowering someone else (see also Hickey 2003: 413). By making an unsolicited shift to the familiar pronoun, speakers express their disappointment with their interlocutors, talk down to them and – more to the point – treat their interlocutors as social inferiors.[4] In a way which is different from common experience in the target community, film dubbing repeatedly introduces shifts to T in the cases of contempt or anger as a result of the frequency of conflictual situations typically represented in films; the latter are used as a means to advance the plot and to make it more involving for the viewer (Cattrysse & Gambier 2008). In *Erin Brockovich*, Erin becomes very angry and upset when she finds out that her absence has been interpreted as a lack of responsibility and that she has been fired. At this point, she storms into her boss's office and – practically shouting – addresses him with *tu* for the first time in the film (4):

(4)
Ed's office

erin to ed	((entering ed's office)) You said to fire me?	((entering ed's office)) hai detto **tu** di licenziarmi? **((shift to T))** [Did you say to fire me?]

On closer inspection, the shifts to T of intimacy and anger described in this section can be interpreted as instances of intersemiotic explicitation, whereby the paralinguistic and non-verbal behaviour in the original version is rendered linguistically as well as by means of a shift in grammatical address in the dubbed version. The translation has an enriching function since it reproduces a sequence in the film (by means of the same images, sounds, intonation). However, at the same time the translation expresses the change in attitude by means of a transition of address modes, which reverberates with additional pragmatic meanings. In addition, intersemiotic explicitation in these cases is at the service of coherence between the translated verbal text and the events or communicative situation represented on screen (Chaume 2004b: 45).[5] In this respect, we may follow Vinay and Darbelnet's definition of explicitation as a translation "technique which consists of making explicit in the target language what remains implicit in the source language because it is apparent from either the context or the situation" (1995: 342). The overall film or film scene, then, represents the context in which the dialogue is embedded, with information spreading across different semiotic levels through translation. As with other instances of the process, a distinction can be drawn between obligatory and optional explicitation, depending on the type of systemic contrast between the two languages involved (Klaudy 1998). With address being a socio-pragmatic phenomenon, absolute obligatoriness in pronoun shifts hardly ever applies. Hence, the translator/adaptor has a degree of leeway and can opt for one mode or another, drawing on the semiotic complex of the film in the knowledge that different interpersonal meanings and effects are obtained by means of different address strategies.

In the discussion of explicitation in address modes, it should be pointed out that non-verbal behaviour may be matched by congruent features of the dialogue, and various linguistic and pragmatic features in the source text may be envisaged as triggers of pronominal changes in the target text. Guillot (2010) provides a systematic account of strategic and tactical solutions centred on such choices of register and pragmatic features in audiovisual translation from French – a language that obligatorily codifies address through pronouns and related morphological features – into English. In that perspective of analysis, shifts in register such as the use of taboo words, the imperative mode and unmitigated, face-threatening acts in English could be viewed as justifying a change of address in Italian. However, the same linguistic features may co-exist with both address pronouns in native Italian and do not necessarily provoke a systematic change in address in the films analysed. Transitions of address in such contexts could be defined as instances of linguistic explicitation (which may work together with intersemiotic explicitation) since a shift from V to T adds an extra dimension to other linguistic choices such as shifts of register, increasing directness or emotional language, all of which can convey a change in interpersonal stance on their own.

Maria Pavesi

The co-existence of linguistic and other semiotic triggers is well exemplified in one of the initial scenes of *The Silence of the Lambs*. An FBI trainee, (Clarice Starling) is sent to interview Hannibal Lecter, a former psychiatrist and psychotic serial killer who is now in jail in the hope that his brilliant insights will be useful in the pursuit of another vicious serial killer. At the beginning of the exchange (5), during the ritual introductions in the Italian version, the two characters exchange respectful pronominal forms until Lecter, having ascertained the young woman's lack of professional status and expertise, unilaterally shifts to T forms:

(5)
Prison, Lecter in his cell

	lecter	((standing)) good morning	((standing)) buon giorno [Good morning]	
→	starling	dr lecter, my name is clarice starling. May I speak with you?	dottor lecter, mi chiamo clarisse starling.. posso parlare con **lei**? **((V form))** [Dr lecter, my name is Clarice Starling. May I speak with you?]	
→	lecter	you're one of jack crawford's, aren't you?	è della squadra di jack crawford, vero? **((V form))** [You're one of Jack Crawford's team, right?]	
	starling	I am, yes	sì, lo sono [Yes, I am]	
	lecter	may I see your credentials?	posso vedere le sue credenziali? [May I see your credentials?]	
	starling	certainly! ((takes credentials out))	certo! ((takes credentials out)) [Certainly!]	
	lecter	closer please… closer! ((both characters move closer, Lecter looking at the papers)) … that expires in one week. you're not real fbi. are you?	più vicino per favore… più vicino ((both characters move closer, Lecter looking at the papers)) … questo scade tra una settimana.. non è proprio dell'fbi, vero? [Closer, please, closer. This expires in one week. You're not really FBI, right?]	
	starling	I'm still in training at the academy	sono ancora in addestramento all'accademia [I'm still in training at the academy]	
	lecter	jack crawford sent a	jack crawford ha mandato una	

Enriching functions of address shifts in film translation

		trainee, to me?	recluta per me? [Jack Crawford sent a trainee to me?]
	starling	yes, I'm a student. I'm here to learn from you.. maybe you can decide for yourself whether or not I'm qualified enough to do that	sì, sono una studentessa. sono qui per imparare da lei.. forse può decidere da sé se sono abbastanza qualificata o no. [Yes, I'm a student. I'm here to learn from you. Maybe you can decide for yourself whether I'm qualified enough or not]
→	lecter	mhm... that is rather slippery of you, agent starling... sit!, please	ahah.. la **tua** è una risposta ingannevole, agente starling... sie**diti**! prego **((shift to T))** [Mhm... your reply is rather deceptive, Agent Starling. sit, please!]

There are several grammatical, pragmatic, paralinguistic and kinetic prompts in the scene that justify the shift to *tu* in the specific turn in which address transition occurs in Italian. Lecter initiates and directs turn-taking, asks questions in an inquisitorial tone and issues unmitigated orders. His general physical attitude is calm, his posture dignified and his gaze cold and searching. Consequently, he takes on a domineering and controlling role with the young woman, who approaches him very apprehensively. The pronominal transition is embedded in a turn where Lecter utters a peremptory imperative ("sit" > *siediti*), preceded by an evaluative judgemental comment, "that is rather slippery of you, agent starling", which in itself signals a position of power. However, the change of address pronoun at that point is clearly a deliberate choice in the translation since *Lei* forms would be equally acceptable given the simultaneous preservation of the formal vocative title plus surname (*agente starling* < "agent starling"). In the Italian dubbing, the option for the pragmatically-marked combination of *tu* and title plus surname linguistically adds and makes explicit the ironic and provocative connotation, which was implicit in the original text.

It should be clear from this example that transitions to *tu* in dubbing translations may be exploited to highlight a differential of power, which may be obvious in the situation but linguistically latent or underrepresented in the original English script. In particular, non-reciprocal shifts – like asymmetric address – index the dominance of one party over the other. As argued by Remael (2003), asymmetries grounded in the dialogue propel the story, a function of address which relates to the narrative dimension of film translation, as will be discussed in the next section.

3. Address shifts in film narrative

The previous sections have shown how address shifts in dubbing from English into Italian typically take place when there are corresponding address shifts in the source texts. In addition, it has been shown that address shifts can also be used as means of increasing the semiotic and linguistic coherence of the audiovisual text. In other words, transitions of address mode in films can be a linguistic device with which the audiovisual target text is enriched through translation. A further function of address shifts that clearly emerges from the analysis is their dramatic role in the fictive worlds represented on-screen. In other words, the transition of address modes occurring in films dubbed from English into Italian do not simply reflect the conventions of the source and target communities or act as intersemiotic and linguistic explicitations. They also acquire a narrative significance specific to the context created on-screen.

The distinction between the translational and fictional dimensions of dubbing (Romero-Fresco 2009) is functional here, with shifts of pronoun being triggered not only by the requirement to transfer dialogue from one language into another within the overall semiotic complex of films, but also by the main aim of these audiovisual texts to narrate a story (Remael 2003, 2008). This is particularly evident when the transitions in address mode are incongruous with the strategies found in real life, which films may implicitly imitate.

It is in fact for the sake of narration that interest is not kindled by static choices of address pronouns, but rather by dynamic transitions from one address mode to the other. Shifts of address pronouns perform several diegetic functions. They may be forward-looking since they point to an intimacy that is growing or, more generally, to the increasing involvement between two characters – either positive or negative. Anticipation is created in the viewer, who is alerted to the development of the story and the characters' future relationships. As is evident from the previous discussion, in many films, there is no consistently predictable point for pronominal switch and quite often translations opt for subjective and creative solutions. When there are many potential triggers or there are no obvious situations in which a shift in the target text is necessarily called for, main characters may be made to adopt informal address from the beginning or very early on in the story. In *Secrets and Lies*, for example, when Hortense speaks for the first time on the phone with Cynthia (her biological mother), she starts by addressing her with *Lei* forms (6). In the telephone call which immediately follows, she switches

Enriching functions of address shifts in film translation

to *tu*, an address pronoun which at this point is quite marked according to Italian standards, as the two women have never met before and are talking on the phone for the first time. In English, no revealing vocative is used by Hortense, who clearly empathises with Cynthia throughout the telephone conversations. In Italian, Hortense maintains a formal address while Cynthia is crying on the phone (*mi spiace, so che questo sarà uno shock per **lei***), but switches to informal address as she resumes the telephone conversation interrupted by Cynthia (*mi spiace tanto / non volevo sconvolger**ti***). The shift propels the story, while at the same time alerting the viewer to the deepening of the relationship between both women.

(6)
At Cynthia's

hortense	((on the phone)) no, it's about elizabeth	((on the phone)) no, riguarda elizabeth [No, it's about Elizabeth]
cynthia	((on the phone)) elizabeth?, elizabeth who?	((on the phone)) elizabeth?, elizabeth chi? [Elizabeth? Elizabeth who?]
hortense	elizabeth purley	elizabeth purley
cynthia	oh!, but she's dead!..	oh!, ma è morta!. [Oh! But she's dead!]
hortense	no, she isn't	non è morta [She isn't dead]
cynthia	she is, darling, I should know!	ma sì, lo saprò io!] [But yes, I should know!]
hortense	I should know!	bè, anch'io [Well, me too]
→ cynthia	look, sweetheart, she's my mother. she went in nineteen sixty one	sen**ti** gioia, è mia madre. se n'è andata nel sessantuno **((T form))** [Listen, love, she's my mother. She went in 1961]
hortense	no, I mean BABY elizabeth purley	no, voglio dire la bambina elizabeth purley [No, I mean baby Elizabeth Purley]

[…]

cynthia	((starts crying))	((starts crying))
→ hortense	look, I'm sorry, I know this must be a	mi dispiace, so che questo sarà uno shock per **lei ((V form))**

349

		shock to you	[I'm sorry. I know this will be a shock for you]
	cynthia	((hangs up and pukes))	((hangs up and pukes))
	cynthia	((phone rings)) ((on the phone)) listen, darling, what is it you want?	((phone rings)) ((on the phone)) che cosa vuoi? [What do you want?]
	hortense	((on the phone)) I'm really sorry	((on the phone)) mi dispiace tanto [I'm really sorry]
	cynthia	you mustn't come round here, sweetheart..	non devi venire da queste parti! [You mustn't come around here]
→	hortense	I didn't wanna upset you	non volevo sconvolger**ti** ((shift to T)) [I didn't want to upset you]

Shifts may also have a backward-looking function, that is, they ratify an attraction, an empathy or a conflict which was already manifest in the characters' behaviour. This function is exemplified in *Finding Forrester* when one of the protagonists, Jamal, a black boy, finally shifts to T with William Forrester, a famous recluse writer who he has been visiting for some time, when they go to the stadium together – cf. (7) infra. The shift takes place towards the end of the story, confirming the intense and prolonged mentor-pupil relationship, and at the same time anticipating a major achievement in William's life as he finally overcomes his long-term agoraphobia. Once again, the transition in address mode does not correspond to any univocal linguistic, visual or behavioural feature of the scene since in both adjacent scenes an informal term of address is used in the source text (i.e., *man* and *William*), which could trigger a shift to *tu* in Italian:

(7)
At Forrester's,
Jamal is typing and discussing with Forrester

	jamal	people LOVE that book, man!	ma i lettori adorano il **suo** libro! **((V form))** [But the readers love your book!]

[…]

In front of Forrester's door,
waiting for him

→   jamal   william, man, I actually   william!, ho speso parecchi soldi
                      spent money on these   per quei biglietti!. **ti** sbrighi?
                      tickets!, come on!   **((shift to T))**
                                                       [William! I spent a lot of money
                                                       on these tickets! Hurry up!]

The excerpt above shows an address shift occurring after a break in the storyline as the scene meaningfully changes from inside Forrester's flat to the doorstep. As a matter of fact, it is not an uncommon device in Italian dubbed films to start new scenes with different pronouns and, in so doing, to avoid the exact moment in which the address shift takes place being represented, and instead to introduce a linguistic change that is required by the development in the interpersonal relationship between the characters. By doing this, the transition is located in an undisclosed part of the story, to be inferred by the viewer, thus expanding the narration beyond the fixed temporal and spatial boundaries of the film, and simultaneously safeguarding its socio-pragmatic coherence.

It should be clear by now that the shift to *tu* can have different semiotic and narrative motivations. It is often the translator's/adaptor's choice to latch onto one or more of the potential triggers available to operate the switch at one point rather than another. A final function performed by the transition of pronominal address in dubbing should also be mentioned here because it gives an important contribution to the diegetic dimensions of films. When the address mode is made to shift at a crucial moment in the story, it imparts additional intensity to that event. In addition, if the shift is backward-looking, it may have a cathartic effect on the viewer. In film translation, this linguistic device is said to perform a climactic or culminating function rarely fulfilled in real life (see also Pavesi forthcoming). In *Dead Man Walking*, Matthew Poncelet, an inmate on death row, addresses with the familiar *tu* form Sister Helen, the nun who has generously been his spiritual advisor for several months and has allowed him to die with dignity but does so only at the very end, on his execution bed – cf. (8). He says, *Ti voglio bene* ('I love you'). These are his last words and the pronominal shift in Italian is purposely and forcefully placed here:

(8)
In the execution chamber

     warden   do you have any last   hai qualcosa da dire, poncelet?...
     to   words, poncelet?..   [Do you have anything to say,

matthew		Poncelet?]
matthew	yes, sir, I do...=	sì, signore...=
matthew to mr delacroix	=mister delacroix--. I don't want to leave this world with any hate in my heart.. I ask your forgiveness for what I done. it was a terrible thing I done in taking your son away from you!	=signor delacroix--.. non lascerò questo mondo con l'odio nel cuore. le chiedo perdono per quello che ho fatto. è stato terribile strapparle suo f-figlio in quel modo! [Mr. Delacroix, I will not leave this world with hate in my heart. I ask your forgiveness for what I have done. It was a terrible thing to snatch your son away from you in that way!]
[...]		
→ mattew to sister helen	=I love you ((keeps looking at her))	=**ti** voglio bene ((keeps looking at her)) **((shift to T))** [I love you]
sister helen	((lips movement: I love you too))	((whispering)) **ti** voglio bene anch'io **((T form))** [I love you too]

The injection procedure starts

4. Conclusions

Pronoun shifts in Italian film translation have been shown to derive from similar phenomena in English source texts. However, transitions in address mode in target texts are not restricted to the transfer of vocative shifts. They also code other semiotic features, point forward or backward to the developing action, as well as amplify the intensity of key narrative moments. Therefore, address shifts in dubbed texts may serve several functions separately or concurrently: mirroring or bending the sociolinguistic norms of the source and target communities, linking to the contextual situations in films, and conveying important narrative meanings. Through intersemiotic and linguistic explicitation, transitions of address modes index and emphasise the interpersonal dynamics in the storyline and significantly enrich the target text, thus proving to be an all-encompassing translational resource within the representational, audiovisual and narrative structure of film.

[1] In English, as in Italian, social and personal distance or proximity can also be conveyed by an array of sociolinguistic and pragmatic features. Here, however, we will concentrate on what is prototypically coded and interpreted as address, that is, a means of performing the two basic functions of summoning and identifying addressees.

[2] The situation may become noticeably more complex with the translation of the full range of vocatives available in English, which express nuanced interpersonal meanings at the informal end of the address spectrum (cf. Bruti and Perego, 2008 on subtitling from English into Italian).

[3] Transcription conventions are reported in Appendix 2. Highlighted features and comments on address are in bold.

[4] Shifts expressing disrespect have been reported to be quite common in literature (cf. Brown and Gilman, 1972); more recently they have been discussed in drama translation (Horton 1999), and in subtitling (Guillot 2010), where they have been shown to co-occur with other address shifts to indicate contextual distancing or rapprochement.

[5] Alternatively, it could be accounted for by relying on a wider definition of synchronization, which goes beyond the matching between lip and body movements and dubbed speech to include the overall matching between images, voices and attitudes portrayed on the screen (cf. Mayoral et al.'s (1988) content synchrony).

References

Biber, Douglas et al. 1999. *Longman Grammar of Spoken and Written English*. London: Longman.
Bonsignori, Veronica. 2009. 'Transcribing Film Dialogue: From Orthographic to Prosodic Transcription' in Freddi, Maria & Maria Pavesi (eds.) *Analysing Audiovisual Dialogue: Linguistic and Translational Insights*. Bologna: Clueb. 185-200.
Brown, Roger & Albert Gilman. 1972. 'The Pronouns of Power and Solidarity' in Giglioli, Pier Paolo (ed.) *Language and Social Context*. London: Penguin. 252-282.
Bruti, Silvia & Elisa Perego. 2008. 'Vocatives in Subitles: A Survey across Genre' in Taylor, Christopher (ed.) *Ecolingua: The Role of E-Corpora in Translation, Language Learning and Testing*. Trieste: EUT. 11-51.
Cattrysse, Patrick & Yves Gambier. 2008. 'Screenwriting and Translating Screenplays' in Díaz Cintas, Jorge (ed.) The Didactics of Audiovisual Translation. Amsterdam: John Benjamins. 39-55.
Chaume, Frederic. 2004a. *Cine y Traducción*. Madrid: Cátedra.
Chaume, Frederic 2004b. 'Synchronization in Dubbing. A Translational Approach' in Orero, Pilar (ed.) *Topics in Audiovisual Translation*. Amsterdam: John Benjamins. 36-52.
Clyne, Michael, Norrby Catrin & Jane Warren. 2009. *Language and Human Relations: Styles of Address in Contemporary Language*. Cambridge: Cambridge University Press.
Díaz Cintas, Jorge. 2004. 'In Search of a Theoretical Framework for the Study of Audiovisual Translation' in Orero, Pilar (ed.) *Topics in Audiovisual Translation*. Amsterdam: John Benjamins. 21-34.
Díaz Cintas, Jorge (ed). 2008. *The Didactics of Audiovisual Translation*. Amsterdam: John Benjamins.

Ervin-Tripp, Susan. 1986. 'Sociolinguistic Rules: Alternations and Co-occurrences' in Gumperz, John J. & Dell Hymes (eds.) *Directions in Sociolinguistics: The Ethnography of Communication*. Oxford: Blackwell, 213-250.

Formentelli, Maicol. 2009. 'Address Strategies in a British Academic Setting' in *Pragmatics* 19(2): 179-196.

Freddi, Maria & Maria Pavesi (eds.). 2009. *Analysing Audiovisual Dialogue: Linguistic and Translational Insights*. Bologna: Clueb.

Guillot, Marie-Noëlle. 2010. 'Film Subtitling from a Cross-cultural Pragmatic Perspective: Issues in Linguistic and Cultural representation' in *The Translator* 6(1): 67-92.

Heiss, Christine & Rosa Maria Bollettieri Bosinelli (eds.). 1996. *Traduzione Multimediale per il Cinema, la Televisione e la Scena*. Bologna: Clueb.

Helmbrecht, Johannes. 2003. 'Politeness Distinctions in Personal Pronouns' in Lenz, Friedrich (ed.) *Deictic Conceptualization of Space, Time and Person*. Amsterdam: John Benjamins, 185-203.

Hickey, Raymond. 2003. 'The German Address System: Binary and Scalar at once' in Taavitsainen, Irma & Andreas H. Jucker (eds.) *Diachronic Perspectives on Address Form Systems*. Amsterdam: John Benjamins. 401-425.

Hirvonen, Johanna & Johanna Sutinen. 2005. 'L'Emploi des Termes d'Adresse dans un Corpus de Films: Comparaison entre le Français et l'Italien'. Paper presented at *XVI Congrès des Romanistes Scandinaves* (Universities of Copenhagen and Roskilde, 24-27 August 2005).

Horton, David. 1996. 'Modes of Address as a Pragmalinguistic Aspect of Translation' in Lauer, Angelika et al. (eds.) *Übersetzungswissenschaft in Umbruch: Festschrift für Wolfram Wilss zum 70. Geburtstag*. Tübingen: Gunter Narr. 69-83.

Horton, David. 1999. 'Social Deixis in the Translation of Dramatic Discourse' in *Babel* 45: 53-73.

Klaudy, Kinga. 1998. 'Explicitation' in Baker, Mona (ed.) *Encyclopedia of Translation Studies*. London: Routledge: 80-84.

Mayoral, Roberta, Dorothy Kelly & Natividad Gollardo. 1988. 'Concept of Constrained Translation: Non-linguistic Perspectives of Translation' in *Meta* 33(3): 356-67.

McCarthy, Michael J. & Anne O'Keefe. 2003. '"What's in a Name?": Vocatives in Casual Conversations and Radio Phone-in Calls' in Pepi, Leistyna & Charles F. Meyer (eds.) *Language Structure and Language Use*. Amsterdam: Rodopi, 153-185.

Morford, Jannet. 1997. 'Social Indexicality in French Pronominal Address' in *Journal of Linguistic Anthropology* 7(1): 3-37.

Murray, Thomas E. 2002. 'A New Look at Address in American English: The Rules have Changed' in *Names* 50(1): 43-61.

Orero, Pilar (ed.). 2004. *Topics in Audiovisual Translation*. Amsterdam: John Benjamins.

Paolinelli, Mario & Eleonora Di Fortunato. 2005. *Tradurre per il Doppiaggio. La Trasposizione Linguistica dell'Audiovisivo: Teoria e Pratica di un'Arte Imperfetta*. Milano: Hoepli.

Pavesi, Maria. 1996. 'L'Allocuzione nel Doppiaggio dall'Inglese all'Italiano' in Heiss, Christine & Rosa Maria Bollettieri Bosinelli (eds.). 1996. *Traduzione Multimediale per il Cinema, la Televisione e la Scena*. Bologna: Clueb. 117-130.

Pavesi, Maria. (forthcoming). 'Exploring the Role of Address Shifts in Film Translation: An Extended Illustration from Crash'. To appear in Chiaro, Delia et al. Bologna: Bologna University Press.

Remael, Aline. 2003. 'Mainstream Narrative Film Dialogue and Subtitling: A case study of Mike Leigh's Secrets & Lies' in *The Translator* 9(2): 225-247.

Remael, Aline. 2008. 'Screenwriting, Scripted and Unscripted Language: What do Subtitlers Need to Know?' in Díaz Cintas, Jorge (ed). 2008. *The Didactics of Audiovisual Translation*. Amsterdam: John Benjamins. 57- 67.

Renzi, Lorenzo. 1995. 'La Deissi Personale e il Suo uso Sociale' in Renzi, Lorenzo, Giampaolo Salvi and Anna Cardinaletti (eds.) *Grande Grammatica Italiana di Consultazione Vol. 3: Tipi di Frase, Deissi, Formazione delle Parole*. Bologna: Il Mulino. 350-375.
Renzi, Lorenzo, Giampaolo Salvi & Anna Cardinaletti (eds.). 1995. *Grande Grammatica Italiana di Consultazione Vol. 3: Tipi di Frase, Deissi, Formazione delle Parole*. Bologna: Il Mulino.
Romero-Fresco, Pablo. 2009. 'The Fictional and Translational Dimensions of the Language used in Dubbing' in Freddi, Maria & Maria Pavesi (eds.) *Analysing Audiovisual Dialogue: Linguistic and Translational Insights*. Bologna: Clueb. 41-55.
Scaglia, Claudia. 2003. 'Deissi e Cortesia in Italiano' in *Linguistica e Filologia* 16: 109-145.
Ulrych, Margherita. 1996. 'Film Dubbing and the Translatability of Modes of Address: Power Relations and Social Distance in The French Lieutenant's Woman' in Heiss, Christine & Rosa Maria Bollettieri Bosinelli (eds.) *Traduzione Multimediale per il Cinema, la Televisione e la Scena*. Bologna: Clueb. 139-160.
Vinay, Jean-Paul & Jean Darbelnet. 1995. *Comparative Stylistics of French and English: A Methodology for Translation*. Amsterdam: John Benjamins.

Filmography

Ae Fond Kiss, Ken Loach (2004), UK.
Bend it like Beckham, Gurinder Chadha (2002), UK.
Billy Elliot, Stephan Daldry (2000), UK.
Crash, Paul Haggis (2004), USA/Germany.
Dead Man Walking, Tim Robbins 1995, USA.
Erin Brockovich, Stephan Soderbergh, 2000, USA.
Finding Forrester, Gus Van Sant, 2000, USA.
Gran Torino, Clint Eastwood, 2008, USA.
Notting Hill, Roger Mitchell, 1999, UK
Ocean's 11, Stephan Soderbergh, 2001, USA.
One Hour Photo, Mark Romanek, 2002, USA.
Secrets and Lies, Mike Leigh, 1996, UK
Sliding Doors, Peter Howitt, 1998, USA/UK.
Thelma and Louise, Ridley Scott, 1991, USA.
The Silence of the Lambs, Jonathan Demme, 1991, USA.

Appendix 1: List of transcription conventions (simplified version from Bonsignori 2009: 200)

=	latching
+some*	overlapping
+1some*	multiple overlapping in succession
((laughter))	comments
((laughing))	comments preceding the whole utterance

Maria Pavesi

((laughing)) +some*	comments preceding parts of an utterance
"some"	reported speech, titles, reading out
(XXX)	unintelligible speech
CAPITALS	emphasis, stress, loud voice tone, first person singular pronoun *I* in the central column with the English soundtrack
(VOICE)	off-screen voice
,	intonation break without pause
.	brief pause (1 second)
..	medium pause (from 1 to 2 seconds)
…	long pause (3 or more seconds)
?	interrogative tone (grammatical function)
!	exclamatory tone
--	hesitation, interrupted speech
-	false start, self-correction
[some]	back translation

Exploring Greetings and Leave-takings in Original and Dubbed Language[1]

Veronica Bonsignori
University of Pisa (Italy)

Silvia Bruti
University of Pisa (Italy)

Silvia Masi
University of Pisa (Italy)

Abstract

Greetings, leave-takings and good wishes are usually regarded as variously 'complex' expressions because of the array of socio-pragmatic meanings that are associated with them (cf. Coulmas 1979) and consequently represent an area of potential difficulty in translation. The present work builds on the premises of previous research (Bonsignori, Bruti & Masi 2011) and describes translating trends for greetings and leave-takings in film language and in translation. Relevant issues in translating trends especially concern the asymmetry of 'good forms', the coherence of register across turns and between characters, along with peculiar choices pertaining to idiolect and connoted slang varieties. Leave-takings, in particular, include 'formulae' with different degrees of 'fixity' as well as a vast range of expressions of phatic communion, which are here distinguished into two subsets. The present analysis is based on a corpus of fifteen recent films, where language varies diatopically, diachronically and diastratically. A pilot reference corpus containing five original Italian films is exploited to investigate the phenomena at issue in original (i.e. not translated) Italian film dialogue.

Keywords
cross-cultural pragmatics, dubbing, English, film language, greetings, Italian, leave-takings, phatic communication

1. Introduction

The purpose of this contribution is to investigate the use of conversational routines (Coulmas 1979, 1981) such as greetings, leave-takings and good wishes in English film language and in Italian dubbed language. The paper resumes and expands on the findings of previous work (Bonsignori, Bruti, Masi 2011) on this topic, and proposes a revised classification of data.

Both our past and present contributions have shown that conversational routines are usually granted much space in film scenarios in spite of their somewhat phatic and redundant nature – because the act of greeting/leave-taking may be quite evident from the visuals – as they establish a relational function among interactants. Hence, although some inevitable asymmetry in the English and Italian repertoires can be observed, a congruent mapping of these formulae should be pursued if the representation of social dynamics in the original and dubbed version is meant to be coherent. In what follows we investigate what happens in the process of transfer, not only when the two languages display dissimilar trends, but also when maintaining register coherence or idiosyncratic choices – e.g. use of slang, verbal habits and the like – seems to be essential to the development of the film narrative. Although we build on a previous classification of conversational routines, we attempt to distinguish different degrees of fixity, especially as far as the category of leave-takings is concerned.

Alterations may occur in the process of translation due to several reasons. In order to evaluate the impact of the translating process on the results for Italian dubbing, we pursue a comparison of conversational routines in translated Italian with the same routines in Italian original films.

The corpus we used in the past now contains fifteen films of British or American productions: the first component consisted of 9 films (*The English Patient* [EP], *Oscar and Lucinda* [OL], *Sliding Doors* [SD], *Bridget Jones's Diary* [BJD], *Love Actually* [LA], *Green Street Hooligans* [GSH], *Match Point* [MP], *Becoming Jane* [BJ], *Music and Lyrics* [ML]), to which we have added six more films (*In Her Shoes* [IHS], *The Devil Wears Prada* [DWP], *The Holiday* [H], *The Duchess* [D], *Revolutionary Road* [RR], *Sex and the City – The Movie* [SC]).

In order to better evaluate the results obtained for translated Italian in dubbing, we have extended a "Pilot" corpus of Italian productions that we started to assemble in our previous contribution (Bonsignori, Bruti, Masi 2011). Now, it counts five films, namely *L'ultimo bacio*, *Ma che colpa abbiamo noi*, *Io e Napoleone*, *Manuale d'Amore 2 (capitoli successivi)* and *Tutta la vita davanti*, whose genres and setting could be compared, to some extent, with those of the films in the main corpus.

The paper has the following layout: section 2 presents a revised version of the classification criteria proposed in our past work, while the subsequent ones are devoted to the discussion of data and concluding remarks.

2. Revision of categories and exemplification

In this work as well as in the previous one the organisation of data has been based on a match of linguistic forms with their marginal, albeit salient, positions in exchanges and their interactional (*vs.* transactional) functions – henceforth functional parameters or macro-functions. On the whole, the choice of linguistic forms covers such heterogeneous material as greetings and leave-takings, vocatives, and expressions of phatic communion (cf. Laver 1981; also see Masi 2008; for a discussion of the interrelatedness, functions and relevance of such expressions to our study, the reader is referred to Bonsignori, Bruti, Masi 2011). Relevant functional parameters are, instead, Openings (O), Introductions (I) – which tend to correlate with sequence initial turns in exchanges – and Closings (C) – which tend to correlate with final turns. In the present account, the functional parameter of Wishes (W) has been added, too – which is rather flexible as to sequential positioning.

Importantly, the present contribution proposes a more explicit and fine-grained description of the linguistic categories fulfilling the macro-functions of Openings, Closings, etc, than our past work. In particular, we have attempted to detect different degrees of fixity within the category of leave-takings – i.e. they have been subdivided into two groups, $\ell 1$ and $\ell 2$ (see below).

Another major point concerns the category of expressions of phatic communion. In fact, the diverse nature of items in this category, as emerging from our findings, has led us to devise a provisional hybrid group – see the label p/x below – which is quite comprehensive and in need of further refinements.

Here is the complete revised list of linguistic categories:

- g > greetings proper, e.g. *hi, hello, hey, good morning*;
- i > introductory formulae, e.g. *nice to meet you, how do you do, pleasure, It's me/ my name is...* (on the phone);
- v > vocatives, e.g. *darling, Mr President, is that Joan?* (in phone calls) – the speaker does not know who is speaking, does not recognise his/her interlocutor and the expression could be replaced with a name;
- $\ell 1$ > leave-takings with formulaic expressions, e.g. *good forms, bye bye, see you, (We/I'll) see you later, farewell*;
- $\ell 2$ > leave-takings with slightly less formulaic expressions. These usually involve additions and/or variations, as well as more restricted applicability to situations of use, *vis-à-vis* more formulaic leave-takings (cf. *see you* or *see you later* vs. the more specific *see you at my wedding*); this category also covers expressions with motion verbs, which are rather fixed in their format, but manifest the intention of leaving rather than expressing a salutation, e.g. *must go, I'm off*;
- w > good wishes, e.g. *good luck, have fun, cheers* (in toasts);

- *p/x* > *p* = more or less formulaic expressions of phatic communion (sometimes also called *small talk*, see Coupland 1992, 2003), e.g. *How are you?, Good to see you!*, along with less formulaic speech acts – e.g. thanking, apologising, promising – that typically start or close the exchange and which have, for example, the function of defusing the potential hostility of silence at the beginning of an exchange or that of mitigating and consolidating at the end (see Laver 1981 and Bonsignori, Bruti, Masi 2011);
- *x* = this stands for a hybrid category of speech acts admittedly in need of further investigation. Although such speech acts represent either a) the very first turn of speech or b) the last one in a conversational exchange, they do not appear to fulfil any of the phatic functions associated with expressions that typically occur in the Opening or Closing phases of interaction. The following example, for instance, proposes an Opening consisting of directive acts which clearly do not have any initiatory or exploratory function (on this and other relevant phatic functions, see Laver 1981): [DWP] *Pick up my shoes from Blahnik and then go get Patricia.* Similarly, the next example shows a Closing consisting of a negatively oriented expressive act with no mitigating or consolidating function (Laver 1981): [ML] *You people disgust me.*

The symbol *m* has been used for classifying mimicry in relevant positions (e.g. bowing, curtsying, waving), while the asterisk '*' has been used to highlight 'fake' tokens of relevant speech acts (see e.g. 6 further on).

Compared to what was proposed in our previous account, the situational categories related to the medium of communication have been expanded too:

- (T) > telephone conversation (including intercom and radio programmes)
- (L) > letters, written messages
- (C) > internet chats
- (sms) > text messages
- (E) > e-mails.

Below are examples of some kinds of matchings of linguistic and functional categories in our classification. Example (1) is a typical case of Opening with an exchange of greetings 'proper'. Examples (2) and (3)

Exploring greetings and leave-takings in original and dubbed language

illustrate some of the expressions that can occur in Closing sequences. Notice, in particular, the difference between $\ell 1$ in (2) and $\ell 2$ in (3). Example (2) also shows a composite sequence of expressions typically occurring in Closing position – where the repeated acts of *thanking* are labelled as *p*, '*see you (later)*' as $\ell 1$ and '*guys*' as *v*.

(1) [IHS]

O-*g*	Jim	[...] Oh, good morning.
O-*g*	Maggie	Hi.

(2) [IHS]

C-*p*-$\ell 1$-*v*	Maggie	So, thanks for the ride. Thanks for the drinks and the fun, and, uh, we'll see you guys later.

(3) [IHS]

C-$\ell 2$	Amy	(to Rose) I gotta go.

Example (4) proposes an Introductory exchange, while (5) is a case of expression of good Wishes – on the occasion of an engagement celebration, namely Rose Feller and Simon Stein's. In example (6), Rose and Simon are going to a wedding and the scene takes place in Simon's car. Rose finds out that one of her shoes has fallen apart, so she takes it off and moves the loose heel repeatedly up and down with her hands, as if it were a puppet's mouth uttering words, a sort of 'fake' speaker in the hands of a ventriloquist through which she expresses her complaints (she is angry because she has no choice but going to her friends' wedding wearing a pair of shoes one of which has a broken heel she was not aware of).

(4) [IHS]

I-*v*-*i*	Ella	Mrs. Lefkowitz, this is my granddaughter Maggie Feller.
I-*g*	Mrs Lefkowitz	Hello!

(5) [IHS]

W-*w*	Stein's father	Mazel tov!

361

(6) [IHS]

| *O-g4 | Rose | (while moving the broken heel of her shoe) "Hi. Hi. Hi! I can talk 'cause I have a mouth." My heel has a mouth! |

Finally, (7) and (8) provide examples of the hybrid category *p/x*. In fact, in such cases, we can hardly speak of expressions of phatic communion. Example (7), for instance, displays a directive act aiming towards the abrupt interruption of any kind of communication – the speaker, Carrie Bradshaw, is a very upset bride on her wedding day who has just found out that her boyfriend, Mr Big, is not going to marry her anymore. Example (8), instead, shows the absence of any interactional turn at the beginning of the exchange – a typical feature of the character of Miranda, who tends to get 'straight to the point' in her conversational exchanges.

(7) [SC]

| C-*p/x* | Carrie | Get me out of here! Get me out of here! |

(8) [SC]

| O-*p/x* | Miranda | (by way of entering resort) You have wifi? |

3. Qualitative analysis

The analysis of data has highlighted different phenomena that deserve attention, which will be discussed in the subsequent sections. The main trends cluster around qualitative asymmetry in the mapping, idiolect, slang and more substantial linguistic variation.

3.1. Asymmetry in mapping

The present section analyses various examples displaying general asymmetry in mapping at different levels and through different means.

A first case of asymmetry is due to **deletion**, that is the cancellation of all linguistic elements in the original opening sequence, thus creating a gap in the dubbed version, as shall be seen in (9) below:

(9) [IHS]

| O-g-v | Rose | Hey, dad! | Ø |
| O-g-v | Dad | Hello, sweetie! | Ciao, tesoro! |

Conversely, there may also be cases in which the dubbed version displays **additional elements** that are not actually present in the original soundtrack. For example, in (10) the opening sequence is simply characterised by the vocative '*Lady*' in the English version, while in the Italian one there is still a vocative – even though the use of an adjective is preferred – followed by a greeting proper (> O-v-g):

(10) [SC]

| O-v | Carrie | Lady! | Bellissima! Ciao! |

Moreover, asymmetry may be conveyed by the use of a different linguistic element with respect to the original sequence, thus producing a **change of category**. For instance, the following example from *The Holiday* shows that the English opening sequence consisting of a vocative in initial position, then followed by a greeting proper and an introduction, is somehow subverted by the use of an expression of phatic communion '*come stai?*' in place of the greeting '*hi*' in the Italian dub (O-v-g-i > O-v-p/x-i):

(11) [H]

| (T) O-v-g-i | Amanda | Iris, hi! It's Amanda! | Iris! Come stai? Sono Amanda! |

Differently, in (12) there is a loss of socio-pragmatic meaning in dubbing, due to the lack of suitable equivalents for the vocative '*mate*', similarly to all other generic descriptors, e.g. *guy, pal, dude, chap, babe,* etc, whose second occurrence in the original is translated as the substantivised quality adjective '*bello*' (roughly, 'beautiful/beauty') in the Italian dub. Also, the multifunctional '*cheers*' is ambiguous between *thanking* and *closing*, and the repetition of Italian '*ciao*' by itself neutralises the effect of peer-to-peer male solidarity which is in fact conveyed by the more overtly colloquial register of the English turn. The impact of lip-synch does not seem to be of much relevance here: although Gerry's face is momentarily focused upon while pronouncing '*cheers*', the character's face and mouth are hardly visible, as they are turned towards the phone receiver.

(12) [SD]

| (T) C-ℓ2-v-ℓ2-ℓ1 | Gerry | Ah, really, mate! No, what a drag! Oh no, yeah. Ok, yeah, sure! Sure, sure, yeah! yeah, I'll help you. Yeah, yeah! Cheers, mate! Cheers! Bye! (hangs up) | Ah, davvero mi dici Ø -- no, che fregatura! No! Sì, sì! Certo, certo, sì! Sì sì! Ti aiuto io! Sì! Sì! Ciao bello! Ciao, ciao! |

Another important way in which asymmetry is conveyed is the **change in the degree of formality**, as shown in (13) below, where Simon uses the colloquial and informal interjection '*hey*' to greet Rose, which is rendered with the more formal Italian greeting '*buongiorno*' in the dubbed version:

(13) [IHS]

| O-g-p/x | Simon | Hey! Danvers got busy. He sent me instead. | Buongiorno. Danvers aveva un impegno e ha mandato me. |

Such changes in the degree of formality are even clearer in extract (14), still from *In her Shoes*. Here, Maggie, who works as a social worker in a rest home in Florida, introduces her sister Rose to some elderly people who are hosted there. As can be observed from the conversational exchange in the original soundtrack, the relationship between Maggie and the group of elderly people is quite confidential, in spite of the difference in age. Indeed, on the one hand, the old ladies/men address to the young woman simply using her name '*Maggie*', and on the other, Maggie employs '*Mr*' or '*Mrs*' followed by quite informal greeting formulae, such as '*hi*', '*hello*' and '*hey*'. In the dubbed version, instead, we can observe the use of different translating options, ranging from the more neutral, less informal and *passepartout* Italian greeting '*salve*', to the definitely informal greeting '*ciao*'. However, Maggie's turn '*Looking good, Mrs Klein!*' has been completely omitted in the Italian dub, probably because its translation would have caused an evident mismatch on the level of formality, with the use of the more formal personal pronoun '*lei*' next or close to more colloquial greeting forms like '*ciao*'. Finally, one last remark on Maggie's last turn. First, she tells her sister Rose about a group of old men she calls 'The Bench', as they are former lawyers, thus highlighting their high position in society. Then, she addresses them using the vocative '*gentlemen*', thus recognising their social status, followed by the informal greeting '*hey*', which mirrors their confidential and close relationship. In the dubbed version, first of all, the term '*lawyers*' is translated into Italian with a higher title, corresponding to the English 'magistrates', probably with the aim of emphasising the importance of their social position. Second, when addressing to them, Maggie uses a pompous and very formal greeting formula corresponding roughly to 'respects', then followed by the vocative, failing in this way to reproduce the same kind of relationship expressed in the original soundtrack.

(14) [IHS]

O-*g-v-i*	Maggie	Hello, ladies! This is my sister.	Salve, signore, questa è mia sorella.
O-*v*	Old Ladies	Maggie.	Ciao, Maggie.
O-*g*	Lady 1	Hi.	Ciao.
	Maggie	Ø	Salve.
O-*g-v*	Lady 2	Hi, Maggie.	Ø
C-*w*	Maggie	Yep. Have a good day!	Arrivederci.
O-*g-v*	(...) Maggie	Hey, guys!	Salve, ragazzi!
O-*g-v*	Old Men	Hi, Maggie!	Ciao, Maggie!
I-*i*	Maggie	This is my sister Rose.	Questa è mia sorella Rose.
I-*g-v*	Old Men	Hello, Rose!	Rose.
O-*p/x-v*	(...) Maggie	Looking good, Mrs Klein!	Ø
O-*g-v*	Woman	Hi, Maggie!	Ciao, Maggie!
O-*g-v*	Maggie	Hi, ladies!	Salve, signore!
O-*v-g*	(...) Maggie	(to Rose) I call these guys "The Bench". They're all former lawyers. (to Old Men) Gentlemen, hey!	E quelli della Poltrona! Sono tutti ex-magistrati. Omaggi, signori!
O-*g-v*	Old Men	Hi, Maggie!	Ciao, Maggie!

3.2. Idiolect and slang

Other interesting cases in the transposition of greetings and leave-takings relate to instances in which linguistic variation is involved, and more specifically **idiolect** and slang.

Typical idiolectal features of a character's way of talking may sometimes be rendered with the same form in the dubbed version. Such features may occur either in the opening or closing sequence. Example (15) shows Miranda's typical opening with an aggressive directive, translated with an apocopic Imperative in Italian:

(15) [DWP]

| O-*p/x* | Miranda | Pick up the polaroids from the lingerie shot. | Va' a prendere le polaroid del servizio sulla lingerie. |

while in (16) the same character closes off debate with the frequent turn of phrase '*that's all*', which is always rendered with the expression '*è tutto*' in the Italian dub. In the original there are seven occurrences, one of which in a telephone conversation, quite a high number given the limited time of a film narrative. The expression in Italian doesn't sound particularly natural and seems to suggest that interference occurred in the translating process. Similar findings are confirmed by Gómez Capuz (2001a: 813, but see also Gómez Capuz 2001b, Chaume, García 2001), who says that

> la interferencia pragmática y cultural en los doblajes peninsulares actuales de películas y serials norteamericanas no es muy acusada. Sin embargo, resulta algo más preocupante la reiteración de ciertos anglicismos pragmáticos: así, el empleo de *¿sí?* (< *yes?*) como rutina discursiva al contestar una llamada (telefónica o de otro tipo), las fórmulas de cierre discursivo *eso es todo* (< *that is all*) y *¡olvídalo!* (< *forget it*).[2]

The Italian translating option '*è tutto*' thus seems to be an instance of translation routine (cf. among others Pavesi 2006: 48-49) – i.e. an expression that tends to occur with regularity in translation but is not necessarily typical of natural conversation.

(16) [DWP]

| C-*p/x* | Miranda | Clearly I'm going to have to do that myself because the last two you sent me were | È chiaro che dovrò pensarci da sola, visto che le ultime due che mi hai mandato erano |

		completely inadequate, so send her in. That's all.	totalmente inadeguate. Perciò falla entrare. È tutto.

However, the presence of idiolectal forms may also lead to divergences in dubbing. For instance, the character of Louise in *Sex & the City* is quite direct and abrupt when speaking on the phone, as shown in example (17), which is characterised by a scanty use of phatic talk in the original soundtrack. Conversely, in the target text explicitation is preferred, with the use of a greeting proper in the opening sequence and an expression of thanking in the closing one, which both make the character sound more polite.

(17) [SC]

(T) O-*i-i*	Louise	(on the phone) Carrie Bradshaw, this is Louise. [...]	Salve, sono Louise da parte della signorina Bradshaw. [...]
(T) C-*p/x*		I'll let her know you called. (hangs up)	Grazie.

A certain linguistic difficulty in translation may also be represented by the use of **slang** in the source text. Indeed, due to the absence of straightforward correspondents in the target language, such slangy expressions often undergo neutralisation in the Italian dub. An example is the closing formula '*so long*' in (18), whose use is both diachronically and diatopically marked. As a matter of fact, the film in which it occurs is *Revolutionary Road*, which is set in the mid-1950s in the suburbs of Connecticut, in the USA. So, the use of such an old American slangy expression in the conversational exchange contributes to providing an element of authenticity to the scene analysed, which is not at all preserved in the Italian version, since it is totally levelled out.

(18) [RR]

C-*w*	April	Have a good day!	Buona giornata!
C-*ℓ2*	Frank	Ok, then. So long.	Bene, allora. A dopo.

However, neutralisation is not the only option in dubbing. In (19), from the same film, the two versions display a clash in the register employed and a lack of internal coherence within the turn in the Italian dub. In English, the middle-aged bourgeois neighbour of April Wheeler, Mrs Givings, employs very colloquial and informal expressions, such as '*scoot*' and '*toodle-oo*', which on the one hand portray the close and friendly relationship between the two women, while on the other the use of the archaic version of 'goodbye', namely '*toodle-oo*', is coherent with the times in which the film is set – i.e. 1955. The Italian version attempts at conveying the same social features with the verb '*schizzare*' for '*scoot*', which however does not seem to be a suitable translating option for the '50s, as it sounds quite modern. Indeed, results from our previous work (Bonsignori, Bruti, Masi 2011) indicate that the Italian verb '*schizzare*' is a frequent choice for the translation of different colloquial English verbs, such as '*dash*' (in BJD) and 'we gotta *book*' (in ML), thus suggesting that it may be an Italian translation routine.

(19) [RR]

| C-ℓ2-ℓ2 | Mrs Givings | I must scoot. Toodle-oo! | Devo schizzare. Baci baci! |

3.3. More substantial variation

Instances of more substantial variation can also be observed in the corpus. For example, there are cases of misinterpretation of mimicry, or at least cases in which the adaptor gives a different interpretation of the meaning conveyed by mimicry. In (20) Maggie gives her answer to her grandmother's offer to help by shaking her head. Her mimicry adds an ancillary shade of meaning of light sarcasm to her positive answer. Conversely, in the Italian dubbed version, apparently a more straightforward interpretation of Maggie's mimicry is preferred, so that she answers negatively, thus irreparably losing the nuance of sarcasm present in the original soundtrack.

(20) [IHS]

| C-p/x | Ella | So you'll call me if you need anything? | Chiamami se ti serve qualcosa. |
| C-p/x | Maggie | (shakes head) Yeah. | No, non credo. |

There are also some cases of literal translation, which convey unnatural and artificial effects to the dubbed version, as in (21) below:

(21) [RR]

| C-p/x | Frank | If it's alright with you, April, I'm gonna go use the bathroom, ok? | Se non hai obiezioni, April, adesso vado a usare il bagno, va bene? |

4. Quantitative analysis

Our quantitative analysis of data proposes: a) some figures from the English film corpus, b) some about the section of films in dubbed Italian, and c) some from our Pilot corpus of Italian films.

4.1. Some figures from the English film corpus

The quantitative overview of functional macro-categories in our corpus of English films shows great representativeness of sequence initial categories (see Figure 1). Openings, that is, are the most frequent macro-function (1,122 tokens out of a total of 2,240, i.e. 50% of macro-categories in our data), followed by Closings (762 tokens, 34%), Introductions (304 tokens, 14%), and, finally, by Wishes (52 tokens, 2%).

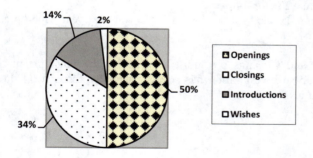

Figure 1. Overview of macro-categories in English (Total 2240)

In our data, the types of combinations of macro-functions with linguistic categories are quite varied. Close inspection, so far, has centred on simpler patterns consisting of one linguistic category per macro-function (see Figure 2). Within Openings, the most frequent type of simple combination is with greetings (cf. O-g, 39% of all Openings), followed by the hybrid category p/x – i.e. expression of phatic communion in need of further refinements, which partly explains the high incidence of the category on total figures, cf. 38% – vocatives (19%), and by introductory formulae (*i*) and mimicry (m) – representing a mere 2% in each case. As to Closings, the most frequent combination is with *p/x* (60%) – probably due to its hybrid nature – followed by *ℓ2* (15%) and *ℓ1* (13%), while less represented combinations are with vocatives and expressions of good wishes (4% in each case), with mimicry and introductory formulae even further down the quantitative scale. In the case of Introductions, the most frequent combination is with introductory formulae (45%), then with greetings (28%), *p/x* (15%), vocatives (11%) and mimicry (1%). Finally, in the macro-function of Wishes we find expressions of good wishes (71%), *p/x* (19%), and vocatives (10%).

In fact, the quantitative complexity of combinatory patterns ranges from a minimum of one linguistic item per macro-category (see examples 22 and 23 below) to a maximum of four in Openings (see example 24, viz. *g* corresponds to '*Hey*', *v* to '*Emily*', *i* to '*it's Andy*', *p/x* to '*Don't hang up, I have a favor to ask you*') and three in Closings (see 25, where *p/x* corresponds to the directive '*Go back to sleep*', *ℓ2* to '*I'll see you next year*' and *ℓ1* to '*Good night*'):

(22) [D] Charles Grey: Morning. O-*g*
(23) [RR] April: Bye. C-*ℓ1*
(24) [DWP] Andy: Hey, Emily, it's Andy. Don't hang up, I have a favor to ask you. (T) O-*g-v-i-p/x*
(25) [SC] Miranda: Go back to sleep. I'll see you next year. Good night. (T) C-*p/x-ℓ2-ℓ1*

As Openings and Closings are, quite expectedly, the most prominent functions, quantitative investigation has so far especially focused on those two macro-categories.

Exploring greetings and leave-takings in original and dubbed language

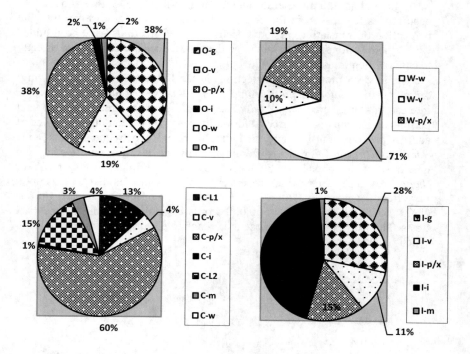

Figure 2. Overview of combination tokens in the corpus

4.2. Data about dubbing

In the following paragraphs types and tokens of greetings and leave-takings are detailed in the dubbing of the films in the corpus.

4.2.1. Greetings

The total number of greetings in English films amounts to 588 instances (see Figure 3). The first six options in terms of frequency are the following: '*hi*', '*hello*', '*hey*', '*good morning*', '*welcome*', '*good evening*', thus showing informal formulae next to slightly more formal good forms. Interestingly, some good forms also occur in their shortened forms (e.g. '*morning*', '*afternoon*') and have thus been considered separately. Among the least frequent options there are also some foreign expressions of salutation, such as '*bonjour*', '*buenos dias*', etc.

371

In the Italian dub the overall number of greetings is 541, thus showing 47 occurrences fewer than in the original. This detail should however not slant perception of translation, as some occurrences of greetings have been added where there is none in the original, so the figure does not correspond directly to cases of non translation.

The first six most frequent greetings in the Italian dub are the following: '*ciao*', '*salve*', '*buongiorno*', '*pronto*', '*ehi*', '*buonasera*' (see Figure 4). The interesting result here is that '*salve*' seems to be a convenient solution, that permits an intermediate degree of formality, very often avoiding the choice of address pronoun. Furthermore, in Italian there are two frequent items – i.e. '*ciao*' and '*pronto*' – which differentiate between face-to-face greeting and greetings on the phone, but which correspond in English to either '*hi*' or '*hello*'. An observation which deserves further attention is that '*ehi*' is not a very frequent word in Italian spontaneous talk: in fact, in the LIP Corpus (1993: 531), which includes 500,000 words of spoken Italian, it appears 9 times. This seems to suggest close adherence to the original and possible lip synch requirements.

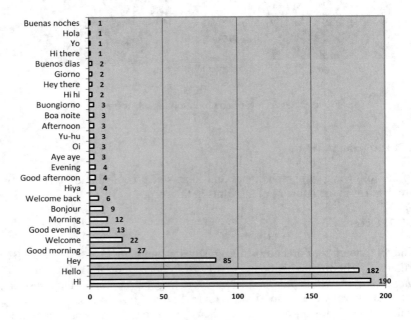

Figure 3. Types of O-g in English (Total 588)

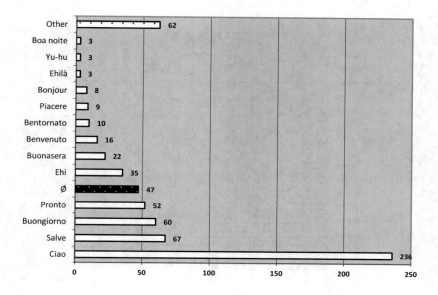

Figure 4. Translating options for O-*g* in Italian dub (Total 541)

4.2.2. Leave-takings

The overall number of greetings in English films amounts to 130 occurrences, many fewer than greetings proper. The first six for frequency of occurrence are: '*bye*', '*good night*', '*see you*', '*goodbye*', '*night*', '*bye bye*' (see Figure 5). As is quite evident, the same forms appear in the more or less formal variants – i.e. '*bye*' and '*bye bye*', '*night*' and '*good night*'.

The reduction in the translation for dubbing is less striking than for greetings, as there are 123 occurrences of leave-takings with formulaic language, still considering that the 7 occurrences fewer are not all 'gaps' as new leave-takings have been introduced. In the Italian dub the first six items for frequency are the following: '*ciao*', '*buonanotte*', '*ci vediamo*', '*arrivederci*', '*addio*' and '*notte*' (see Figure 6). At least in the case of '*buonanotte*' and '*notte*', the same variation that is observed in the original is kept. The occurrence of '*ci vediamo*' as the third most frequent item is quite surprising, as the comparison with the Pilot Italian corpus confirms (see Section 5). The inclusion of '*addio*' in the list of top frequent occurrences is also quite astonishing as it is highly formal and obsolete – so adequate in costume dramas but not in contemporary scenarios – also given that there is also '*arrivederci*', which translates more or less the same meaning.

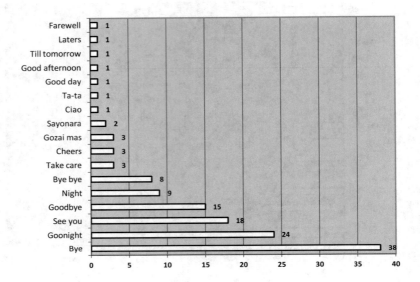

Figure 5. Types of C- $\ell 1$ in English (Total 130)

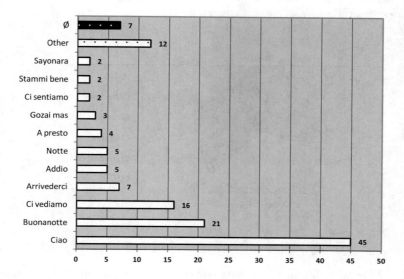

Figure 6. Types of C- ℓ1 in Italian dubbing (Total 123)

5. Pilot Italian Film corpus

The Pilot Corpus of Italian films was enlarged with respect to the original one analysed in our previous work (Bonsignori, Bruti, Masi 2011), with the addition of two films, reaching a total of five (see Section 1). Such a change produced interesting results with reference to both greetings and more formulaic leave-takings, ℓ1. The last category type was here analysed for the first time, since in our previous work we only focused on greetings in Italian film language comparing it to Italian dub.

As regards greetings, Figure 7 below gives a general overview of the most frequent forms that occur in the five Italian films analysed. Interestingly, the most frequent greeting form is '*ciao*' with 48 tokens on the total 129, and not '*buongiorno*', as shown by the preliminary analysis in Bonsignori, Bruti, Masi (2011), which however represents the second most frequent form (43 occurrences). Both greeting types comply with the findings on the Italian dub (see Section 4.2.1.), even though another striking difference can be noticed if comparing the two genres. More specifically, a very frequently used greeting option in dubbing is the *passepartout* '*salve*', which is ranked in the second position, while in Italian film language it does not seem to be a very typical greeting form, with only 2 occurrences. Indeed, '*salve*' is part of the general category named 'Other', together with other expressions such as '*ehi*', '*benvenuto/i*', '*ué*', '*bentornata*' and mimicry.

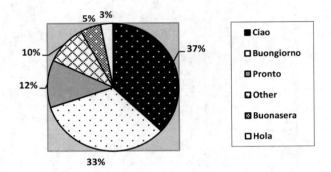

Figure 7. Overview of O-*g* Types in the Pilot Italian film Corpus

As regards formulaic leave-takings (see Figure 8), the form that is mainly used is '*ciao*', with 84 occurrences out of the total 157, followed at a remarkable distance by '*arrivederci*' (21 occurrences), '*buonanotte*' (16 occurrences) and '*addio*' (9 occurrences). These results seem to comply with those relating to the Italian dub (see Section 4.2.2.), even though the quite frequent translating option '*ci vediamo*' never occurs in Italian filmic speech, where we can find only 3 occurrences of a similar expression, namely '*ci vediamo dopo*', which is classified in the category 'Other'.

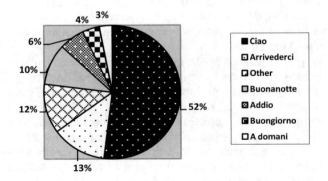

Figure 8. Overview of C-ℓ*1* Types in the Pilot Italian film Corpus

6. Conclusion

What has emerged from this study is that conversational routines are numerous and crucial in the description of characters and their relationships. Both the choice of types and their translation are strongly influenced by film genre: to give just one example, in the film *The Duchess* there are no Closings with formulaic leave-takings, but 16,7% of Closings are performed through mimicry – e.g. silent bowing and curtseying (C-*m*) – whereas, still in the same film, Openings with greetings proper are not very frequent (3,5%) when compared with Openings with vocatives (28,15), due to the rather rigid and hierarchical nature of social relationships at the time when the story is set.

Another general trend emerging is a certain tendency to employ some so-called 'pragmatic anglicisms' (cf. Gómes Capuz 2001: 813 for Spanish) – e.g. expressions that are translated literally and whose form and usage in the target language do not sound natural. A case in point is the closing formula *'that's all'* > *'è tutto'* in [DWP], but also *'schizzare'* as a translating option for different expressions across different films in the corpus (see Section 3.2.).

The quantitative comparison of data also suggested that omissions of forms – i.e. instances of greetings, leave-takings and good wishes that are not translated – are counterbalanced by additions – i.e. cases where translators have inserted other instances in different places.

Generally speaking, a tendency towards greater accuracy in translation has been noticed in more recent films, especially in terms of coherence in register and characters' portrayal – with some reservations for *Revolutionary Road*. Yet, overall, a higher register is often adopted in translation, as has been shown for *g* in § 4.2.1. and 5. above.

Much work still needs to be done, especially in three directions: first, the category labelled *p/x* should be accounted for by way of a finer-grained analysis, as it currently accommodates very disparate items. Different types of speech acts (now part of *p/x*), that is, should be classified on a cline from 'most' to 'least' or 'non phatic'. Preservation, in translation, of the same level of phatic quality is indeed tantamount to a faithful and consistent portrayal of relationships between characters and of their evolution within a film. Second, the comparison of dubbed Italian with original Italian film language has shed some light on possible interference phenomena and trends in translation and should be pursued further. Finally, suggestions from neighbouring disciplines – e.g. anthropology, behavioural studies – should also complete the picture, as there seem to be cultural preferences for choosing ways to greet or to take leave which strongly skew numerical results. For instance, leave-taking (in a broad sense) is perceived in the UK as a very delicate matter at the end of a conversation, so much so that it is taken care of with a series of formulae, often reiterated, which contribute to the same general function and slowly build up Closing sequences (Fox 2004). In particular, similar insights would indeed be beneficial to a more accurate account of the fuzzy category of phatic expressions – within Closings as well as in Openings – mentioned above.

---

[1] The research was carried out by all authors together. Paragraph 6 was written jointly; Veronica Bonsignori wrote paragraphs 3, 3.1., 3.2., 3.3., 5.; Silvia Bruti wrote paragraphs 1., 4.2., 4.2.1., 4.2.2.; Silvia Masi wrote paragraphs 2., 4., 4.1.

[2] Translation: "Pragmatic and cultural interference in Spanish dubbing of North-American audiovisual products is not particularly marked. Undoubtedly the reiteration of certain pragmatic Anglicisms it is often more serious: among these the use of ¿sí? (< yes?) as a discursive routine to answer a call (on the phone or otherwise), the closing formula eso es todo (< that is all) and ¡olvídalo! (< forget it)"

References

Bonsignori, Veronica, Silvia Bruti & Silvia Masi. 2011. 'Formulae across Languages: English Greetings, Leave-Takings and Good Wishes in Italian Dubbing' in Lavaur, Jean-Marc, Anna Matamala & Adriana Serban (eds.) *Audiovisual Translation in Close-Up: Practical and Theoretical Approaches*. Bern: Peter Lang. 23-44.

Chaume Varela, Frederic & Cristina García de Toro. 2001. 'El Doblaje en España: Anglicismos Frecuentes en la Traducción de Textos Audiovisuales' in *Rivista Internazionale della Tecnica della Traduzione* 6: 119-137.

Coulmas, Florian. 1979. 'On the sociolinguistic relevance of routine formulae' in *Journal of Pragmatics* 3: 239-266.

Coulmas, Florian. (ed.). 1981. *Conversational Routine: Explorations in Standardized Communication Situations and Prepatterned Speech*. The Hague: Mouton de Gruyter.

Coupland, Justine. 2003. 'Small Talk: Social Functions' in *Research on Language and Social Interaction* 36 (1): 1-6.

Coupland, Justine & Nikolas Coupland. 1992. "How Are You?': Negotiating Phatic Communion' in *Language in Society* 21: 207-230.

De Mauro, Tullio, Federico Mancini, Massimo Vedovelli & Miriam Voghera. 1993. *Lessico di frequenza dell'italiano parlato (LIP Corpus)*. Milano: ETAS Libri.

Fox, Kate. 2004. *Watching the English: The Hidden Rules of English Behaviour*. London: Hodder & Stoughton.

Gómez Capuz, Juan. 2001a. 'Usos Discursivos Anglicados en los Doblajes al Español de la Películas Norteamericanas: Hacia una Perspectiva Pragmática' in De La Cruz Cabanillas, Isabel (ed.) *La Lingüística Aplicada a Finales del Siglo XX: Ensayos y Propuestas (Vol. 2)*. Alcalá: Universidad de Alcalá. 809-814.

Gómez Capuz, Juan. 2001b. 'Diseño de Análisis de la Interferencia Pragmática en la Traducción Audiovisual del Inglés al Español' in Sanderson, John D. (ed.) *¡Doble o Nada!' Actas de las I y II Jornadas de Doblaje y Subtitulación*. Alicante: Publicacions de l'Universitat d'Alacant. 59-84.

Laver, John. 1981. 'Linguistic Routines and Politeness in Greeting and Parting' in Coulmas, Florian (ed.) *Conversational Routine: Explorations in Standardized Communication Situations and Prepatterned Speech*. The Hague: Mouton de Gruyter. 289-304.
Masi, Silvia. 2008. 'Verbal Greetings and Leave-Taking Formulae across Time and Situational Settings' in Gotti, Maurizio & Susan Kermas (eds.) *Socially-Conditioned Language Change: Diachronic and Synchronic Insights*. Lecce: Edizioni Del Grifo. 115-136.
Pavesi, Maria. 2006. *La Traduzione Filmica: Aspetti del Parlato Doppiato dall'Inglese all'Italiano*. Roma: Carocci.

Filmography

Becoming Jane (2007), Julian Jerrold, UK.
Bridget Jones's Diary (2001), Sharon Maguire, UK.
Green Street Hooligans (2005), Lexi Alexander, UK/USA.
In Her Shoes (2005), Curtis Hanson, USA/Germany.
Io e Napoleone (2006), Paolo Virzì, Italy.
L'ultimo bacio (2001), Gabriele Muccino, Italy.
Love Actually (2003), Richard Curtis, UK/USA.
Ma che colpa abbiamo noi (2003), Carlo Verdone, Italy.
Manuale d'Amore 2 (*capitoli successivi*) (2007), Giovanni Veronesi, Italy.
Match Point (2005), Woody Allen, USA/UK/Luxembourg.
Music and Lyrics (2007), Marc Lawrence, USA.
Oscar and Lucinda (1997), Gillian Armstrong, UK/USA/Australia.
Revolutionary Road (2008), Sam Mendes, USA/UK.
Sex and the City – The Movie (2008), Michael Patrick King, USA.
Sliding Doors (1998), Peter Howitt, UK/USA.
The Devil Wears Prada (2006), David Frankel, USA.
The Duchess (2008), Saul Dibb, UK/Italy/France.
The English Patient (1996), Anthony Minghella, USA.
The Holiday (2006), Nancy Meyers, USA.
Tutta la vita davanti (2008), Paolo Virzì, Italy.

What AVT Can Make of Corpora: Some Findings from the *Pavia Corpus of Film Dialogue*

Maria Freddi
University of Pavia (Italy)

Abstract

This contribution reports on a research project aimed at identifying frequent phraseology in both original and translated filmic speech. Findings based on the *Pavia Corpus of Film Dialogue*, a parallel corpus of original British and American film dialogues and their dubbed Italian versions, are presented and discussed with a view to showing how corpus methods can be of use to audiovisual translation (AVT). It is argued that, on the one hand, corpus investigations provide a deeper understanding of film dialogue and the ways in which such dialogue functions. On the other, quantitative information gleaned from observation of translators' recurrent behaviour can help pinpoint linguistic and translational areas that are specific to the genre and, consequently, develop translators' awareness, improve translation quality and thus foster alignment with acceptability standards.

Keywords

corpus-based translation studies, dubbing, film dialogue, parallel corpus, phraseology

1. Background

The field of translation studies has recently benefited from the use of both parallel and comparable corpora allowing observations on recurrent patterns of translation – sometimes called 'universals' – such as source-language interference and source-text transfer, simplification and explicitation, and levelling (see Laviosa 1998; Mauranen and Kujamäki 2004), and facilitating large-scale comparative and contrastive language studies. This has launched what is considered a methodological shift in the theory of translation and in translators' training alike, called Corpus-based Translation Studies (CTS) (see Baker 1995, 1996; Laviosa 2004; Olohan 2004). AVT research, in particular, has only just started to look at corpora as a resource for the study of recurrent translation solutions within and across texts, alignment and disalignment with target-language norms, for example, in film dubbing, (Pavesi 2005, 2008, 2009; Romero-Fresco 2006, 2009; Bruti & Pavesi 2008), translator variability (Freddi 2009) and creativity (Heiss & Soffritti 2008; Valentini 2008).

Particularly, hypotheses on the routinised nature of dubbed language have been tested against various linguistic features of fictional – television and film – dialogue and by comparing different kinds of corpora. For example, Pavesi (2009) has studied the distribution and functions of personal pronouns by contrasting translated with non-translated Italian film dialogue. Romero-Fresco (2006, 2009) has compared the sitcom *Friends* dubbed into Spanish with the original in-house version of the popular TV show, *Siete Vidas*. Also, corpora of natural conversation have been taken as reference as is the case in Pavesi's (2008) work on syntactic phenomena in dubbed Italian vs. natural conversation. This approach – at times source-oriented and at times target-oriented – has tried to show the extent of source-text influence on the translation process by quantifying the semantic and structural calques, the constraints inherent in this type of translation (duration of the original speech, that is, the length of the lines and quality of performance as related to the articulation of the speech and kinesics) and also the degree to which dubbese is the natural result of filmese, the 'prefabricated orality' posited by Chaume for English–Spanish (2001, 2004a, 2004b, recently reprised in Baños-Piñero and Chaume 2009), and by Taylor (1999, 2004, 2006) for English–Italian. Taylor has concluded that the frequency of given linguistic elements is associated with particular scenes and scene types in both original and translated film dialogue.

This is the background for the present contribution, which discusses some results of a cutting-edge research project carried out at the University of Pavia and drawn up with a view to compiling an annotated parallel corpus of both American and British films and their Italian dubbed versions to study features of dubbed language. With the recent exception of *Forlixt* (see Valentini 2007), the Pavia film corpus is perhaps the first attempt to represent the language of Italian film dubbing on a wider scale. Such an empirical approach responds to the call for context-sensitive analyses of large bodies of translations advanced by researchers in CTS, especially Baker (2004), but also in AVT, particularly Díaz Cintas (2004: 28, 32) and Chaume (2004c) (see Chaume's suggestion that an analysis of the texts focusing on each of the signifying codes of cinematographic language can contribute to the study and understanding of AVT). It is argued that quantitative information gleaned from observation of translators' recurrent behaviour can help pinpoint linguistic and translational areas that are problematic, develop translators' awareness, improve translation quality and thus foster alignment with acceptability standards.

2. Data and methodology

As mentioned in Section 1, the analysis is based on the *Pavia Corpus of Film Dialogue*, a parallel corpus consisting of both American and British films released in the period between 1995 and 2005 together with their Italian dubbed versions. Findings were subsequently tested on a smaller set of data collected by the author according to the same sampling criteria to see if similar trends were observable and why, and to check for factors such as sample size and representativeness, that is, is the Pavia corpus big enough to provide a reliable indicator of the language of film dialogue with its most common translations?

The *Pavia Corpus of Film Dialogue* (Freddi & Pavesi 2009) consists of the orthographic and prosodic transcriptions of films all characterised by face-to-face conversations in contemporary settings and – as a guarantee of their status and diffusion within the cultures that produced and consumed them – successful both with critics and the general public.

The dialogues were transcribed. Subsequently, the original dialogues and the translations were aligned and annotated with paralinguistic and contextual information. A database was developed to facilitate the cross-examination of the translations and translators in order to identify continuity patterns that cut across individual variation as well as idiosyncrasies and individual behaviour in the linguistic mediation process. Table 1 shows the composition of the Pavia Corpus of Film Dialogue, while Table 2 summarises the second data set, including the total number of running words in each corpus.

Table 1. Composition of the *Pavia Corpus of Film Dialogue*
(taken from Freddi and Pavesi 2009: 99)

Film Title	Year of release in Italy	Film Director	Screenwriter	Translator - dialogue writer	Runtime	No. of running words (Eng)	No. of running words (It)
Ae Fond Kiss	2004	Ken Loach	Paul Laverty	Federica Depaolis	104'	8,624	8,828
Bend it like Beckham	2002	Gurinder Chadha	Gurinder Chadha	Elettra Caporello	112'	9,582	9,729
Billy Elliot	2001	Stephen Daldry	Lee Hall	Carlo Cosolo	110'	5,507	5,354
Crash	2005	Paul Haggis	Paul Haggis	Filippo Ottoni	112'	9,639	8,709
Dead Man Walking	1996	Tim Robbins	Tim Robbins	Lorena Bertini	122'	12,447	11,382

Film	Year	Director	Screenwriter	Translator	Runtime	Original words	Translated words
Erin Brockovich	2000	Steven Soderbergh	Susannah Grant	Marco Mete	130'	13,714	12,842
Finding Forrester	2001	Gus Van Sant	Mike Rich	Elettra Caporello	136'	10,379	10,591
Notting Hill	1999	Roger Michell	Richard Curtis	Francesco Vairano	124'	10,438	9,661
Ocean's Eleven	2001	Steven Soderbergh	Ted Griffin	Marco Mete	116'	9,784	9,273
One Hour Photo	2002	Mark Romanek	Mark Romanek	Carlo Valli	96'	5,731	5,231
Secrets & Lies	1996	Mike Leigh	Mike Leigh	Elisabetta Bucciarelli	142'	13,229	11,926
Sliding Doors	1998	Peter Howitt	Peter Howitt	Francesco Vairano	99'	8,882	8,339
Whole corpus					1403'	117,956	111,865

As can be seen in Table 1, the corpus comprises about 23 hours of film in each language, totalling almost 118,000 words of original dialogue and slightly fewer words in the translations–adaptations (almost 112,000). The second data set consists of only four films, the total size of the corpus being roughly 60,000 words between the two languages, thus adding almost another 8 hours of film for each version. The sampling frame is the same as in the Pavia corpus, American and British films, each constituting fifty per cent of the sample. The time span covered is the same but for the slight update represented by *Michael Clayton*, and so are the translators–dialogue writers with the exception of Fiamma Izzo, who is a new entry. However, also the genre of the films chosen matches those in the Pavia corpus:[1] both *Lost in Translation* and *Love Actually* can be considered romantic comedies, like, for example, *Notting Hill* and *Sliding Doors*. *Snatch* is a heist film, very much like its American counterpart represented by the *Ocean's* saga, while *Michael Clayton* is a lawyer movie like *Erin Brockovich* in the other corpus.

Table 2. Composition of the test data set

Film Title	Year of release in Italy	Film Director	Screenwriter	Translator-dialogue writer	Runtime	No. of running words (Eng)	No. of running words (It)
Lost in Translation (US)	2003	Sofia Coppola	Sofia Coppola	Elisabetta Bucciarelli	102'	4,172	3,769
Love Actually (UK)	2003	Richard Curtis	Richard Curtis	Fiamma Izzo	135'	10,368	10,360
Michael Clayton (US)	2007	Tony Gilroy	Tony Gilroy	Francesco Vairano	119'	10,067	9,071
Snatch (UK)	2001	Guy Ritchie	Guy Ritchie	Marco Mete	103'	6,499	5,602
Whole corpus					459'	31,106	28,802

Typical tools of corpus analysis are frequency counts of individual words, frequency counts of multi-word sequences (or clusters), aligned concordances and the annotation of language data with non-linguistic information that might be relevant to the identification of language patterns. In the case of spoken filmic dialogue, the kind of non-linguistic information which can be encoded in the corpus will include the setting and scene type, the paralinguistic behaviour and kinetic features associated with a character uttering a line, the name of the translator–dialogue writer, the latter to relate style preferences to a given translator. In the next section, findings obtained through each of the tools will be discussed one at a time with a view to identifying patterns of filmic speech in both the original and translated versions. The results will then be further tested on the smaller data set to see if variation occurs or if the same patterns are found (following Sinclair 1996 reprinted as Sinclair (2004: Chapter 2) and Sinclair 2003).

3. Results and discussion

As far as simple frequency counts are concerned, a comparison can be made of the most frequent clusters in the English originals and in the Italian translational subcorpus respectively. Clusters are defined as sequences of words of varying length, found to co-occur repeatedly and thus calculated exclusively on the basis of their frequency. Lists of clusters can easily be generated with a concordancing program such as *Wordsmith Tools* (version 4.0), as shown in Tables 3 and 4, which contain the most frequent 3-word clusters. As is clear from the two tables, clusters do not necessarily display any sort of lexico-grammatical integrity, but rather show how words combine with each other, producing chunks that might indicate the type of texts sampled in the corpus. The two far right-hand columns in both tables display the number of texts in which each cluster is found also expressed as a percentage. However, while Table 3 is ranked according to frequency (with the most frequent cluster on top of the list), Table 4 is re-sorted according to the number of texts in which each cluster appears, which shows how dispersed each cluster is in the overall corpus. Dispersion is a way to measure the pervasiveness of the most frequent clusters. By comparing Tables 3 and 4, it is evident how frequent clusters also tend to occur in all or most of the films sampled in the corpus. In fact, when resorted according to dispersion, the top four clusters remain unaltered (see Tables 3 and 4).

Table 3. Top 3-word clusters in the English subcorpus ranked by frequency

N	Cluster	Freq.	%	Texts	%
1	I DON'T KNOW	124	0.10	12	100
2	WHAT DO YOU	88	0.07	12	100
3	WHAT ARE YOU	67	0.06	12	100
4	DO YOU THINK	51	0.04	12	100
5	ARE YOU DOING	49	0.04	11	92
6	YOU KNOW WHAT	45	0.04	10	83
7	I DON'T WANT	40	0.03	10	83
8	DO YOU KNOW	37	0.03	11	92
9	DO YOU WANT	36	0.03	11	92
10	HERE WE GO	33	0.03	9	75
11	HOW ARE YOU	33	0.03	11	92
12	WHY DON'T YOU	32	0.03	10	83
13	YOU WANT TO	32	0.03	10	83
14	A LOT OF	31	0.03	11	92
15	OUT OF THE	31	0.03	8	67
16	A COUPLE OF	30	0.03	12	100
17	WANT YOU TO	30	0.03	10	83
18	ARE YOU GONNA	29	0.02	9	75
19	DON'T WANT TO	29	0.02	10	83
20	THIS IS THE	28	0.02	12	100
21	I THOUGHT YOU	26	0.02	11	92

22	HOW DO YOU	25	0.02	8	67
23	OH MY GOD	25	0.02	8	67
24	TO DO WITH	25	0.02	9	75
25	A LITTLE BIT	24	0.02	9	75
26	I WANT YOU	24	0.02	10	83
27	LOOK AT ME	24	0.02	10	83
28	TO MEET YOU	24	0.02	7	58
29	TO SEE YOU	24	0.02	11	92
30	WHAT IS IT	24	0.02	9	75
31	WHAT'S GOING ON	24	0.02	7	58
32	YOU ALL RIGHT	24	0.02	9	75
33	YOU DON'T KNOW	24	0.02	10	83

Table 4. Top 3-word clusters in the English subcorpus ranked by dispersion or consistency[2]

N	Cluster	Freq.	%	Texts	%
1	I DON'T KNOW	124	0.10	12	100
2	WHAT DO YOU	88	0.07	12	100
3	WHAT ARE YOU	67	0.06	12	100
4	DO YOU THINK	51	0.04	12	100
5	A COUPLE OF	30	0.03	12	100
6	THIS IS THE	28	0.02	12	100
7	WANT ME TO	21	0.02	12	100
8	ARE YOU DOING	49	0.04	11	92
9	DO YOU KNOW	37	0.03	11	92
10	DO YOU WANT	36	0.03	11	92
11	HOW ARE YOU	33	0.03	11	92
12	A LOT OF	31	0.03	11	92
13	I THOUGHT YOU	26	0.02	11	92
14	TO SEE YOU	24	0.02	11	92
15	DO YOU MEAN	22	0.02	11	92
16	I TOLD YOU	22	0.02	11	92
17	YOU KNOW WHAT	45	0.04	10	83
18	I DON'T WANT	40	0.03	10	83
19	WHY DON'T YOU	32	0.03	10	83
20	YOU WANT TO	32	0.03	10	83
21	WANT YOU TO	30	0.03	10	83

22	DON'T WANT TO	29	0.02	10	83
23	I WANT YOU	24	0.02	10	83
24	LOOK AT ME	24	0.02	10	83
25	YOU DON'T KNOW	24	0.02	10	83
26	I DON'T THINK	23	0.02	10	83
27	YOU HAVE A	23	0.02	10	83
28	DO YOU HAVE	19	0.02	10	83
29	TO GO TO	19	0.02	10	83
30	YOU KNOW I	19	0.02	10	83
31	HERE WE GO	33	0.03	9	75
32	ARE YOU GONNA	29	0.02	9	75
33	TO DO WITH	25	0.02	9	75
34	A LITTLE BIT	24	0.02	9	75
35	WHAT IS IT	24	0.02	9	75
36	YOU ALL RIGHT	24	0.02	9	75

Even before commenting on the sequences found, we can do the same for the Italian subcorpus and what we obtain are the data in Tables 5 and 6.

Table 5. Top 3-word clusters in the Italian subcorpus ranked by frequency

N	Cluster	Freq.	%	Texts	%
1	NON LO SO	80	0.07	12	100
2	UN PO DI	65	0.06	12	100
3	HA DETTO CHE	31	0.03	10	83
4	NO NO NO	31	0.03	9	75
5	NON È VERO	30	0.03	9	75
6	UN PAIO DI	28	0.02	10	83
7	OH MIO DIO	27	0.02	9	75
8	QUESTO È IL	26	0.02	10	83
9	IO NON HO	24	0.02	8	67
10	È IL MIO	21	0.02	8	67
11	UN SACCO DI	21	0.02	8	67
12	NON HO MAI	20	0.02	11	92
13	LA PG E	19	0.02	1	8
14	UNO DUE TRE	19	0.02	4	33
15	NON È CHE	18	0.02	9	75
16	NON È UN	18	0.02	10	83
17	NON VOGLIO CHE	18	0.02	8	67

18	QUESTA È LA	18	0.02	8	67
19	TUTTO QUELLO CHE	18	0.02	9	75
20	È UN PO	17	0.02	10	83
21	NON FA NIENTE	17	0.02	8	67
22	DETTO CHE NON	16	0.01	8	67
23	DI QUELLO CHE	16	0.01	8	67
24	MI DISPIACE TANTO	16	0.01	6	50
25	PIÙ O MENO	16	0.01	8	67
26	TANTI AUGURI A	16	0.01	3	25
27	CHE NON È	15	0.01	7	58
28	CI POSSO CREDERE	15	0.01	5	42
29	IL FATTO CHE	15	0.01	7	58
30	LO SO CHE	15	0.01	8	67
31	NON CI POSSO	15	0.01	5	42
32	NON CREDO CHE	15	0.01	9	75
33	QUAL È IL	15	0.01	8	67

Table 6. Top 3-word clusters in the Italian subcorpus ranked by dispersion or consistency

N	Cluster	Freq.	%	Texts	%
1	NON LO SO	80	0.07	12	100
2	UN PO DI	65	0.06	12	100
3	NON HO MAI	20	0.02	11	92
4	HA DETTO CHE	31	0.03	10	83
5	UN PAIO DI	28	0.02	10	83
6	QUESTO È IL	26	0.02	10	83
7	NON È UN	18	0.02	10	83
8	È UN PO	17	0.02	10	83
9	NO NO NO	31	0.03	9	75
10	NON È VERO	30	0.03	9	75
11	OH MIO DIO	27	0.02	9	75
12	NON È CHE	18	0.02	9	75
13	TUTTO QUELLO CHE	18	0.02	9	75
14	NON CREDO CHE	15	0.01	9	75
15	NON SE NE	13	0.01	9	75
16	CHE NON TI	12	0.01	9	75
17	IO NON HO	24	0.02	8	67
18	È IL MIO	21	0.02	8	67

19	UN SACCO DI	21	0.02	8	67
20	NON VOGLIO CHE	18	0.02	8	67
21	QUESTA È LA	18	0.02	8	67
22	NON FA NIENTE	17	0.02	8	67
23	DETTO CHE NON	16	0.01	8	67
24	DI QUELLO CHE	16	0.01	8	67
25	PIÙ O MENO	16	0.01	8	67
26	LO SO CHE	15	0.01	8	67
27	QUAL È IL	15	0.01	8	67
28	È UNA COSA	14	0.01	8	67
29	IO NON VOGLIO	14	0.01	8	67
30	CHE È SUCCESSO	13	0.01	8	67
31	È STATO UN	13	0.01	8	67
32	CHE TU NON	12	0.01	8	67
33	SI PUÒ SAPERE	12	0.01	8	67

The data rearranged like this lend themselves to comparative observations about English and Italian considered independently from one another. First, the English clusters in the table show a high incidence of second- and first-person pronouns (*you* mostly, but also *I*, see no. 21 in Table 3 *I thought you* or no. 16 in Table 4 *I told you*) orienting the analyst towards the interactional nature of the text type under consideration (i.e., film dialogue). Second, some sequences partially overlap. For example, *what do you* overlaps with *do you think*, *do you know* and *do you want*. This reveals a larger pattern where variation takes place within fixedness. In fact, it is the lexical verb that changes while the interrogative pattern remains fixed. The same is true of *what are you* (ranking third with 67 occurrences), *how are you* (ranking eleventh with 33 occurrences) and *are you doing*, which forms another two interrogative sequences, namely *What are you doing?* and *How are you doing?* Questions of this kind seem to be prominent at least quantitatively and point to what is potentially a genre-specific feature (see below for a discussion).

Furthermore, some chunks correspond to routine expressions which are either common in natural conversation (e.g., the expletive *oh my God*) or whose high frequency might be associated with the particular type of interaction going on (e.g., *here we go* or *to meet you* as part of the greeting formula *Nice to meet you*). Also of interest is the sequence *you know what*, for which the full concordance is worth looking at to see if it corresponds to the utterance launcher, also common in natural conversation, functioning as an attention-getting device (see Biber et al. 1999). From the same conversational perspective, the sequences *I don't know* (the top-most cluster in the list) and *I don't want* are among those found by Biber and Conrad (1999: 184) to typify conversation as opposed to written academic prose. However, notice that Biber and Conrad were dealing with 4-word clusters (e.g., *I don't know what*, *I don't know how* and *I don't want to*).

The high frequency and consistent distribution of *look at me, what is it, what's going on* and *you all right*, which can indeed be considered semantically complete sequences, deserve a different explanation. Evidence from the smaller corpus will confirm the suggestion that these expressions are common in scripted dialogue and that they help build the conflict situations which are crucial in film plots and are functional to carrying the action forward.[3] The remaining set of clusters also showing prominence comprises quantifiers (e.g., *a lot of, a couple of, a little bit*) specifying a non-exact amount, and, finally, the deictic sequence *this is the* (ranked sixth in Table 4 because of the 28 occurrences over twelve films). All these will be commented on in comparison with the corresponding Italian chunks (see below).

Similar observations can be made for the Italian clusters, with *non lo so* (80 occurrences) at the top of the list, followed by *un po' di* (with 65 occurrences). Interestingly, there is a big gap in terms of frequency between the top two and the clusters that follow (see nos. 3 and 4 in Table 5, *ha detto che* and *no no no*, which occur only 31 times each). If compared with the English list, this implies a higher number of less frequent clusters and less overlap (see *ha detto che, non è vero, non ho mai, non è un, tutto quello che*, etc.). Overlap is restricted to *ci posso credere* and *non ci posso* (together forming a 4-word cluster translating both *I don't believe it* (9 times) and *I can't believe it* (the remaining 6 times)) and – to a lesser extent – to *io non ho* and *non ho mai* (indeed *io non ho mai* occurs only 5 times in the corpus).

Related to the dramatic drop in the frequencies is the presence of the cluster 'la pg e', which occurs 19 times but is limited to one film only, namely *Erin Brockovich*, where PG&E is the name of the company involved in the law suit portrayed in the film. This idiosyncratic cluster obviously disappears from the list when the data is reorganised according to dispersion (i.e., the number of films in which a given cluster is found to occur) leaving room for *di quello che, più o meno, lo so che*, etc. all found to occur in eight out of the twelve films (see Table 6). This is the first striking difference between the original and the dubbed corpus in that, while the data in Table 3 are never restricted to less than 60% of the corpus, Table 5 contains phrases found in only a few films. Indeed, sequences such as *mi dispiace tanto* – however fixed they may be – appear in only half of the films in the dubbed corpus (ranked twenty-fourth in Table 5).

When compared, the English and Italian lists differ in their distribution for the obvious structural differences between the two languages involved in the translation process. Clusters are sensitive to such differences. So, for example, the fixedness associated with *what*-questions in English (with the auxiliary preceding the obligatory subject pronoun as in *what do you* and *what are you*) is predictably not mirrored in the Italian 3-word cluster list because of the different way in which questions are formed. Grammatical functions are taken on by morphological variation in Italian and are therefore less likely to generate fixed patterns. Along the same lines, *look at me* (ranked twenty-fourth in Table 4) will not have its equivalent in the 3-word cluster list (see *guardami* and *guardi me*). Apart from *I don't know* and *non lo so*, both at the top of each list, and the quantifiers *un po' di, un paio di* and *un sacco di*, which also appear as prominently as their English counterparts *a lot of, a couple of* and *a little bit*, the relative distribution is different. Moreover, translator variability might affect the ranking of potential equivalents in that not all frequent English clusters are translated in the same way. An example would be the phrase *you know what*, for which no equivalent cluster appears on the Italian list. On the other hand, convergence on a fixed solution on the part of the translators might be suggested by the positions occupied by the expletives *oh my God* and *oh mio Dio*, the latter slightly higher in frequency than the English with 27 vs. 25 instances.

However, these indications need to be substantiated by looking at the concordances and the dialogue lines in which clusters are found to occur. Thus, the second stage of the analysis is concerned with both the monolingual and aligned concordances. The aligned concordances are used to check for translation adequacy and acceptability. Finally, the annotated corpus is used to relate the translation solutions retrieved to the various translators–dialogue writers and to explore translator variability.

Findings derived from the reading of concordances in the original version are of two types in that frequent formulas reflect either the diegetic or the mimetic purpose of film dialogue. The former often take on a polemic function and are used to challenge the interlocutor's stance, thus typifying film dialogue as a genre in which conflict is a propelling force of narration (i.e., the many *wh*-questions from *What do you want?* to *What's going on?* or *What is it?*). Conversely, the frequent formulas which reflect the mimetic purpose of film dialogue represent the many ritualised acts of our daily routine such as greetings (e.g., *Nice/pleased/lovely to meet you, How are you (doing)?*), exclamations (e.g., *Oh my God!*) and various other forms of allocution (e.g., *You know what?, Look at me!*). This interpretation is reinforced by the analysis of the translations that help disambiguate the pragmatic role of such routines. In Table 7, the repeated co-occurrence of the gerund together with the weak connective *ma* in initial position is both indicative of the fixed quality of this type of formula in the original versions and a mark of the semantic and structural calques (see Pavesi (2008: 87), who has shown how *e* 'and' and *ma* 'but' tend to be overused weak connectives in dubbed language). Here, fixedness is ascribable to the diegetic function of the type of source expressions considered, which, by being preserved in the target texts, becomes a recognisable marker of the genre for the target audience as well.

Table 7. A selection of *What are you doing?* and its translations from the *Pavia Corpus of Film Dialogue*

Film	Cue	Language	Character	Text	Translator-dialogue writer
Ae Fond Kiss	105	Eng	TAHARA	What are you doing?	
Ae Fond Kiss	105	Ita	TAHARA	Cosa stai combinando?	Federica Depaolis
Ae Fond Kiss	233	Eng	DANNY	What are you doing? You stupid bastard.	
Ae Fond Kiss	233	Ita	DANNY	Ma guarda che hai combinato!	Federica Depaolis
Ae Fond Kiss	300	Eng	CASIM	What are you doing?	
Ae Fond Kiss	300	Ita	CASIM	Che cosa stai facendo?	Federica Depaolis
Bend it like Beckham	846	Eng	JULES	What are you doing?	
Bend it like Beckham	846	Ita	JULES	Ma che state facendo?	Elettra Caporello
Bend it like Beckham	900	Eng	JESS	Tony, *What are you doing?*	
Bend it like Beckham	900	Ita	JESS	Tony! Tony, *ma che vuoi fare?*	Elettra Caporello
Billy Elliot	33	Eng	GEORGE WATSON	(..) This is man-to-man combat, not a bloody tea dance. *What are you doing, man?* Hit him! He's just pi...	
Billy Elliot	33	Ita	GEORGE WATSON	(..) È un combattimento corpo a corpo, non un tè danzante! *Dove accidenti vai?* Colpiscilo!	Carlo Cosolo

Maria Freddi

Billy Elliot	91	Eng	DAD	Chris ti prende… *What are you doing?*	
Billy Elliot	91	Ita	DAD	*Che stai facendo?*	Carlo Cosolo
Billy Elliot	136	Eng	TONY	Got enough food there, scab? *What are you doing, eh?*	
Billy Elliot	136	Ita	TONY	Hai preso abbastanza da mangiare, crumiro? *Che stai facendo, eh?*	Carlo Cosolo
Billy Elliot	251	Eng	BILLY	*What are you doing?*	
Billy Elliot	251	Ita	BILLY	*Che stai facendo?*	Carlo Cosolo
Billy Elliot	445	Eng	BILLY	*What are you doing?*	
Billy Elliot	445	Ita	BILLY	*Cosa stai facendo?*	Carlo Cosolo
Dead Man Walking	344	Eng	SISTER HELEN	(..) a friend comes to visit and he sees him reading the Bible. The friend says "W.C., you don't believe in God, *what are you doing* reading the Bible?"	
Dead Man Walking	344	Ita	SISTER HELEN	(..) un amico va a trovarlo e vede che legge la Bibbia, allora gli chiede: "W.C. tu non credi in Dio, *ma che fai* leggi la Bibbia"?	Lorena Bertini
Erin Brockovich	168	Eng	ERIN	*What are you doing*, making all that goddamn noise?	
Erin Brockovich	168	Ita	ERIN	*Come vi salta in mente* di fare tutto questo casino?	Marco Mete
Finding Forrester	404	Eng	JAMAL	*What are you doing?*	

394

Finding Forrester	404	Ita	JAMAL	Ma che sta facendo?	Elettra Caporello
Ocean's Eleven	95	Eng	BARRY	What are you doing?	
Ocean's Eleven	95	Ita	BARRY	Ma che fai?	Marco Mete

Among the recurrent routines which are mimetic of natural conversation in English (e.g., *Here we go, Nice to meet you, You all right?*), there seems to be a large degree of variation taking place in terms of translation solutions. Table 8 exemplifies the use and translations of *You know what?* If we look at the underscores, it is difficult to spot any patterned solution (compare *Sai che ti dico, (la) sai una cosa* and *senta/senti*) unless we consider those instances where the expression is completely left out, that is, omission, as showing regularity. However, most of the omissions come from the film *Crash*. Parts of the film which contained the relevant dialogue lines were watched and a plausible reason for the omission of the expressions seemed to be the duration of the line, or quantitative sync. Translator–dialogue writer Filippo Ottoni (personal communication) has confirmed that the rhythm of the characters' speech was so tight to convey their nervousness in those scenes that he did not have enough room to fit the whole Italian text. Consequently, he opted to omit the pragmatic marker *you know what*.

Table 8. Concordances of *You know what?* and its translations from the *Pavia Corpus of Film Dialogue*

Film	Cue	Language	Character	Text	Translator dialogue-writer
Bend it like Beckham	855	Eng	MRS PAXTON	Yeah. Oh, and *do you know what?* One of those England girls' players is a maths teacher as well and she's happily married with a baby!	
Bend it like Beckham	855	Ita	MRS PAXTON	Sì. Uh, *la sai una cosa?* Una delle ragazze della nazionale inglese fa la professoressa di matematica e è felicemente sposata e ha un bambino.	Elettra Caporello
Crash	149	Eng	JEAN	I would like the locks changed again in the morning. And *you know what?* You might mention that we'd appreciate it if next time they didn't send a gang member.	

Maria Freddi

Crash	149	Ita	JEAN	Io voglio cambiare ancora le serrature.. domattina! E Ø tu dovresti anche dire alla ditta di non mandarci ancora un malvivente questa volta.	Filippo Ottoni
Crash	266	Eng	CHRISTINE	(..) You weren't afraid that all your good friends at the studio were gonna read about you in the morning and realize "*you know what?* He's actually black!"	
Crash	266	Ita	CHRISTINE	(..) Non avevi paura che i tuoi amici bianchi allo studio avrebbero letto il giornale e detto: "*Ecco, visto?* Non è altro che un negro, in fondo!"	Filippo Ottoni
Crash	401	Eng	DANIEL	You... *You know what?* Why don't you just pay for the lock and I won't charge you for the time.	
Crash	401	Ita	DANIEL	*Senta*... mi paghi solo la serratura e lasci perdere la mano d'opera.	Filippo Ottoni
Crash	690	Eng	FLANAGAN	(..) And you're arguing with me that maybe we're not being fair to him? *You know what?* Maybe you're right. Maybe you're right. Maybe Lewis did provoke this. Maybe he got exactly what was coming to him. (..)	
Crash	690	Ita	FLANAGAN	(..) E lei ora sta dicendo che noi non siamo giusti con lui? Ø Magari lei ha ragione, magari Louis se l'è cercato e magari ha avuto quello che si meritava (..)	Filippo Ottoni
Crash	797	Eng	DANIEL	Hey, *you know what?* Hey, I got fifty dollars. Here.	
Crash	797	Ita	DANIEL	Ehi, *senti, okay*. Ti do, ehi, ho qui cinquanta dollari, tieni.	Filippo Ottoni
Crash	811	Eng	JEAN	I sent her out for groceries, and that was two hours ago, Carol. Well, *you know what?* You are one to talk. You go through, like, six	

				housekeepers a year? I'm not snapping at you! I am angry. Yes! At them! Yes! (..)	
Crash	811	Ita	JEAN	L'ho mandata a fare la spesa e sono già passate due ore, Carol. Beh, Ø senti chi parla! Proprio tu che cambi cinque o sei donne l'anno. Non ti sto facendo un rimprovero, è che sono incazzata! Sì, con quelli! Sì, (..)	Filippo Ottoni
Erin Brockovich	641	Eng	ERIN	No. See? See? That's what those arrogant PG&E fucks want me to think. But *you know what?* They're wrong.	
Erin Brockovich	641	Ita	ERIN	No, lo vedi? Lo vedi? E' proprio quello che vogliono farmi pensare quegli arroganti di merda della PG&E, ma *sai che ti dico?* Si sbagliano!	Marco Mete
Erin Brockovich	679	Eng	ERIN	Okay. Um, well, I'm a little busy here, honey. I mean, we invited all these people here. Ed and I have to… Hey, I'm sorry. Okay. *You know what?* I have an idea. Please, please, I have an idea. (..)	
Erin Brockovich	679	Ita	ERIN	D'accordo. Beh, amore, io ho un po' da fare, cioè, le abbiamo invitate noi queste persone, Ed e io dobbiamo… Ehi, mi dispiace… Allora, *sai che ti dico?* Ho un'idea… (..)	Marco Mete
Erin Brockovich	704	Eng	ERIN	No, no, no, no. *You know what?* Can you just give me one just give me one second.	
Erin Brockovich	704	Ita	ERIN	No, no, no, no, no… Ehm… *Sai una cosa?* Mi puoi dare solo… Dammi un secondo.	Marco Mete
Erin Brockovich	708	Eng	ERIN	Thank you. Thank you. Oh, my, oh my God. Uh, *you know what?* Why don't, why don't you guys go ahead without me and I will get a ride with Ed.	

Maria Freddi

Erin Brockovich	708	Ita	ERIN	Ehm... *Facciamo così.* Perché non andate avanti senza di me e io mi faccio riaccompagnare da Ed.	Marco Mete
Erin Brockovich	848	Eng	THERESA	*You know what?* Why don't I take Erin down the hall so we can start on this stuff? (..)	
Erin Brockovich	848	Ita	THERESA	*Sai che ti dico?* Magari porto Erin con me nell'altra stanza, così possiamo cominciare con questa roba, (..)	Marco Mete
Erin Brockovich	901	Eng	ERIN	Oh, *you know what?* That is bullshit!	
Erin Brockovich	901	Ita	ERIN	Ah, *smettila, Ed*, è una cazzata!	Marco Mete
Erin Brockovich	1066	Eng	ERIN	I did a job. You should reward me accordingly. It's not complicated. *You know what?* That is the fucking problem. All you lawyers do is complicate situations that aren't complicated. (..)	
Erin Brockovich	1066	Ita	ERIN	No, io ho fatto un lavoro, tu dovresti premiarmi di conseguenza, non è complicato, *lo sai?* Questo è il problema, cazzo. Voi avvocati non fate altro che complicare situazioni che non sono complicate. (..)	Marco Mete
Secrets & Lies	118	Eng	SISTER-IN-LAW	Listen, *you know what?* You could split the whole house in two, right?	
Secrets & Lies	118	Ita	SISTER-IN-LAW	Te lo dico io, *sai cosa facciamo?* Divideremo la casa in due parti. Capito?	Elisabetta Bucciarelli

The same is true of *Here we go*, whose varying translations show how translators–dialogue writers skilfully exploit the flexibility and often peripheral usage of pragmatic markers by resorting to a wide range of equivalent colloquial expressions (see, for example, *ecco a lei, ecco fatto, ci siamo, ricominciamo, sei pronto?, allora ci riproviamo*). When looking at the concordances, even the apparent correspondence between *this is the* and two frequent clusters from the Italian list, namely *questo è il* and *questa è la* (see

Table 5, ranks 8 and 18), becomes less evident. These pronominal references can be used to translate a variety of English presentative patterns including *There's the...*, *Here's the...* and often replace the distal identification *That's the/my...*, which is roughly as frequent as the proximal one. Moreover, the fixedness of *questo/a è il/la* also accounts for interrogative patterns as in *Is this the truth?* or *Is this your club?*

When moving from the target text to the source text (rather than from the source text to the target text), we find that *non fa niente*, which occurs 17 times over eight films, is the stock equivalent form for – in descending frequency order – *It's okay, That's okay, That's fine, It's fine, I'm okay, it's alright* and the non-standard *it don't matter*. Besides, *non fa niente* counts as a 3-word cluster, while the contracted forms in the English original contribute to creating 2-word clusters (this is because of word tokenisation with *Wordsmith*). Analogously, *mi dispiace tanto* systematically translates as *I'm so/terribly/really sorry* and if we take *si può sapere* at the bottom of Table 6, we see that it is always used to render the challenging functions of the *what*-questions, which are so frequent in the original (e.g., *What do you want from me, man?*, *What the hell is wrong with you?*, *What on earth's going on here?*, *What the bloody hell were you thinking?*). However, convergence on translational routines seems to be limited to the very few cases observed. Even the fifth most frequent cluster *non è vero*, when looking at the concordances, is used as a fixed equivalent for the English question tags in less than half of the cases, the other instances corresponding to the proposition *it's not true*. Along the same line, the frequency of *un po' di* is boosted by its functioning as a marker of vague language variously translating quantifiers such as *some, a little, a bit of, a couple of, a wee*, but even occasionally added anew to the target text or used to play down the swearing in the original texts (see *the fucking weight - un po' di peso, Take your goddam hand off my door - Vedi un po' di levare quella manaccia dalla mia porta*). In conclusion, convergence on translational routines seems to be motivated by genre-specific features and arises only when no equivalent structure is available in the target language or target-text type in terms of frequency and distribution (e.g., the maintenance of the gerund or alternatively the stock expression *si può sapere* to translate the frequent *what*-questions).

As a last stage of this research, the smaller sample consisting of 4 movies was examined. The list of the most frequent 3-word clusters from both the original and the translational component shows a repertoire that is very similar to the one observed in the Pavia corpus. Interestingly, the top-most sequences both by frequency and distribution over texts are identical: *I don't know* is followed by *what do you*, at least partially overlapping with *do you think, do you want* and *do you mean* (Table 9, rank nos. 3, 4 and 27 respectively); *what are you* occupies rank no. 6, partly extending to *are you doing*, rank no. 9. These chunks point to the same kind of interrogatives already observed in the larger corpus. A look at the concordances that they belong to has confirmed the same challenging function already ascribed to some of them (e.g., *What do you want?*, *What do you mean?*), whereby character A questions character B in a way that is somewhat redundant and therefore predictable for the viewer, but a way which contributes to the tension of the scene and moves on the story. See, for example, the following exchange taken from one of the last scenes in *Michael Clayton*, where Michael finally unmasks litigator Karen Crowder's whole scheme while she is offering him hush money. Significantly, Karen's question is echoed in the first part of Michael's turn to stress his annoyance (see underscores).

KAREN   What do you want?
MICHAEL What do I want? I want more. I want out! And with this, I want everything.

Another example comes from *Snatch*, where the expression *What do you mean* is followed by infinitives and used to ask for clarification about something which is puzzling "Bullet-Tooth" Tony (played by actor Vinnie Jones). The same type of question expressing surprise and annoyance, while at the same time fulfilling a plot-structuring function, has been reported for the Pavia Corpus (see Freddi (2009: 112-113) for the examples).

AVI   Well, let's have a look, shall we, Tony?
TONY   What?
AVI   Have a look in the dog.
TONY   What do you mean have a look in the dog?
AVI   I mean open him up.
TONY   It's not a fuckin' tin of baked beans, what do you mean open him up?
AVI   I mean open him up.
TONY   That's a bit strong, isn't it?

The fact that many clusters from the new sample are common to the list in Table 3 confirms the hypothesised fixedness of the dialogues under study and their genre-specificity as scripted filmic speech (see also *you want to, to meet you, a lot of, oh my God, I don't want, how are you, nice to meet* and *you know what*). In this case too, repetition is associated with either the fictional dimension of the world narrated or else with the mimicking of naturalness as reproduced by expletives and conversational routines (*Oh my God!, Nice to meet you, You know what?*, etc.). The odd clusters in Table 9 –

despite their frequency – all come from just one film in the second set of data. For example, *it in my* together with *feel it in* belong to *I feel it in my fingers, in my toes*, the refrain of the song frustrated rock and roll legend Bill Mack, performed by Billy Nighy, is recording at the studios in the film *Love Actually*. This shows that a small sample like this is skewed by the presence of one or two films, which do not, however, influence the consistent distribution of the very frequent clusters across the four movies. Along the same lines, the cluster *you know what* (found to occur 9 times in three films) deserves special attention. A look at the concordance lines shows that most of its occurrences come from *Michael Clayton* and they are part of questions such as *You know what I just heard?* or *You know what he's doing?*, including one instance of the utterance launcher as in *You know what, guys?*, generally indicating the high incidence of questions as related to conflictual situations and possibly to films where conflict is especially constitutive of the plot.

Table 9. Top 3-word clusters in the English test-corpus ranked by frequency

N	Cluster	Freq.	%	Texts	%
1	I DON'T KNOW	44	0.13	4	100
2	WHAT DO YOU	31	0.09	4	100
3	DO YOU THINK	17	0.05	4	100
4	DO YOU WANT	17	0.05	4	100
5	I LOVE YOU	17	0.05	3	75
6	WHAT ARE YOU	17	0.05	4	100
7	TO MEET YOU	14	0.04	3	75
8	YOU WANT TO	14	0.04	4	100
9	ARE YOU DOING	13	0.04	4	100
10	I DON'T WANT	12	0.04	3	75
11	IT IN MY	12	0.04	1	25
12	OH MY GOD	12	0.04	3	75
13	WHAT THE HELL	12	0.04	2	50
14	A LOT OF	11	0.03	4	100
15	FEEL IT IN	11	0.03	1	25
16	I AM NOT	11	0.03	1	25
17	NO NO NO	11	0.03	2	50
18	HOW ARE YOU	10	0.03	3	75
19	NICE TO MEET	10	0.03	2	50
20	DID YOU GET	9	0.03	3	75

21	TO BE A	9	0.03	4	100
22	YOU HAVE TO	9	0.03	4	100
23	YOU KNOW WHAT	9	0.03	3	75
24	ALL I WANT	8	0.02	1	25
25	ALL THE TIME	8	0.02	2	50
26	DO YOU KNOW	8	0.02	3	75
27	DO YOU MEAN	8	0.02	3	75
28	DON'T KNOW WHAT	8	0.02	3	75
29	I FEEL IT	8	0.02	1	25
30	I WANT TO	8	0.02	3	75
31	LOVE LOVE LOVE	8	0.02	1	25
32	OUT OF THE	8	0.02	4	100
33	THIS IS A	8	0.02	3	75

An analogous list can be drawn up for the Italian dubbed version, ranked according to dispersion (Table 10) which contains many of the same clusters already observed in the larger corpus (see Tables 5 and 6), notably *non lo so* occupying the first rank, *è il mio*, *un sacco di*, *un paio di*, *ha detto che*, *questo è il*, *tutto a posto* and *non fa niente*, the last two coinciding with the already-mentioned stock expressions. However, the list quickly drops down to clusters which are skewed by the presence of just one or two films in the corpus (chiefly *Love Actually* and *Michael Clayton*, which are the ones with the highest number of words):

Table 10. Top 3-word clusters in the Italian test-corpus ranked by dispersion or consistency

N	Cluster	Freq.	%	Texts	%
1	NON LO SO	27	0.09	4	100
2	NON È UN	9	0.03	4	100
3	QUESTO È UN	7	0.02	4	100
4	IO NON SO	6	0.02	4	100
5	È IL MIO	5	0.02	4	100
6	NON RIESCO A	5	0.02	4	100
7	SOLO CHE NON	5	0.02	4	100
8	UN SACCO DI	5	0.02	4	100
9	HA DETTO CHE	11	0.04	3	75
10	QUESTO È IL	8	0.03	3	75
11	TUTTO QUELLO CHE	8	0.03	3	75

12	TUTTO A POSTO	7	0.02	3	75
13	A NEW YORK	6	0.02	3	75
14	DA QUALCHE PARTE	6	0.02	3	75
15	SI TRATTA DI	6	0.02	3	75
16	UN PAIO DI	6	0.02	3	75
17	CHE NON TI	5	0.02	3	75
18	E NON È	5	0.02	3	75
19	NON È IL	5	0.02	3	75
20	NO NO NO	11	0.04	2	50
21	NON FA NIENTE	8	0.03	2	50
22	UNA COSA CHE	8	0.03	2	50
23	QUESTA È LA	7	0.02	2	50
24	DELLA MIA VITA	6	0.02	2	50
25	È QUELLO CHE	6	0.02	2	50
26	IN QUESTO MOMENTO	6	0.02	2	50
27	MILIONI DI DOLLARI	6	0.02	2	50
28	CHE NE DICI	5	0.02	2	50
29	È LA MIA	5	0.02	2	50
30	NO NON FA	5	0.02	2	50

4. Conclusions

The analysis carried out has shown how the language of original film dialogue is characterised by a certain amount of predictability as a result of its diegetic features as well as simulated spontaneity meant to reproduce natural conversation.

Frequency observations together with the qualitative analysis of the concordances have revealed two sets of patterns. On the one hand, routines which serve a plot-advancing function (*what*-questions such as *What's going on?* and *What are you talking about?*), while on the other hand conversational formulas with either a textual cohesive or interpersonal function typical of dialogic interaction tout-court (e.g., *You know what?*, *How are you doing?*, *You all right?*). As for the first kind of fixed expressions, they have been explained by resorting to the dramaturgical principle of conflict underlying screenwriting (see Aimeri 2007). Although often redundant with regard to the situations portrayed on-screen, dialogue contributes to the construction of dramatic events which can be resolved only at the end of the story and therefore its features ought to be fully described and understood by linguists and translators alike (in line with the dialogue analysis suggested by Remael (2004)). However, it does become apparent that limitations to this kind of approach arise because of the fact that the corpus is not – at this stage at least – multimodal. Consequently, the impact of the technical constraints on the translation outcome runs the risk of being obscured unless manually checked (e.g. lip-synchronisation as well as isochrony).

As for the relevance of this study and generally Corpus-based Translation Studies to AVT research, we have tried to demonstrate that regularities in the translation outcomes become evident only through repeated observations of principled collections of language data (here corpora of originals and translations in parallel), where continuity across translations can be detected as well individual creativity. The analysis of the translational corpus clusters independent of the source texts has revealed a different patterning from the original one, partly because of the structural differences between the two language codes involved in the translation process, and partly because translator variability seems to override repetition. The comparative study of source texts and target texts has demonstrated that source-text transfer and convergence on translational routines take place only where there is no equivalent structure in the target language and in the target-text type in terms of frequency and distribution (e.g., the maintenance of the gerund together with the addition of a weak connective or alternatively the stock expression 'si può sapere' to translate the genre-specific *what*-questions). Therefore, it is filmese, which is responsible for the occasionally stilted sound of dubbed dialogue, without however diminishing the overall acceptability of the Italian translations with respect to the English chunks.

To answer the question of whether the *Pavia Corpus of Film Dialogue* is big enough to provide a reliable indicator of the language of film dialogue with its most common translations, two measures have been used: frequency and dispersion (or consistency), the latter to control skewing effects. In addition, findings have been tested on a smaller sample, which – for the most part – yielded the same results. This confirms the formulaicity of filmic speech originally hypothesised and the consequent repetition of some of the translations. Further research is required to investigate variation across film genre (e.g., action films, dramas, romantic comedies) and the geographical origins of the films – whether American or British – so that distribution can be used to adjust the sampling criteria of the overall corpus.

---

[1] Although no strict genre categorizations guided the sampling of the *Pavia Corpus of Film Dialogue* (see Freddi & Pavesi (2009: 98)), categorizations did emerge from the films included. Some of the traditional screenplay types found were, for example, drama, comedy, crime, thriller, noir with the consequent exclusion of costume films, science-fiction as well as westerns. Notice also that categorizations are often fuzzy. In fact, romantic comedies are sometimes

described as *dramedies*. In addition, there are possible overlaps (e.g., between a thriller, a lawyer movie or courtroom drama, and an action movie).

[2] See Scott and Tribble (2006: 29) on consistency concerning the tendency some items have of being used consistently in several texts in a corpus instead of being restricted to only some of them.

[3] On conflict as an essential driving principle of screenwriting, see Cerami (1996 cited in Aimeri 2007: 36 [1998]) "Non sempre l'idea prefigura una storia o una situazione immediatamente propizia a una drammaturgia. (..) Sempre però esso contiene, più o meno espresso, un conflitto. E sarà proprio questo conflitto a dar vita a una drammaturgia: non esiste una drammaturgia senza conflitto e viceversa" [This always contains some conflict. And it is this conflict that will originate the dramaturgy: there is no dramaturgy without conflict and vice versa] (my translation).

References

Aimeri, Luca. 2007. *Manuale di Sceneggiatura Cinematografica: Teoria e Pratica*. Torino: Utet.
Baker, Mona. 1995. 'Corpora in Translation Studies: An Overview and Some Suggestions for Future Research' in *Target* 7(2): 223-243.
Baker, Mona. 1996. 'Corpus-Based Translation Studies: The Challenges that Lie Ahead' in Somers, Harold (ed.) *Terminology, LSP and Translation: Studies in Language Engineering in Honour of Juan C. Sager*. Amsterdam: John Benjamins. 175-186.
Baker, Mona. 2004. 'A Corpus-Based View of Similarity and Difference in Translation' in *International Journal of Corpus Linguistics* 9(2): 167-193.
Baños-Piñero, Rocío & Frederic Chaume. 2009. 'Prefabricated Orality: A Challenge in Audiovisual Translation' in Special Issue on The Translation of Dialects in Multimedia of inTRAlinea 2009. Online at http://www.intralinea.it/specials/dialectrans/eng_more.php?id=761_0_49_0_M
Biber, Douglas & Susan Conrad. 1999. 'Lexical Bundles in Conversation and Academic Prose' in Hasselgard, Hilde & Stig Oksefjell (eds.) *Out of Corpora: Studies in Honour of Stig Johansson*. Amsterdam: Rodopi. 181-190.
Biber, Douglas et al. 1999. *Longman Grammar of Spoken and Written English*. London: Longman.
Bruti, Silvia & Maria Pavesi. 2008. 'Interjections in Translated Italian: Looking for Traces of Dubbed Language' in Martelli, Aurelia & Virginia Pulcini (eds.) *Investigating English with Corpora: Studies in Honour of Maria Teresa Prat*. Monza: Polimetrica. 207-221.
Chaume, Frederic. 2001. 'La Pretendida Oralidad de los Textos Audiovisuales y Sus Implicaciones en Traduccion' in Agost, Rosa & Frederic Chaume (eds.) *La Traducción en los Medios Audiovisuales*. Castelló de la Plana: Publicacions de la Universitat Jaume I. 77-87.
Chaume, Frederic. 2004a. *Cine y traduccion*. Madrid: Cátedra.
Chaume, Frederic. 2004b. 'Discourse Markers in Audiovisual Translating' in *Meta* 49(4): 843-855.
Chaume, Frederic. 2004c. 'Film Studies and Translation Studies: Two disciplines at Stake in Audiovisual Translation' in *Meta* 49(1): 12-24.
Díaz Cintas, Jorge. 2004 'In Search of a Theoretical Framework for the Study of Audiovisual Translation' in Orero, Pilar (ed.) *Topics in Audiovisual Translation*. Amsterdam: Benjamins. 21-34.

Freddi, Maria. 2009. 'The Phraseology of Contemporary Filmic Speech: Formulaic Language and Translation' in Freddi, Maria & Maria Pavesi (eds) *Analysing Audiovisual Dialogue. Linguistic and Translational Insights*. Bologna: Clueb. 101-123.

Freddi, Maria & Maria Pavesi (eds.). 2009. *Analysing Audiovisual Dialogue. Linguistic and Translational Insights*. Bologna: Clueb.

Heiss, Christine & Marcello Soffritti. 2008. 'Forlixt 1: The Forlì Corpus of Screen Translation: Exploring Microstructures' in Chiaro, Delia, Christine Heiss & Chiara Bucaria (eds.) *Between Text and Image: Updating Research in Screen Translation*. Amsterdam: John Benjamins. 51-62.

Laviosa, Sara. 1998. 'Universals of Translation' in Baker, Mona (ed.) *Encyclopaedia of Translation Studies*. London: Routledge. 288-291.

Laviosa, Sara. 2004. 'Corpus-Based Translation Studies: Where does it Come from? Where is it Going?' in *Language Matters* 35(1): 6-23.

Mauranen, Anna & Pekka Kujamäki (eds.). 2004. *Translation Universals: Do they Exist?* Amsterdam: John Benjamins.

Olohan, Maeve. 2004. *Introducing Corpora in Translation Studies*. London: Routledge.

Pavesi, Maria. 2005. *La traduzione filmica: Aspetti del Parlato Doppiato dall'Inglese all'Italiano*. Roma: Carocci.

Pavesi, Maria. 2008. 'Spoken Language in Film Dubbing: Target Language Norms, Interference and Translational Routines' in Chiaro, Delia, Christine Heiss & Chiara Bucaria (eds.) *Between Text and Image: Updating Research in Screen Translation*. Amsterdam: John Benjamins. 79-99.

Pavesi, Maria. 2009. 'Dubbing English into Italian: A Closer Look at the Translation of Spoken Language' in Díaz Cintas, Jorge (ed.) *New Trends in Audiovisual Translation*. Clevedon: Multilingual Matters. 201-213.

Remael, Aline. 2004. 'A Place for Film Dialogue Analysis in Subtitling Courses' in Orero, Pilar (ed.) *Topics in Audiovisual Translation*. Amsterdam: John Benjamins. 103-126.

Romero-Fresco, Pablo. 2006. 'Spanish Dubbese: A Case of (Un)idiomatic Friends' in *The Journal of Specialized Translation* 6: 134-151. Online at http://www.jostrans.org/issue06/art_romero_fresco.php

Romero-Fresco, Pablo 2009. 'Naturalness in the Spanish Dubbing Language: A Case of Not-So-Close Friends' in *Meta* 54(1): 49-72.

Scott, Mike & Christopher Tribble. 2006. *Textual Patterns: Key Words and Corpus Analysis in Language Education*. Amsterdam: John Benjamins.

Sinclair,, John. 2003. *Reading Concordances*. London: Longman.

Sinclair, John. 2004. 'The Search for Units of Meaning' chap. 2 of *Trust the Text: Language, Corpus and Discourse*. London: Routledge. 24-48.

Taylor, Christopher. 1999. 'Look Who's Talking: An Analysis of Film Dialogue as a Variety of Spoken Discourse' in Lombardo, Linda et al. (eds.) *Massed Medias: Linguistic Tools for Interpreting Media Discourse*. Milano: Led. 247-278.

Taylor, Christopher. 2004. 'The Language of Film: Corpora and Statistics in the Search for Authenticity. Notting Hill (1998) – A Case Study' in *Miscelanea* 30: 71-86.

Taylor, Christopher. 2006. "I Knew He'd Say That!': A Consideration of the Predictability of Language Use in Film' in MuTra 2006 – Audiovisual Translation Scenarios, EU-High-Level Scientific Conference Series. Online at http://www.euroconferences.info/proceedings/2006_Proceedings/2006_Taylor_Christopher.pdf)

Valentini, Cristina. 2007. 'Developing AVT Corpora for a Quantitative Approach to Language Transfer in Cinematic Products' in Mus, Fernando (ed.) *Selected Papers of the CETRA Research Seminar in Translation Studies 2006*. Online at http://www.kuleuven.be/cetra/papers/papers.html

Valentini, Cristina 2008. 'Forlixt 1: The Forlì Corpus of Screen Translation: Exploring Macrostructures' in Chiaro, Delia, Christine Heiss & Chiara Bucaria (eds.) *Between Text and Image: Updating Research in Screen Translation*. Amsterdam: John Benjamins. 37-50.
Wordsmith Tools v. 4.0. Oxford: Oxford University Press.

Multisemiotic and Multimodal Corpus Analysis in Audio Description: TRACCE

Catalina Jiménez
Universidad de Granada (Spain)

Claudia Seibel
Universidad de Granada (Spain)

Abstract
This contribution presents the results of the TRACCE Project, whose objective has been to design the structure of an accessible audiovisual product database. In an initial step, over 300 films with audio description in Spanish were collected, stored and inventoried. This corpus was complemented by a further 50 films in English, French and German. Throughout the project, the audio-description scripts constituted the main object of study, since they form the basis of the semantic tagging and are therefore the source of the knowledge base. Subsequently, a conceptual framework underlying the semantic tagging system was developed, which operated on three distinct levels: (1) narratology, (2) cinematography and (3) grammar. This allowed us to establish comparisons and patterns of equivalence between the three levels. The three-tier tagging system was later integrated into a single software application known as *Taggetti*. In the first two phases of the project, two independent applications were designed for tagging Narration (*Taggetti 1.4.*) and Image (*Taggetti Imagen 1.4.*). In a final stage, these were fused into the definitive software application combining the three tagged dimensions: (1) Narration, (2) Image and (3) Grammar.

Keywords
audio description, corpus linguistics, multimodal corpus analysis, multisemiotic corpus analysis

1. Introduction

This contribution explains how to apply corpus linguistic analysis to a multimodal corpus (Baldry & Thibault 2006). Following Salway (2007) and Ädel and Reppen (2008), we assert that a multimodal corpus can be tagged to extract different types of information. In our research project, this information has been used to create a database, which is a useful tool for computer-aided audio description.

The first section of this contribution briefly describes the transformation that corpus linguistics has undergone over the past decades and its impact on research and analysis in the field of audio description. It also discusses the compatibility of corpus-based methods with research issues in text linguistics and its subfields. The second part of this contribution shows how recurrent semiotic patterns in an audio described film can be analysed and integrated into a unified model. This process involves the segmentation and specification of visual units of analysis with a view to tagging and linking them to a narrated text in the audio description script. Although our corpus contains language-only text – which has been semantically tagged – this linguistic information is related to the conceptual grammar of the visual semiosis codified in film scenes, as well as to the narratology of the film.

2. Corpus data to validate multimodal text analysis

Corpus linguistics arose with the need to collect real data about language and to perform empirical studies. In order to have a scientific basis for multimodal text research and be able to examine how such texts create meaning, it is necessary to have a large amount of data available as well as an appropriate method of analysis. Today, any meaningful research on text types and text linguistics must be preceded by the elaboration of a representative corpus or a large collection of running text with several million words (i.e., types and tokens). Corpora are often analysed by using software programs for the semi-automatic extraction of conceptual, lexical and pragmatic information.

Consequently, it is crucial for texts in a corpus to be organised in such a way that the data extracted by the software analysis program are reliable and thus lead to meaningful results. This means that a corpus should be a collection of real texts that are representative of a specific text type or text types. The design of the corpus depends on the nature of the research project and its objectives. Therefore, an adequate design is of great importance. In corpus compilation, the type of data to be collected and the analysis to be performed are crucial. The effectiveness of any corpus approach depends on how effectively data are gathered, the nature of the corpus, and how the corpus is tagged. It goes without saying that a corpus must be representative, balanced and sufficiently large for its projected use.

In order to be representative, a corpus should be in direct relation with the text type that is the object of investigation. Thus, a corpus should be a microcosm of a larger phenomenon. Accordingly, its equilibrium and size are directly related to its representativity and – in a certain sense – depend on it. A corpus is not representative if it is not balanced or if it does not have a suitable size. However, the equilibrium of a corpus also depends on other factors. For example, in our corpus, the majority of texts were narrated by six different people. In other words, of approximately three hundred films, we have examples of only six different voices. This logically affected the representativeness of the corpus to a certain extent.

3. Tagging a multimodal corpus

Generally speaking, multimodal corpora are composed of recordings of spontaneous conversations. They often include recordings of facial expressions, movements, posture and all types of body language. Allwood (2008: 208) describes multimodal corpora as follows:

> (A multimodal corpus) in a slightly narrow sense, (...) would only include material that has been digitized, i.e. the films would have to be digitized rather than just available in an archive ... a multimodal digitized corpus is a computer-based collection of language and communication related material drawing on more than one sensory modality or more than one production modality. In a still more narrow sense, we might require that the audiovisual material should be accompanied by transcriptions and annotations or codings based on the material.

The multidimensional nature of such corpora is determined by the range of semiotic systems used. These include running text, static and dynamic images, hyperlinks, etc.

At the beginning of our research project, *Evaluación y gestión de los recursos de accesibilidad para discapacitados sensoriales a través de la traducción audiovisual: La audiodescripción para ciegos. Protocolo para formar a formadores* (TRACCE),[1] the accessibility of audiovisual media for the handicapped was not regulated, and there was an evident need for more research studies to help establish criteria and guidelines for quality evaluation, user expectations and successful communication in this area.

For this reason, in the initial phases of TRACCE, it was necessary to set up an in-depth study of the current state of affairs in Spain with regard to audio description for the blind. For this purpose, a methodology was used in our project that took into account not only the technical and technological dimensions of multimodal text analysis but also all contextual, pragmatic, cultural, functional and linguistic aspects that determine and influence the reception of this audiovisual product for the visually impaired. This objective was achieved by integrating experimental and descriptive methods for multimodal corpus linguistics and discourse analysis (Baldry & Thibault 2006; O'Halloran 2006). Our multimodal corpus of audio described films provided the basic data for our study of the audio-description process as the generation of a new text type as well as a new modality of translation (Jiménez Hurtado 2007).

3.1. Corpus design and building

In order to systematise the analysis of the texts in our corpus and facilitate the access, retrieval and re-use of the information, we collected, stored and inventoried approximately 300 audio described films in Spanish. These films were complemented by another 50 audio described films in English, French and German. Since there is a general scarcity of audio described films – except for a few that are commercially available – most of the Spanish audio described films in our research came from the film archives of the ONCE (Spanish National Organization for the Blind), who kindly allowed us to use the films for research purposes. The CEIAF and Mundovision corporations also generously allowed us to use their movie scripts and audio described films. The audio described films in English, French and German were acquired commercially.

We also transcribed the audio description scripts (ADSs). These ADSs were the focal element of our study since these texts were given semantic tags and, thus, became the foundation of our knowledge base.[2] However, given the fact that the texts analysed are accessible multimodal texts, the theoretical and analytical tools used had to be tailored to their multimodal nature and focus on the relations between different codes (Jiménez Hurtado 2010a, 2010b).

The classification of this material was carried out according to the following three parameters: (1) classification of texts according to language,[3] (2) classification of texts according to film genre and (3) classification of texts according to their degree of compliance with AENOR regulations.[4] This triple classification allowed us to perform a wide range of studies and analyses. For example, some of our work measured the degree of accessibility of audiovisual texts (Bourne & Lachat 2010). Other substudies contrasted different languages and cultures. Still others analysed different types of discourse strategies used in the audio description of film genres or the shift that occurred when professionals in the field began to apply AENOR regulations.

3.2. Conceptual framework for the semantic tagging of ADSs

The conceptual framework underlying the system of semantic tagging has three levels. This multilevel system enabled us to manage the information more effectively. It also allowed us to compare different languages, and to find parameters and correspondences that interact in the audio-description process. These levels of analysis include the film narrative (i.e., a story event that takes place in a given space and time), the camera language (types of camera shots, framing, and focus), and the set of recurring grammatical structures in the ADSs.

This multiple tagging system for audio described texts facilitated the identification and codification of certain morphosyntactic, lexical-semantic, and pragmatic-discursive patterns that generally occur in this type of intersemiotic translation, as well as the automation and systematisation of this information for its subsequent study and exploitation. Figures 1, 2 and 3 show the conceptual maps corresponding to our three-level system of semantic tagging (i.e., *Narrative [Mise-en-scène]*, *Image* and *Grammar*).

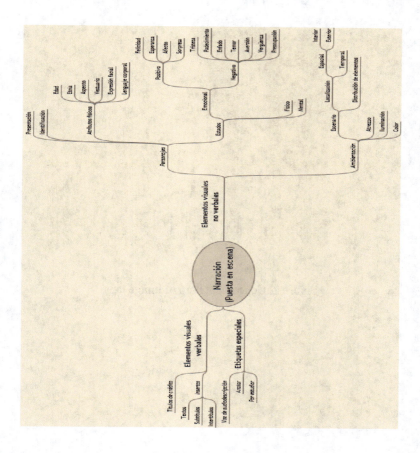

Figure 1. Conceptual map of narrative tags

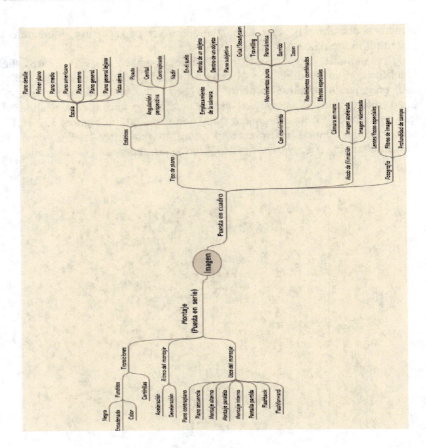

Figure 2. Conceptual map of image tags

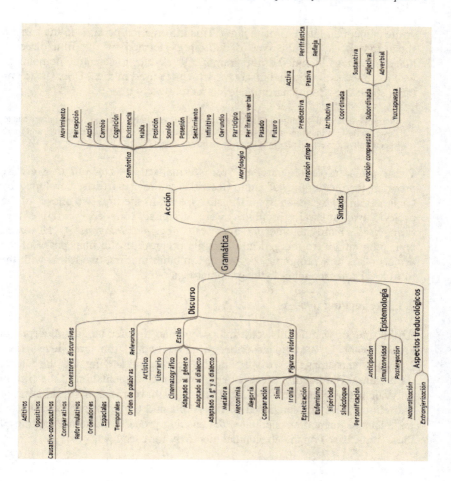

Figure 3. Conceptual map of grammar tags

As can be observed in Figures 1, 2 and 3, each tagging level is based on a conceptual organisation that depends on the sphere of focus. The organisation of all the tagging elements at each level is hierarchical and the elements are configured from the most general levels to more specific ones.

Each level is analysed in accordance with its nature. For example, in the analysis of the film (i.e., the source text), it is first necessary to examine the narrative structure of the story. Thus, the tags refer to the characters and their actions, as well as to the space and times during which the actions occur (narrative tags). Similarly, it is also necessary to tag the audiovisual structure or the camera language (image tags). This information pertains to the camera shots and focus and the type of editing performed by the film director. Finally, the tags included at the grammar level refer to semantic domains as well as to the syntactic and discourse structures used in the ADSs. Coste and Pier (2009: 295) define narrative levels as follows:

> Narrative levels (also referred to as diegetic levels) is an analytic notion whose purpose is to describe the relations among the plurality of narrating instances within a narrative, and more specifically the vertical relations between narrating instances.

These semantic tag hierarchies were formalised in *Taggetti*, a software program for the tagging of audio described audiovisual texts, developed by Gizer.net and the University of Deusto (Spain). In the first two phases of the project, two software programs were designed: one for narrative tags (*Taggetti 1.4*) and the other for image tags (*Taggetti Imagen 1.4*). However, both programs were merged into a single program in the final phase of the project. This new program, *Taggetti 2,* combines the first two levels with the third level corresponding to the grammar tags.

3.3. The tagging process

At the time of writing this contribution, we had finished tagging a corpus of approximately 270 audio described films at two of the three levels (i.e., Narrative and Image). We were in the process of tagging the third level (Grammar). The tagging process begins with the segmentation of the film in polyvalent Meaning Units (MUs). These units have a maximum duration of one minute, and are composed of the ADSs and the associated audiovisual text. This segmentation facilitates the ensuing process of manual tagging of these units, based on the conceptual hierarchy for each level.

Multisemiotic and multimodal corpus analysis in audio description

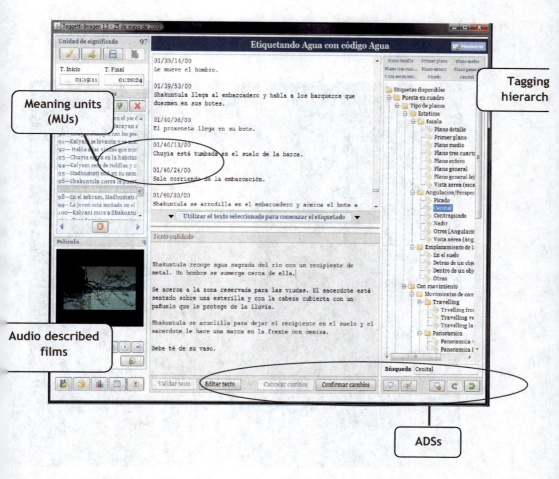

Figure 4. Screen capture of *Taggetti Imagen 1.4* during the tagging process

For example, Figure 4 shows the tagging process at the image or the camera-language level. As can be observed, the meaning units (MUs) are listed in the left column. These units are actually short clips from the film, which are segments lasting approximately one minute. These segments are linked to their corresponding section of the audio description script (ADSs) (see the upper middle column). The actual tagging takes place in the lower part of the middle column. The menu of possible tags appears in the column at the right.

417

Once the film is tagged, it is possible to retrieve any previously analysed segment or segments. Figures 5, 6 and 7 show examples of types of data that can be retrieved.

Pinocchio and Jiminy Cricket [ACC#ACCION]se sientan [fin_ACC#ACCION] [AMB#LOC#ESP#LEXT]en el porche[fin_AMB#LOC#ESP#LEXT] [PERS#EST#MENT]pensativos[fin_PERS#EST#MENT] y [PERS#EST#EMOC#NEG#TRIS]tristes[fin_PERS#EST#EMOC#NEG#TRIS].

Figure 5. Tagging of the cognitive domain of emotions. Pinocchio (Disney 1940)
[Pinocchio and Jiminy Cricket are sitting on the porch, pensive.]

Multisemiotic and multimodal corpus analysis in audio description

[AMB#ATREZZO]La espada
[AMB#COLOR]plateada[fin_AMB#COLOR].Harry
[ACC#ACCION]lee[fin_ACC#ACCION] la
inscripción[fin_AMB#ATREZZO] [ACC#PAR]grabada[fin_ACC#PAR] en
la hoja

Figure 6. Tagging of props. Harry Potter and the Secret Chamber (2002)
[The silver sword. Harry reads the inscription engraved on the blade]

[AMB#LOC#TEMP]Al amanecer[fin_AMB#LOC#TEMP], las viudas [ACC#ACCION]realizan[fin_ACC#ACCION] los ritos del funeral de Buhá.

Figure 7. Tagging of Temporal location. Water (2005)
[At dawn the widows perform the Buhá funeral rites]

The software application generates a .xml file, which includes the TCR (time code reading) of each MU and the ADS segment that corresponds to the film segment, tagged at the corresponding level. These .xml files are stored in the database for future access and retrieval. These files provide valuable data for the semi-automatic text analysis of the corpus.

3.4. Web interface of the database

The audiovisual texts that were tagged with *Taggetti* were incorporated in a knowledge base that is available at the Tracce project website (http://www.tracce.es). This interface has various tools, including a search engine for the retrieval of tags as well as statistical information pertaining to tags, which facilitate the effective retrieval of data obtained from a range of different perspectives (see Figures 8 and 9). These search tools are complemented by an independent software program for the generation of tagging statistics. This program allows the comparison and exploitation of data in the knowledge base for research, training, and professional purposes.

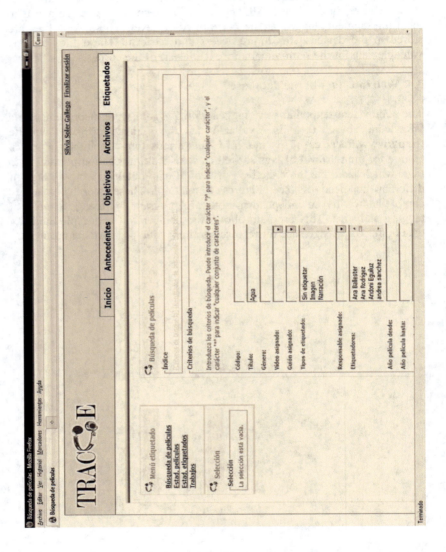

Figure 8. Interface of the TRACCE knowledge base: Film search screen

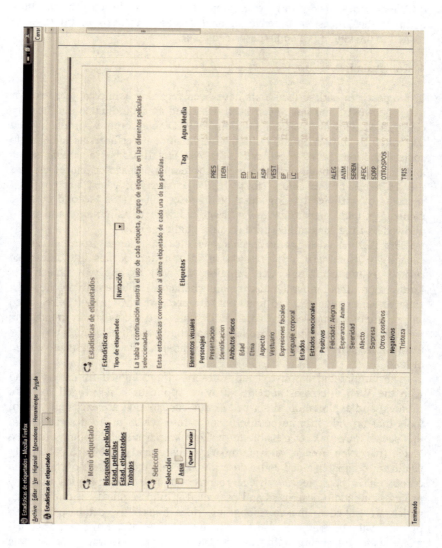

Figure 9. Interface of the TRACCE knowledge base: Tagging statistics

Based on the data record of each film (with the fields of *Genre, Author, Title, Year, Source Text Language*, etc.), these software applications make it possible to generate statistics pertaining to patterns and structures (in the different film subcorpora) concerning film genres. In conclusion, they optimise the processes of retrieval, analysis, and synthesis of information related to the tagging of audio described texts.

4. Conclusions

In the past, audio described texts have been regarded as incomplete texts or as pseudo-texts, and have even been described as subordinated and heavily constrained. However, in our opinion, the AD is a complex, multi-leveled text which is fully adequate in its own right since it performs an undeniable social function. More specifically, the AD that describes a certain scene appears at the moment in which there is a temporal space or pause between the dialogues of the actors (first creative challenge); when that temporal space is of sufficiently long duration to insert the ADSs (second creative challenge); and when the scene is described with the simplicity and depth allowed by time constraints (third creative challenge).

The AD encodes narrative characteristics that range from adequacy, capacity of summary, compression of information or absolute relevance related to the communicative function, as well as apparent objectivity. Furthermore, this innovative text type is characterised by a convergence of a singular set of semantic and functional features, which is why it is regarded an extremely specialised text type. As linguists and specialists in translation, we are faced with an extraordinary challenge, which is to create a new theoretical framework and methodology of analysis for this innovative type of text.

The multimodal corpus of audio described and tagged film texts along with the Web interfaces and the software applications developed for data retrieval and exploitation, described in this contribution are extremely useful tools that provide infinite possibilities for research in audio description. In this sense, they make it possible to perform searches that combine the three levels (narration, image, and grammar). Consequently, they are potentially useful for computer-aided audio description. From the database of the tagged corpus, it is possible to retrieve recurrent translation strategies used by professional audio describers and presented in film segments of one minute, which are linked to the corresponding video clips. This database can also provide valuable information for the elaboration of multimedia teaching materials for e-learning platforms, which can be applied to train professionals in the field of audio description.

---

[1] Evaluation and management of accessibility resources for the handicapped through audiovisual translation: audio description for the visually impaired.

[2] The audio described films in our project come from different sources, such as television channels, the video library of the ONCE (Spanish National Organization of the Blind), and commercial DVDs in Spain, other European Union countries, and the USA.

[3] This project provides corpus data from the analysis of the Spanish corpus only.

[4] The name of the audio describer was also included when this information was available.

References

Ädel, Annelie & Randi Reppen (eds.). 2008. *Corpora and Discourse: The challenges of different settings.* Amsterdam: John Benjamins.
Allwood, Jens. 2008. 'Multimodal corpora' in Lüdeling, Anke & Merja Kytö (eds.) *Corpus Linguistics: An International Handbook.* Berlin: Mouton de Gruyter. 207-224.
Baldry, Anthony P. & Paul J. Thibault. 2006. *Multimodal Transcription and Text.* London: Equinox.
Bourne, Julian & Christina. Lachat. 2010. 'Impacto de la Norma Aenor: Valoración del Usuario' in Jiménez Hurtado, Catalina, Ana Rodríguez & Claudia Seibel (eds.) *Un Corpus de Cine: Teoría y Práctica de la Audiodescripción.* Granada: Tragacanto. 319-330.
Coste, Didier & John Pier. 2009. 'Narrative Levels' in Hühn, Peter et al. (eds.) *Handbook of Narratology.* Berlin: de Gruyter. 295-308.
Jiménez Hurtado, Catalina. 2007. 'Una Gramática Local del Guión Audiodescrito: Desde la Semántica a la Pragmática de un Nuevo Tipo de Traducción' in Jiménez Hurtado, Catalina (ed.) *Traducción y Accesibilidad: Subtitulación para Sordos y Audiodescripción para Ciegos: Nuevas Modalidades de Traducción Audiovisual.* Frankfurt: Peter Lang. 55-79.
Jiménez Hurtado, Catalina. 2010a. 'Fundamentos Teóricos de la Audiodescripción' in Jiménez Hurtado, Catalina, Ana Rodríguez & Claudia Seibel (eds.) *Un Corpus de Cine: Teoría y Práctica de la Audiodescripción.* Granada: Tragacanto. 13-64.
Jiménez Hurtado, Catalina. 2010b. 'Fundamentos Metodológicos y Aplicados de la Audiodescripción' in Jiménez Hurtado, Catalina, Ana Rodríguez and Claudia Seibel (eds.) *Un Corpus de Cine: Teoría y Práctica de la Audiodescripción.* Granada: Tragacanto. 65-114.
O'Halloran, Kay L. 2006. 'Towards a Unified Theory of Text: A Systemic Functional Multimodal Discourse Analysis (SF-MDA) Approach to Mathematics' in Amano, Masachiyo (ed.) *Multimodality: Towards the Most Efficient Communications by Humans.* Nagoya: Nagoya University. 65-81.
Salway, Andrew. 2007. 'A Corpus-Based Analysis of the Language of Audio Description' in Díaz Cintas, Jorge, Pilar Orero & Aline Remael (eds.) *Media for All: Accessibility in Audiovisual Translation.* Amsterdam: Rodopi. 151-174.

Notes on contributors

Junichi Azuma is professor of English as a Foreign Language and Media and Communication Studies at the University of Marketing and Distribution Sciences, Kobe, Japan. His research covers the use of innovative media in TEFL, e-learning and future communication systems employing universal visual symbols.

Dominique Bairstow holds a PhD position in cognitive psychology at the University of Montpellier 3, where she works as teaching assistant. She studies the influence of subtitles on film perception, comprehension and memorisation as well as their effects on language learning. She has presented her work at various international congresses and has published in international psychology reviews.

Veronica Bonsignori holds a PhD in English Linguistics and has carried out her research at the Department of English studies of the University of Pisa. She currently has a scholarship as a temporary researcher at the University of Siena. Her research interests are in the fields of pragmatics, sociolinguistics and audiovisual translation. She has published various articles on audiovisual translation, focussing on the study of linguistic phenomena pertaining to orality in English filmic speech in comparison to Italian dubbing.

Silvia Bruti holds a PhD in English from the University of Pisa and is Associate Professor of English Language and Linguistics at the University of Pisa. Her research interests include text-linguistics, discourse analysis, (historical) pragmatics, corpus linguistics and translation. She has published widely in these areas and spoken at national and international conferences in these areas. She has recently investigated issues in intercultural pragmatics and audiovisual translation, including the translation of compliments and terms of address in inter-linguistic subtitles and dubbing.

Mary Carroll was founder and Managing Director of Titelbild Subtitling and Translation GmbH, Berlin until June 2011. She has extensive experience as an AVT consultant and lecturer on subtitling and AVT trends and profiles and has published widely in the field. She is a member of the Transmedia Research Group, the Transforum Coordination Committee for Interpreting and Translation Practice and Teaching in Germany and the German Federal Association of Interpreters and Translators. Her current research interests focus on AVT as well as mediation and interpreting.

Notes on contributors

Agnieszka Chmiel is Assistant Professor in the Department of Translation Studies at the School of English, Adam Mickiewicz University in Poznan. Her research interests include memory, psycholinguistic aspects of conference interpreting, audiovisual translation and audio description. She works as an interpreter and translator and has trained conference interpreters at AMU for 11 years. She currently heads the Post-Graduate Programme in Audiovisual Translation at AMU.

Lucile Desblache is Reader in Translation and Comparative Literature and Director of the Centre for Research in Translation and Transcultural Studies. Her main research interests lie in two areas: music and translation on the one hand, and environmental and animal representation in contemporary literature on the other. She is the editor of JoSTrans, The Journal of Specialised Translation and convenes the MA in Audiovisual Translation at Roehampton University, London.

Maria Freddi holds a PhD from the Catholic University of Milan. She is Assistant Professor of English Language and Linguistics at the University of Pavia, Italy, where she teaches courses on English grammar, text and corpus linguistics. For the past five years she has been involved in an audiovisual translation research project aimed at designing a computer-readable corpus of film dialogue (original and dubbed). Together with the project's principal investigator, she co-edited a collected volume entitled *Analysing Audiovisual Dialogue. Linguistic and Translational Insights*, 2009.

Nazaret Fresno Cañada holds an MA in Comparative Literature and Literary Translation from Universitat Pompeu Fabra (Barcelona, Spain) and an MA in Audiovisual Translation from Universitat Autònoma de Barcelona (Spain). She is currently working towards her PhD, which focuses on the reception of characters in audio described films. She has been working as a professional audio describer of opera for three years and teaches audio description in the postgraduate programmes in Audiovisual Translation at the Universitat Autònoma de Barcelona, the Universitat Pompeu Fabra and the University of Texas at Brownsville.

Henrik Gottlieb holds a PhD in Translation Studies. He worked as a subtitler from 1980 till 1992. He is Associate Professor at the University of Copenhagen and has lectured extensively in Europe and abroad. Recent publications include "Multilingual Translation vs. English-fits-all in South

African Media" (2010). *Across Languages and Cultures;* "English-inspired Post-9/11 Terms in Danish Media" (2010) in *Translating Information* Roberto A. Valdeón (ed.), Ediciones de la Universidad de Oviedo. His main fields of reseach are translation theory, audiovisual translation, lexicography, contact linguistics and linguistic borrowing.

Catalina Jiménez Hurtado is a lecturer in linguistics and translation at the Department of Translation and Interpreting at the Universidad de Granada. She is interested in the relation between lexical semantics and translation and the modulation of both fields in the development of different types of meaning representation and controlled languages. Further research interests include the connection between text linguistics and terminology management within the field of local grammars, multimodal discourse analysis and multimodal corpus linguistics applied to the description of audio description.

Jean-Marc Lavaur lectures and conducts research in cognitive psychology at the University of Montpellier 3. His basic research relates to the organization and functioning of multilingual lexicon, focusing on links between translation equivalents in memory and the effects of language change (the cost of switching) on processing. His applied research centers on the cognitive processing of audiovisual information (with particular emphasis on subtitled audiovisual programmes).

Carmen Mangiron is a lecturer and researcher at the Universitat Autònoma de Barcelona. She is a member of the research group TransMedia Catalonia and the Centre for Ambient Intelligence and Accessibility in Catalunya. She has participated in several international conferences and has extensive experience as a translator, specialising in software and game localisation. Her main research interests are game localisation, game accessibility, and serious games.

Silvia Masi is a researcher in English Linguistics at the Faculty of Foreign Languages and Literature of the University of Pisa, Italy, where she received a Ph.D. in Linguistics of Modern Languages in 2004. Her research interests are in the fields of lexical semantics, pragmatics, text linguistics and translation and she has published several articles in national and international journals and collections.

Iwona Mazur is Assistant Professor at the Department of Translation Studies, School of English, Adam Mickiewicz University in Poznan. Her research interests include audiovisual translation in general and audio description in particular. She is currently Head of Postgraduate Studies in Specialized Translation at AMU and Executive Board member of ESIST, the European Association for Studies in Screen Translation.

Alex Mc Donald is currently a part-time PhD student at the University of Leeds, developing a multimodal transcription tool for the in-vision BSL interpreter in TV drama. He is also an invited lecturer on the MA in Applied Translation Studies at the University of East Anglia, and is working as an interpreter at Alexander Communications, of which he is the founder, a company that provides British Sign Language interpreters who specialise in Theatre, Media and Education.

Vincenza Minutella is a lecturer in English Language and Translation at the University of Turin. She holds a PhD in Translation Studies from the University of Warwick. She has conducted research in theatre translation, film adaptation, Shakespearean translation and audiovisual translation. Her current research focuses on audiovisual translation of multilingual films and films for children and on the use of computerised corpora in Translation Studies.

Juan Martínez Pérez was a journalist at Swiss Broadcasting from 1996 to 2002, responsible for news and public relations. He studied Translation Studies at the Zurich University of Applied Sciences Winterthur (ZHAW). From 2006 to 2008, he was a lecturer in Computational Linguistics at the ZHAW. Since 2008, he has been a consultant and instructor in speech recognition and respeaking. He currently works with state and private broadcasters in different European countries.

Minako O'Hagan, PhD, is a senior lecturer at Dublin City University (DCU) affiliated with the DCU Centre for Translation and Textual Studies. She has been involved in interdisciplinary, cutting-edge translation research with a main interest in the impact of emerging technologies on the practice of translation. Funded research projects include a feasibility study on Machine Translation, eye-tracker studies on translation tools and fan translator studies. More recently her research focus has been on empirically-oriented studies of video game localisation and user studies of social media platforms.

Pilar Orero holds a PhD from UMIST. She works in the CAIAC Research Centre of the Universitat Autònoma de Barcelona and is director of the Online European MA in Audiovisual Translation http://mem.uab.es/metav/.

Her recent publications include: *Media for All: Subtitling for the Deaf, Audio Description and Sign Language* (2007) Rodopi, co-edited with Jorge Díaz Cintas and Aline Remael; *Listening to Subtitles: SDHoH* (2010) Peter Lang, co-edited with Anna Matamala and *Voice-over: An Overview* (2010) Peter Lang, co-authored with Anna Matamala and Eliana Franco. She leads numerous research projects funded by the Spanish and Catalan Government as well as TransMedia Catalonia http://grupsderecerca.uab.cat/transmedia catalonia. She is a partner of the EC project DTV4ALL http://www.psp-dtv4all.org/.

Maria Pavesi is Professor of English Language and Linguistics at Pavia University. Her research has recently focused on spoken language in film translation and language acquisition via audiovisual input. She has published several articles on these topics, authored *La traduzione filmica* (2005) and co-edited *Analysing audiovisual dialogue* (2009). She is the coordinator of the international project *English and Italian audiovisual language: translation and language learning*.

Aline Remael is Professor of Audiovisual Translation and Translation Theory at the Department of Translators and Interpreters of Artesis University College. Her main research interest is in audiovisual translation (intralingual and interlingual subtitling, live subtitling and audio description). She has published widely on the subject and is the co-author with Jorge Díaz Cintas of *Audiovisual Translation: Subtitling* (St Jerome, 2007). She is a member of TransMedia, chief editor of *Linguistica Antverpiensia New Series, Themes in Translation Studies* (www.lans-tts.be) and board member of EST.

Pablo Romero-Fresco is a senior lecturer in audiovisual translation at Roehampton University. He also teaches for the MA on Audiovisual Translation at Universidad Autònoma de Barcelona. As a member of the research group TransMedia Catalonia / CAIAC, he has published and carried out research on dubbing, subtitling and audio description and has coordinated the subtitling section of DTV4ALL, an EU-funded research project exploring the possibility of providing a common standard for Subtitling for the Deaf and Hard of Hearing in Europe. He is author of *Subtitling through Speech Recognition: Respeaking* (St Jerome). His research interests also include film and he collaborates regularly with the London Spanish Film Festival and the online film radio station FRED.

Claudia Seibel is a lecturer in translation and terminology at the Department of Translation and Interpreting at the Universidad de Granada. She is interested in terminology management and the relation between technical-scientific translation and different types of meaning representation. Further interests include controlled language and the application of audio description to local grammar. She is member of the research and development team *AMATRA*, which aims to promote accessibility in the media for the blind, the deaf and the hard-of-hearing.

Anna Vermeulen is a senior lecturer at the University College of Translation Studies in Ghent where she teaches subtitling and audiovisual translation. Her research interests and publications focus on translation strategies and linguistic variation in audiovisual translation. As a visiting professor she held conferences and workshops at the Universities of Madrid, Santander, Aranjuez, Salamanca, Valencia, Castellón, Las Palmas de Gran Canaria, Buenos Aires and México.

Anika Vervecken studied drama prior to commencing studies in translation in Antwerp where she focused on surtitling for her M.A. thesis. She works with various theatres, theatre companies, opera houses and surtitling software companies. She currently lives in Vancouver and works internationally as a surtitler.

Monika Woźniak is Associate Professor of Polish Language at the Faculty of Human Sciences of the University of Roma "La Sapienza". She has conducted research in literary translation and the history of Italian literature and has published numerous essays related to these topics. She is also a literary translator. Her recent research interests focus on the translation children's literature and audiovisual translation. She has been guest editor of two special issues of „Przekładaniec. Journal of Literary Translation" (Cracow) dedicated to audiovisual translation (2008) and fairy tales in translation (2010).

Index

Aarseth, Espen J., 45, 57
Abdullah, Rayan, 81, 83
Ädel, Annelie, 409, 425
Aenor 167, 412
Agost, Rosa, 269, 405
Aijmer, Karin, 268, 269, 270, 271
Aimeri, Luca, 403, 405
Allwood, Jens, 411, 425
Altbach, Philip, 98, 103, 106
Amano, Masachiyo, 425
Amer, Terek S., 78, 83
Americans with Disabilities Act 48
Anderman, Gunilla, 187, 228, 245, 268, 269, 270, 271, 272, 292
Aparicio, Xavier, 280, 292
Aristotle 147, 167
Arumi Ribas, Marta, 135, 136, 144, 145
Asselin de Beauville, Jean-Pierre, 146
Assis Rosa, Alexandra, 297, 311
Au, Kenneth K.L., 270
Auer, Peter, 312
Austin, Michael Holquist, 204
Azuma, Junichi, 7, 17, 61, 69, 83, 427
Bahan, Benjamin, 194, 204
Baines, Roger, 205
Bairstow, Dominique, 8, 19, 273, 274, 278, 280, 283, 292, 427
Baker, Colin, 316, 332
Baker, Mona, 40, 91, 106, 297, 311, 316, 333, 354, 381, 382, 405, 406
Bakhtin, Mikhail M., 200, 204
Balázs, Béla, 148, 167
Bald, Wolf-Dietrich, 261, 272
Baldridge, Jason, 327, 333
Baldry, Anthony, 205, 409, 411, 425
Ballester, Ana, 149, 167
Baños-Piñero, Rocio, 382, 405
Baranauskienė, Reda, 214
Bartoll, Eduard, 326, 333
Bartrina, Francesca, 203, 204
Baumgarten, Nicole, 212, 227
Beaudry, Guylaine, 93, 103, 106
Beaumont, Jean-François, 131
Beentjes, Johannes, 291, 292
Belczyk, Arkadiusz, 210, 227
Benecke, Bernd, 149, 167, 174, 178, 187
Beninatto, Renato, 33
Berman, Antoine, 297, 312
Berruto, Gaetano, 316, 333

Berry, David 26, 39
Bey, Youcef, 28, 39
Bhabha, Homi, 88, 103, 104, 106, 107
Biber, Douglas, 337, 353, 391, 405
Bierre, Kevin, 48, 50, 51, 57
Björk, Bo-Christer, 93, 103, 106
Blanc, Nathalie, 275, 292
Blaževičienė, Rasa, 214
Blicher, Henrik, 271
Blissymbolics 71, 72, 83, 84
Block, Bruce A., 201, 204
BOAI 86, 105
Bogucki, Lukasz, 211, 227
Boismenu, Gérard, 93, 103, 106
Boisvert, Maryse, 131
Boitet, Christian, 39
Bollettieri Bosinelli, Rosa Maria, 246, 333, 354, 355
Bonsignori, Veronica, 8, 20, 314, 333, 353, 355, 357, 358, 359, 360, 368, 375, 378, 427
Bordwell, David, 148, 167
Böttger, Claudia, 227
Boulianne, Giles, 131
Bourne, Julian, 412, 425
Braffort, Annelies, 194, 204
Brandeau, A., 146
Brant, Rosemary, 251, 269
Braun, Sabine, 175, 187
Brouard, Thierry, 146
Brousseau, Julie, 131
Brown, Roger, 353
Brunette, Louise, 27, 33, 40
Bruti, Silvia, 8, 20, 353, 357, 358, 359, 360, 368, 375, 378, 381, 405, 427
Bucaria, Chiara, 406, 407
Burch, Noël, 196, 204
Burton, Jonathan, 229, 230, 231, 235, 239, 245
Burton, Tim, 151, 152, 167
Caili, Eric, 58
Camhy, Daniela G. 84
Cardinal, Patrick, 131
Cardinaletti, Anna, 355
Cardwell, Sarah, 201, 204
Carlson, Marvin, 229, 230, 231, 234, 243, 245
Carroll, Mary 7, 11, 13, 276, 292, 333, 427

Index

Cartmell, Deborah, 196, 204
Cassella, Maria, 97, 103, 106
Cattrysse, Patrick, 353
Chafe, Wallace, 112, 113, 130, 131, 136, 144, 146, 180, 187, 188
Chandler, Heather M., 58
Chapdelaine, Claude, 131
Chatman, Seymour, 148, 167
Chaume, Frederic, 191, 204, 269, 298, 312, 336, 345, 353, 366, 378, 382, 405
Chiaro, Delia, 315, 326, 333, 354, 406, 407
Chmiel, Agnieszka, 7, 18, 173, 176, 177, 179, 180, 187, 188, 428
Clyne, Michael, 336, 337, 342, 353
Cokely, Dennis, 203, 204
Comeau, Michael, 131
Conrad, Susan, 391, 405
Constantini, Erica, 166, 167
Corbin, Zoëb, 87, 104, 107
Corson, Yves, 292
Coste, Didier, 416, 425
Coulmas, Florian, 357, 378, 379
Coupland, Justine, 359, 378
Coupland, Nikolas, 378
Cowdery, Ron, 193, 205
Craven, Jenny, 101, 104, 107
Cronin, Michael, 101, 103, 104, 107
Crossley, Rob, 43, 58
Crystal, David, 62, 83
Cubbison, Laurie, 29, 39, 40
d'Ydewalle, Géry, 270, 274, 292
Dahl, Roald, 151, 168
Danan, Martine, 285, 291, 292
Darbelnet, Jean, 345, 355
Davis, Desmond, 204
Davis, Philip, 85, 86, 104, 107
Davis, William S., 190, 202, 205
De Caluwe, Johan, 298, 312
De Higes Andino, Irene, 326, 333
De Houwer, Annick, 312
De La Cruz Cabanillas 378
De Mauro, Tullio, 378
DeBruycker, Wim, 274, 292
Delbeke, Tijs, 146
DePalma, Don, 27, 32, 33, 34, 40
Desblache, Lucile, 7, 17, 85, 245, 428
Désilets, Alain, 27, 28, 33, 40
Dewolf, Linda, 246
Di Fortunato, Eleonora, 338, 340, 343, 354

Díaz Cintas, Jorge, 11, 13, 21, 25, 29, 36, 38, 40, 90, 104, 107, 131, 135, 146, 168, 187, 204, 228, 237, 239, 245, 246, 249, 255, 269, 270, 271, 272, 273, 292, 297, 312, 326, 330, 333, 336, 353, 354, 382, 405, 406, 425, 430, 431
Dillman, Don, 155, 168
Directory of Open Access Journals 92, 93, 98, 105
Dosch, Elmar, 167, 174, 178, 187
Dries, Josephine, 210, 214, 227
Du Bois, John W., 180, 187
Duchowski, Andrew, 130, 131, 145
Duden 82, 83
Dumouchel, Pierre, 131
Dunger, Hermann, 249, 250, 269
Durastanti, Sylvie, 246
Ebner, Martin, 69, 83
Eco, Umberto, 88, 104, 107
Ellis, Barry, 48, 54, 58
Emerson, Caryl, 204
Ervin-Tripp, Susan, 337, 354
European Commission 55, 252, 269
European Research Council 86, 105
Fels, Deborah, 175, 188, 235, 246
Filipović, Rudolf, 254, 269
Findlay, John M., 144, 146
Fischer, Roswitha, 268, 269
Fong, Gilbert, 270
Formentelli, Maicol, 337, 354
Foster, Edgar M., 168
Fouces, Oscar Diaz, 105, 108
Fox, Kate, 378
Franco, Eliana, 209, 212, 226, 227, 228, 430
Freddi, Maria, 8, 20, 314, 333, 338, 353, 354, 355, 381, 383, 400, 404, 406, 428
Fresno, Nazaret, 7, 18, 147, 428
Funredes 102, 104, 107
Furiassi, Christiano, 270
Gambier, Yves, 191, 204, 215, 227, 235, 246, 269, 270, 311, 344, 353
Garcarz, Michal, 211, 214, 227
García de Toro, Cristina, 378
Garcia, Ignacio, 28, 33, 40, 88, 104, 107
Geeraerts, Dirk, 298, 311, 312
Gellerstam, Martin, 250, 268, 269
Gerzymisch-Arbogast, Heidrun, 333
Giglioli, Pier Paolo, 353
Gile, Daniel, 146
Giles, Jim, 27, 40

Index

Gilman, Albert, 353
Glaser, Gabrielle, 210, 227
Glinert, Eitan, 47, 58
Gollardo, Natividad, 354
Gómez Capuz, Juan, 255, 269, 366, 378
Gomez, Jeff, 96, 104, 107
Goossens, Jan, 298, 312
Görlach, Manfred, 250, 268, 269
Gotti, Maurizio, 379
Gottlieb, Henrik, 8, 19, 216, 227, 235, 246, 249, 250, 251, 255, 256, 257, 268, 269, 270, 311, 316, 333, 428
Graddol, David, 262, 270
Graedler, Anne-Line, 268, 270
Graham, Joseph, 40
Grammenos, Dimitri, 50, 58
Gregersen, Frans, 262, 270
Greimas, Algirdas, 147, 168
Griesel, Yvonne, 229, 230, 231, 233, 237, 239, 244, 245, 246
Grigaraviciuté, Ieva, 216, 227
Grignon, Pamela, 275, 292
Grutman, Rainier, 296, 312
Guillot, Marie-Noëlle, 338, 345, 353, 354
Gumperz, John J. 354
Hanke, Ken, 152, 168
Harder, Peter, 270
Hartmann, Reinhard, 269
Hasegawa, Machiko, 78, 83
Hasselgard, Hilde, 405
Haton, Jean-Paul, 146
Haugen, Einar, 268, 270
Havelock, David, 292
He, Yuanjian 270
Hehner, Barbara, 71, 83
Heiss, Christine, 246, 297, 312, 326, 330, 333, 354, 355, 381, 406, 407
Helmbrecht, Johannes, 336, 354
Hendrickx, Paul, 214, 227
Hendrykowski, Marek, 210, 227
Herbst, Thomas, 193, 201, 204, 228, 250, 270
Hickey, Raymond, 337, 340, 344, 354
Hicks, Diana, 86, 104, 107
Hildyard, Angela, 131
Hinskens, Frans, 312
Hirvonen, Johanna, 339, 342, 354
Hoc, Jean M., 292
Hoffman, Eva, 89, 104, 107
Holland, Andrew, 175, 187
Horn, Robert, 71, 84
Horton, David, 338, 342, 353, 354

House, Juliane, 227, 297, 312
Howe, Jeff, 25, 26, 31, 40
Hübner, Roger, 81, 83
Hühn, Peter, 425
Hurt, Christina, 246
Hyks, Veronika, 175, 187
Hymes, Dell, 354
IBM 46, 58, 120, 134
ISO 9241-11 47
ITC 174, 175, 179, 187
Ivarsson, Jan, 227, 276, 292
Ivir, Vladimir, 271
Jackson, Rodhri, 104, 107
Jackson, Sherri L., 155, 168
Jarvad, Pia, 250, 271
Jenkins, Henry, 25, 40
Jiménez Hurtado, Catalina, 9, 20, 167, 409, 411, 412, 425, 429
Jørgensen, Merete K., 271
Jucker, Andreas H., 354
Kachru, Braj B., 316, 327, 333
Kageura, Kyo, 39
Kalogjera, Damir, 271
Kammerer, Matthias, 312
Kan, Yun-Feng, 274, 292
Karlin, Daniel, 250, 271
Kearns, John, 40
Keen, Andrew, 26, 40
Kelly, Dorothy 354
Kelly, Nataly, 27, 32, 34, 40
Kermas, Susan, 379
Kerswill, Paul, 312
Kitaoka, Akiyoshi, 78, 84
Klaudy, Kinga, 345, 354
Konerding, Klaus-Peter, 312
Koolstra, Cees M., 249, 271, 274, 291, 292
Kozloff, Sarah, 212, 227
Kriouille, Abdelaziz, 146
Kristiansen, Tore, 250, 271
Krzyżaniak, Wojciech, 215, 227
Kujamäki, Pekka, 381, 406
Kuwano, Sonoko, 292
Kvaran, Guðrún, 268, 270
Kyle, Jim G., 190, 204
Kytö, Merja, 425
L.L. 244, 246
Lachat, Christina, 412, 425
Ladouceur, Louise, 298, 312
Lahiri, Jhumpa, 89, 104, 107, 314, 324, 333
Laitinen, Sauli, 47, 58

435

Index

Lambert, Sylvie, 137, 146
Langeveld, Arthur, 297, 312
Langham-Brown, Jo, 204, 228
Lauer, Angelika, 354
Lauri, Lari, 103, 106
Lavaur, Jean-Marc, 8, 19, 187, 273, 274, 275, 280, 283, 287, 292, 378, 429
Laver, John, 359, 360, 379
Laviosa, Sara, 381, 406
Lavolee, Bruno, 231, 246
Laxen, Janika, 280, 292
Lee, Mina, 274, 292
Lehr, Andrea, 312
Leijten, Mariëlle, 146
Lejeune, Fanch, 194, 204
Lenz, Friedrich, 354
Leonard, Sean, 28, 40
Levy, Emanuel, 152, 168
Lewis, Philip, 30, 40
Lilllo-Martin, Diane, 205
Linder, Gion, 145
Linguistica Antverpiensia New Series 89, 104, 107, 431
Liversedge, Simon P., 131, 144, 146
LoCos 71, 72
Lommel, Arle, 58
Looms, Peter Olaf, 144, 146
Lopes Cavalheiro, Lili, 297, 312
Lorenzo García, Lourdes, 269
Losse, Kate, 27, 33, 40
Luca, Joseph, 83
Lucas, Ceil, 194, 204
Lüdeling, Anke, 425
Luyckx, Bieke, 137, 146
Luyken, Georg-Michael, 190, 204, 214, 228
Mackenzie, Fraser, 250, 271
Mahal, Baljinder K., 318, 321, 322, 333
Majid, Amir A., 102, 104, 107
Mancini, Federico, 378
Mangiron, Carmen, 7, 17, 43, 429
Mari, Jean-Francois, 103, 146
Marinetti, Cristina, 205
Marleau, Lucien, 251, 271
Maron, Nancy L., 87, 107
Martelli, Aurelia, 405
Martínez Pérez, Juan, 7, 17, 133, 145, 430
Martínez Tejerina, Anjana, 268, 271
Mascarenhas, Renata, 150, 168
Masi, Silvia, 8, 20, 357, 358, 359, 360, 368, 375, 378, 379, 429

Matamala, Anna, 11, 21, 131, 146, 168, 187, 210, 226, 228, 231, 246, 292, 378, 430
Mateo, Marta, 230, 231, 232, 235, 246
Mauranen, Anna, 381, 406
Maurer, Hermann, 83, 84
Mayoral, Roberta, 353, 354
Mazur, Iwona, 7, 18, 173, 176, 177, 179, 180, 187, 188, 429
McCarthy, Michael, 337, 354
McCloud, Scott, 79, 80, 81, 84
McDonald, Alex, 8, 18, 189, 193, 199, 203, 204
McGonigle, Francis, 149, 168
McNaughton, Shirley, 71, 84
Media Consulting Group 291, 292
Meir, Irit, 192, 204
Melchers, Gunnel, 268, 269, 270, 271
Merriam Webster's Online Dictionary 45, 58
Merschmann, Helmut, 152, 168
Meyer, Charles F. 354
Microsoft 44, 46, 58, 64
Miller, Christopher, 271
Millerson, Gerald, 201, 204
Minutella, Vincenza, 8, 19, 20, 313, 430
Mitchell, William.J.Thomas, 103, 104, 106, 107
Monti, Alessandro, 320, 333
Monti, Silvia, 326, 327, 330, 333
Monzó, Esther, 105, 108
Morford, Jannet, 337, 354
Morrison, Heather, 104, 107
Möttönen, Riikka, 274, 292
Motz, Markus, 227
Munday, Jeremy, 255, 271, 333
Muños Sánchez, Pablo, 29, 40
Murray, Thomas E., 337, 354
Muthiah, Subbiah, 317, 318, 321, 333
Muysken, Pieter, 316, 333
Myers-Scotton, Carol, 315, 333
Nair, Mira, 314, 330, 333, 334
Nakatsu, Ryohei, 62, 84
Nauert, Sandra, 333
Nava, Sophie, 274, 275, 292
Neesbye-Hansen, Nicolai, 253, 271
Neves, Josélia, 11, 21, 131, 146, 203, 204, 273, 292
Ngom, Fallou, 262, 271
Nichols, Bill, 212, 228
Nisato, Catherine, 246

436

Nornes, Abé Mark, 25, 28, 30, 31, 38, 40, 249, 271
Norrby, Catrin, 353
O'Hagan, Minako, 7, 16, 25, 28, 29, 40, 430
O'Halloran, Kay, 411, 425
O'Keefe, Anne, 337, 354
OFCOM 113, 121, 131, 149, 168, 189, 204
Office of Public Sector information (OPSI) 204
Oksanen, Susanna, 229, 246
Oksefjell, Stig, 405
Olohan, Maeve, 381, 406
Olson, David, 131
Onysko, Alexander, 250, 271
Orero, Pilar, 7, 11, 13, 21, 131, 149, 150, 166, 168, 174, 175, 179, 185, 188, 204, 209, 210, 214, 226, 228, 231, 246, 251, 270, 271, 353, 354, 405, 406, 425, 430
Osterrath, Frédéric, 131
Ota, Yukio, 71, 84
Ouellet, Pierre, 131
Palomo, Alicia, 149, 168
Paolinelli, Mario, 338, 340, 343, 354
Park, Ji-Hong, 94, 104, 107
Pavesi, Maria, 8, 20, 314, 333, 335, 337, 338, 339, 340, 342, 351, 353, 354, 355, 366, 379, 381, 382, 383, 393, 404, 405, 406, 431
Pedersen, Jan, 249, 252, 271
Peeters, Allerd L., 271, 274, 292
Pepi, Leistyna, 354
Perego, Elisa, 210, 228, 270, 353
Pereira Rodríguez, Ana María, 269
Pérez González, Lewis, 29, 40
Perteghella, Manuela, 205
Pfanstiehl, Cody, 174, 188
Pfanstiehl, Margaret, 174, 188
Pianesi, Fabio, 167
Pier, John, 416, 425
Pollatsek, Alexander, 115, 131, 145, 146
Poplack, Shana, 268, 271
Potter, Cherry, 201, 204
Preisler, Bent, 252, 271
Prete, Michela, 167
Probst, Julia, 227
Propp, Vladimir, 147, 148, 168
Puigdomènech, Laura, 149, 168
Pujol, Joaquim, 175, 188
Pułaczewska, Hanna, 268, 269

Pulcini, Virginia, 270, 405
Radd, David, 43, 58
Rai, Sonali, 179, 188
Rajendran, Lawrence, 145
Ramos Pinto, Sara, 297, 312
Rander, Anni, 144, 146
Ranson, Maureen, 103, 106
Ravindran, Sury, 78, 83
Ray, Rebecca, 27, 40, 58
Rayner, Keith, 115, 116, 119, 131, 138, 144, 146
Redish, Janice, 102, 105, 108
Rehabilitation Act 48, 102
Reid, Helene, 204, 228
Reimer, Robert C., 190, 202, 205
Remael, Aline, 7, 11, 13, 21, 25, 36, 38, 40, 135, 146, 149, 168, 174, 176, 188, 237, 239, 245, 246, 273, 292, 297, 312, 326, 330, 333, 336, 347, 348, 354, 403, 406, 425, 430, 431
Renzi, Lorenzo, 337, 340, 342, 355
Reppen, Randi, 409, 425
Rocks, Siobhán, 190, 193, 199, 203, 205
Rodríguez, Ana, 425
Rogers, Margaret, 268, 269, 270, 271, 292
Romero-Fresco, Pablo, 7, 17, 111, 112, 113, 115, 116, 118, 120, 129, 130, 131, 134, 135, 136, 138, 144, 145, 146, 306, 312, 348, 355, 381, 382, 406, 431
Roosr, Annikk, 103, 106
Roskos-Ewoldsen, Beverly, 274, 292
Roskos-Ewoldsen, David, 292
Russell, Ian, 102, 105, 108
Russo, Mariachiara, 193, 205
Sajavaara, Kari, 250, 271
Salaün, Jean-Michel, 95, 105, 108
Saldanha, Gabriela, 40
Salmon Kovarski, Laura, 316, 333
Salvi, Giampaolo, 355
Salway, Andrew 409, 425
Sams, Mikko, 274, 292
Sánchez, Diana, 11
Sanderson, John, 246, 269, 270, 271, 378
Sandler, Wendy, 192, 204, 205
Sandøy, Helge, 250, 271
Sankoff, David, 271
Santana Hernández, Rafael, 114, 131
Sanz, Elena, 326, 333
Sario, Marjatta, 229, 246
Savidis, Anthony, 50, 58

Index

Scaglia, Claudia, 337, 342, 355
Schäler, Reinhard, 28, 40
Scott, Anthony Oliver, 152, 168
Scott, Mike, 405, 406
Seibel, Claudia, 9, 20, 409, 425, 431
Selby, Keith, 193, 205
Serban, Adriana, 187, 292, 378
Shevchenko, Tatiana, 114, 131
Shlesinger, Miriam, 246
Sinclair, John, 385, 406
Skantze, P.A., 239, 245, 246
Slimane, Mohamed, 146
Sloan, David, 102, 105, 108
Smith, Kirkby, 87, 104, 107
Snyder, Joel, 149, 174, 175, 188
Sobchack, Vivian, 217, 228
Soffritti, Marcello, 381, 406
Solaz, Lucía, 152, 168
Sørensen, Knud, 250, 271
Spinhof, Herman, 204, 228, 271, 274, 292
Stephanidis, Constantine, 57, 58
Stiven, Agnes Bain, 249, 271
Stoddart, Jonathan, 205
Stolze, Radegundis, 246
Storrer, Angelika, 312
Stubenrauch, Robert, 84
Subbotko, Donata, 211, 228
Suber, Peter, 86, 105, 108
Surowiecki, James, 27, 40
Sutinen, Johanna, 339, 342, 354
Sutton-Spence, Rachel, 192, 194, 205
Svavarsdóttir, Ásta, 255, 271
Szarkowska, Agnieszka, 213, 228
Szubert, Andrzej, 268, 271
Taavitsainen, Irma, 354
Taeldeman, Johan, 298, 312
Taler, Izabella, 93, 105, 108
Tannen, Deborah, 180, 188
Tanriverdi, Belgin, 284, 291, 293
Tapscott, Don, 26, 27, 41
Tate, Erin, 194, 205
TAUS 28, 39, 41
Taylor, Christopher, 193, 205, 353, 382, 406
TED 25, 28, 31, 32, 33, 34, 35, 36, 37, 38, 41
The World Bank, 44, 58
Theofanos, Mary Frances, 102, 105, 108
Thibault, Paul J., 193, 205, 409, 411, 425
Thimm, Caja, 312
Thompson, Roy, 202, 205
Tirkkonen-Condit, Sonja, 250, 272

Todorov, Tzvetan, 148, 168
Tomaszkiewicz, Teresa, 210, 214, 228
Torrance, Nancy, 131
Torres Monreal, Santiago, 114, 131
Tribble, Christopher, 405, 406
Trosborg, Anna, 270
Turner, Victor, 191, 205
Tveit, Jan-Emil, 228, 249, 272
UA-Games 58
Udo, John Patrick, 175, 188, 235, 246
Uglova, Natalia, 114, 131
Ulrych, Margherita, 337, 338, 355
UN Universal Human Rights Declaration 48
UsabilityNet 47, 58
Valdeón, Roberto, 297, 306, 312, 429
Valentini, Cristina, 381, 382, 406, 407
Van Kerkhoven, Marianne, 231, 247
Van Tol, Richard, 53, 58
Van Waes, Luuk 146
Vanattenhove, Miel, 231, 247
Vandekerckhove, Reinhilde, 298, 311, 312
Vedovelli, Massimo, 378
Venturini, Gilles, 146
Venuti, Laurence, 30, 41, 297, 313, 333
Vercauteren, Gert, 149, 168, 174, 179, 185, 188
Vermeulen, Anna, 8, 19, 295, 431
Vervecken, Anika, 8, 19, 229, 231, 232, 237, 241, 243, 245, 247, 432
Viereck, Wolfgang, 261, 272
Vilaró, Anna, 166, 168
Vinay, Jean-Paul, 345, 355
Voghera, Miriam, 378
Vorländer, Michael, 292
Walsh, Catarina, 104, 107
Waltham, Mary, 93, 97, 99, 105, 108
Wang, An-Hsiang, 274, 292
Wang, Jian, 86, 104, 107
Warren, Jane, 353
Weinreich, Uriel, 268, 272
Weippl, Edgar R., 83
White, Sarah J., 131, 146
Williams, Anthony, 26, 27, 41
Winge, Vibeke, 253, 272
Wise, Louis, 232, 247
WKYC 44, 58
Wolf, Michaela, 89, 105, 108
Wolksi, Werner, 312
Woll, Bencie, 190, 192, 204, 205
Wolverton, Gary S., 116, 131, 145, 146

Wordsmith Tools 386, 407
Woźniak, Monika, 8, 18, 209, 432
Wurm, Svenja, 190, 191, 205
Yang, Moon-hee, 274, 292

Yuksel, Dogan, 284, 291, 293
Yuste, Elia, 39
Zola, David, 116, 131, 145, 146

Printed in the United States
by Baker & Taylor Publisher Services